Concise Guide to Jazz

EDITION
7

MARK C. GRIDLEY

PEARSON

Boston   Columbus   Indianapolis   New York   San Francisco   Upper Saddle River
Amsterdam   Cape Town   Dubai   London   Madrid   Milan   Munich   Paris   Montréal   Toronto
Delhi   Mexico City   São Paulo   Sydney   Hong Kong   Seoul   Singapore   Taipei   Tokyo

Editorial Director: Craig Campanella	*Senior Operations Specialist:* Diane Peirano
Editor in Chief: Sarah Touborg	*Senior Art Director:* Pat Smythe
Senior Publisher: Roth Wilkofsky	*Interior and Cover Designer:* Wanda Espãna, Wee Design Group
Editorial Assistant: Christopher Fegan	*Cover Photo:* Courtesy of John Sobczak
Director of Marketing: Brandy Dawson	*Senior Digital Media Project Editor:* David Alick
Senior Marketing Manager: Kate Mitchell	*Digital Media Project Manager:* Rich Barnes
Marketing Assistant: Paige Patunas	*Full-Service Project Management:* GEX Publishing Services
Senior Managing Editor: Melissa Feimer	*Composition:* GEX Publishing Services
Production Liaison: Joe Scordato	*Printer/Binder:* LSC Communications
Senior Operations Supervisor: Mary Fischer	*Cover Printer:* LSC Communications

Portions of the Louis Armstrong coverage in chapter 4 originally appeared in *Jazz Educators Journal*, Vol. XIV (1984), No. 3, pp. 71–72 as "Why Is Louis Armstrong So Important?" and are reproduced by permission of the editors. Portions of the section designated "The Popularity of Bebop" in chapter 6 originally appeared in *Popular Music and Society*, Vol. IX (1984), No. 4, pp. 41–45 as "Why Have Modern Jazz Combos Been Less Popular Than Swing Big Bands?" and are reproduced by permission of the editors. Portions of the first ten paragraphs of chapter 10 originally appeared in *Popular Music and Society*, Vol. IX (1983), No. 2, pp. 27–34 as "Clarifying Labels: Jazz, Rock, Funk, and Jazz-Rock" and appear here by permission of the editors. The first six paragraphs of chapter 8 are adapted from "Clarifying Labels: Cool Jazz, West Coast, and Hard Bop" in *Tracking: Popular Music Studies*, Vol. 2 (1990), No. 2, pp. 8–16, and are used by permission of the editors.

This book was set in 12/14 Goudy Oldstyle BT

Credits and acknowledgments borrowed from other sources and reproduced, with permission, in this textbook appear on appropriate page within text.

Library of Congress Cataloging-in-Publication Data
Gridley, Mark C.,
  Concise guide to jazz / Mark C. Gridley. —Seventh ed.
    pages cm.
  Includes bibliographical references and index.
  Sixth edition published as: Gridley, Mark C. Concise guide to jazz. Upper Saddle
River, New Jersey : Pearson, 2009.
  ISBN-13: 978-0-205-93700-4
  ISBN-10: 0-205-93700-4
  1. Jazz—History and criticism. I. Title.
  ML3506.G736 2012
  781.65—dc23

2012039508

ISBN: 0-205-93700-4	Book Alone
ISBN: 0-205-93749-7	A La Carte version
ISBN: 0-205-93741-1	CourseSmart
ISBN: 0-205-93738-1	*Jazz Classics 2CD set for Concise Guide to Jazz 7E*
ISBN: 0-13-601098-9	*Demonstration CD*
ISBN: 0-13-601053-9	*Listening to Jazz DVD by Steve Gryb*
ISBN: 0-13-602643-5	*Prentice Hall Jazz History DVD*
ISBN: 0-205-17896-0	*The Prentice Hall Jazz Collection CD*

The following packages are available that offer students discounts when these items are purchased together:

ISBN: 0-205-95902-4	*Book with Jazz Classics 2CD set*	ISBN: 0-205-95523-1	Ebook and MySearchLab
ISBN: 0-205-95901-6	*Book with Demonstration CD*	ISBN: 0-205-94140-0	Book with Demonstration CD, Jazz
ISBN: 0-205-94085-4	*Book with Jazz Classics 2CD set and*		Classics 2CD set, and Prentice Hall
	Demonstration CD		Jazz Collection CD
ISBN: 0-205-93868-X	*MySearchLab Instant*	ISBN: 0-205-94086-2	Book with Prentice Hall Jazz Collection
ISBN: 0-205-93850-7	*MySearchLab Standalone*		CD and Jazz Classics 2CD set
ISBN: 0-205-95523-1	*Book with MySearchLab*		

PEARSON

www.pearsonhighered.com

Student Edition:
ISBN-10: 0-205-93700-4
ISBN-13: 978-0-205-93700-4

Instructor's Resource Copy:
ISBN-10: 0-205-93739-X
ISBN-13: 978-0-205-93739-4

7 2021

Contents

PRENTICE HALL JAZZ COLLECTION

Available separately as ISBN 0-205-17896-0.
Order by phone: 800-526-0485 web: *http://www.mypearsonstore.com*. This CD is available bundled with Concise Guide's Jazz Classics 2CD set (ISBN: 0-205-95902-4) or with Concise Guide's Demonstration CD and the Jazz Classics 2CD set (ISBN: 0-205-10233-6).

Structural analysis-style listening guides are available for each of these selections at http://www.pearsonhighered.com/gridley. (Click on "Concise Guide to Jazz," then click on "Supplements.")

1. **"Wolverine Blues"** (Jelly Roll Morton) June 10, 1927 by Jelly Roll Morton, Johnny Dodds, Baby Dodds; 3' 19"

2. **"Seven Come Eleven"** (Benny Goodman & Charlie Christian) November 22, 1939 by Benny Goodman, Charlie Christian, Lionel Hampton, Fletcher Henderson, Artie Bernstein, Nick Fatool; 2' 44"

3. **"Groovin' High"** (Dizzy Gillespie) February 28, 1945, by Dizzy Gillespie, Charlie Parker, Clyde Hart, Remo Palmieri, Slam Stewart, Cozy Cole; 2' 43"

4. **"Round Midnight"** (Thelonious Monk) November 4, 1968 by Thelonious Monk; 3' 48"

5. **"Four Brothers"** (Jimmy Giuffre) December 27, 1947 by Woody Herman Big Band featuring Zoot Sims, Herbie Steward, Stan Getz, and Serge Chaloff; 3' 16"

6. **"Blue Rondo a la Turk"** (Dave Brubeck) August 18, 1959 by Dave Brubeck, Paul Desmond, Gene Wright, Joe Morello; 6' 44"

7. **"Work Song"** (Nat Adderley) January 27, 1960 by Nat Adderley, Wes Montgomery, Bobby Timmons, Sam Jones, Percy Heath, Louis Hayes; 4' 15"

8. **"Fables of Faubus"** (Charles Mingus); May 5, 1959 by Shafi Hadi, John Handy, Booker Ervin, Jimmy Knepper, Horace Parlan, Charles Mingus, Danny Richmond; 8' 10"

9. **"Civilization Day"** (Ornette Coleman) September 9, 1971 by Ornette Coleman, Don Cherry, Charlie Haden, Billy Higgins; 6' 03"

10. **"Birdland"** (Joe Zawinul) January 1977 by Weather Report: Joe Zawinul, Wayne Shorter, Jaco Pastorius; 5' 57"

11. **"Express Crossing"** (Wynton Marsalis) 1993 by Wynton Marsalis (trumpet) and Kent Jordan (piccolo) from *Jazz: Six Syncopated Movements* (Columbia: CK 66379); 6' 11"

12. **"Kidnapping Kissinger"** (Dave Douglas) 2001 by Dave Douglas, Chris Speed, Mark Feldman, Eric Friedlander; 3' 04"

Preface

The *Concise Guide to Jazz* originated because both professors and students asked for an introduction to jazz that was as clear and accurate as *Jazz Styles* but without as much detail. Many professors also said they wanted a book that was easy to complete in one semester. Some said the ideal introductory text would focus on only about ten major figures. Reducing jazz history to a maximum of ten musicians was not feasible, however, because few authorities agree on which ten to discuss. But by increasing the minimum number of musicians to a little over 50 names, we were able to accommodate the combined preferences from most authorities' "top ten" lists and still not overload students. Though this approach neglects some of the richness of jazz history, it also makes conveniently comprehensible a diversity of styles in a way that provides a basis for further explorations.

THE BOOK AND ITS SUPPLEMENTS

✓•–Study and Review on mysearchlab.com

We are offering an online learning center, called *mysearchlab* (www. mysearchlab.com), that will greatly enhance student learning. Instructors may order *mysearchlab* to accompany new copies of the text or students can order it online at www.mypearsonstore.com. Throughout the book, we've called attention to features in mysearchlab that will help students in completing the course. Beyond the usual chapter questions and summaries, there are:

- Interactive eText
- Streaming audio
- Active Listening Guides for 33 classic jazz recordings discussed in the text
- Audio-Visual Tutorials to review jazz concepts
- Video clips of jazz performances
- Documentaries of jazz performers
- Chapter quizzes and flashcards for self-study

Jazz Classics 2CD Set

This set includes all 36 of the pieces that are analyzed by listening guides in the text. See contents for Jazz Classics 2CD set listed on inside front cover. We highly recommend that all students purchase this CD set or the online streamed format for the complete pieces along with the book so they may maximize their learning. The streaming format is available with purchase of MySearchLab with Pearson eText (ISBN 0-205-93850-7).

Listening to Jazz DVD and Demonstration CD

These two resources are specifically designed with non-majors in mind. They demonstrate key concepts in how jazz is made. These can be taught along with the book's Elements of Music Appendix and Chapter 2, "How to Listen to Jazz," at the beginning of the semester to orient students to the listening they will be doing later in the book. See contents for DEMONSTRATION CD listed on inside back cover. Listening to Jazz is Steve Gryb's video version of Mark Gridley's audio Demonstration CD.

Prentice Hall Jazz Collection CD

Twelve historic recordings collected to supplement the Jazz Classics 2CD set. Most are by artists who are missing from the Jazz Classics 2 CD set. This CD is available for students who buy the book with the Jazz Classics 2CD set. See complete contents listed on page iv.

The Prentice Hall Jazz History DVD

The mysearchlab supplement offers historic films of major jazz performers, from Bessie Smith through Weather Report. A full list of the clips is available on the mysearchlab website.

Book and Supplements Combination Packages

All of these supplements, in any combination, may be packaged with the book to save additional expense. Your local sales representative can outline these options to you. Or see http://www.pearsonhighered.com, and click on "Music," then on "Introduction to Jazz," then on "Concise Guide to Jazz," then on "Pearson Choices" or "Packages."

DESIGNING YOUR COURSE

In designing a semester-long or quarter-long course in jazz appreciation, instructors need to tally their own priorities, not necessarily the same topics that appear in this book. Topics, musicians, and entire chapters can be skipped without doing serious damage to a brief Introduction to Jazz or Understanding Jazz course. For example, if emphasis is placed on in-depth appreciation of particular recordings and the musicians on them, an entire class period can be devoted to each one. Dissecting a given selection, chorus by chorus, phrase by phrase, and then replaying it five times is not excessive if students are led to focus on a different aspect each time. Therefore, a respectable course could be constructed around only eight to ten major figures, perhaps just Louis Armstrong, Lester Young, Duke Ellington, Charlie Parker, Dizzy Gillespie, Miles Davis, Ornette Coleman, and John Coltrane, and in-depth appreciation of just ten to fifteen selections from the *Jazz Classics CDs*.

WHAT IS NEW TO THIS EDITION?

The first six editions of *Concise Guide to Jazz* have been successfully used at over 400 high schools, colleges, and universities throughout the country in their Jazz History and Intro to Jazz courses for non-majors. We are committed, however, to continually updating the book to give students an even more powerful resource for their learning.

The most exciting addition to the text is *mysearchlab*. This is a resource available to every student who purchases a copy of the book. *Mysearchlab* should help students to better understand jazz history and its key performers through many interactive features.

The following changes will be seen throughout the book:

- Updated "Music Buying Strategies" appendix
- Updated recommended further reading, listening, and viewing for every chapter
- New "call-outs" for listening and viewing on supplementary CDs, DVDs, and mysearchlab features
- 19 full-color photographs
- Online listening guides for all selections on the Prentice Hall Jazz Collection CD of 12 historic recordings
- New selection on the Jazz Classics CD2 and listening guide for a celebrated concert recording of free jazz by Cecil Taylor
- New selection on Jazz Classics CD2 and in-depth listening guide for a concert recording by the Miles Davis fusion band of 1970 featuring Chick Corea
- In-depth audio-visual explanations on mysearchlab for blues poetic form, blues chord progression, A-A-B-A song form, instrument timbres, trombone styles, saxophone styles, tempo, meter, and syncopation

ACKNOWLEDGEMENTS

Because this book is basically an abridged version of *Jazz Styles: History and Analysis*, all the people who helped put together the first eleven editions of *Jazz Styles* deserve thanks for working on this book as well. Their names are found in the acknowledgments sections of those volumes. I am especially grateful to the hundreds of students who spoke with me, wrote critiques, and corresponded with me about the best ways to approach the preparation of this book. Their names are too numerous to mention because this project has been a continual process since 1973.

A few individuals who are mentioned in the acknowledgments sections of *Jazz Styles* must be singled out for their hefty contributions to this volume. The biggest influence on the thinking and organization in this material is Harvey Pekar, who contributed almost continuously to my work since 1971. His original ideas and penetrating observations can be found in every chapter. Much of the research for these books was made possible by Pekar's generosity in giving me unlimited access to his collection of over 14,000 albums and his intimate knowledge of jazz history. He always shared his latest research with me and continued to keep me abreast of changing currents in jazz. Chuck Braman served as a technical consultant and a copy editor on five editions of *Jazz Styles* as well as a copy editor and prime figure in the conceptualization for the first edition of the *Concise Guide to Jazz*. He was additionally helpful in choosing photos. As in the past editions of *Jazz Styles*, Bill Anderson has continued to provide indispensable suggestions and updating regarding discography, videography, bibliography, and overall organization.

Two substitutions were made on Jazz Classics CD2 for this new seventh edition of *Concise Guide to Jazz*. A new listening guide was prepared for "Jitney #2" from Cecil Taylor's *Silent Tongues* album, in place of "Mars" from John Coltrane's *Interstellar Space* album. Several observations by David Such and Franck Amsellam were retained for it from an earlier rendition of the guide that had appeared in several editions of the *Jazz Styles* text. Useful comments on several drafts of this new guide were contributed by Merce Robinson. A new guide was prepared for Chick Corea's solo on "Spanish Key" from the *Black Beauty* album of Miles Davis in place of Corea's "Captain Marvel" from the *Light as a Feather* album of Return to Forever. Structural harmonic analyses were provided by Bob Fraser and Bart Polot. Additional comments on Corea's harmonic thinking in this solo were contributed by Marc Copland, Howie Smith, and Paul Rinzler. Suggestions for improving several drafts of the guide were supplied by Chuck Braman, George Gridley, Merce Robinson, and Jon Goldman.

The Album Buying Strategies appendix was retitled Music Buying Strategies and updated with the advice of Stephen Toombs (of Case Western Reserve University), Jon Goldman (formerly of Case Western Reserve University), Bill Anderson (formerly of Cleveland Public Library and Cleveland State University), James White (University of Northern Colorado), David Caffey (University of Northern Colorado), and the results of student surveys that were conducted by Pete Ford at Adrian College, Rob Foster at Augusta State University, Rob Hoff at Mercyhurst University, Michael Shirtz at Terra State Community College, Wayne Bumpers at Miami Dade Community College, Brian Kozak and Gary Scott at Cuyahoga Community College.

In order to provide representative illustrations, I am grateful for the loan of a banjo by Charles Coleman; a sousaphone by Christian Secrist and Tiffin University; a baritone saxophone by John Owen and Heidelberg College; a fluegelhorn, a trombone, and mutes by Ed Adams and Forte Music; a cornet, a trumpet, an acoustic guitar, a Fender bass guitar, and an upright string bass by Don Mossman and Mossman Music; and a soprano saxophone, Albert-system clarinet, late 1920s-model baritone saxophone, and 1914-model Holton bass saxophone by John Richmond. Rob Ledwedge and Dan Morgan photographed the musical instruments for this book. I remain deeply grateful to Jim Schafer for his patience, generosity, resourcefulness, and skill in digitally preparing the musician photos and instrument photos for the electronic form required by my publisher.

The accuracy of coverage in this textbook is due in part to the cooperation of many musicians whose music is discussed on its pages. Unfortunately, several of them passed away before seeing the finished product. The following players helped by means of conversations, proofreading, and/or correspondence with the author: Benny Goodman, Stan Kenton, Bill Evans, Wayne Shorter, Joe Zawinul, Eric Gravatt, David "Fathead" Newman, Herbie Hancock, Tony Williams, William Parker, Chris Speed, Fred Anderson, Bob Belden, Joe Henderson, Michael Brecker, Joe Venuti, Chuck Wayne, Al McKibbon, Dizzy Gillespie, Paul Smith, Richard Davis, Bob Curnow, Jimmy Heath, Jaco Pastorius, Red Rodney, and others who are mentioned in the acknowledgments sections of the first ten editions of *Jazz Styles*.

What Is Jazz?

Sonny Rollins. Photo by Bob Parent, courtesy of Getty Images

THE WORLD OF JAZZ

The world of jazz includes many different kinds of music. Some is light and happy. Some is heavy and serious. Some makes you want to dance. Some makes you think. Some is filled with surprises. Some is smooth and easy. Some is fast and complicated. Some is slow and mellow. Jazz is played by big bands and small groups. It has been played on almost every musical instrument. It comes in varieties called Dixieland and swing, bebop and cool, hard bop and fusion. But most jazz has no style designation. We refer to the sounds just by naming the musicians—for instance, Duke Ellington, Miles Davis, or John Coltrane.

Jazz is heard in numerous settings. Many bands present it as serious music in concert halls. Some jazz is played in ballrooms for dancers. There is jazz in background music on the radio. A lot of jazz is offered in nightclubs, where people gather to hear music while they drink and talk with their friends.

Jazz has an impressive reputation. It is so interesting that it is played and analyzed in hundreds of colleges. Almost every high school and college has at least one jazz band. Though it originated in America, jazz is so compelling that musicians on every continent have played it, and today there is no city without it. The sounds of jazz have influenced the development of new styles in popular music and the work of symphonic composers. Jazz is so sturdy that the old styles are still being played, and new styles are always being developed. In fact, jazz is regarded as a fine art, not just a passing fad.

DEFINING JAZZ

The term "jazz" has a variety of meanings because it has been used to describe so many kinds of music. And the term has different meanings according to who is using it. Different people use different ways to decide whether a given performance is "jazz." Some consider only how it makes them feel. Some rely on what it reminds them of. Some people decide it must be jazz if the performers have a reputation for jazz. Others consider how the music is made. They look at what techniques are being used. But despite these different attitudes toward defining jazz, there are two aspects that almost all jazz styles have in common—improvisation and swing feeling.

Improvisation

To improvise is to compose and perform at the same time. Instead of saying "improvise," many people say "ad lib" or "jam." This means that *jazz musicians make up their music as they go along. Much of their music is spontaneous. It is not written down or rehearsed beforehand.* This is like the impromptu speaking all of us do every day when we talk "off the cuff." We use the same words and phrases that we have used before. But now we improvise by using them in new ways and new orders that have not been rehearsed. A lot of originality can result. This is significant because being original is very important to jazz musicians. They try to be as spontaneous as possible. In fact, they try never to improvise the same way twice. Several versions of a tune made during the same recording session may be entirely different from each other because of this.

Improvisation is essential to jazz. If you are not very familiar with jazz, however, you might not be able to tell what has been written or memorized beforehand from what is being improvised. One clue is that if part of a performance sounds improvised, it quite often is. Improvised parts sometimes sound less organized than the written or memorized parts.

Another clue comes from knowing about a routine that most jazz musicians use. The players begin with a tune they all know. First they play it once all the way through. The melody is played by the horns. The accompaniment is played by the piano and bass. Then the piano and bass keep doing what they did before. But this time the horns make up and play new melodies of their own. *They improvise their own melodies to the tune's accompaniment chords.* The way the chords progress in that accompaniment guides the notes they choose to play for their new melodies, which we call improvisations. In other words, when the melody of the piece itself ends, what follows is improvised. Then it is all improvised until that same melody begins again. This kind of improvisation distinguishes the practices of jazz musicians from most pop musicians, who merely decorate a tune by changing some of its rhythms or adding notes to it.

Even though improvisation is the big emphasis in jazz, not everything is spontaneous. Most jazz bands use arrangements of some sort. In the case of large jazz bands where the players are seated with written arrangements in front of them, a player is usually improvising when he stands up alone and takes a solo. Otherwise the music is coming from the written parts. In the next chapter, we will examine more practices that can help us know what parts in a jazz performance are worked out in advance.

Swing Feeling

Next we are going to consider the way that jazz makes people feel. This has been called "jazz swing feeling." To begin, let's discuss a few elements that contribute to swing feeling in all music, not just jazz. If music makes you want to dance, clap your hands, or tap your feet, it has the effect we call "swinging." This effect can be created by almost any kind of music that keeps a steady beat and is performed with great spirit. In that sense, many non-jazz performances can be swinging. But to specify the unique ways a jazz performance swings, let's first discuss the general characteristics of swinging. Then we can discuss the characteristics that are specific to jazz swing feeling.

◀ Charles Mingus, jazz bassist known for his composing and improvising. He is important for getting his musicians to improvise their own parts to fit with his written music in colorful and provocative ways.

Photo by Paul Hoeffler, courtesy of Getty Images

▲ Joe Zawinul, Wayne Shorter, Manolo Badrena, Alex Acuna, and Jaco Pastorius, leading musicians in jazz of the 1960s and 70s.
Photo by Andrew Putler, courtesy of Getty Images

Listening to Jazz by Steve Gryb
Demo DVD Track 15

One of the clearest causes of swing feeling is a steady beat. This helps us distinguish it from the kinds of symphonic music where conductors are free to vary the tempo while playing a piece. A steady beat is nearly always kept in jazz pieces. Constant tempo brings a certain kind of momentum that is essential to swing feeling. Much of the excitement in jazz comes from musicians in the band tugging against this very solid foundation by playing notes slightly before or after the beat.

To call music "swinging" also means that the performance conveys a lilting feeling. This property is also sometimes referred to as a "groove." In fact, verbs derived from the nouns "swing" and "groove" are commonly applied to the sound of jazz: "The band is swinging tonight." "That pianist is really grooving." For many listeners, swinging simply means pleasure. A swinging performance is like a swinging party. Both are very enjoyable. Jazz has a reputation for being highly spirited music. In fact, the word "jazzy" is sometimes used instead of the word "spirited." To "jazz up" and to "liven up" are often used interchangeably, and some people call clothes "jazzy" if they are gaudy or extraverted.

"Boogie Woogie" by Count Basie
on the *Prentice Hall Jazz History
DVD*. Basie was one of the great
masters of swing music.

Music that swings, then, has constant tempo and is performed with lilt and spirit. But for music to swing in the way peculiar to jazz, more conditions have to be met. One is an abundance of syncopated rhythms. "Syncopating" means accenting just before or just after a beat. You might think of syncopation as off-beat accenting, or the occurrence of stress where it is least expected. Jazz swing feeling requires certain combinations of these off-beat accents. The tension generated by members of a band accenting opposite sides of the beat is essential to jazz swing feeling.

Dizzy Gillespie, modern jazz trumpeter who devised a highly syncopated style of improvising. He specialized in rhythmic surprises.

Photo by Lee Tanner

One more component of jazz swing feeling is not actually a rhythmic element. It is the continuous rising and falling motion in a melody line. This pattern makes you alternately tense and relaxed, tense and relaxed, over and over again.

We must keep in mind that listeners disagree about whether a given performance swings, and, if so, how much. So, just as we often hear that "beauty is in the eye of the beholder," it is also true that swing is in the ear of the listener. In other words, *swinging is an opinion, not a fact about the music.* Ultimately this becomes another reason that it is difficult to reach a workable definition for jazz. We find that the same music one listener calls jazz will not necessarily be what another calls jazz because the listeners disagree about whether it swings.

STUDYING DIFFERENT JAZZ STYLES HISTORICALLY

Jazz comes in many varieties. The easiest way to introduce a lot of these varieties is to group them into categories called styles. Every jazz musician has a personal style of playing. But this can be a confusing way to use the word "style" because we also use it to designate a larger category of ways musicians like to play. These larger categories have names such as bebop and Dixieland. Each of these styles includes particular ways the musicians like to improvise and the types of accompaniment harmonies and rhythms they prefer. Throughout this book we will be examining the particular styles of famous jazz musicians. But we also have to categorize them within the larger styles, such as Dixieland and bebop, so that we can divide the book into chapters. Grouping the players in these ways is not always fair because styles vary considerably, and some players from the same era don't play at all like each other. But because some musicians' approaches have more in common than other musicians', we rely on the common aspects to help us decide which musicians to discuss in each chapter.

As we study styles in a chronological order, it is important to keep in mind several considerations. First, the musicians discussed in this book did not create their styles entirely by themselves. Their work reflects the influence of other players in addition to their own original ideas. Second, jazz history is not a single stream of styles that developed smoothly from Dixieland to swing to bebop and so forth. Several streams exist at the same time, and streams overlap, merge, and influence each other all the time. Third, each new style does not render the previous ones obsolete. Many different styles of jazz exist at the same time, though some are more popular during one era than another. Fourth, jazz history is not merely a series of reactions in which one style made musicians angry and so they invented another to oppose it. However, many journalists and historians believe this because they look for conflict, and they attach great drama to the development of new styles. The truth is that most musicians find their own favorite ways of playing. Often it is an existing style they like. Sometimes they choose one traditional approach and modify it to suit their tastes and capabilities; sometimes they combine different approaches to make a mixture they like. Many players stick with that style for good; some change their styles whenever they become bored with what they are doing or whenever they hear something new that they like more.

▶ Ella Fitzgerald, singing with the Dizzy Gillespie big band, with Gillespie looking on from his seat, bassist Ray Brown in background.

Photo by William P. Gottlieb, courtesy of the Library of Congress

Fifth, the origination of most new jazz styles cannot necessarily be traced to non-musical forces such as politics and sociocultural conflicts, though some historians believe that they can. Certainly, jazz does not exist in a vacuum, yet the media have exaggerated the contributions of non-musical factors. Usually, jazz innovators draw primarily upon their own extraordinary individual creativity, and they frequently adapt methods and materials from previous jazz styles, pop music, classical music, and world music.* In other words, in making their music, the originators tend to gather far more from music itself than from the non-musical world around them.

A sixth consideration is also important to keep in mind. Many people tend to think that jazz is just the music that they first heard termed "jazz." They are not aware of the diversity of styles that have been tagged "jazz." On the other hand, some people who are aware of numerous styles prefer that certain styles not be included in the jazz category. For instance, during the 1970s and 80s many people felt that jazz-rock fusion should not be called "jazz." As recently as 2013 there were still many jazz purists who did not want the most popular styles such as "smooth jazz" to be called "jazz." Granted, different jazz styles do convey different rhythmic feelings, and some even use different instruments and differing amounts of improvisation. But classical music fans and popular music fans find jazz styles more distinguishable from classical music and popular music than from each other. No matter how sticky these controversies get, though, remember that learning how to label the styles is just a handy way to keep track of what you want to hear. The most important goal is to increase your enjoyment of jazz.

SUMMARY

1. Defining jazz is difficult because there are so many varieties.

2. The most common elements that appear in definitions of jazz are improvisation and swing feeling.

3. Improvisation means making it up as you go along, as with impromptu speaking.

4. Jazz musicians usually begin by playing a tune they all know. After that, they make up their own music and guide their improvisations by the accompaniment chords that came with the original tune.

5. Swing feeling is the rhythmic property perceived by listeners who enjoy a particular performance.

6. Jazz swing feeling seems to be perceived in listeners when music has a certain combination of:

   a. steady tempo
   b. a certain kind of off-beat accenting
   c. a continuous rising and falling of the melodic line

7. Listeners do not always agree that a given performance is jazz. One reason is that jazz swing feeling is an opinion about how the music feels, not a fact.

8. Jazz style designations are often more expedient than accurate. Style designations are made in this book to present a variety of musicians in the smallest number of chapters.

*For an in-depth discussion regarding controversies about the role of politics in the emergence of bop and free jazz, see "Misconceptions in Linking Free Jazz with the Civil Rights Movement." *College Music Symposium*, Vol. 47, 2008, pages 139–155; available at http://www.jazzstyles.net/illusory.html.

FURTHER RESOURCES

✓● Study and Review on mysearchlab.com

This is the complete web supplement for this text. As a start, test your knowledge with the chapter quiz.

VIEW

The Prentice Hall Jazz History DVD
> 21 historic clips of performances by key artists.

Listening to Jazz DVD by Steve Gryb
> Demonstrates how jazz musicians go about making their music. Illustrates all the instruments; constitutes a video version of the Gridley *Demo CD* audio demonstrations.

LISTEN

Demonstration CD by Mark Gridley, 157 narrated demonstrations of how musicians make jazz.

What Is Jazz? by Leonard Bernstein, Columbia CL 919, LP, 1956; reissue: in *Bernstein Century: Bernstein on Jazz,* SONY SMK 60566, CD, 1998. The best introduction to jazz, it explains improvisation, the blues, A-A-B-A song form, Dixieland, swing, bebop; Louis Armstrong, Bessie Smith, Miles Davis, John Coltrane, and other musicians illustrate Bernstein's narration. (Alternate versions are on *Demo CD* and mysearchlab.com.)

READ

Feather, Leonard. 1957, 1965, 1976. *The Book of Jazz.* New York: Horizon-Dell.

Gridley, Mark, Robert Maxham, and Robert Hoff. 1989. "Three Approaches to Defining Jazz." *Musical Quarterly,* 73(4):513–31; reprinted and updated in Lewis Porter, *Jazz: A Century of Change.* New York: Schirmer, 1997, and at http://www.jazzstyles.net/ThreeApproach.html.

Ostransky, Leroy. 1960. *Anatomy of Jazz.* Seattle: University of Washington Press, reprinted 1973 by Greenwood, Westport, CT.

Joe Lovano, at the 2001 Tri-C Jazz Festival, Cleveland. Photo by Jeff Forman

OPEN YOUR EARS

Much pleasure can be derived from listening to jazz improvisation. But many people say that they cannot enjoy it because they do not understand it. If you are one of those people, this chapter will be quite helpful. Remember that with knowledge and practice, listening to jazz becomes easier, and it becomes more and more fun.

Hearing the improvised lines of a jazz soloist as melodies in themselves should help you enjoy much of jazz. Experienced listeners get as much pleasure from hearing their favorite improvisations as most people get from hearing their favorite songs. It might help to keep in mind that *some jazz improvisers strive to invent lines that are as catchy as the melodies in pop tunes and classical pieces.* On the other hand, many improvisers tend toward more elaborate lines. Some passages in their improvisations are more melody-like than others. For this reason many listeners pay close attention as the improvisations are unfolding. They want to notice when the line becomes particularly melodic. Then they can have the pleasure of hearing a new song being composed. There are gems of inspired melody hidden in many improvisations just waiting to be discovered by attentive listeners. We need to remember, however, that melody is more important in some styles than in others. For instance, in some avant-garde and jazz-rock fusion performances the music focuses instead on variations in mood, sound qualities, and rhythms. Sometimes the mood alone may be the most prominent aspect instead of only part of the effect.

One way a lot of jazz fans listen is to **imagine layers of sound, one on top of another, all moving forward in time. Each layer can represent the sound of a different instrument**. Once you become skilled in visualizing separate sounds, you will begin to notice relationships between the sounds. **Try to imagine a graph of the solo line**. The horizontal side of the graph represents time passing. The vertical dimension represents highness and lowness of pitch. Your graph can be embellished by colored shapes and textures representing the accompanying sounds of piano chords, drums, cymbals, bass, and so on.

Some people hum the original tune to themselves while listening to the improvisations that are guided by its chord changes. Try to synchronize the beginning of your humming with the beginning of a solo improvisation, and then keep the same tempo as the performer. You will become aware of two compositions based on the same chord changes: the original tune and the improvised melody. As you become more aware of how they go together, your appreciation of jazz will deepen considerably.

To help follow the music in a jazz performance, you might **try to divide the sounds into the functions they serve**. For instance, there are two kinds of roles that instruments have in a jazz combo: (1) the **soloist role** and (2) the **accompanist role**. The soloist role can be assumed by any melody instrument, though saxophones and trumpets are the most common. Jazz fans think of accompanists as members of a **rhythm section.** The standard instruments in rhythm sections are (a) bass, (b) drums, and (c) a chording instrument such as piano, organ, or guitar.

Demo CD Track 32 |

Rhythm section The part of a jazz combo that provides the accompaniment for the soloists

HOW DO MUSICIANS KEEP THEIR PLACE WHILE IMPROVISING?

To improvise is to compose and perform at the same time. Jazz musicians make up their music as they go along. Most jazz is guided by the musicians agreeing beforehand to maintain a given (1) tempo, (2) key, and (3) progression of accompaniment chords. They then invent and play their own melodies and accompaniments in a way that is compatible with those chords. Frequently, the agreed-upon harmonies are borrowed from a familiar melody, and the melody itself is played before and after the improvisations. This is easy because jazz musicians tend to know many of the same tunes in the same keys.

Jazz musicians often keep the original melody in mind while they improvise. This helps them keep their place in the progression of accompaniment chords that guides them. Despite this, *the improvised lines are not*

Saxophonist Lester Young soloing in front of his rhythm section accompanists (left to right): drummer, bassist, pianist and guitarist.

Photo courtesy of Frank Driggs

usually variations on the original melody. They are entirely different melodies. The improvised melodies and the original melody have only a progression of accompaniment chords in common. To understand what goes into creating jazz, try learning the melody of a piece. Then try to keep your place in the improvised section of a jazz performance of that piece by listening for patterns that you remember hearing under the melody.

Another help in following a jazz improvisation is the form of the piece being played. For instance, when a jazz group plays a blues, the melody of the piece is usually played twice by everyone. (See page 277 and listen to *Demo CD* Track 19.) Then the soloists improvise over the progression of chords in its accompaniment. **One complete progression of accompaniment chords is called a chorus.** Each soloist ordinarily improvises for several choruses. When one soloist ends an improvisation, another soloist takes over. The chords continue to progress in a cycle that never varies. In that way, the whole group stays together. That particular progression of chords and its tempo are the glue that holds the music together. After all the solos are taken, the group concludes by playing the melody to the piece twice more.

Jazz musicians often improvise over tunes written in the form of four sections. The most common arrangement for such pieces has one section called the A-section and another called the B-section or **bridge.** The A-section is played two times in a row. Then the B-section is inserted, followed by the A-section again. The sequence is **A-A-B-A,** and thousands of tunes composed from the 1920s through the 50s were organized in such

Chorus A single playing through of the structure being used to organize the music in an improvisation

Bridge The B part of an A-A-B-A composition

A-A-B-A A sequence used to structure many popular songs, beginning with a first part ("A") repeated once, followed by a new melody ("B" or bridge), and concluding with a return to the "A" part

((● **Listen** on
mysearchlab.com
Listen to audio-visual explanation of A-A-B-A song form on mysearchlab.com

a format. You might recall the format if you hum the melody to the Christmas carol "Deck the Halls." The same format is used for "(Meet the) Flintstones." When jazz musicians play an A-A-B-A tune, they usually play its melody once before and once after the solo improvisations. Each solo fits the tune's **chord progression** so that the A-A-B-A chorus structure is repeated over and over again. The cycle continues A-A-B-A-A-A-B-A-A-A-B-A, and so forth. (See page 278.)

(See page 278.)

INSTRUMENT ROLES

When you listen to a jazz performance, the large number of different sounds might be overwhelming to focus on. If this happens to you, try focusing only on one instrument's role at a time. Then after you become a more skilled listener, you will be able to identify combinations of instruments. You will also be able to move your focus of attention quickly from one activity to another.

One of the easiest parts to follow is the bass line. In jazz styles that were common from the 1930s through the 1960s, the bassist plucked a string once per beat. This (1) kept time for the band and (2) gave the group's sound a buoyancy. This style of playing is called **walking bass.** The notes played by the bassist are chosen from important notes in the accompaniment chords that are guiding the solo improvisation.

Demo CD Track 33 explains A-A-B-A form.

Chord progression
Harmonies in a particular order with specified durations

Walking bass A style of bass line in which each beat of each measure receives a separate tone, thus creating a moving sequence of quarter notes in the bass range

Demo CD Track 23

acoustic bass
Photo courtesy of Frank Driggs

bass guitar
Photo by Tom Copi, courtesy of Getty Images

▶ **Left:** Ron Carter playing a string bass, also known as acoustic bass, bass viol, or upright bass.

Right: Jaco Pastorius playing an electric bass guitar. Though it looks like a guitar, the electric bass can be differentiated from the solid body electric guitar by having four instead of six tuning pegs, one for each string.

((•— **Listen** on
mysearchlab.com

Listen to audio-visual demonstration of piano comping on mysearchlab.com

Comping Syncopated chording accompaniment for an improvised solo

Also try to follow the sounds of the accompaniment pianist. Find a recording in which a trumpet or saxophone soloist is accompanied by piano, bass, and drums. When you listen, ignore the horns, bass, and drums. Listen only to how the pianist plays chords that support the soloist. Notice how the piano supplies a syncopated commentary on the solo. The pianist provides both harmonies and rhythms. The pianist uses both hands at the same time to play chorded rhythms behind a soloist. What the pianist is doing is called **comping.** This term is short for the word accompanying.

A particularly interesting role to follow is the drummer's. In styles rooted in jazz of the 1930s to the 1960s, the drummer uses his right hand to play rhythms that provide both (1) regular pulse and (2) swing feeling. The drummer plays these rhythms on the **ride cymbal** suspended over the drum set. (Listen to *Demo CD* Track 3.) These rhythms are called **ride rhythms.** Occasionally they consist of one stroke per beat and they sound like "ting, ting, ting, ting." Usually they are more complicated, sounding like "ting tick a ting tick a ting tick a ting" or "ting ting ting tick a ting" or "ting tick a ting tick a ting tick a tick a ting." The drummer may play ride rhythms on other drums and cymbals, too.

The drummer's left hand is free to decorate the group sound by striking the **snare drum** that sits on a stand close to his lap. The snare drum has a crisp, crackling sound. (Listen to *Demo CD* Track 5.) The combinations of sounds made by striking the snare drum are often called **"fills"** because they fill in a musical gap left by the soloist. The snare drum can also be played to provide an undercurrent of activity that seems to be "chattering" while the band is playing.

A drummer often interrupts the series of ride rhythms to strike a **crash cymbal.** (Listen to *Demo CD* Track 4.) This particular cymbal is chosen for its splashy sound quality and the quickness with which its sound disappears. This contrasts with the *ride cymbal* that is chosen for the quality of its "ting" and the fact that its sound sustains longer than that of a crash cymbal.

The drummer reinforces every other beat by pressing his left foot on a pedal that closes two cymbals together, making a "chick" sound. This apparatus is called a **high-hat.** It will produce a "chick" sound if the pedal is depressed and very briefly held in closed position. (Listen to *Demo CD* Track 2.) It can then be opened and closed again for another "chick." Sounds can also be extracted from the high-hat if it is struck with a drumstick or a wire brush. (Listen to *Demo CD* Tracks 12 and 13.)

The drummer uses his right foot to press a pedal, which, in turn, causes a mallet to strike the bass drum. (Listen to *Demo CD* Track 1.) The drummer sometimes plays the bass drum lightly on every beat. It can also be used to provide accents and "bombs."

Ride cymbal A cymbal suspended over the right of the drum set. Its sound sustains, and the rhythms played on it provide a time keeping function

Ride rhythm The pattern a drummer plays on the ride cymbal to keep time

Fills Anything a drummer plays in addition to basic timekeeping patterns

((◄●—[**Listen** on **mysearchlab.com**
Listen to audio-visual demonstration of cymbals on mysearchlab.com

High-hat Two cymbals that strike together by means of a foot pedal

Listening to Jazz DVD Tracks 2–14.

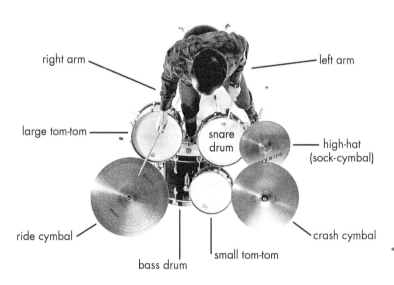

right arm — left arm

large tom-tom — snare drum — high-hat (sock-cymbal)

ride cymbal — small tom-tom — crash cymbal

bass drum

((◄●—[**Listen** on **mysearchlab.com**
Listen to a drummer keeping time with wire brushes on mysearchlab.com

◄ Aerial view of drummer at drum set

▶ Audience view of drum set

Photo of Elvin Jones by Lee Tanner

Prentice Hall Jazz History DVD: "Build A New World" by Art Blakey's Jazz Messengers. Art Blakey was one of the greatest drummers in jazz. Try to identify the techniques discussed in this chapter while watching this video.

Demo CD Tracks 8, 31, and 32

((•─ Listen on
mysearchlab.com

Listen to interactive drumming on mysearchlab.com

The public often considers drummers merely to be timekeepers for a band. Though this is true in some bands, throughout jazz history drummers have also added sounds and rhythms that make music more colorful and exciting. Many of these colorful sounds do show where the beat is. However, much jazz percussion work does more than keep time. It dramatizes. In other words, **the drummer acts as a colorist in addition to acting as a timekeeper**. In fact, some bands have employed drummers exclusively for coloristic playing instead of timekeeping. Instead of "drummer," we say "percussionist" to describe that role.

The drummer not only (1) keeps time and (2) decorates the group sound, but also (3) **kicks and prods the soloist**. Drummers also (4) underscore the playing of the other band members by playing the same rhythm that the others have arranged for a particular moment in the piece. These tendencies expanded after the 1930s. By the mid-1960s jazz drumming had changed so much that the sounds made by drummers were often in the forefront of the band. They were as obvious as melody instruments. During this period of change in jazz styles, the amount of interplay between drummers and other group members also increased. Also keep in mind that a drummer's playing can control (1) the loudness level, (2) sound texture, and (3) mood of a combo's performance, much as a conductor does with a symphony orchestra.

ARE SOLO IMPROVISATIONS COMPLETELY ORIGINAL?

Though we have said that jazz musicians make up their music as they go along, an improviser's lines are not totally original in each and every performance. There are themes in the improvisations that the musician has used before. In fact, these themes combine with the player's own unique

◀ Jim Hall, an improviser known for devising solos that are largely free of familiar patterns.

Photo by Chuck Stewart

tone qualities and rhythmic tendencies to help us identify the player's improvising style. Using such themes is an accepted practice. Beginners are advised to collect favorite "licks," those very themes that we later hear in their music. Most improvisers tend to play bits and pieces of lines they have played before. They also play melodic figures they have practiced and pet phrases of other improvisers. An improviser may actually play portions of a solo he remembers from another musician's recording. Sometimes an improviser will quote snatches of a pop tune or a classical piece. The separate parts of an improvised solo may not themselves be original, but the way in which they are combined usually is. However, there are a few extraordinarily gifted and disciplined improvisers, including Jim Hall and Wayne Shorter, who manage to devise lines that are largely free of familiar patterns.

SUMMARY

1. Unwritten rules are followed that enable jazz improvisers to piece together performances without rehearsal.

2. Musicians know many of the same tunes, and they follow common practices when performing tunes having 12-bar blues and A-A-B-A construction.

3. Jazz musicians play the melody before and after they play improvisations. Both the melody and the improvisations are guided by the same cycle of chord patterns in the accompaniment.

4. Walking bass style involves playing notes that keep time for the band as well as outlining the chord progression for the improvisers.

5. The jazz drummer uses bass drum, ride cymbal, and high-hat cymbals to keep time for the band and crash cymbal and snare drum to kick and prod soloists and dramatize their ideas.

6. Comping is the accompaniment style in which the pianist feeds chords to the improvising soloist in a flexible and syncopated way.

7. People can listen to jazz by

   a. humming the original tune to themselves while listening to the improvisations that are guided by the same progression of accompaniment chords
   b. imagining a graph of the solo line
   c. imagining layers of sound moving forward in time
   d. hearing the improvised lines of a soloist as melodies in themselves
   e. listening for variations in mood, tone qualities, and rhythms

8. Jazz musicians improvise by reorganizing phrases they have played before. However, some of the best manage to devise lines off the cuff that are largely free of familiar patterns: Jim Hall and Wayne Shorter, for instance.

KEY TERMS

A-A-B-A	comping	ride cymbal
bridge	fill	ride rhythm
chord progression	high-hat	walking bass
chorus	rhythm section	

FURTHER RESOURCES

✓•─[Study and Review on mysearchlab.com

Test your knowledge with the chapter quiz.

VIEW
Listening to Jazz, Demonstration DVD by Steve Gryb 0-13-601053-9
   Demonstrates instruments and their roles through short film clips.

LISTEN
What Is Jazz? by Leonard Bernstein, Columbia CL 919, LP, 1956; reissue: *Bernstein Century: Bernstein on Jazz*, SONY 60566, CD, 1998. This contains demonstrations and explanations for many of the concepts and techniques discussed in this chapter.

Demonstration CD by Mark Gridley 0-13-601098-9
   Contains audio demonstrations for most of the concepts and techniques discussed in this chapter.

READ
Kernfeld, Barry. 1995. *What to Listen for in Jazz.* New Haven, CT: Yale University Press. Includes a CD of illustrations in historic jazz recordings.

The Origins of Jazz

Superior Orchestra, 1910. Photo courtesy of Frank Driggs

BEGINNINGS

Jazz originated from brass band and ragtime piano styles of the 1800s that were blended to satisfy social dancers. During the 1890s, jazz began to be recognizable as a style of its own. By the 1920s, it was fully formed and recorded in New York, Los Angeles, and Chicago. At least three essential trends had led to the birth of jazz: (1) The practice of taking liberties with the melodies and accompaniments of tunes as they were being performed. This led to what we today call *improvisation*. (2) Taking liberties with tone qualities. For instance, musicians cultivated rough and raspy sounds to add to their collection of smooth tone qualities. (3) African Americans creating new kinds of music such as ragtime and the blues. **Ragtime** (a) provided some of the *jazz repertory* and (b) made *syncopated rhythms* popular. The **blues** (a) provided another portion of jazz repertory, (b) popularized the practice of *toying*

Ragtime A popular turn-of-the-20th century style of written piano music involving pronounced syncopation

Blues A style of African American song, originally consisting of a vocal with guitar accompaniment, that often expresses a lonesome or sad feeling

with a melody tone's pitch to produce a soulful effect, and (c) popularized the practice of manipulating the starting times for sung notes and phrases. Such delays are technically classified as *rhythmic displacement*.

A glance back at the experiences of Africans in America will help us understand how these different kinds of music came together. When Africans were taken as slaves to the New World, they were not allowed to bring their musical instruments. They were not even grouped with their own families or members of the same language community who could help perpetuate their musical customs. Slaves were expected to learn the music of their masters. In some regions, especially New Orleans, they were occasionally allowed to recreate their own music, but such situations decreased as the twentieth century neared. Considering those situations, African musical tastes and practices could have simply died out, having been overpowered by the European musical tastes and practices of the majority culture. The African traditions were sufficiently robust, however, to be retained in new forms of music and creative alterations of European music. This may explain why European music often sounded different when played in the New World by musicians of African ancestry. For example, some slaves modified European church hymns, folk songs, and dance music to suit their own tastes and traditions.

There are numerous ways in which African tastes and traditions were retained in the New World despite their contrast with the musical tastes and traditions of the majority culture:.

1. Some children's games were highly rhythmic and physical. A few used the player's own body as a drum. Some children's activities involved highly syncopated songs, a few of which required juggling complicated rhythmic parts.

2. African American church music kept a few African musical traditions alive. Slaves had spiced up European church hymns by altering rhythms, adding **pitch bends** and new tone qualities. They also made otherwise bland, non-swinging phrases more rhythmically emphatic in their execution.

Pitch bend A purposeful raising or lowering of a tone's pitch; usually done for coloration or expressive purposes

Demo CD Tracks 50–58. illustrates pitch bends.

3. Imaginative flexibility of pitch is also common. It is obvious in *work songs* and ways devised by workers for communicating in the fields called *field hollers*.

4. There were examples of undiluted African music performed in public. Some African music was made in social clubs that existed year-round, particularly in New Orleans. They managed to keep African music and dance traditions alive since at least as early as the 1880s. These organizations' existence was made conspicuous during Mardi Gras celebration in New Orleans, though Mardi Gras is not their reason for being. They often comprised uninvited paraders appearing on side streets and after the officially sanctioned paraders had passed. Though dressed as Native American Indians, these paraders were African Americans, and their music was essentially African. They were informally known as Mardi Gras Indians. (*Note:* A wide assortment of

invited paraders are today termed Mardi Gras Indians, some of whom have nothing to do with perpetuating African practices.)

5. The popularity of blues singing since the end of the 1800s made African musical practices continuously accessible.

6. Much of the music that was coming from Latin America and the Caribbean during the 1800s and the first part of the 1900s originated by fusing African and Spanish music. The popularity of this "Latin" music in the United States made African characteristics continuously available to Americans.

NEW ORLEANS

Let's first examine the setting in which jazz was born. We will begin with the history of different groups of people who settled in New Orleans, paraphrased here from *The Creoles of Color of New Orleans* by James Haskins (Crowell, 1975). France began building New Orleans in 1718, and 147 black slaves were brought there in 1719. There were free blacks there as early as 1722. In 1763 France gave the territory of Louisiana to Spain. Despite Spanish rule, the language and customs there remained primarily French. In 1801, Spain gave Louisiana back to France. But Spain still continued to rule the territory until the United States bought it in 1803.

◀ The levee in New Orleans shown in a Currier and Ives print from the middle 1800's.

Library of Congress

Significant social patterns can be traced back to that period of Spanish rule. At that time, marriage between the different ethnic groups in Louisiana occurred frequently. Furthermore, the Spanish freed many slaves. This increased the number of free blacks—there were 1,147 by 1789. Under Spanish rule, **free people of color began to be regarded as a class that was separate from the whites and the slaves. Their status was closer to that of whites.** Many light-skinned women of color became mistresses to white men and were set up as second families to the men in separate houses. The children from some of these unions were called **Creoles of Color**. Their ancestry was part African and part French. This distinguished them from the white Creoles, whose background was Spanish and French. Creoles of Color were never referred to as Negro. The term Negro was reserved for blacks who had little or no white ancestry.

By 1810, the number of free people of color living in New Orleans had increased to 5,000. As these population changes occurred and people of African or part-African ancestry became the largest ethnic group, the small white (non-Creole) population reacted to their own minority status with fear. The whites captured business and governmental power in New Orleans. With that power they made laws that took status away from the Creoles of Color and eventually placed them in the same position as Negroes.

A sharp separation existed between the two groups of New Orleans residents who had African ancestry. Negroes lived in a racially mixed neighborhood, a large portion of which was uptown. They worked primarily as house servants and unskilled laborers. Most of the white Creoles and the Creoles of Color lived downtown in the area of New Orleans known today as the French Quarter. Creoles of Color were mostly well-educated, successful people—businessmen, doctors, landowners, and skilled craftsmen. They spoke French. Many owned slaves and often required their slaves to speak French, too. Children in Creole of Color families often received high-quality musical training, some even traveling to Paris for study at a conservatory. (See photo on page 21.) The Creoles of Color maintained a resident symphony orchestra and supported an opera house. This reinforced the intensely musical orientation of New Orleans, a city that had three opera houses, far more than any other American city of comparable size. By comparison with residents in other regions, they took the pleasures of music and dance more seriously.

Creoles of Color, like the white Creoles, wholeheartedly favored European music. European concert traditions were maintained by Creole music. Meanwhile, some music played by Negroes retained aspects of African musical practices. Though many Negro musicians received formal training, their music was generally less refined than that of the Creoles. It may have included improvisation. Moreover, it is significant to understand that the vocal music of the uptown blacks in New Orleans contained new blends of European and African vocal traditions.

The social history outlined here pertains to jazz for two reasons. First, it helps us appreciate how exceptionally musical New Orleans was. Second, it gets us thinking about how people of African and European-African

Creole of Color A person who has mixed French and African ancestry and was born in the New World

New Orleans Creole clarinetist Sidney Bechet, one of the first great solo improvisers in early jazz.

Photo courtesy of Jazzsign/Lebrecht Music & Arts

descent combined their own traditional tastes to create a new form of music in their new American home.

THE BLUES

The term "blues" refers to several different kinds of music. The first kind was a black folk music that began developing long before outside observers noticed and took it seriously enough to describe. This was long before the invention of the recording machine in 1877. So we really don't know for certain how all its roots and developmental stages sounded. We do know, however, that it didn't come from Africa. It was developed in America by African slaves and their descendants. Researchers believe the blues originated from other vocal idioms such as (1) *field hollers*, which slaves devised from highly varied pitches and rhythms for the purpose of communicating among themselves while working in fields; (2) *ballads*, which come partly from European traditions for songs that tell stories; and (3) music devised for dances, such as the *ring shout*.

Performing the blues involves some of the same techniques that are used by singers and musicians who play stringed instruments in Senegal and Gambia, the northern parts of West Africa. For example, the earliest recorded blues have enormous variety in the ways notes are sung. In particular, what might sound like moans and wails may be merely the vocabulary of drops and scoops of pitch in vocal music of the parent culture. Or what may sound to us like odd starting and stopping points in the phrases probably reflects the rich variation of rhythms common to the music that

((•— **Listen** on
mysearchlab.com
Listen to audio-visual explanation
for blues lyrics on mysearchlab.com

▶ Guitar and banjo, instruments used in African American music that led to jazz. The banjo was invented in the New World by African slaves. The guitar was brought to America from Europe. The guitar was an important instrument for accompanying blues singing. The banjo was common in minstrel bands and ragtime music.

((•∎ **Listen** on
mysearchlab.com

Listen to audio-visual explanation of 12-bar blues chord progression on mysearchlab.com

influenced the blues. Creatively toying with the rhythms and pitches in the melody notes was commonplace. The effect of these manipulations became known as "bluesy" or "soulful." Twentieth-century recordings of Son House, Charley Patton, and Robert Johnson indicate how the earliest forms of blues probably sounded.

In the beginning, blues was a form of unaccompanied solo singing. After blues began to develop, singers began to accompany themselves on the guitar or banjo. The earliest accompaniments did not necessarily use chords or chord progressions. Their accompaniments often had only 1 note at a time or 2 notes played together. Eventually the singers began to use chords. But, at first, they used only whatever chords they already knew. They didn't necessarily go and learn a set of harmonies that would, in turn, dictate the notes they were allowed to use in the melody, as jazz musicians later did. Usually only a few chords were employed. There was much repetition, not only in the accompaniment but also in the lyrics. Then, as the blues evolved, a certain pattern of accompaniment chords became customary. It was similar to the pattern used in church hymns. (See Elements of Music Appendix, pages 270–271, for full explanation and illustration.)

As the blues, developed, the pattern of words and the rhythms of words in the lyrics began to become more and more standardized. It had become fairly well developed by 1910. Eventually a rhyme scheme was adopted that had its own rhythm. (See the example of paired couplets in iambic pentameter, "Fine and Mellow," on page 275 of Elements of Music Appendix and listen to "Reckless Blues" by Bessie Smith on the

Jazz Classics CD1 Track 5.) *Underneath that rhyme scheme, a given progression of accompaniment chords became standardized.* This pattern of chords, in turn, set the pace for the twentieth-century tradition of blues performances that had no singing. (Listen to the trumpet, trombone, and piano solos on "West End Blues" on *Jazz Classics CD1* Track 3.) *Instrumental blues, as it has been called, evolved as its own idiom.* By the 1930s, many chord changes were being made by jazz bands when playing the blues. By the mid-1950s, quite challenging harmonies had been explored within the blues form. (Listen to the saxophone solo improvisations on "Two Bass Hit" on *Jazz Classics CD1* Track 23; see page 300 for chord progressions.)

When trumpeters, clarinetists, saxophonists, and trombonists began playing jazz, they sometimes imitated the scoops and drops of pitch that blues singers used. They also decorated their songs with odd rhythms and tone qualities that had been demonstrated by blues singers. These nuances of rhythm and inflections of pitch allowed instrumentalists to spice up bland melodies by making their rhythms less predictable and the tone qualities and pitches of melody notes more flexible. Occasionally instrumentalists also picked tunes that had been first introduced by blues singers. So you see that *the blues tradition contributed to jazz in at least three important respects:* (1) modeling novel sounds, (2) offering a standard set of accompaniment harmonies, and (3) furnishing part of the jazz repertory.

After jazz and blues had both become recognizable forms, blues continued to change over the years, parallel to but usually separate from the course of development that jazz followed. Its progress occasionally overlapped with jazz, however. For instance, many blues singers hired jazz musicians to accompany them. And many jazz bands routinely featured a blues singer. Eventually blues became a major part of popular music in America and provided one of the roots for rock and roll. Jazz, on the other hand, became more complicated, less popular, and some of it was considered art music, instead of popular music.

((◦● **Listen** on
mysearchlab.com
Listen to blues poetic form by Bessie Smith on mysearchlab.com

BRASS BANDS

Historian-musicologist Karl Koenig has come up with a way to help us appreciate the musical setting that gave birth to jazz. He encourages us to imagine life at the beginning of the twentieth century. Consider for instance that there were no electronic devices. Trying to have fun on a night in New Orleans would be very different than it is now. You could not listen to any radio or television programs, CDs, or tapes. You could not call anyone on the telephone or visit movie theaters or video arcades. Candlelight would be needed for reading. However, you could go to the town square, which would be lit by gas lamps. There you could buy flavored ices from a vendor, exchange pleasantries with your neighbors, and take a walk in the moonlight. You could also listen and dance to the local band. In other words, there almost had to be *live* music. A town without a band was a very dull place to be. The social and fraternal organizations knew this, as did the newspapers and businesses. Therefore sponsorship was provided for most of the local bands by churches, social and benevolent clubs, fraternal clubs, fire departments, townships, undertakers, and plantation owners.

A black military brass band of the Civil War period.

Photo courtesy of the collections of the Library of Congress

A band was present at almost every social activity, most of which took place outdoors: picnics, sporting events, political speeches, or dramatic presentations at the town hall, and dances in the open-air pavilions. The band played before the event and for the dance that followed. Dancing was the main social activity of the nineteenth century. A large brass band was used so that the music could be heard in outdoor settings. Note that in the narrowest sense, a "brass band" has only brass instruments, bass drum, cymbal, and snare drum. But the early Louisiana bands also included a clarinet and later a saxophone. When the social activity was held indoors, a large band was not needed. There the smaller "string band" was suitable. It was usually comprised of cornet, violin, guitar, bass, and piano or some combination of those instruments (see photo on page 26).

There had been brass bands in the New Orleans area long before the Civil War. Then, during the war, occupation by Union troops had exposed the city to many more. About thirty different regimental bands of the occupying forces were stationed in and around New Orleans. They were very conspicuous. They played for the many military ceremonies and for concerts of patriotic and popular music. Their presence was an additional stimulus for the band tradition in New Orleans.

RAGTIME

Another trend was important to the birth of jazz. By the end of the 1800s, ragtime was very popular in New Orleans. The word "rag" refers to a kind of music that was put together like a military march and had rhythms borrowed from African American banjo music. You could tell ragtime music because many of the loud accents fell in between the beats. This is called syncopation. Musicians would use syncopation on all kinds of different tunes and say they were "ragging" those tunes. So the term "to rag" came to mean giving the rhythms in a piece of music a distinctly syncopated feeling.

Photo courtesy of Michael Ochs Archives/Getty Images

◀ Scott Joplin, the most important ragtime composer.

"Ragtime" ordinarily refers to a kind of written piano music that first appeared in the 1890s. The most famous composer of this style was Scott Joplin (1868–1917). The term has also been used to identify an entire era of music, not exclusively written piano music. For example, between the 1890s and the 1920s there were also ragtime bands, ragtime singers, ragtime banjo players, etc.

Many of the musicians we classify today as "jazz" musicians called themselves "ragtime" musicians back then. Because of this, some scholars consider ragtime to have been the first jazz style. However, ragtime does not qualify as a jazz style by the strictest definition of jazz because it lacked what today is called jazz swing feeling. Instead we can say that (1) ragtime was a forerunner of jazz and (2) contributed tunes to jazz repertory. (3) It popularized using accents before and after the beat instead of always directly on it. This was its syncopation, which gave ragtime its distinct character and charm. Today jazz musicians play "around" the beat partly because ragtime made the practice popular.

COMBINING INFLUENCES

During the 1890s, there were bands in almost every small town and settlement in southern Louisiana. Their music reflected several influences. It combined march music and ragtime. Moreover, these two styles were interrelated. John Philip Sousa, the famous bandleader, had included ragtime pieces in his band concerts. Ragtime pianists often performed Sousa marches in a ragtime style. Another significant force in New Orleans culture of that time was music of the Mexican bands that visited the city.

Musicians from these bands settled in and around New Orleans, and some became music teachers. Their music was respected and enjoyed so much that it influenced the styles of New Orleans trumpeters.

Band music directly influenced jazz for several reasons. By the beginning of the twentieth century, New Orleanians were accustomed to hearing brass bands such as Sousa's, having already heard many military bands of the Gulf Coast Command. Dances held in the middle 1800s were often provided with music by the military band that was stationed in the region. In fact, the march form was sometimes modified and used as dance music. Later a popular dance called the "two-step" was done to march-like music. Moreover, the way that passages were organized in a ragtime piece followed the pattern found in marches. Eventually roles of various instruments were transferred from marching band to jazz band. For instance, flute and piccolo parts in marches were imitated by jazz clarinetists, and drum parts for marches developed into styles for playing drums in jazz.

THE PARTY ATMOSPHERE

In addition to the brass band movement there were other factors that made New Orleans an ideal setting for the birth of jazz. New Orleans was a center for commerce because of its nearness to the mouth of the Mississippi River, a flourishing trade route for America, the Caribbean, and Europe. Because the city was a seaport, it catered to travelers from all over the world, and New Orleans maintained a party atmosphere. There were numerous taverns and dance halls. One aspect of the entertainment it provided was a famous prostitution district known as Storyville. **The reason the party atmosphere of New Orleans is important to the beginning of jazz is that it generated so much work for musicians. There was so much demand for live music that there was a constant need for fresh material. This caused musicians to stretch styles. They blended, salvaged, and**

▶ Ory's Woodland Band, an early New Orleans "string band," posing during an outdoor picnic gig.

Courtesy of William Ransom Hogan Jazz Archive, Tulane University

continuously revised odd assortments of approaches and material. This ultimately became jazz.

Early jazz musicians have said that their repertory was constructed primarily to accompany dances such as the mazurka, schottische, quadrille, and one-step. These musicians were not hired specifically to play jazz. At the beginning of the twentieth century, New Orleans parade bands (photo below) and dance bands shared the same musicians and much of the same repertory. It was almost as though the musicians walked directly from the street parade into the dance hall, often putting down a brass instrument and picking up a violin. The performing groups that accompanied dances were termed "string bands" or "orchestras"—violin, guitar, bass viol, and one or two wind instruments, played by the same musicians who had paraded with trumpet and trombone. (See photo on page 26.) To satisfy the demands of dancers, these musicians often combined music from different sources. Sometimes they ended up creating new sounds that were very compelling rhythmically, such as "ragging" march music to make it more jumpy.

These approaches became the core of jazz style, and their manner of playing led to the idea that jazz is not *what* you play, but *how* you play it. In other words, **jazz was an outgrowth of treatments for many kinds of music being played on the demand of dancers.** Today we call these same musicians "jazz musicians," and their music "New Orleans jazz" or "Dixieland."

◀ Eureka Brass Band, a New Orleans brass band, playing in a funeral procession.

Photo by Bill Russell, courtesy of William Ransom Hogan Jazz Archive, Tulane University

Another trend also led to jazz style. In parades as well as dance halls, small bands were trying to perform music originally written for large bands. This led to what became standard Dixieland style. In trying to fill out the sound, more activity was required of each player, so musicians improvised parts to order. They got in the habit of improvising, and as jazz evolved, this habit changed from being a necessity to being a choice. In essence, the musicians in New Orleans were combining diverse materials to please people who had a taste for special kinds of musical excitement.

SUMMARY

1. Jazz originated in New Orleans around the beginning of the twentieth century.

2. New Orleans was the ideal site for the birth of jazz because it was an intensely musical city with a history of rich ethnic diversity, especially French and African.

3. African American forms of music such as the blues and ragtime blended with European dance music and church music.

4. Jazz emerged when brass bands were at a height of popularity.

5. Ragtime was in such high demand that brass bands and string bands were improvising rag-like syncopations into their pieces to please dancers.

6. New Orleans musicians combined diverse materials to please people who had a taste for special kinds of musical excitement.

7. Jazz came out of the combination of instruments, repertory, and musical practices used by brass bands and string bands in New Orleans before the 1920s.

8. Improvisation became common as small bands attempted to perform music originally intended for large bands. Musicians improvised parts to order.

KEY TERMS

blues	pitch bend	ragtime
Creole of Color		

FURTHER RESOURCES

✓•—[Study and Review on mysearchlab.com

Watch the Documentary on "Jazz in New Orleans"
Test your knowledge with the chapter quiz.

LISTEN

Early Band Ragtime 1899–1909 (Smithsonian/Folkways RBF 38)

Jazz, Vol. 1: The South (Smithsonian/Folkways 2801)

Jazz, Vol. 2: The Blues (Smithsonian/Folkways 2802)

Riverside History of Classic Jazz (Riverside/Fantasy 005, 3CD Set, 1900–1954)

That's My Rabbit, My Dog Caught It: Traditional Southern Instrumental Styles (New World 226)

Come and Trip It: Instrumental Dance Music 1780s–1920s (New World 80293)

The Sousa and Pryor Bands: Original Recordings 1901–1926 (New World 282)

Steppin' On the Gas: From Rags to Jazz 1913–1927 (New World 269, LP, 1977)

Jazz: Some Beginnings 1913–1926 (Smithsonian/Folkways RF 31)

Street Cries and Creole Songs of New Orleans (Folkways FA 2202)

Roots of the Blues (New World 80252)

African Journey: A Search for the Roots of the Blues (Sonet 667; Vanguard SRV 73014/5)

That Devilin' Tune Vol. 1 (1985–1927) WHRA-6003.

New World Records are available at www.newworldrecords.org

Smithsonian/Folkways are available at www.si.edu/folkways

READ

Abbott, Lynn, and Doug Seroff, eds. 2003. *Out of Sight: The Rise of African American Popular Music, 1889–1895*. Jackson: University of Mississippi Press.

Abbott, Lynn, and Doug Seroff, eds. 2007. *Ragged but Right: Black Traveling Shows, Coon Songs, and the Dark Pathway to Blues And Jazz*. Jackson: University of Mississippi Press.

Bebey, Francis. 1975. *African Music: A People's Art*. Chicago: Lawrence Hill Books (translation).

Berlin, Edward A. 1980. *Ragtime: A Musical and Cultural History*. Berkeley: University of California Press.

Berlin, Edward A. 1994. *Scott Joplin: King of Ragtime*. New York: Oxford University Press.

Brooks, Tim. 2005. *Lost Sounds: Blacks and the Birth of the Recording Industry, 1890–1919*. Urbana: University of Illinois Press.

Evans, David. 1982. *Big Road Blues: Tradition and Creativity in the Folk Blues*. Berkeley: University of California Press.

Gushee, Lawrence. 2005. *Pioneers of Jazz: The Story of the Creole Band*. New York: Oxford University Press.

Haskins, James. 1975. *The Creoles of Color of New Orleans*. New York: Crowell.

Hasse, John, ed. 1980. *Ragtime: Its History, Composers and Music*. Berkeley: University of California Press.

Kebede, Ashenafi. 1982. *Roots of Black Music: The Vocal, Instrumental, and Dance Heritage of Africa and Black America*. Upper Saddle River, NJ: Prentice-Hall.

Koenig, Karl. 2002. *Jazz in Print (1856–1929): An Anthology of Selected Early Readings in Jazz History*. Hillsdale, NY: Pendragon.

Lowe, Allen. 2001. *That Devilin' Tune: A Jazz History*. Berkeley, CA: Music and Arts Programs of America.

Marquis, Donald M. 1978, 1993, 2005 (rev. ed.) (Da Capo reprint, 1980). *In Search of Buddy Bolden: First Man of Jazz*. Baton Rouge: Louisiana State University Press.

Nketia, J. H. Kwabena. 1974. *The Music of Africa*. New York: Norton.

Oliver, Paul. 1970. *Savannah Syncopators*. New York: Stein and Day (with a 2-LP set of records available as *Savannah Syncopators* from CBS [England] 52799).

Roberts, John Storm. 1998. *Black Music of Two Worlds*. 2nd ed. New York: Schirmer (with 3-LP set of records available as Smithsonian Folkways FE 4602).

Schafer, William J. 1977. *Brass Bands and New Orleans Jazz*. Baton Rouge: Louisiana State University Press.

Smith, Michael P. 1994. *Mardi Gras Indians*. Gretna, LA: Pelican.

Early Jazz

Ma Rainey and her Georgia Jazz Band. Photo courtesy of Frank Driggs

A NEW STYLE

Early jazz musicians often began improvising by embellishing the melodies of pop tunes. As jazz evolved across the 1920s, the embellishments sometimes became more important to a performance than the tunes themselves. In some performances of the 1930s, all that remained was the original tune's spirit and chord progressions. What is today called improvising was sometimes referred to by early jazz musicians as embellishing, riffing, "jassing," or "jazzing up."

Early jazz differs from its ragtime, blues, and brass band roots in several important respects:

1. Much of each performance was improvised.
2. Rhythmic feeling was looser and more relaxed, thus anticipating jazz swing feeling.
3. It generated much of its own repertory of compositions.
4. Collective improvisation created a more complex musical product than was typical in ragtime, blues, or marching band music.

Combo jazz began in New Orleans, and that city contributed several very important musicians. The best known were trumpeter Louis Armstrong and composer-arranger Jelly Roll Morton.

It was in Chicago that many black New Orleans musicians were first recorded in the early 1920s. Black New Orleans style jazz as played between 1900 and 1922 in New Orleans was not recorded. We can't say we know exactly what it sounded like. According to interviews and a few early records, the earliest forms of jazz featured **collective improvisation**, with all group members playing at the same time. This took place when every player created phrases which complemented every other player. This is a very exciting effect, and it captivated many listeners.

In the collective improvisation of early jazz, instruments tended to fulfill set musical roles similar to those established in brass bands. The trumpet often played the melody. The clarinet played busy figures with many notes. The clarinet part decorated the melody played by trumpet. The trombone would play simpler figures. The trombone's music outlined the chord notes and filled in low-pitched harmony notes. The trombone created motion in a pitch range that was lower than that of clarinet and trumpet.

((•—Listen on **mysearchlab.com**
Listen to Oliver's Creole Jazz Band on mysearchlab.com

Collective improvisation
Simultaneous improvisation by all members of a group together

Photo courtesy of Pictorial Press Ltd/Alamy

◄ Original Dixieland Jass Band (also called Original Dixieland Jazz Band), 1916. Left to right: Tony Spargo [Sbarbaro, Sparbaro] (drums), Eddie Edwards (trombone), Nick LaRocca (cornet), Alcide Nunez (clarinet),Henry Ragas (piano), the first jazz group to make records.

New Orleans jazz was first recorded in Chicago and New York, not in New Orleans. **The Original Dixieland Jazz Band** made the first recordings. This was a collection of white New Orleans musicians who organized a band in Chicago during 1916 and played in New York in 1917. They used cornet, clarinet, trombone, piano, and drums. Under the leadership of cornetist Nick LaRocca (1889–1961), the band recorded its first 78 rpm record in 1917. They played "Livery Stable Blues" on one side and "Dixie Jazz Band One-Step" on the other. It sold very well and was widely imitated. Even during the 1990s, musicians were forming Dixieland jazz bands in the style of this group.

((•—Listen on **mysearchlab.com**
Listen to collective improvisation by Creole Jazz Band on mysearchlab.com

((•─ Listen on mysearchlab.com

Recorded February 26, 1917, in New York by Nick LaRocca (cornet), Larry Shields (clarinet), Eddie Edwards (trombone), Henry Ragas (piano), and Tony Spargo (drums) by Victor Records.

This record was made in New York by a group of white New Orleans musicians who had come together in Chicago the preceding year. They called themselves the Original Dixieland Jass Band (ODJB). "Dixie Jazz Band One-Step" (also known as "Original Dixieland One-Step") was on the reverse side of "Livery Stable Blues," one of the most popular discs in the first decade of recorded jazz. Worldwide sales of the record are said to have reached about a million copies by the late 1930s.

This is the first instrumental jazz recording ever released, and music by the ODJB has continued to influence musicians, partly because this band made the first jazz records. The roles that the different instruments assume on this recording were associated with what is known today as New Orleans, Chicago, or Dixieland style jazz. We can consider this record to be an example of music that was popular in New Orleans during this period because most of the fashions heard here were already common in New Orleans ragtime bands by 1917. So even though it was the first to be recorded, the ODJB was not necessarily the first or the "Original" band of its kind, as its name implies.

Of the five instruments playing here, the clarinet is the most evident, and the piano is least evident. The cornet and trombone sounds frequently blend so closely that you may have difficulty distinguishing them, though many trombone smears are conspicuous. As was typical for New Orleans drummers of the period, Spargo frequently switches instruments. At various moments he can be heard playing snare drum, woodblock, and cowbell. He uses the cymbal sparingly, and a cymbal crash usually signifies a climactic moment in the music.

Many of the different sounds heard here are so close in pitch and rhythm that they blend together in your ear and disguise each other. But the more often you listen, the more distinct they will become. Can you remember peering at a trick sketch on a comic book, trying to recognize a tiger hidden in jungle ferns where overlapping lines camouflaged its contours? Your search for separate instruments here might resemble the experience you had with the trick sketch.

The ODJB's roots in the brass band tradition are reflected in this piece's opening. The rhythm of the first four-measure sequence is called a "roll-off," a device usually played by a parade band's drummer to prepare the musicians to march. By listening closely, you can hear the drummer playing the roll-off pattern underneath the horns. His rhythm is the same as theirs. The trombone smear in the third group of four beats coincides with a drum roll. Like other march-style popular music of this period, the "Dixie Jazz Band One-Step" was used to accompany a dance called the "one-step."

The first two themes in this piece were written by the band members. The third theme was composed by Joe Jordan. To guide you through the events in this recording, we will break the music into beats and groups of four beats, each of which is called a "measure." At the beginning we will identify what happens on each beat. This will clarify the drum roll model the ODJB used for playing their parts. After that, we will refer to each section of the piece in terms of what happens for each group of measures.

0' 00"	**First Theme**			
	First Measure:	*bang*	*bang*	*silence*	*silence*
	(numbered beats):	*1*	*2*	*3*	*4*
	Second Measure:	*bang*	*bang*	*silence*	*silence*
	(numbered beats):	*1*	*2*	*3*	*4*
	Third Measure:	*trombone smear*			
	(numbered beats):	*1*	*2*	*3*	*4*
	Fourth Measure:	*smear ends*	*silence*	*crash*	
	(numbered beats):	*1*	*2*	*3*	*4*

0' 03" **Fifth, Sixth, Seventh, and Eighth Measures:**

Band plays a new theme, with clarinet playing around the cornet and trombone parts. The drummer plays a military snare drum rhythm as a counteractivity to the rhythms of the horn lines.

0' 07" **Repeat of the First Theme, but with different ending**

0' 15" **Second Theme**

0' 23" **Repeat of the Second Theme, but with different ending**

0' 30" **Repeat of First and Second Themes in above order**

1' 00" **Third Theme** ("That Teasin' Rag" by Joe Jordan)

Trombone exchanges with clarinet in a call-and-response fashion, playfully trading descending smears; "clickety-clacking" of the drummer's sticks sound military rhythms on the woodblock for the first eight measures, then alternately striking woodblock and cowbell.

Trombone plays descending smears in unison with piano, as a "call." Cornet and clarinet harmonize a bobbing little figure as a "response." This section ends with the horn parts going in different directions. A robust trombone part emerges with a repeating figure near the end. Intensity builds and then culminates with a high-pitched descending clarinet smear.

1' 16" **Third Theme, with different ending**

First beat is played by the drummer striking his cymbal for a crash. Then he plays woodblock and cowbell. The trombone then briefly carries a melody of its own, using a style similar to the tuba parts of march arrangements. Near the end, the cornet chimes in with a sustained tone on an offbeat.

1' 32" **Third Theme**

Drummer begins this section by emphasizing his cowbell, and he uses woodblock less than before. Notice the descending trombone smears. A quick, high-pitched clarinet smear ends the section.

1' 48" **Repeat of Third Theme, with different ending**

Drummer begins with a cymbal crash, then plays patterns on woodblock. He interrupts his pattern during the middle of this section and strikes the bass drum twice in succession.

2' 03" **Third Theme**

If you listen closely during the last half of this section, you will hear the piano pounding out bass patterns. This section ends with a descending clarinet smear.

2' 18" **Third Theme, with different ending**

Recorded October 5, 1923, in Richmond, Indiana, by Joe Oliver and Louis Armstrong (cornet), Johnny Dodds (clarinet), Stump Evans (saxophone), Honore Dutrey (trombone), Lil Hardin (piano), Johnny St. Cyr (banjo), unknown but probably Charlie Jackson (tuba), Baby Dodds (drums, woodblock, cymbals); composed by Alphonse Picou and Joe Oliver.

Terms to know from tracks on *Demo CD*: break (34), clarinet (69), woodblock (10), trombone (78), banjo (91).

Joe Oliver's Creole Jazz Band was the first African American group to make records containing a substantial amount of improvisation. They made a number of different recordings in 1923, and "Alligator Hop" is one of their most lively. It was used for a social dance called a "one-step." Though billed as the "Creole" Jazz Band, they had only one true Creole musician in the band at this time, Honore Dutrey. The "Creole" term apparently carried marketing value because it was faintly exotic. In fact, there was another Creole Jazz Band before Oliver's.

The first recordings of this band are also significant because Louis Armstrong is present. Many historians consider Armstrong to be the most important musician in the first forty years of jazz, and some still rank him as the most important musician in all of jazz history. Reverence for these recordings runs so deep that when the building in which they were made was being dismantled in 1960, jazz fans from all over America collected its bricks as souvenirs to that legacy.

Oliver's playing was the main model for Armstrong's style. The two men knew each other in their native New Orleans before Oliver relocated to Chicago in 1918. Oliver called Armstrong from Chicago in 1922 to leave New Orleans. He asked Armstrong to join his Creole Jazz Band at a steady engagement they were playing. This was a very significant event because if Armstrong had remained in New Orleans, the course of jazz history would have been forever altered. Oliver's pianist Lil Hardin also exerted a significant influence. It was Hardin who eventually persuaded Armstrong to leave the Creole Jazz Band and go out on his own, thereby expanding his visibility. Armstrong began playing with a series of different bands and made recordings as a leader. These recordings set the pace for major developments in jazz. Hardin and Armstrong also married each other.

The approach to making this music is often termed "collective improvisation" because the musicians seem to be making it up as they go along, and they are all playing different lines at the same time. Rather than "counterpoint," in which each note has another note sounding at the same time to "counter" it, the term "non-imitative polyphony" better describes the music on "Alligator Hop." Polyphony means many (poly) sounds (phony). "Non-imitative" means that the lines are not imitating each other or themselves. Modern jazz small groups improvise collectively, too; but modern jazz differs from the earliest jazz in that modern jazz usually features solos, and relegates the accompanying instruments during solo passages to the background. It does not sound several lines of equal importance in the foreground as we hear in this selection.

Despite our description of this music as "collective improvisation," the music is not entirely spontaneous. It has been rehearsed. How else would the moments at which everybody stops playing except the one who takes the solo break be so cleanly coordinated by all the band members? A common practice was for all the members of the band to agree ahead of time to stop playing entirely at the beginning of the 13th measure of each 16-measure section. When the band stops, as prearranged, one soloist continues, usually the clarinet. A few breaks are filled by saxophone. Note also that the musicians are all following the same organization of themes in the piece. Besides rehearsal, something else makes "collective improvisations" possible: a pre-established structure. The prearranged plan allocates four measures for an introduction, 16 measures for an "A-section," which is then repeated. Another 16 measures is allocated for a "B-section" (also known as a "bridge" or "trio strain"). The sections are sequenced as **Intro-A-A-B-A-A-B-B-B**. Then there is a very brief section attached to the end at about 2′ 21″. This is termed a "tag."

Careful listening will also reveal other parts that obviously have been worked out in advance. For example, the recording contains a melody you might detect in the cornet part, especially from about 0′ 56″ to 1′ 08″ and in the saxophone part at about 1′ 30″. Furthermore, clarinet parts played during the breaks are similar enough to each other that we know the clarinetist is not always improvising.

Oliver's musicians packed about a half hour's worth of music into just two and a half minutes. Your job is to air it out, expanding the fleeting moments into major sensations. Make sure you use the pause switch on your CD player every so often to help you digest what just happened. Then replay several times to verify your impressions. This will be necessary because the music sounds chaotic to most listeners the first few times they hear it. There is a lot going on, and it is going by very fast. Therefore it is not realistic to expect to grasp more than a fraction of it the first few times you listen.

To help make sense out of the sonic complexity in "Alligator Hop," keep in mind that all the musicians are following the same progression of accompaniment chords that came with the original melody. They are also adhering to a number of unwritten rules such as:

1. Don't get in each others' way.
2. Try to invent lines that complement each others' lines.
3. Strive to create an exciting feeling.
4. Make music so rhythmically compelling that people will want to dance to it.

One way to sort out the density of activity in "Alligator Hop" is to focus on the sound of just one instrument at a time. One sound that should be easy to detect is the drummer clacking away on woodblock much of the time. This is particularly evident at the beginning of the piece and at 1′ 39″. The clarinet is the most prominent instrument. Solo breaks occupy the 13th and 14th measures ("bars") of most sections, and clarinet fills many of these. So you would do well to concentrate on its sound first. This is easy when it is alone in breaks as at 0′ 17″, 0′ 34″, and 0′ 51″. Often the pattern played there is a sequence of chord notes played one at a time. This is the pattern technically termed *arpeggio*. You can also hear clarinet weaving lines around the other horn parts the rest of the time, in a manner technically known as *obbligato*. The slide trombone offers us a lead-in at the very beginning. So if you can stay with its sound, you should be able to track its contributions throughout the piece.

The saxophone also has some feature time and should be identifiable, particularly at 1′ 30″. What may sound like a banjo solo a few moments later is actually a purposeful manipulation of saxophone sound. The tone of the saxophone has been drastically altered by the way the notes are started with the player's tongue at 1′ 53″ and 1′ 59″. Ordinarily the tongue interrupts the airflow but stays out of the way enough that listeners don't notice its involvement. If the tongue stays on the reed of the saxophone mouthpiece too long, however, it affects the tone quality, and this is what is happening at the moments indicated below as "slap-tongued."

The lines played by the two cornets are often difficult to distinguish. It is especially challenging to determine when they are going their own separate ways and when they are playing harmony parts that they worked out in advance. (Harmonized cornets can be heard joined by the trombone at 2′ 17″.) You might postpone tackling that puzzle until after you are comfortable with easier aspects of the music.

The piano is often hard to hear, but it does come in and out of the foreground frequently, as at 1′ 36″ and 1′ 42″. It is prominent in the accompaniment, playing emphatically under the cornet solo at 1′ 30″. So when it emerges, you could try to follow its sound as it recedes into the mix. Keep in mind that when it is not prominent, piano is briskly striding in a "uum chuck uum chuck" rhythm. The banjo is also hard to hear when everyone else is playing.

Once we begin to notice the various lines, we might marvel at how so many of them can coexist without clashing. It is like rush hour traffic in a big city. If you watch it carefully, you find people tend most of the time to stay in their own lane, but when they do decide to change lanes, they are especially considerate of others. Thus, astonishingly—given so many cars—there is rarely a collision, and everybody manages to get home in one piece!

Remember that the musicians created quite an elaborate texture at a quick tempo. So practice taking it in small doses. In that way you will give yourself a good chance to keep up with this busy ensemble. The reward will be discovering how much is revealed.

Introduction (4 bars)

0′ 00″   Trombone slides up in pitch as a lead-in to the downbeat.

0′ 05″ **A-section** (16 bars)

Cornets play melody. Clarinet plays an obbligato, decorating the cornets. Trombone outlines harmony with low-pitched notes, emphasizing downbeats. Piano is chording. Woodblock is clacking.

0′ 17″   break by clarinet on a descending arpeggio (chord notes played one at a time)

A-section (16 bars)

0′ 21″   two cornets playing harmony while clarinet weaves an obbligato
Drummer is striking his woodblock. Piano is striding. Banjo is strumming.

0′ 34″   Clarinet plays descending arpeggio.

B-section (16 bars)

0′ 38″   two cornets and clarinet in harmony

0′ 45″   Break features clarinet.

0′ 51″   Break features clarinet on ascending arpeggio.

A-section (16 bars)

0′ 56″   Joe Oliver cornet solo improvisation, clarinet obbligato, woodblock prominent

1′ 08″   break for clarinet

1′ 13″ **A-section** (16 bars)

1′ 26″   Clarinet plays descending arpeggio.

B-section (16 bars)

1′ 30″   embellished bridge melody by saxophone (piano playing very emphatically on every beat; tuba playing on every other beat)

1′ 36″   break for piano

1′ 39″   Sax solo resumes; drummer is playing woodblock.

1' 42"	solo break for piano, double-timing; concluded by cymbal crash
1' 45"	Saxophone finishes the phrase.
1' 46"	very syncopated lead-in by cornets in harmony
1' 47"	**B-section** (16 bars)
	collective improvisation; saxophone countermelody; clarinet countermelody
1' 53"	break for saxophone to play a descending line, second half of which is slap-tongued, significantly changing the tone quality
1' 59"	break for saxophone, slap-tongued
2' 03"	**B-section** (16 bars)
	tuba playing on every other beat
2' 04"	flutter/growl tone lead-in by cornet
2' 10"	descending smear by growling trombone
2' 16"	break by two cornets and trombone in harmony
	Tag
2' 21"	Come again? Done twice as though to be sure it is really done?

◀ Joe "King" Oliver's Creole Jazz Band of 1923. (Oliver is standing rear left.) This group of New Orleans musicians performed steady engagements in Chicago. Pianist Lil Hardin was the band's only non-New Orleanian, and she married Louis Armstrong, fourth from left.

Photo courtesy of Frank Driggs

Chicago was the center for a very active jazz scene during the 1920s. Musicians there can be described in terms of three main categories: (1) The transplanted New Orleans African American musicians, (2) their white New Orleans counterparts, and (3) young white Chicagoans who imitated the older players. That third category is today called "The **Chicago School**" or the "Chicagoans." Eventually the Chicago musicians and the transplanted New Orleans musicians mixed with New York musicians. By the late 1920s, a strong jazz scene had also developed in New York.

Jazz piano styles were evolving in places other than New Orleans prior to 1920. In fact, many outstanding jazz pianists of the 1920s were from the East Coast. Many of them played unaccompanied. Early jazz piano styles evolved from ragtime. Playing ragtime did not always necessitate reading or memorizing written music. Once the style had been absorbed, skilled pianists appeared who could improvise original rags as well as embellish written ones. One jazz piano style with roots in ragtime is known as **stride** style. This uses percussive, fast-moving, left-hand figures in which low bass notes alternate with mid-range chords, while the right hand plays melodies and embellishments in a very energetic fashion. This is a difficult style to play. The best players kept a perfect stride going continuously.

INSTRUMENTS IN EARLY JAZZ BANDS

The **front line** of most early jazz combos included trumpet, clarinet, trombone, and occasionally saxophone. The rhythm section was made up of

Chicago School A group of young white Chicagoans who emulated the styles of New Orleans musicians in the mid-1920s

Stride Left-hand style used by early jazz pianists. It usually employs a bass note on the first and third beats of each measure and a chord on the second and fourth

Front line Musicians appearing directly in front of the audience; this designation is sometimes used to separate hornmen (because they stand in the front of a combo) from accompanists (who usually appear behind them)

▶ A Sousaphone, an instrument often used in early jazz marching bands, because it was easier to carry than a conventionally shaped tuba

several instruments, which might include guitar, banjo, tuba, bass saxophone, string bass, piano, and drums. No bands had all these instruments playing at the same time, but most drew some combination from that collection. It was not unusual for early jazz combos to be without string bass, and many early jazz recordings were made without drums. Some groups substituted tuba for string bass.

((•— Listen on
mysearchlab.com
Listen to audio-visual comparison of clarinet and soprano saxophone on mysearchlab.com

◄ Clarinet and soprano sax.

Early jazz drummers are poorly heard on records because early studio equipment was not well-suited to recording drums. At that time, records were made by playing into acoustic recording horns (see page 57). The small end of the horn was connected to a cutting needle that made grooves in a cylinder or a disc. Any loud sound, especially a blow to the bass drum, could knock the needle off the cutting surface. Many recordings during this period consequently represent working bands minus their drummers. Many of the recordings that do employ drummers either omit most drum equipment entirely or muffle it so much that, when combined with low recording quality, drum sounds are almost inaudible. We are often left with little more than the clickety clicking sound of drumsticks striking a small block of wood that has been hollowed out to increase resonance. This was one of the only sounds drummers were allowed to produce when engineers were hesitant to attempt recording loud sounds.

Demo CD Track 10 for the sound of the woodblock.

Though the drumming sound described above was particularly convenient in adapting to the restrictions imposed by early recording situations, it represents only one sample in a range of sounds commonly generated by the earliest jazz drummers. Light, staccato sounds were also produced by striking a cowbell or the shell or rim of the bass drum, rather than the drum head that usually receives the blow. These sounds were also employed in some early recording sessions. A large cymbal or gong was sometimes used to signal a dramatic height in the music. When playing on the light-sounding instruments, many of the earliest drummers chose patterns from military and ragtime drumming.

EARLY JAZZ INNOVATORS

Jelly Roll Morton

Jelly Roll Morton (1890–1941) was a pianist, composer-arranger, and bandleader from New Orleans. He was one of the first jazz pianists as well as the first jazz composer. Morton performed in both the ragtime style and the jazz style. He developed rhythmic techniques to make his lines swing. By doing this and reducing adornment, Morton played with a lighter and more swinging feeling than was typical of ragtime. It was the first style of piano playing that warrants the label of "jazz."

Morton's piano style was quite complex. He often played two or three melodic lines at a time, like a band. It was as though trumpet parts, clarinet parts, and trombone parts were all being heard coming from a piano! Morton put a variety of themes and dramatic devices within a single piece. Morton mixed ragtime with less formal, more blues-oriented New Orleans styles.

▶ Jelly Roll Morton (pianist) and his Red Hot Peppers. In this 1926 studio recording band, Morton combined the free-wheeling spirit of New Orleans jazz with a more highly arranged format. Morton was the first important jazz composer.

Photo courtesy of Frank Driggs

Morton's best known bands were a series of recording groups in Chicago called the Red Hot Peppers. Morton's compositions and arrangements on those recordings are still respected by jazz composers and scholars. Morton employed many of the same New Orleans-born musicians shared by other black Chicago groups. Under Morton's leadership, the resulting sounds were equally high-spirited but better organized. In summary, Jelly Roll Morton is historically notable because:

1. He was the first important jazz composer, and several of his pieces became well known in rearranged form when played by other bands.
2. He was one of the first jazz musicians to balance composition with improvisation while retaining the excitement of collectively improvised jazz.
3. He recorded piano solos that were well-organized, forcefully executed musical statements with horn-like lines.
4. He bridged the gap between the piano styles of ragtime and jazz by loosening ragtime's rhythmic feeling and decreasing its embellishments.

James P. Johnson

James P. Johnson (1894–1955) was born in New Jersey. He was part of the East Coast jazz piano tradition that was developing at about the same time as combo jazz was developing in New Orleans. Like Morton, his work smoothed the transition from ragtime to jazz. One of the first jazz musicians to broadcast on the radio, Johnson was already a prominent figure by the time jazz began to be recorded. He wrote his famous "Carolina Shout" in 1914 and recorded it in 1921. Johnson is considered "the father of stride piano." This is a style in which the pianist uses fingers on his left hand to play a bass note the first and third of every four beats and a mid-range chord on the second and fourth beats. These sounds are made very percussively. The right hand then plays melodies very energetically. The left hand motion resembles a striding kind of leg motion made by a person walking, hence the name. The technique is extremely demanding. Johnson's title of "Father" was earned because his own brand of stride did the most to spread this style and because he was the best of the earliest stride masters.

Johnson's playing tended to be lighter, faster, and less bluesy than Morton's. He relied less on dramatic devices and more on a breathtaking flow, demonstrating great virtuosity. Like Morton, he perfected an orchestral approach to jazz piano playing, as though he were a one-man band. Many musicians feel that he was never surpassed in this style. At a time when informal competitions among solo pianists were common in New York, Johnson is said to have won more contests than anyone else. His speed, precision, dexterity, and imagination amazed musicians. The force and swing of his pianistic feats are legendary. Johnson influenced most pianists who emerged during the 1920s, including Fats Waller and Duke Ellington.

Prentice Hall Jazz Collection CD: "Wolverine Blues" by Jelly Roll Morton. This track features only piano, clarinet (Johnny Dodds), and drums (Baby Doods), with the first minute and a half played by Morton. He imitates the sound of a full band in his imaginative and complex piano playing.

Jazz Classics CD1 for *Jazz Styles* (ISBN 0-205-03686-4): "You've Got to Be Modernistic" by James P. Johnson.

Photo courtesy of Frank Driggs

► James P. Johnson, the greatest of all stride-style pianists.

Fats Waller

Fats Waller (1904–1943) was one of the most popular figures in jazz history. Six of his recordings hit number one position on the sales charts, and many more rose into the top ten. Some were million-sellers. He was almost equally well known for three different talents: song writing, piano playing, and entertaining. From 1922 he was making records, and from 1923 he was broadcasting regularly on the radio. He collaborated in writing music for several Broadway shows. Some of his tunes remain among the most enduring in American music. "Ain't Misbehavin'," "Honeysuckle Rose," and "Jitterbug Waltz" are the best known. Waller was capable of bringing a tremendous sense of fun to almost any endeavor. Anyone who ever heard his music or saw him in movies could not help but smile. Much of his material was novelty songs, some of which he composed. While accompanying himself on the piano, he cleverly half talked, half sang the lyrics. He often added witty remarks that he improvised during the performance. In these ways he was an important entertainer and a major figure in popular music as a whole, not just in jazz.

Waller was most important to jazz as an improvising pianist. He was probably the most gracefully swinging of all the stride-style pianists during

Jazz Classics CD1 for *Jazz Styles* (ISBN 0-205-03686-4): "Handful of Keys" by Fats Waller.

Photo courtesy of Frank Driggs

◀ Fats Waller, the most popular jazz pianist-composer of the 1920s and 30s.

the 1920s and 30s. He was the first to conquer the difficult style so well that it came out light and springy. He managed to extract a full, pretty tone quality from the piano, no matter how hard he was swinging nor how fast he was playing. His sense of rhythm was near perfect. His melodic ideas seemed to flow from a boundless imagination.

Some listeners have trouble deciding upon Waller's stature in jazz history. They overlook the extent of Waller's achievement for two reasons. First, he made his work sound so easy because he was such a good pianist and improviser. His skill combined with the lively, happy character of his music to make his playing sound so casual that it is hard to take seriously. The second reason is that piano listeners can get distracted by his vocals and clowning remarks. Yet his improvisations had real substance, and they often contained imaginative twists of harmony and rhythm that were quite subtle. In fact, many pianists were so impressed that they chose to imitate Waller's playing while developing their own styles. Art Tatum, Count Basie, and Dave Brubeck are just a few of the better known pianists who did this.

Photo courtesy of Frank Driggs

▶ Earl Hines, the pianist known for his trumpet-style approach to improvising. His style spanned early jazz and swing to influence modern styles. Hines' big bands were heard by radio broadcasts from Chicago during the 1930s. This photo was taken in 1928, the year Hines recorded "West End Blues" with Louis Armstrong.

Earl Hines

Earl Hines (1903–1983) was an early jazz pianist who significantly influenced piano playing styles of the 1930s and 40s. Born in Pittsburgh, Hines moved to Chicago in 1924. He brought with him an assortment of different jazz techniques, all combined in the form of one catchy style. His playing began its enormous influence during the late 1920s when he recorded with trumpeter Louis Armstrong and made a series of important records of his own. This impact extended during the 1930s by way of radio broadcasts and tours with the big band he led at the Grand Terrace Ballroom from 1928 to 1939. Musicians as far away as Kansas and Texas heard his broadcasts. His style had a clear impact on Teddy Wilson, Nat Cole, Art Tatum, and Count Basie. Hines had an influence on modern jazz because these players, in turn, influenced the development of modern styles.

Much of the piano music made by Hines can be called "brassy." This is partly because of the great physical force Hines used to strike the piano keys. Even when Hines played in a flowery way, a roughness remained in his sound. Rarely was anything sustained, and nearly everything had a punching quality. These properties combined with his method of phrasing to lend that brassy quality to the sound of the piano. Because his right-hand lines sometimes sounded like jazz trumpet playing, the Hines approach earned the title of **trumpet-style** or **horn-like**. His piano lines even seemed to breathe at the moments a trumpeter would breathe. Additionally they contained phrases and rhythms preferred by trumpeters rather than pianists. This manner stems partly from Hines having originally begun his musical training with the goal of becoming a trumpeter instead of a pianist, and also came from what Hines did to be heard over loud band instruments. We must remember that he was playing long before electronic amplification came to the aid of pianists. To manage the task of cutting through, he played very hard, phrased like a trumpeter, and doubled his right-hand melody lines in octaves.

Demo CD Track 41 to hear octave-voiced piano lines.

Hines' "trumpet-style" approach is historically significant because, by playing more as a horn and less in the standard piano styles, Hines paved the way for modern jazz pianists who solo with essentially the same conception that is used by jazz trumpeters and saxophonists. It is less flowery and more direct. It is less classically pianistic and more swinging. Additionally, it is important to realize that the Hines approach is more flexible than the ragtime and stride approaches.

Louis Armstrong

Trumpeter Louis Armstrong (1901–1971) is often called the "father of jazz." In fact, musicians often refer to him as "Pops." No list of jazz greats omits him, and most start with him. Born in New Orleans, he left in 1922 to join Joe Oliver's New Orleans style band in Chicago. The band's best known piece, "Dippermouth Blues," takes its title from another Armstrong nickname, a reference to his mouth being as large as a dipper. A third nickname, Satchmo, is a variation on the same idea: Satchel Mouth.

Armstrong's earliest appearances on record are in collective improvisations, with everyone playing together. But his most significant recordings were made in 1927 and 1928 with him presenting a dramatic solo style.

Prentice Hall Jazz History DVD: "Tiger Rag" by Louis Armstrong; this film was made in 1931, when Armstrong was at the height of his performing powers.

Photo courtesy of Frank Driggs

((•○ **Listen** on **mysearchlab.com**

Listen to Louis Armstrong's trumpet style on mysearchlab.com

◀ Louis Armstrong, the most widely imitated trumpeter in the first twenty years of jazz. His improvised ideas were so well formed and swinging that he influenced pianists, saxophonists, and trombonists, not just trumpeters. Pictured here in 1927, near the time he made his most stirring recordings.

Composed by Joe Oliver; recorded June 6, 1928, in Chicago by Louis Armstrong (trumpet and vocal), Jimmy Strong (clarinet), Fred Robinson (trombone), Earl Hines (piano), Mancy Cara (banjo), and Zutty Singleton (drums).

0' 00" **Introduction**

The opening phrases in this piece are among the most famous in jazz history. Note the drama as Armstrong reaches up to his highest note, the one he sustains. Then listen to the manner in which he gradually descends to finish with a note that makes you eager to hear what follows. Notice his warm, brassy tone and his sure-footed manner. This introduction is a masterpiece that you might want to hear several times before listening to the rest of the performance.

The idea of a bravura solo style, particularly an unaccompanied solo passage like this, was common in light classical music that was popular in America around 1900. Virtuoso cornet soloists were frequently featured in band concerts at that time. In addition, the trumpet sounds of Mexican bands that visited New Orleans had impressed musicians there. When Louis Armstrong devised this stirring opening, he was drawing, either consciously or unconsciously, from that tradition in light classical music, and he was establishing a tradition in jazz.

0' 13" Full band plays a chord.

0' 16" **First Chorus** (a 12-bar blues played slowly)

Melody Played by Armstrong on Trumpet

Notice Armstrong's firm, deliberate manner and quick vibrato.

Accompaniment includes:

soft, sustained trombone notes (often preceded by a smear of pitch that begins well below the ultimate note);

sustained tones of clarinet, sometimes paralleling the motion of the trumpet line (listen for the clarinet's edgy timbre and fast vibrato);

trombone and clarinet notes together indicating the chords changing underneath the trumpet;

piano chords sounded in unison with banjo chords played staccato on each beat ("chomp chomp chomp chomp . . .")

0' 50" **Second Chorus**

Trombone Solo

The trombonist uses the high register and many smears of pitch.

Accompaniment includes:

staccato chording from banjo;

The music that he played in those recordings became a model for the swing era that followed.

Louis Armstrong appeared in about fifty movies and sang in most of his post-1930 performances. During 1964, his vocal on "Hello, Dolly" was #1 for one week on the popularity charts. This put him ahead of the phenomenally

tremolo chords from piano;

slow ride rhythm played by drummer on a hand-held "Bock-a-da-Bock" apparatus that brings together two cymbals that are each about three inches wide, played by drummer cupping the apparatus in his hand as in playing spoons.

1' 25" **Third Chorus**

Improvised Duet Between Clarinet and Armstrong's Vocal

This chorus employs a call-and-response format, with the vocal supplying the responses. It is an early example of "scat" singing. Piano and banjo are chording in a staccato manner on each beat. The duet's last phrase is done in harmony. No percussion instruments are used here or in the next chorus.

2' 00" **Fourth Chorus**

Unaccompanied Piano Improvisation by Earl Hines

First Four Measures

Pianist's left hand is contributing legato chording in stride style while right hand improvises flowery figures.

2' 10" *Second Four Measures*

Style of playing by right hand switches to brash character and pounds out a double-time figure voiced in octaves. This is the famous "trumpet-style" piano playing of Earl Hines.

2' 20" *Third Four Measures*

Style returns to flowery character.

2' 32" **Fifth Chorus**

Trumpet Solo

First Four Measures

Sustained high note from trumpet for 16 beats; Accompaniment includes staccato chords from piano on each beat, sustained trombone notes, and sustained clarinet notes.

2' 45" *Second Four Measures*

Trumpet line features double-timing.

2' 55" *Third Four Measures*

Horns stop playing for 12 beats while piano plays a descending sequence of chords, striking each in bell-like fashion, linking them with a glissando. Piano sustains a chord. Armstrong returns with a long, drawn-out bluesy figure played in a markedly slowed pace. It is accompanied by long tones harmonized by trombone, clarinet, and piano to form three different chords that conclude the piece.

popular Beatles. With the success of the 1988 revival of his "What a Wonderful World" (in the movie *Good Morning Vietnam*), Armstrong chalked up the longest career on the national singles charts, even outdistancing singers Bing Crosby and Frank Sinatra. Understandably then, the post-1930s public knows Armstrong more as an entertainer than as an innovative jazz improviser. Even though they have heard his name, most people are not aware of Armstrong's monumental contributions to the history of jazz.

Armstrong was the most widely imitated jazz improviser prior to the appearance of modern saxophonist Charlie Parker in the 1940s. Armstrong's style is especially easy to detect in the most prominent trumpeters of the 1930s and 40s. His influence extended not only to trumpeters, but to saxophonists, pianists, guitarists, and trombonists, too. Swing era players almost always cite Armstrong's influence. Moreover, pieces of his tunes and improvisations continued to be found in the work of post-swing era innovators.

Let's examine a few aspects of Armstrong's work that musicians appreciated so much:

1. Armstrong showed that the New Orleans technique of collective simultaneous improvisation was not the only approach to jazz horn work. Intelligently developed solos could be effectively improvised apart from the lines of other band members. In other words, **Armstrong was one of the first great soloists in jazz history.** Partly because of him, post-Armstrong styles usually stressed solo improvisation instead of group improvisation.

2. Armstrong was one of the first jazz musicians to refine a rhythmic conception that
    a. abandoned the stiffness of ragtime
    b. employed swing eighth-note patterns
    c. gracefully syncopated selected rhythmic figures. Sometimes he staggered the placement of an entire phrase, as though he were playing behind the beat. This projected a more relaxed feeling than ragtime and exhibited more variety in the ways that notes seemed to tug at opposite sides of the beat.

    These rhythmic elements combined to produce one of the first jazz styles with what is today called "jazz swing feeling."

3. Despite the excellent players who came after Armstrong, few equal him as musical architects. Few had his degree of control over the overall form of a solo. He calmly forged sensible lines that had both the flow of spontaneity and the stamp of finality. His improvisations are well-paced, economical statements. The organization of Armstrong's phrases suggests that he was thinking ahead, yet the phrases manage to sound spontaneous, rather than calculated.

4. He brought a superb sense of drama to jazz solo conception. His pacing was careful, allowing a solo to build tension. His double-time solo breaks were constructed to achieve maximum excitement. His high-note endings ensured a properly timed peak of intensity and resolution of tension.

5. At that time most improvisers were satisfied simply to embellish or paraphrase a tune's melody. Armstrong himself was a master at both, but he did much more. He frequently broke away from the melody,

and improvised original, melody-like lines that were compatible with the tune's chord progressions. This became the main approach for improvisation in the next fifty years of jazz history.

6. Armstrong's command of the trumpet was possibly greater than that of any jazz trumpeter before him. It became a model to which others aspired. He had an enormous, brassy tone, and remarkable range. Altogether with his rhythmic and dramatic sense, he conveyed a certainty and surging power. Even during the final decades of his career, Armstrong maintained a tone quality that was unusual for its weight, breadth, and richness.

7. Armstrong popularized the musical vocabulary of New Orleans trumpet style and then extended it.

8. Armstrong's tremendously fertile melodic imagination provided jazz with a repertory of phrases and ways of going about constructing improvisations. In other words, he extended the vocabulary for the jazz soloist.

These next two contributions are less central to his reputation among jazz musicians, but they remain significant in the broadest sense of jazz history.

9. The Armstrong singing style influenced many popular singers, including Louis Prima, Billie Holiday, and Bing Crosby. In this way, he affected American music beyond the boundaries of jazz. Armstrong's influence was so pervasive that Leslie Gourse titled a book about American jazz singers *Louis' Children.*

10. Armstrong popularized scat singing, a vocal technique in which lyrics are not used (*Jazz Classics CD1* for *Jazz Styles, 11th Edition*, Track 11; *Jazz Classics CD1* for *Concise Guide to Jazz,* Track 3). The voice improvises in the manner of a jazz trumpeter or saxophonist. Recent examples of the technique can be found in the work of George Benson, Al Jarreau, and Bobby McFerrin.

Bix Beiderbecke

Bix Beiderbecke (1903–1931) was the most influential trumpeter of the 1920s, aside from Louis Armstrong. Even in 2013 jazz musicians were still studying his recordings. Beiderbecke offered listeners an approach that contrasted with Armstrong's. Whereas Armstrong was usually hot, Beiderbecke was usually cool. Whereas Armstrong liked to play loudly and feature high notes, Beiderbecke often played in a more subdued manner. Like Armstrong, Beiderbecke put solos together quite intelligently. But, unlike Armstrong, he played their rhythms with considerable restraint.

Beiderbecke was particularly interested in stringing together unusual note choices. He is widely admired for the modern tendencies in his improvisations. Similarly, he is known for rich harmonies in his compositions. Like the French composers Claude Debussy and Maurice Ravel, whom he favored, Beiderbecke composed piano pieces that combined

((•▪ **Listen** on
mysearchlab.com

Listen to Bix Beiderbecke's cornet style on mysearchlab.com

Recorded May 9, 1927, in New York by Bix Beiderbecke (cornet), Frankie Trumbauer (C-Melody saxophone), Doc Ryker (alto saxophone), Don Murray (clarinet), Bill Rank (trombone), Eddie Lang (guitar), Itzy Riskin (piano), Chauncey Morehouse (drums); composed by Hoagy Carmichael; recorded by Okeh, reissued many times by Columbia Records.

Terms to know from tracks on *Demo CD*: break (34), saxophone (72), clarinet (69), stride piano (38), guitar chording (88), trombone (78).

Cornetist Bix Beiderbecke showed melodic imagination, and he delivered his inventions with a bearing that alternated between polite, authoritative, and verging on explosive. Beiderbecke fans consider his improvisations on "Riverboat Shuffle" to be among his best on record. His improvisations were sophisticated compositions in and of themselves. For example, in selecting tones for his solo at 1' 00", Beiderbecke is using almost all the chord notes from a progression in which the chords are rapidly changing.

Like much jazz of the 1920s, this performance has intentionally playful moments. Notice the raucous trombone breaks at 1' 36", 1' 40", 1' 48", and the humorous saxophone break at 2' 50". This recalled the hokum (very corny, intentionally silly) tradition that provided employment for many musicians in tent show minstrel and vaudeville contexts during the late 1800s and early 1900s. But don't let the humor distract or mislead you into overlooking the serious artistry of Bix Beiderbecke.

This piece does not follow the 12-bar blues or 32-bar A-A-B-A form. Its organization includes two strains, broken into smaller parts. The first strain is termed a "verse." It is sixteen measures long. A 4-measure introduction precedes it. We first hear the verse at 0' 04", and the band performs it in a question and answer ("call and response") manner. The horns play the figure that constitutes a question. Then guitar answers them. The second section has longer portions. It is in a different key and is termed a "chorus." We first hear it at 0' 23". The organization of the chorus is A-B-A'-C, in which each section lasts eight measures. Like the verse, the first A-section of the chorus is performed in a question-answer pattern. The horns pose a question, and the guitar answers it. Performance of the second A-section is similarly organized, but the clarinet plays an answer. The overall organization of this selection is **Intro-Verse-Chorus-Chorus (cornet solo)-Verse-Chorus (clarinet solo)-Chorus**.

The second time we hear the chorus section of the piece, it features Bix Beiderbecke's cornet solo. Then the band returns to the verse at 1' 35". This time the trombone, not the guitar, provides the answers. This verse is followed at 1' 52" with a chorus-long solo by clarinet. The entire band returns to play the next chorus at 2' 29". The peak of excitement in that final chorus is at 2' 55" with the explosive rip by Beiderbecke's cornet. That leads into the C-section. Thereafter, we should pay close attention to the continuation of the cornet line. Beiderbecke takes the lead and improvises authoritatively to the end. This is termed a "ride-out" in which the lead player performs the final passage, blowing over top the lesser lines of his fellow band members.

The improvisation on this recording is tied closely to the compositional form. The events follow a start-stop pattern. Most improvisation on "Riverboat Shuffle" is found in moments when the full band sound is interrupted by breaks. Most of these end with a cymbal crash. At one time or another, every band member except the drummer gets to improvise in a break. Collective improvisation occupies more passages than solo improvisation. It is particularly prominent at 0' 21", 1' 44", 2' 32", and 2' 48". (See the listening guide for "Alligator Hop" to review the terminology and listening strategies for this kind of collective improvisation.) Extended solo improvisation is limited to the cornet's 32-bar excursion that Beiderbecke begins politely at about 1' 00". The extent of improvisation in the clarinet solo is far less than in the cornet solo. The first half of the clarinet solo at 1′ 52″ constitutes a new melody that was, however, not freshly improvised at this record date. The second half, beginning around 2′ 11″, has aspects that seem more spontaneous. Most of the second half, though, sounds like stock patterns that were selected by the clarinetist for this recording.

0′ 00″	**Introduction** (4 bars)	
	Band plays brief figure, answered by cymbal crash.	
0′ 01″	same sequence	
0′ 03″	Band plays figure 3 times before cymbal crash.	
	Verse (16 bars)	
0′ 05″	new band figure, answered by guitar, then cymbal crash	
0′ 10″	new band figure, answered by guitar	
0′ 13″	swinging full band improvises collectively with cornet lead	
0′ 18″	band figure, answered by guitar, then cymbal crash	
	Chorus (32-bar A-B-A′-C) key change and new theme	
0′ 22″	**A**	Cornet plays lead while clarinet and saxophone embellish it.
0′ 26″		break filled by guitar chording
0′ 30″		chorded break by guitar
0′ 32″	**B**	cornet, clarinet, saxophone weaving lines around each other, trombone outlining chord notes, guitar strumming on every beat
0′ 38″		break filled by piano flourish
0′ 41″	**A**	band returns
0′ 43″		clarinet break
0′ 45″		band returns to improvise collectively
0′ 50″	**C**	
0′ 56″		Break allows cornet to begin solo.
	New Chorus (32-bar A-B-A′-C) **Bix Beiderbecke Cornet Solo**	
1′ 00″	**A**	Bix Beiderbecke cornet solo improvisation, accompanied only by strumming guitar, striding piano, drums
1′ 07″	**B**	
1′ 14″		break for cornet, ended by cymbal crash
1′ 16″	**A**	cornet solo accompanied only by strumming guitar, striding piano, drums
1′ 25″	**C**	
1′ 33″		break filled by horns in harmony
	Verse (16 bars)	
1′ 35″	return to opening phrases of piece, answered by cymbal crash	
1′ 36″	low-pitched trombone response to band figure	
1′ 40″	repeated band figure, answered by trombone	

| 1' 44" | collective improvisation |
| 1' 48" | Ensemble plays opening phrases of piece, answered by cymbal crash. |

Chorus (32-bar A-B-A'-C) **Don Murray Clarinet Solo**

1' 52"	clarinet solo accompanied just by strumming guitar, striding piano
2' 09"	break for clarinet solo
	Clarinet solo is occasionally embellished by the drummer.
2' 26"	break for horns in harmony

Final Chorus (32-bar A-B-A'-C)

2' 29"	**A**	collective improvisation by entire band
2' 31"		break filled by cornet improvisation
2' 36"		break filled by hokum-style saxophone improvisation
2' 39"	**B**	
2' 45"		break filled by chorded guitar improvisation
2' 47"	**A**	collective improvisation
2' 49"		break filled by hokum-style saxophone solo
2' 55"		Dramatic rip into a high note by cornet introduces high-pitched, explosive Bix Beiderbecke cornet improvisation.
2' 57"	**C**	collective improvisation by entire band, with Beiderbecke playing lead

▶ Bix Beiderbecke, the first "cool jazz" musician.

Photo courtesy of Frank Driggs

twentieth-century harmonies with ragtime rhythms. His "In a Mist" is one example, and it was recorded in 1927 with Beiderbecke himself playing piano.

VOCAL BLUES

Vocal blues has always been important to some segments of jazz. Even during the 1990s a vocalist singing a blues occasionally occurred in concerts of jazz bands. Vocal blues belonged to a stream of styles that were somewhat separate from ragtime-derived instrumental styles. Much popular music, especially rock and roll, drew upon traditions in vocal blues. The singing style was also significant for jazz because hornmen often decorated their melody lines with the ornaments of pitch and tone quality that blues singers used.

Photo courtesy of Frank Driggs

((•─Listen on
mysearchlab.com
Listen to audio-visual explanation for 12-bar blues chord progression on mysearchlab.com

◀ Bessie Smith, Empress of the Blues.

POPULARITY OF EARLY JAZZ

The earliest jazz had a wide appeal, especially to young audiences and particularly to social dancers. This roughly parallels the kind of popularity that rock music had during the 1950s and 60s. But it contrasts dramatically

Recorded January 14, 1925, in New York by Bessie Smith (vocal), Louis Armstrong (cornet), and Fred Longshaw (harmonium); composed by Fred Longshaw.

Terms to know from tracks on *Demo CD*: chord progression (16–19), 12-bar blues (19), blue notes (54–58), and plunger mute (67). Terms to learn from Elements of Music Appendix: blues poetic form, chord change, 12-bar blues chord progression, blue notes, and plunger mute.

In this recording of "Reckless Blues" we have a double advantage because we hear the most famous blues singer—Bessie Smith, and the most famous early jazz hornman—Louis Armstrong. Smith had enormous talent and influenced generations of singers, both inside and outside the field of jazz. She was known as the "Empress of the Blues." Her voice was so powerful that it could be heard over the sound of a band, even without using a microphone. Her songs were quite simple, and most were similar. But her impact did not depend upon anything fancy. It relied on soulful emotions that appealed to millions of listeners. The lyrics she chose were often about disappointment and sorrow in love affairs. Most people could easily identify with these topics.

Smith surrounded herself with first-rate jazz improvisers. We can hear them play countermelodies while she is singing. Their work is conspicuous whenever the singer pauses because they fill those gaps with improvised lines of their own. Such an instrumental device is therefore termed a "fill." In "Reckless Blues," Armstrong improvises lines for a 4-measure introduction and many such fills. In doing this, he uses two techniques that were not common in his later work. The first is that Armstrong uses a plunger mute to toy with his cornet's pitch and tone quality. They sometimes sound like "wah wah," particularly at about 0' 12" and 0' 26". The second technique is blue pitches, as at 1' 07", 1' 45", and 1' 59", 2' 26". These are intentionally out-of-tune notes, played for expressive purposes and timed with exacting deliberation.

The instrument providing the chording underneath Smith is called a harmonium, also known as a reed organ. It is like a church organ. If you can get past its wheezy tone quality, you might notice that its player Fred Longshaw is contributing a flowing sequence of chords that move gracefully. Armstrong draws from these chord movements to lend direction to the lines in his improvised fills. That strategy is especially evident at 0' 51" where he plays a new figure for each chord, and at 2' 54" where he selects notes that clearly indicate the chord change. Note that chord changes here are far more involved than

with public response to modern jazz of later eras. Whereas modern jazz recordings rarely penetrated the hit parade, the Original Dixieland Jazz Band had several records that stayed near the top of the popularity charts. Early jazz giants such as Louis Armstrong and Jelly Roll Morton were known to a wide public.

New Orleans and Chicago styles did not just live and die with the 1920s. The music has persisted. For instance, there was a revival of interest in New Orleans combo jazz during the 1940s, and several players who

those of guitarist-blues singers such as Robert Johnson, Charley Patton and Son House. Bessie Smith might have sounded rough and soulful, but she and her accompanists were sophisticated musicians who can be easily distinguished from the folk blues tradition represented by Robert Johnson.

0' 00"   **Introduction**
         Armstrong improvises cornet solo over harmonium for introduction.

         First Chorus ("When I Was Young . . . ")
0' 14"   Smith begins singing.

         Final Two Measures of First Chorus
0' 51"   Cornet improvises a fill that indicates the chord progression.

         Second Chorus ("Then I Am Growing Old")
0' 57"   Smith singing new chorus

         Final Two Measures of Second Chorus
1' 31"   improvised cornet fill

         Third Chorus ("My Momma Says I'm Reckless")
1' 38"   Smith singing new chorus

         Final Two Measures of Third Chorus
2' 10"   improvised cornet fill

         Fourth Chorus ("Daddy, Momma Wants Some Lovin'")
2' 19"   Smith singing final chorus

         Second Fill in Fourth Chorus
2' 41"   Cornet gets fancy, double-timing its line.

had left music returned to careers in performing. The music at New Orleans' Preservation Hall, since 1962, has been so popular that they have always had to have several bands on hand. That way some could be on tour and at least one could be in residence. For many years it has been common to find a few good Dixieland bands in every major American city. In addition, many regions of the United States sport yearly festivals of traditional jazz.

SUMMARY

1. The first forms of jazz resulted from blending improvisational approaches to ragtime, blues, spirituals, marches, and popular tunes.

2. The first jazz bands used the instruments of brass bands: trumpet, clarinet, trombone, tuba, drums, and saxophone.

3. The earliest jazz was not recorded. We can only infer how it sounded on the basis of recordings made by New Orleans players after they had moved to Chicago.

4. The first jazz group to record was the Original Dixieland Jazz Band in 1917.

5. Chicago was the jazz center of the world during the 1920s.

6. The earliest significant New Orleans pianist-composer was Jelly Roll Morton.

7. James P. Johnson was considered the "father" of stride piano.

8. Fats Waller was one of the most popular jazz musicians of the 1920s and 30s, as well as a prolific composer.

9. Waller brought a lightness and springy quality to stride style.

10. Earl Hines devised the "trumpet-style" of piano playing in which phrases are more "horn-like" than pianistic.

11. Louis Armstrong was one of the first combo players to effectively demonstrate solo improvisation instead of retaining the New Orleans tradition of collective improvisation.

12. Louis Armstrong possessed a larger tone, wider range, and better command of the trumpet than most early players. His solo improvisations were especially well constructed.

13. Bix Beiderbecke was one of the first "cool style" jazz improvisers.

KEY TERMS

Chicago School	front line	stride
collective improvisation		

FURTHER RESOURCES

✓•⌐Study and Review on **mysearchlab.com**

Watch documentaries on Louis Armstrong and Jelly Roll Morton.

Test your knowledge with the chapter quiz.

VIEW

Prentice Hall Jazz History DVD (ISBN 0-13-602643-5) Bessie Smith, "St. Louis Blues," Louis Armstrong, "Tiger Rag", and Fats Waller, "Honeysuckle Rose"

Louis Armstrong: The Portrait Collection (Hip-O, c 2008). Performances from 1933, 1952, and 1959, along with an extensive interview with Armstrong about his life and music.

Bix: "Ain't None of Them Play it like Him Yet" (Playboy Home Video, 1981, 1994, 2002). Documentary on Beiderbecke's life and times.

LISTEN

Numerous pieces by Louis Armstrong, Bix Beiderbecke, Earl Hines, James P. Johnson, Jelly Roll Morton, Fats Waller, and other early jazz musicians are on *Smithsonian Collection of Classic Jazz* and *Ken Burns Jazz* (Sony/Legacy C5K 61432 5 CD set, 1917–1992). *Prentice Hall Jazz Collection* (ISBN 0-205-17896-0) has "Wolverine Blues" by Jelly Roll Morton and Johnny Dodds. *Jazz Classics CD1* for *Jazz Styles, 11th Edition* (ISBN 0-205-03686-4) has Bix Beiderbecke's "Singin' the Blues."

READ

Armstrong, Louis. 1954 (Da Capo reprint, 1986). *Satchmo: My Life in New Orleans*. Upper Saddle River, NJ: Prentice-Hall.

Brothers, Thomas. 2007. *Louis Armstrong's New Orleans*. New York: Norton.

Brown, Scott E., and Robert Hilbert. 1986. *James P. Johnson: A Case of Mistaken Identity*. Metuchen, NJ: Scarecrow.

Charters, Samuel B. 2008. *A Trumpet Around the Corner: The Story of New Orleans Jazz*. Jackson, Mississippi: University Press of Mississippi.

Dance, Stanley. 1975 (Da Capo reprint, 1983). *The World of Earl Hines*. New York: Scribner.

Hadlock, Richard. 1965 (Da Capo reprint, 1986). *Jazz Masters of the Twenties*. New York: Macmillan.

Lomax, Alan. 1973, 2001. *Mister Jelly Lord*. Berkeley: University of California Press.

Sandke, Randall. 2010. *Where the Dark and the Light Folks Meet: Race and the Mythology, Politics, and Business of Jazz*. Lanham, Massachusetts: Scarecrow.

Schuller, Gunther. 1968. *Early Jazz*. New York: Oxford.

Shapiro, Nat, and Nat Hentoff. 1955 (Dover reprint, 1966). *Hear Me Talkin' to Ya*. New York: Rinehart.

Sudhalter, Richard M. 1974, 1975. *Bix: Man & Legend*. Arlington; Schirmer.

Sudhalter, Richard M. 1994. *Lost Chords: White Musicians and Their Contributions to Jazz, 1915–1945*. New York: Oxford University Press.

Williams, Martin. 1970 (Da Capo reprint, 1978). *Jazz Masters of New Orleans*. New York: Macmillan.

◀ Original Dixieland Jazz Band playing into acoustic recording horns. This was the method for making records before the advent of electric microphones.

Photo courtesy of William Ransom Hogan Jazz Archive, Tulane University

5 Swing

Count Basie's 1938 band. Courtesy of Frank Driggs

HOW SWING DIFFERS FROM EARLY JAZZ

A looser, less stiff rhythmic feeling developed in jazz during the 1920s, causing jazz to swing more. This was a gradual change that continued into the 1940s. Most jazz from the mid-1930s to the mid-40s is called "swing music." Since much of it was played by bands of ten or more musicians, it is also called music of the "big band era." **Swing was the most popular style in jazz history,** and it attracted millions of dancers. Several of the big dance bands were very important in jazz because of their soloists and the ways the bands combined written with improvised parts. There was a resurgence of interest during the 1990s when swing dancing once again became a fad.

Before we examine those particulars, let's look at a few ways that swing differs from early jazz:

1. The preferred instrumentation for swing was **big band** rather than combo. This made for greater reliance on written arrangements during the swing era.
2. **Saxophones** were more common in swing.
3. **Bass viol** appeared more often in swing (*Demo CD* Track 22).
4. **High-hat** cymbals were used more (*Demo CD* Track 2).
5. Collective improvisation was rare in swing.
6. Overall **rhythmic feeling was smoother.**
7. Swing musicians usually showed a **higher level of instrumental proficiency** in terms of speed, agility, tone control, and playing in tune.

INSTRUMENTS IN SWING BANDS

Big bands were made up of ten or more musicians whose instruments fall into three categories: brass, saxophones, and rhythm section. The brass section included trumpets and trombones. Although saxophones are also made of brass, they are technically called woodwinds because they originated from instruments traditionally made of wood (clarinet, flute, and oboe). They are also played in the manner of traditional wooden instruments. Because most saxophonists also play clarinet, and both sax and clarinet have cane reeds attached to their mouthpieces, the sax section was often called the "reed section." This label was retained in later decades, even when saxophonists began adding flute, a non-reed instrument.

Demo CD Tracks 69–75

The alto and tenor saxophones were the most frequently used saxes. By the late 1930s, most bands had also adopted the baritone saxophone. The

((•– **Listen** on **mysearchlab.com**
Listen to trombone section on mysearchlab.com

((•– **Listen** on **mysearchlab.com**
Listen to saxophone section on mysearchlab.com

((•– **Listen** on **mysearchlab.com**
Listen to audio-visual comparison of alto and tenor saxophones on mysearchlab.com

◀ Left to right: Alto, tenor, and baritone saxophones.

sax section contained from three to five musicians. Saxophonists did not usually play one instrument to the exclusion of the others. Some musicians, for instance, were required to alternate from clarinet to alto and baritone saxophones. Eventually a section of two altos, two tenors, and a baritone became standard.

The size of the trumpet section varied from two to five musicians. Most had three during the late 1930s and early 1940s. The lead trumpeter usually sat in the middle. The trombone section ranged from one to five musicians, with two or three being standard. The lead trombonist was in the center.

With the growth of big bands came an increase in the use of written arrangements. These had not been as necessary with small combos. As bands became bigger, it was more difficult to improvise a respectable performance, though some big bands did succeed in playing without written arrangements. Eventually, however, musicians had to learn to read and write arrangements to have a big enough repertory on hand. A newcomer had much less difficulty learning the music if a band worked from written arrangements rather than memorized routines.

The compositional devices employed in most of the arrangements were simple. Melodies were played by the entire band in unison or in harmony. Then jazz improvisation followed, accompanied both by the rhythm section and by figures scored for other members of the group. These figures were usually short, simple phrases called *riffs*. The melodies and accompanying figures were taken up in turn by one section of the band and then another.

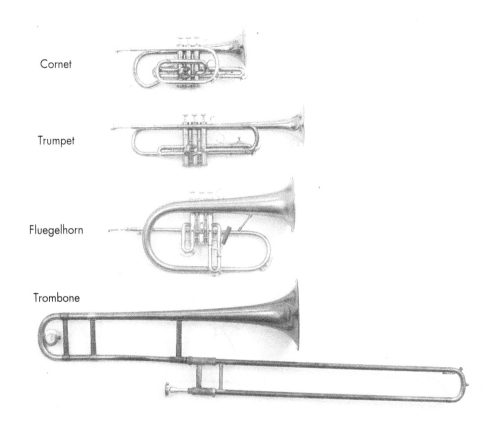

Cornet

Trumpet

Fluegelhorn

Trombone

Saxes might state the "A-section," brass state the bridge, and so forth. Besides pop tune melodies, arrangements often contained variations on those themes. Some of those variations were actually as good as improvised solos. These were offered as passages for one section of the band to play while another accompanied them or remained silent. Sometimes, portions within the passages were passed back and forth. This sounded as though one section of the band posed a question and another section answered it. This technique is called **call and response** style.

The rhythm section ordinarily contained piano, guitar, bass, and drums. **Rhythm guitar** disappeared from most big bands during the late 1940s. Although the banjo had been present in early-style bands, it dropped out of sight during the 1930s. Tuba had preceded string bass in some bands, but had been abandoned by the mid-1930s. Before the guitar and string bass became firmly established, guitarists often alternated on guitar and banjo, and bassists alternately played both tuba (brass bass) and string bass (bass viol).

The **pianist** in the rhythm section occasionally played melody instead of just chords and embellishments. Comping was not the common accompaniment style during the swing era, though Count Basie did use it. Pianists of the swing era used stride style or played a chord on every beat or every other beat.

Guitar and bass were usually assigned timekeeping duties. The guitarist strummed one chord on each beat. This was known as **rhythm guitar style.** The **bassist** generally played a note on the first and third of every 4 beats, **two-beat style,** or on every beat, **walking style.** Bassists during the swing era remained in the background.

Call and response A compositional technique in which one section states a theme as a question and another section states another theme as an answer to it

Demo CD Track 88 illustrates a rhythm guitar part.

Demo CD Track 20 illustrates comping.

Rhythm guitar style Guitarist strumming one chord on each beat

Two-beat style Bassist playing on the first and third of every 4 beats

Walking style Bassist playing a note on every beat, pitches of which "walk" up and down

((•—**Listen** on **mysearchlab.com**
Listen to trombones call and muted trumpets respond on mysearchlab.com

((•—**Listen** on **mysearchlab.com**
Listen to saxophones call and muted trombone respond on mysearchlab.com

◀ Jimmy Blanton, Duke Ellington's bassist from 1939 to 1941. Not only was Blanton a superbly swinging timekeeper, but he was also a soloist Ellington used in the manner of a horn. This was revolutionary for its time, and Blanton was idolized by bassists for many years thereafter.

Photo courtesy of Frank Driggs

Sonny Greer, Duke Ellington's drummer from 1919 to 1951. This photo shows some of the instruments used by swing era drummers. We can see only the top of the bass drum in the bottom center of our picture, but an assortment of attached instruments are clear: two cowbells and a woodblock mounted close to its rim, large tom-toms mounted to tilt toward Greer, four cymbals on stands. Greer is using wire brushes to strike his cymbals.

Photo by William P. Gottlieb

Most big band drummers during this period limited themselves to making the beat obvious for dancers and lending swing feeling to the band. It was a matter of simple timekeeping with occasional dramatic effects. Swing drummers tended not to play new or provocative rhythms that ran counter to the horn lines. This came with modern jazz during the 1940s, when drummers began offering a parallel line of activity instead of just keeping time.

SWING ERA SOLOISTS

Roy Eldridge

Trumpeter Roy Eldridge (1911–1989) was one of the most advanced improvisers of the swing era. He is often considered a link between swing and

Roy Eldridge, the most daring trumpeter of the 1930s. Eldridge frequently improvised in the manner of a saxophonist by using long, swooping, scale-like lines. He also liked to dart into the highest register of his instrument and make his sound explode like fireworks. His style formed the beginning for Dizzy Gillespie's new bebop style.

Photo courtesy of Frank Driggs

modern jazz. Eldridge had a fiery, aggressive style and unprecedented mastery over the trumpet. His imaginative choice of notes and sax-like lines bridged the gap between the style of Louis Armstrong and the modern approach pioneered by Dizzy Gillespie. Eldridge also creatively varied the size, texture, and vibrato of his tone. Sometimes it was clear and warm, at other times brittle and edgy. His high-register playing had a sweeping scope. In that register, he gave his entrances a rhythmic feeling that suggested modern jazz inflections to come.

Roy Eldridge demonstrated that long, sinewy lines were possible on trumpet. These, though easy to execute on saxophone, do not lend themselves to the mechanics of the trumpet. Eldridge influenced modern trumpeters to cultivate greater instrumental facility and to improvise in more intricate and unpredictable ways than their early jazz counterparts. Eldridge's influence extended into the 1950s because Dizzy Gillespie built his own influential modern style upon the foundation of Eldridge's bristling high-register work, unorthodox choice of notes, and saxophone style of phrasing.

Coleman Hawkins

The man generally considered to be the first important jazz tenor saxophonist is Coleman Hawkins (1904–1969). Prior to his arrival on the jazz scene in the 1920s, the saxophone was considered little more than a novelty.

Break The portion of a piece in which all band members stop playing except the one who improvises a solo

Photo by William P. Gottlieb, courtesy of Library of Congress

◀ Coleman Hawkins, father of jazz tenor saxophone.

Recorded November 10, 1938, in New York by Roy Eldridge (trumpet), Chu Berry (tenor saxophone), Clyde Hart (piano), Danny Barker (guitar), Artie Bernstein (bass), Sid Catlett (drums); originally issued by Commodore Records.

Terms to know from the *Demo CD* tracks include solo break (34), staccato (45), legato (44), brushes (12), snare drum (5), stride style piano (38), trumpet (59), tenor sax (73), rhythm guitar (88), walking bass (23), and chorus (33).

When a jazz combo has a steady gig, it is customary to let guests join them to improvise solos during their regular performance; this is termed "sitting in." In the past, particularly the era when this recording was made, musicians often went to hear other jazz musicians and sometimes sat in with them. Jazz musicians still sit in occasionally with other bands on nights when they do not have a gig of their own or when their gig ends much earlier than another band's gig. (Perhaps because "playing" is the description of their job, it helps us understand that jazz musicians enjoy their work so much they want to continue long after their own gigs finish.) The full version of this recording originally began with a conversation between Eldridge and Berry about not being tired after their regular gig. Berry suggested, "Let's go some place and swing." They went to a place where a friend was playing, and ultimately Berry told Eldridge, "Come on … Get your horn out!" This sense of fun propels the performance from start to finish.

The musicians never actually play the melody "Bill Bailey (Won't You Come Home?)" from which their progression of accompaniment chords is borrowed. The piece is comprised of four different 8-bar sections (roughly conceivable as A-B-A'-C), all of which lend themselves to being stopped for the final 8 beats to form a solo break. In keeping with the idea of "sittin' in," trumpeter Eldridge begins improvising immediately. In fact he starts during the moment the rest of the band stops playing. This is called a **break** and corresponds to the final 4 measures in the previous chorus. It sounds as though we entered the nightclub during the middle of the piece and missed the theme statement. But this band never plays the melody at the end, either.

Notice how Eldridge darts all over the range of his horn and how he does this almost as easily as a saxophonist. We must recognize that this is not easy for most trumpeters. We also need to recognize that he is inventing a huge number of highly varied melodic figures. These are a few of the virtues that make Eldridge exceptional and cause us to label him "innovative."

Tenor saxophonist Chu Berry was one of the most outstanding Coleman Hawkins disciples. His prominence was sufficient during the 1930s to win popularity polls run by jazz magazines. Berry's lines were less complicated and more graceful than Hawkins', but he delivered them with just as much force. Both men played as though supercharged. As with Hawkins, there is a powerful sense of authority in his work. Berry used a deep, dark, heavyweight tone. He kept this tone full-bodied while flowing throughout his solo in an almost syrupy manner. Unlike Eldridge on "Sittin' In," Berry did not use any staccato articulation; he preferred exclusively legato phrasing. Instead of being full of surprises like Eldridge's work, Berry's solo is mostly long strings of continuous eighth notes. He also used much less syncopation than Eldridge used.

Berry and Eldridge chose one of the best available combinations for their rhythm section. Both pianist Clyde Hart and drummer Sid Catlett were among the most in-demand accompanists of the 1930s and 40s. Even the revolutionary trumpeter Dizzy Gillespie hired them for his first bebop recordings during 1945 and 1946. They are joined by Danny Barker strumming guitar on each beat, and Artie Bernstein providing walking bass lines. Like these other musicians, Barker and Bernstein worked with the top bands of the period. What we are getting from "Sittin' In" is a glimpse of small combo jazz in the swing era and how exciting it could be.

A tempo as brisk as that of "Sittin' In" might give other swing era improvisers difficulty. Berry and Eldridge, however, manage to keep dreaming up fresh ideas and executing them every moment, without faltering. Toward the end of "Sittin' In," the two hornmen additionally alternate 4-measure sections with each other. This is termed "trading fours." This means they were rapidly playing ever more licks before their brief recording time expired. The creativity and pace with which Berry and Eldridge generated so many themes anticipated the high value that modern jazz placed on playing fast and packing as many themes as possible into each improvisation.

0′ 00″   Trumpet improvises in break.

First Chorus (Roy Eldridge Trumpet Solo)
0′ 03″   Trumpet improvisation is accompanied by piano striding, guitar strumming each beat, bass walking, drummer keeping time with wire brushes on snare drum.

Final 2 Measures of First Chorus, plus 8 Beats (Chu Berry Sax Break)
0′ 29″   Saxophone improvises entrance in break.

Second Chorus (Chu Berry Tenor Saxophone Solo)
0′ 32″   Rhythm section resumes accompaniment as saxophonist improvises solo.

Third Chorus (Clyde Hart Piano Solo)
0′ 59″   improvised piano solo

Second Half of Third Chorus (Chu Berry Saxophone Solo)
1′ 13″   Saxophone solo resumes.

Final 2 Measures of Third Chorus, plus 8 Beats (Sid Catlett Drum Solo)
1′ 25″   Drummer plays solo break.

Fourth Chorus (Horns Trading 4's)
1′ 28″   Trumpet improvises with rhythm section for 4 measures.
1′ 32″   Saxophone improvises with rhythm section for 4 measures.
1′ 37″   Trumpet improvises with rhythm section for 4 measures.
1′ 39″   Saxophone improvises with rhythm section for 2 measures.

Final 2 Measures of Fourth Chorus (Artie Bernstein Bass Solo)
1′ 41″   Bass plays solo break.

Fifth Chorus
1′ 42″   Trumpet improvises with rhythm section for 4 measures.
1′ 46″   Saxophone improvises with rhythm section for 4 measures.
1′ 49″   Trumpet and saxophone collectively improvise for 8 measures.
1′ 56″   Horns and piano construct a tie-it-up figure that neatly concludes the piece.

Recorded in 1939 in New York by Coleman Hawkins (tenor saxophone), Gene Rogers (piano); composed by Johnny Green; issued by Victor Records.

This is the most famous recording in the career of tenor saxophonist Coleman Hawkins. Prior to Lester Young, Hawkins had the largest number of imitators of any saxophonist in jazz. The song had been recorded previously by other jazz musicians and singers. This version, however, contained more improvisation than other recordings. The most adventuresome musicians liked the song because it had so many different chords in its accompaniment and because it changed keys several times. They liked the way Hawkins used all these chords in his lines and sometimes put his own chords in place of the ones the composer had used. Musicians consider this to be a virtuoso performance. It probably was the most complicated sax solo improvisation to appear on record up to this time. In these ways it attracted musicians who were then developing modern jazz, which ultimately emphasized all these characteristics.

This recording is also significant because it garnered high sales, thereby representing an exception to the general rule that best sellers are usually characterized by simplicity and lots of repetition. Jazz historians and musicians remain puzzled by its commercial success because this Hawkins performance is complicated and contains no repetition. Some have guessed that its popularity might stem from accumulated popularity of the song itself. This explanation is problematic, however, because Hawkins refers to the tune's melody in an obvious way only in his first 8 measures, at about 0' 10" to 0' 32". In the remainder of the performance, any relationship between the Hawkins solo and the pop tune itself is found only in the accompaniment chords and the way Hawkins tends to construct lines partly by incorporating several notes from each chord as it goes by. In some passages, the soloist offers a new phrase for almost every chord and starts and stops his line accordingly. Another possible reason the solo became so popular is that this aspect of the performance allows us to follow the saxophonist's thinking. Of course this should affect popularity only among listeners who like to follow an instrumentalist's improvisatory thinking.

The popularity of "Body and Soul" by Hawkins might just reflect appreciation for the sheer power of the performance. That is an appealing explanation because Hawkins does play quite convincingly and with great force. In fact, there is considerable drama in his final A-section. Beginning around 2' 32" he reaches for high notes several times and makes his tone gruff when he sounds the highest one. Having built tension throughout the performance, these gruff high notes evoke a climax. Once

Hawkins' supercharged playing on it brought recognition to the horn. His command of the instrument and his deep, husky tone became a model for other saxophonists. As a result, tenor sax became one of the most popular instruments in jazz (*Demo CD* Track 73). In fact, it symbolizes jazz for many people. Hawkins also demonstrated more interest in chord progressions than most other premodern saxophonists. He loved to play over complex chord progressions, such as those in his famous rendition of "Body and Soul." He was less interested in devising new melodies than in investigating the chord progressions that could be added to a tune's original accompaniment. Because of his attitude, some listeners consider Hawkins primarily a harmonic improviser rather than a melodic improviser.

again, however, this explanation is problematic because solos on many other Hawkins recordings are exceedingly powerful, yet none of them attained popularity.

So we are left with a pleasant mystery. Jazz recordings that have high artistic quality have rarely enjoyed great popular success. Hawkins' "Body and Soul" is an exception in having achieved both.

Introduction

0' 00"		piano chord on the downbeat then sustained, high-pitched melodic response; chord on the downbeat and sustained, high-pitched melodic response; chord, mid-register melodic response

First Chorus (A-A-B-A)

0' 10"	**A**	Saxophone plays melody with considerable self-ornamentation that outlines the chord movements.
0' 32"	**A**	Saxophone departs from original melody, improvises fresh lines.
0' 51"	**Bridge** (key change)	Hawkins offers strings of eighth notes, occasionally interrupted by a pause.
1' 11"	**A**	Hawkins sometimes outlines the passing chords by playing their notes in succession.

Second Chorus (A-A-B-A)

1' 32"	**A**	Hawkins plays a new lick for every chord.
1' 33"		Sustained tones by horns accompany Hawkins.
1' 52"	**A**	
2' 12"	**Bridge**	
2' 32"	**A**	Hawkins reaching into high register, roughening his tone, increasing tension
2' 50"		Break
2' 57"		Hawkins improvises chord notes for each of 4 chords that conclude the piece; joined by horn chord to reinforce the very end.

SWING ERA BANDLEADERS

Kansas City Style

During the 1920s and 30s there was a thriving jazz scene in Kansas City, Missouri. A number of historically significant jazz musicians worked there and are associated with "Kansas City style jazz," though few were born there. Count Basie (from New Jersey) and Lester Young (from Louisiana) were the most famous. Their music was neither as glossy nor as elaborate as that of their New York counterparts; it was lighter, more relaxed, and exceptionally swinging.

Listen on
mysearchlab.com

*Listen to big band riff style on
mysearchlab.com*

Head arrangement Band
arrangement created extemporaneously by the musicians and
not written down

Kansas City style was not based on the interweaving lines of the collectively improvised New Orleans style. Arrangements were based instead
on short musical phrases called **riffs** that are repeated again and again. Riffs
serve two functions. Sometimes they are (1) theme statements, and sometimes they are (2) backgrounds for improvised solos. Some of these riffs were
written down and became the basis for tunes. Many, though, were created
spontaneously during a performance ("off the top of someone's head"),
learned by ear, and kept in the heads of the players. Arrangements of this
kind are called **head arrangements,** and they are basic to the Kansas City
riff band style. For example, "Taxi War Dance" has no theme. It consists
solely of riffs and improvisations over the chord progression accompaniment
of "Willow Weep for Me" (see page 70).

Count Basie

Musicians generally agree that the most swinging big band was that of
Count Basie (1904–1984). When compared with all others from the swing
era, Basie's never seemed out of breath nor the least bit frantic, and it always
seemed to swing more. Basie led a big band almost continuously from 1937
until his death. Every edition of the band had at least two players who made
important contributions to jazz history. Some editions had four or five.

Basie was originally a stride-style pianist. Basie's touch was unique among
jazz pianists. It was very light and extremely precise. His choice of notes
was near perfect. His impeccable sense of timing was equivalent to a good
drummer's. In fact, Basie originally began his musical career as a drummer,
not a pianist. Succinct and compact statements are hallmarks of Basie's style.
When he soloed, he artfully used silence to pace his lines.

Prentice Hall Jazz History DVD:
"Boogie Woogie" by Count Basie

Listen on
mysearchlab.com

*Listen to Count Basie's solo piano
style on mysearchlab.com*

▶ Count Basie

Photo by William P. Gottlieb, courtesy of Library of Congress

Basie led the first rhythm section in jazz history that consistently swung in a smooth, relaxed way. That famous rhythm section consisted of Basie himself (piano), Freddie Green (rhythm guitar), Walter Page (string bass), and Jo Jones (drums). Among the special **qualities of the Basie rhythm section** were:

1. An excellent sense of tempo.
2. The ability to keep time and swing consistently without using a hard-driving, pressured approach.
3. Quiet, relaxed playing, which conveyed a feeling of ease.
4. Placing a fairly even amount of stress on each beat instead of on every other beat.
5. Emphasis on buoyancy rather than intensity.

Bassist **Walter Page** (1900–1957) contributed:

1. A supple walking bass sound. In fact he is considered to be one of the first masters of the walking style.
2. A strong, articulated sound with life in it.
3. Playing all beats evenly (*Demo CD* Track 23).
4. Balancing his sound to mesh smoothly with piano, bass, and guitar.

Guitarist **Freddie Green** (1911–1987) was noted for:

1. His crisp strokes on unamplified guitar that sounded his rhythm chords with unerring steadiness and propulsive swing feeling (*Demo CD* Track 88).
2. His close coordination with bass and drums.

Drummer **Jo Jones** (1911–1985) was distinguished for:

1. A loose, assured manner that was precise without being stiff.
2. Quieter bass drum playing than was common in the swing era. Jones sometimes omitted bass drum entirely, sometimes using it only for off-beat accents (*Demo CD* Track 1).
3. Quiet use of wire brushes on high-hat (*Demo CD* Track 2).
4. Ride rhythms played on high-hat continuously as the apparatus was opening and closing. Jones let his cymbals ring prominently between strokes, thereby creating a sustained sound that smoothed the time-keeping pattern instead of leaving each stroke as an abrupt sound.

The Basie rhythm section was well balanced among the sounds of each member. The four parts were so smoothly integrated that one listener was inspired to compare the effect to riding on ball bearings. If you listen carefully to recordings of the band, you will notice that it is unusual for one member to stick out. Guitar, bass, and drums are all carefully controlled to avoid disturbing the evenness and balance of sound.

In Basie's interjections, jazz piano had the bounce, syncopation, and flexibility of what became known as comping. This is playing accompanying chords as accents behind the soloist. It requires the pianist to listen carefully and play interactively. Though he did not invent it, Basie is so

LISTENING GUIDE
"Taxi War Dance" by Count Basie and Lester Young

((•[Listen on **mysearchlab.com**

Recorded March 19, 1939, in New York by the Count Basie Band (four trumpets, three trombones, four saxophones), Count Basie (piano), Freddie Green (guitar), Walter Page (bass), and Jo Jones (drums); composed by Count Basie and Lester Young; originally issued by the Vocalion firm, subsequently reissued many times by Columbia Records.

Terms to know from tracks on *Demo CD:* piano comping (20), boogie-woogie style (38), walking bass (23), ride rhythm on high-hat cymbals (2), trombone (78), tenor saxophone (73), mutes (68).

The music of the "Taxi War Dance" recording demonstrates the Kansas City jazz style of the 1930s. Basie's music is relaxed but firm and spirited but disciplined. It evokes an easy, unhurried swing feeling. This selection also gives us a sample of Lester Young's eloquent style of improvising with the tenor saxophone. Young said he was pleased with this recording.

This selection provides a good example of the Count Basie Band acting like a small jazz combo. This means two things. (1) Little of this music was arranged in advance. In fact, we never hear a real theme statement at all. Most of the music here was improvised. This includes both the accompaniments and the solos. It is not elaborate. For instance, when more than one horn is playing at a time, such as the trombones at 1' 50" and 2' 27", we hear only brief riffs. These were probably devised spontaneously and learned by rote. They did not come from a formal, written arrangement. This is why early Basie music is termed "riff band style." (2) Much of the recording has only an improvising soloist and the rhythm section playing instead of entire collections of brasses and saxophones. Such passages represent a small jazz combo, not a big band.

At the beginning of the piece, Basie plays a boogie-woogie figure on the piano to establish a rhythmic groove. This figure originated in a solo piano style that was popular in Kansas City and Chicago during the 1920s. Boogie-woogie usually adhered to a chord progression of the 12-bar blues. "Taxi War Dance" is not a 12-bar blues. It borrows the chord progression of "Willow Weep for Me," which is a pop tune organized in a 32-bar, A·A·B·A form.

Lester Young begins his improvisation by quoting the opening phrase of the Broadway show tune "Ol' Man River." Then he develops it but changes course when Basie stops his boogie-woogie figure and begins comping.

After Young's first solo, we hear a full chorus solo by trombonist Dicky Wells, beginning at 0' 47". Pay attention to how he bases his solo on simple phrases to be developed by repetitions and slight alterations. His first three phrases follow logically from each other. Sometimes it sounds like Wells is poking fun, as at 0' 51". At 0' 53" he repeats the same idea four times at different positions relative to the underlying pulse. His lines are clear and logical. He outlines the descending chords of the bridge section, beginning at 1' 05". In this way he lends direction to his own invention and alerts us to the relationship of harmonies in the piece.

After the trombone solo, we hear a tenor saxophone solo by Buddy Tate at 1' 37". Tate splits the third chorus with pianist Count Basie, who improvises the bridge at 1' 41". If you have trouble distinguishing Tate's tenor saxophone playing from Young's, try focusing on tone quality. Tate's is coarser, darker, and sounded with a faster vibrato. Then listen for overall effect. Tate's execution has less poise and does not swing as much as Young's.

Lester Young returns in the fourth chorus at 2' 04". The contrast with Tate's sound is particularly distinctive because Young conveys a light feeling and plays higher pitches, also known as "using the upper register" of his instrument.

The ending section and its new progression of chords is what musicians call a "tag." The performers divide it into a series of brief breaks. Soloists are playing for only 2 measures apiece (8 beats). This is termed "trading two's." Such organization forces improvisers to abruptly create concise remarks and swing at the same time.

Introduction

Four Measures

0' 00"   Basie plays boogie-woogie figure on piano with left hand.

Jo Jones plays ride rhythms on high-hat cymbals.

Four Measures

0' 04"   Trumpets punctuate in unison with piano.

Trombones are "walking."

First Chorus (32-bar A-A-B-A)   Lester Young Tenor Saxophone Solo

0' 09"   **A**   Saxophone quotes first phrase of "Ol' Man River" to begin improvisation.

Timekeeping is by piano comping, guitar strumming each beat, bass walking, drummer playing ride rhythms on opening and closing high-hat.

0' 17"   **A**   Boogie-woogie piano figure returns.

0' 22"   Boogie-woogie figure is replaced by comping.

0' 27"   **B**   Saxophone solo continues.

0' 37"   **A**   Saxophone solo continues.

Two-Measure Introduction to the Second Chorus

0' 45"   Trumpets punctuate in unison with piano.

Boogie-woogie figure returns.

0' 46"   **Second Chorus** (32-bar A-A-B-A)   **Dicky Wells Trombone Solo**

0' 51"   It sounds like Wells is poking fun.

0' 53"   Wells plays one idea four times at different positions in relation to the beat.

1' 05"   The solo notes outline the descending chords.

1' 19"   *Final 2 Measures of Last A-section*

Trombone solo stops, and Basie plays up and down the scale on the piano.

Third Chorus (32-bar A-A-B-A)   Call and Response Passage

1' 23"   Trombones call. Trumpets respond.

1' 27"   Buddy Tate improvises a tenor saxophone solo.

1' 32"   Trombones call. Trumpets respond.

1' 36"   Buddy Tate improvises a tenor saxophone solo.

1' 41"   Bridge: Count Basie Piano Solo

1' 49"   Trombones call. Trumpets respond.

1' 55"   Buddy Tate improvises a tenor saxophone solo.

Fourth Chorus (32-bar A-A-B-A)   **Call and Response Passage**

        A   *Four Measures*

1' 58"   Trombones call. Trumpets respond with a syncopated figure that alternates muted with unmuted sound. Basie plays boogie-woogie figure.

           Four Measures

2' 04"   Lester Young improvises a tenor saxophone solo

        A   *Four Measures*

2' 09"   Trombones call. Trumpets respond with a syncopated figure that alternates muted with unmuted sound.

           Four Measures

2' 13"   Lester Young improvises a tenor saxophone solo

2' 16"   **Bridge:** Count Basie Piano Solo

        A   *Four Measures*

2' 27"   Trombones call. Trumpets respond with a syncopated figure that alternates muted with unmuted sound.

           Four Measures

2' 31"   Lester Young improvises saxophone solo, rapidly alternating bright and dark tone quality.

        Ending (Two-Measure Unaccompanied Solo Sections)

2' 36"   Basie improvises a solo break.

2' 38"   Young improvises a solo break.

2' 40"   walking bass alone

2' 42"   sticks on snare drum alone

2' 44"   Horns play a tie-it-up figure.

2' 47"   High-hat cymbals "chick" shut.

A written transcription of Young's solo is available in *You Got to Be Original, Man!: The Music of Lester Young* by Frank Buchmann-Moeller (New York: Greenwood, 1990).

thoroughly associated with comping that he might as well have. His comping was very sharp and lively. Basie comped so well and with such relaxed swing feeling that he provided the most-used model for it. To appreciate how far ahead of its time Basie's comping was, consider this. Though Basie had been doing it for over ten years, many other pianists of the 1940s continued in the predominant styles of the 1920s and 30s, accompanying by (1) stride style, (2) playing a chord on each beat in the manner of a rhythm guitarist, or (3) playing flowery countermelodies and embellishments. But by the end of the 1940s, the other pianists had caught on, and comping had become central to modern jazz.

Demo CD Tracks 20 (comping), 38 (stride style), and 88 (rhythm guitar).

Lester Young

Many of the best jazz trumpeters and saxophonists of the 1930s and 40s played with Count Basie at one time or another. Basie's most notable soloist during this period was tenor saxophonist Lester Young (1909–1959). This musician was so good that he was nicknamed "Pres" (or "Prez"), which is an abbreviation for "president of tenor saxophone players." His style served as a model for modern jazz saxophonists, and an entire subcategory of modern jazz that was called "cool jazz." Even trumpeters and guitarists were inspired by the way Young improvised. He became one of the five most influential saxophonists in jazz history.

Young played lines which were fresher and more smoothly swinging than those of any previous improvisers. He paved the way for modern saxophone tone color, vibrato, rhythmic conception, and phrasing. **Young offered a clear alternative to the complicated style of Coleman Hawkins with its heavy tone and fast vibrato.** Young's light tone, slow vibrato, and loping, buoyant phrases became the model for an entire generation of saxophonists, who often copied his solos note for note.

To explore Lester Young's improvisatory style, let's compare it with Coleman Hawkins'. Often, where Hawkins seemed to be chugging, Young seemed to be floating. Hawkins made improvisation sound like hard work. Young made it seem easy, like talking. Whereas Hawkins accented hard and often directly on main beats, Young was more subtle. Furthermore, Young tended to accent off-beats and lightly stress portions of beats that made his lines swing with ease. Young's playing was not as intricate as Hawkins', but his melodic ideas were certainly as advanced. He just made it sound easier.

((•—Listen on
mysearchlab.com

Listen to Lester Young's saxophone style on mysearchlab.com

Photo courtesy of Metronome/Archive Photos/Getty Images

◀ Tenor saxophonist Lester Young and drummer Jo Jones. Young was the swing era saxophonist who offered a model for the beginnings of modern jazz "bebop" and "cool" styles. The most melodic of all improvisers, Young generated lines that floated above the band with remarkable grace and a lilting swing feeling never heard before. Jo Jones was the swing drummer important for loosening rhythmic feeling and playing ride rhythms on high hat cymbals.

Young concerned himself with only a core of melodic material. He didn't incorporate afterthoughts into his phrases, as Hawkins was prone to do. He practiced deliberate restraint. He could pace a solo so well that it seemed an integral part of the written arrangement. His gift for inventing new, easily singable melodies while he improvised is unsurpassed in jazz history. He often improvised long lines that had a fresh, expansive feeling. There is an overriding sense of continuity in Young's improvisations that is very satisfying. Young possessed a musical storytelling talent which surfaced in nearly every improvisation.

Benny Goodman

Demo CD Tracks 69 (clarinet) and 97 (vibraphone).

Prentice Hall Jazz Collection CD Track 2: "Seven Come Eleven" by Benny Goodman

During the 1930s and 40s, clarinetist Benny Goodman (1909–1986) led the best-known jazz-oriented big band. His group had a very hard-driving sound and showcased Goodman's swinging and highly agile clarinet playing. His name was so well known, so often on the popularity charts, that he ranks above all but five other artists making recordings between 1890 and 1954. This means that Goodman was one of the most popular figures in the music industry as a whole, not just in jazz. Today he ranks with Louis Armstrong and Dave Brubeck as one of the best-known musicians in all of jazz history. In addition to his impact as a clarinetist, he influenced the course of jazz by providing exposure for other outstanding improvisers. His small combos were especially effective for bringing wide recognition to such swing era standouts as pianist Teddy Wilson, guitarist Charlie Christian, and vibraphonist Lionel Hampton.

▶ Benny Goodman (standing in foreground, holding clarinet), the most popular jazz musician of the swing era. Pictured here leading his big dance band of 1936.

Photo courtesy of Chicago History Museum/Archive Photos/Getty Images

Duke Ellington

Duke Ellington (1899–1974) is one of the most outstanding figures in jazz history. His contributions were threefold: he was significant as (1) a bandleader, (2) a pianist, and (3) a composer-arranger. He led one of the

◀ The Duke Ellington Band of 1938, the vehicle for its leader's innovative composing and arranging ideas.

Photo from Frank Driggs Archives, courtesy of Getty Images

first jazz-oriented big bands, beginning in 1923, and only his death in 1974 ended the band's run. **Ellington's group was the most stable and longest-lived big band in jazz history.** Some of the musicians remained for twenty to thirty years at a stretch. His musicians had strong, unique styles of their own. Together they made up an all-star unit. Many of their improvisations were so good that they became permanent parts of the band's pieces, as though composed. Ellington knew their musical personalities so thoroughly that he wrote tunes especially for them. He imaginatively mixed and matched their work with his own. The result was a breadth and depth of repertory that was superior to every other jazz group in history.

Ellington was **the single most creative and prolific composer-arranger in jazz history.** He wrote more than two thousand compositions and many arrangements and rearrangements for them. He began composing and arranging before 1920 and continued productively until his death. Recording more than any other jazz group, the Ellington band and its leader's compositions can be heard in hundreds of albums.

As a piano soloist, Ellington performed often in the stride style. He also performed in his own original style, which was still quite percussive though much sparser than the stride style. Elllington's playing sparkled and popped. His notes had unerring swing feeling. Ellington stood out for his unusual harmonies. He showed the same imagination, but with more restraint, in playing for his orchestra. His sidemen valued his accompanying for its vitality and the complementary way he framed their phrases. His comping was full of spirit, and his timing and taste were near perfect.

Ellington wrote many tunes, often in collaboration with his sidemen. Some of these became popular songs when lyrics were added. A few were hits when recorded by singers apart from the Ellington band. Among his best-known songs are "I'm Beginning to See the Light," "Solitude," "Mood Indigo," and "Don't Get Around Much Anymore." Nearly all jazz musicians have played at least one Ellington tune during their careers. Many

Prentice Hall Jazz History DVD: "It Don't Mean A Thing (If It Ain't Got That Swing)" by Duke Ellington

Photo by William P. Gottlieb, courtesy of Library of Congress

► Cootie Williams, Duke Ellington's star trumpeter, who specialized in growl-style use of the plunger mute. Ellington featured his unmuted playing on "Harlem Airshaft."

have devoted entire albums to his music, more albums than have honored any other jazz composer.

Ellington also wrote hundreds of instrumentals. **Some of them paint musical portraits of famous personalities** such as the great stride pianist Willie "The Lion" Smith ("Portrait of the Lion") and the comedian Bert Williams ("Portrait of Bert Williams"). **Others paint musical pictures of places** such as "Warm Valley" and "Harlem Airshaft," or sensations such as "Transblucency."

Ellington also wrote many longer pieces. **He is widely acclaimed for having taken jazz into the format of "extended works,"** as these longer pieces were termed. His most respected such work is "Black, Brown, and Beige," a fifty-minute tone poem describing the history of the American Negro. Some of his longest pieces were film scores. A favorite of musicians and critics is his music for "Anatomy of a Murder," the Otto Preminger movie starring Jimmy Stewart.

Ellington's Compositions and Repertory

((•-Listen on
mysearchlab.com
Listen to saxophone section on mysearchlab.com

An important element of the Ellington sound is what is called **voicing across sections of the band.** Most arrangers, including Ellington, routinely write passages that pit the sound of one section of the band, such as the saxes, against another section of the band, such as the brasses. But Ellington was innovative because he often wrote passages to be played by combinations of instruments drawn from different sections of the band. The most famous example is in his 1930 recording of "Mood Indigo." There he voiced clarinet with muted trumpet and muted trombone. This piece combined instruments from three different sections of the band: trumpet section, trombone section, and saxophone section. In his 1940 recording of "Concerto for Cootie," he voiced pizzicato bass notes in unison with the horns. This was unusual because bass was primarily assigned to a timekeeping role as a member of the rhythm section and rarely played melody parts.

Photo by Lee Tanner

◀ Johnny Hodges, Duke
Ellington's star soloist, the
most widely imitated alto
saxophonist of the swing
era. Even modern giants
like John Coltrane were
influenced by his style.

Another notable technique employed by Ellington was placing a
wordless vocal in an arrangement. Sometimes called *instrumentalized
voice,* this became identified with Ellington. He was applauded for its use
in his 1927 recording of "Creole Love Call" and his 1946 recording of
"Transblucency."

Ellington was also famous for his exotic "jungle sounds." These
originated with his jobs playing for floor shows at New York nightclubs that wanted stylized presentations of African atmosphere. To do
this, he wrote parts for trumpeter Bubber Miley and trombonist "Tricky
Sam" Nanton playing into plunger mutes, achieving what has become
known as *growl style* (*Demo CD* Track 67). He also used clarinets playing un-usual harmonies in an intense, wailing fashion. Even years later,
when he was no longer playing for these floor shows, he continued to
employ these exotic sounds. They contributed to his group's reputation
as a "hot band."

Diversity and breadth characterized Ellington's music. The pieces in
Ellington's repertory were filled with variety, and the lack of repetition
within each piece is striking. Ellington's arrangements presented a larger
number of different themes and rhythmic figures than those of other swing
bands. Accompanying figures also reflected a greater assortment than
was customary. In addition, Ellington's overall repertory was also diverse.
It was so varied that we can summarize it as a number of separate books:
(1) an impressionistic book with arrangements that place more emphasis
on orchestral colors and shading than on swinging; (2) a book of romantic
ballads; (3) a book of exotic pieces; (4) a concert book in which each piece
is a long work with much less improvisation than was usually found in his
music; (5) a book of concertos in which each piece frames the style of one

((•─ **Listen** on
mysearchlab.com
*Listen to alto saxophone by Johnny
Hodges on mysearchlab.com*

Recorded in 1940 in New York by the Duke Ellington band: three trumpets, three trombones, five saxophones (Barney Bigard doubling on clarinet), piano, guitar (Freddie Guy), bass (Jimmy Blanton), and drums (Sonny Greer); composed by Duke Ellington; made by RCA Victor Records.

Terms to know from tracks on *Demo CD:* walking bass (23), rhythm guitar (88), wire brushes (12), high-hat cymbals (2), snare drum (5), plunger mute (81), trombone (78), trumpet (59), clarinet (69), pitch bends (50–53), blue notes (54–58), A-A-B-A form (33).

"Harlem Airshaft" is a monumental achievement in jazz history by what most historians consider Duke Ellington's greatest band. This piece combines the gritty, soulful nature of New Orleans combo jazz with the sophisticated big band writing associated with 1930s New York. The harmonies assigned to the saxophones are slick, East Coast renderings. The earthy clarinet improvisations that are swooping and swirling around the band sound are supplied by Barney Bigard, a Creole from New Orleans. Trumpet improvisations are provided by Mobile, Alabama, native Cootie Williams. You might detect the influence of New Orleans natives Louis Armstrong and Joe Oliver in Williams' searing style. Notice his manipulations of tone quality and his sliding into and out of the main pitches, as at about 1′ 16″ and 1′ 30″. Pay attention to Williams' percussive attacks for selected notes, as at 1′ 00″ and 2′ 33″.

Ellington delivers the incredible sound of three to five different layers of activity at almost every moment in "Harlem Airshaft." Despite the inherent potential for internal conflict, the saxophone parts never clash with the trumpet and trombone parts. Instead, they bounce off and complement each other. In addition, there is occasionally an improvised clarinet line weaving around several composed lines. For instance, note the relationship at 2′ 36″ between Bigard's improvised figures on clarinet and the composed ones being played by the band. It all fits together despite the spontaneity. All the while, an extremely propulsive force is coming from the rhythm section combination of rhythm guitar, string bass, and drums. The action is heightened at 2′ 51″, where three different lines are running at the same time over the hard swinging rhythm section. It seems as though the music may break into chaos but it doesn't.

One strategy that can make listening fun is to rotate your attention from one part, such as brasses, to another, such as saxophones. Later, you might try to hear their parts interlocking. At several junctures, you will notice more than one melody sounding at the same time. For instance, at 1′ 35″ you may detect one melody played in harmony by muted trombones, a second by saxophones, and a third improvised by clarinetist Barney Bigard. Then try to notice the walking bass of Jimmy Blanton driving this effect. Blanton was a powerhouse in Ellington's rhythm section.

Breaks also provide some of the drama in "Harlem Airshaft." Notice the harmonies and vibratos of the saxophones when timekeeping rhythms are suspended at 0′ 55″ and 1′ 06″.

In "Harlem Airshaft" there is so much going on that you should not hesitate to use the pause switch on your CD player to digest it. You will often need to replay passages to catch what you missed. In some passages, such as 0′ 54″ to 0′ 59″, there is something new and important occurring every second.

Introduction

0′ 00″   *First 4 Measures*

         Brass instruments call in harmonized sustained tones.

         Saxophones respond with a melodic figure.

         Rhythm guitar, walking bass, and wire brushes on snare drum play timekeeping.

0′ 05″   *Second 4 Measures*

         Saxophones play the lead in harmony.

0' 10'		*Third 4 Measures*
		Trombones play the lead.
0' 13"		answered by baritone saxophone
0' 14"		Trombones play harmonized punching figures.

First Chorus (32-bar A-A-B-A)

0' 16"	**A**	Saxophones play simple melody in unison while muted trumpets repeat a background figure in harmony.
0' 25"	**A**	Saxophones play simple melody in unison while muted trumpets repeat a background figure in harmony.
0' 35"	**B**	Saxophones call in harmony.
0' 37"		"Tricky Sam" Nanton replies by blowing his trombone into a plunger mute.
0' 45"	**A**	Saxophones play simple melody in unison while muted trumpets repeat a background figure in harmony.
0' 55"		Sonny Greer ends the passage by striking a cymbal then quickly grabbing it to prevent ringing.

Second Chorus (32-bar A-A-B-A)

	A	*First 4 Measures*
0' 56"		Rhythm section stops playing.
		Saxophones play a harmonized part with sustained tones.
0' 57"		Drum roll underneath final saxophone tones.
0' 59"		Drummer plays syncopated figures for trumpet solo.
		Second 4 Measures
1' 00"		Cootie Williams opens his trumpet improvisation by percussively stating the same note repeatedly in an off-the-beat fashion. He uses the high register and shakes one of his tones as it ends.
		Saxophones play syncopated, harmonize.d line underneath trumpet solo.
1' 06"	**A**	same strategy as first A-section
1' 09"		repeated high notes from trumpet, each figure landing on a shaken tone
1' 16"	**B**	Saxophones are repeating a climbing figure under trumpet solo.
1' 25"	**A**	same strategy as first A-section
1' 31"		Cootie Williams roughens his tone and slowly slides down from his last high note's pitch.

Third Chorus (32-bar A-A-B-A)

1' 35"	**A**	Trombones play a harmonized melody in foreground, as clarinetist Barney Bigard improvises around it, and saxophones play another series of interjections underneath.
1' 45"	**A**	Trombones play a harmonized melody in foreground, as clarinetist Barney Bigard improvises around it, and saxophones play another series of interjections underneath.
1' 55"	**B**	Trumpets join trombones to repeat a sustained tone while clarinet improvisation continues, and saxophones make sporadic interjections.
2' 03"		Bigard ends bridge section with a shake.
2' 05"	**A**	same formula as in first A-section. Notice Bigard's blue notes.

Fourth Chorus (32-bar A-A-B-A)

Band Starts Softly, Gradually Getting Louder and Louder

2' 14"	**A**	Horns softly play a syncopated, low-register melody while clarinet solo spills into the first 3 measures of this chorus.
		Rhythm guitar and walking bass are easier to hear now.
2' 19"		Cootie Williams begins muted trumpet solo.
2' 23"	**A**	Trumpet solo continues.
2' 33"		Williams percussively states the final 4 notes of his solo directly on each beat.
2' 34"	**B**	Band plays a composed call.
2' 36"		Clarinet improvises a reply.
2' 43"	**A**	Brass call, and saxophones answer repeatedly, clarinet improvising throughout.
2' 51"		Saxophones repeat a new riff of their own.
		Clarinet enters the high register.
		Ending has brass sustaining a chord and baritone saxophone sounding a low note.

The complete score and parts are available from *www.jalc.org*.

Ellington sideman; (6) a book of swinging instrumentals, each with jazz solos, catchy ensemble themes, and punching accompaniment figures; (7) a book of music for sacred concerts. This was a context that brought Ellington to present new shows and use choirs, new vocal soloists, organ, and dancers. It inspired writing for different moods, such as that of prayer. It also inspired extensive lyrics.

Duke Ellington's contributions were indeed vast. You could explore a few hundred selections and then realize that Ellington also composed several operas, a couple of ballets, and about ten musical shows. We should also remember that the Ellington band's music never really fell into any fixed category—early jazz, swing, or modern. It was always unique. Ellington created a jazz classification that was practically his own. And it maintained its creative energy for more than four decades.

The influence of Ellington's music was also vast. Other big bands played his compositions and were influenced by his writing style as early as the 1930s. There was an echo of Ellington in the work of several outstanding arrangers of the 1950s and 60s. Revivals of Ellington's work were frequent during the 1980s and 90s. Even a few avant-garde bands and composers of this period drew upon Ellington for inspiration. Ellington's piano style was also influential. His approach inspired a number of players, including the highly individualistic modernists Thelonious Monk and Cecil Taylor.

This recording preserves what was an almost nightly event in the life of the touring Duke Ellington band. Based on a song written by Duke Ellington and originally recorded with a vocal in 1941, this became a feature number for the ballad artistry of Ellington's star alto saxophonist Johnny Hodges (1907–1970). It demonstrates his huge, lush sound and his exceedingly sensual craftsmanship with timing of pitch bends. Notice the reverence Hodges gave to every note. On this recording the saxophonist sticks fairly close to Ellington's original melody. The bulk of his improvisation here takes the form of ornamentation and paraphrase. Most listeners find the result to be quite romantic.

Though we often associate Ellington with the swing era of the 1930s and 40s, the Ellington band continued to tour and record into the 1970s. This particular recording was made in 1961 with many of the same musicians Ellington had been using since the 1940s. The piano introduction is contributed by Jimmy Jones, and the arrangement is by Billy Strayhorn for five trumpets, three trombones, five saxophones, piano, bass, and drums. Ellington himself does not play on this recording.

VOCALISTS

Billie Holiday

Billie Holiday (1915–1959) is the most influential singer associated with jazz since the early 1930s. Many vocalists began their careers imitating her. Some devoted albums to tunes they first heard Holiday sing. Nicknamed "Lady Day," she is also the singer most frequently cited by jazz musicians when asked what music they would take to a desert island. This is quite an endorsement because most jazz musicians prefer instrumental music and rarely name a vocal recording among their favorites.

Prentice Hall Jazz History DVD: "Fine and Mellow" by Billie Holiday

Holiday did not possess the power of Bessie Smith, the deep, rich voice of Sarah Vaughan, or the speed and range of Ella Fitzgerald. Yet why is she so revered? First, she was original and fresh. Second, the depth and sincerity of emotion that she communicated are unparalleled. She made lyrics come alive. Holiday conveyed the song's meaning as though speaking directly to you. The agony she portrayed in sad songs could tear your heart out. Her renditions of "Gloomy Sunday," "Strange Fruit," and a tune she herself co-authored, "God Bless the Child," had intense effects on listeners. On the other hand, some of her late 1930s recordings convey a carefree spirit of joy unmatched by her contemporaries. No matter the mood, her tender, knowing delivery grabbed you right away. (Listen to her "She's Funny That Way" in *Smithsonian Collection of Classic Jazz.*)

Photo courtesy of Frank Driggs

▶ Billie Holiday, the most
influential singer in jazz
after the early 1930s.

A third reason for Holiday's stature is jazz flavor. Though she was not really a blues singer—her repertory was mostly pop and show tunes—Holiday often formed her tones as a jazz hornman would, with a whine that had blues flavor. Like jazz instrumentalists, she did not always give songs a straight reading, even though she had excellent diction. Instead, she varied her delivery creatively. One of the ways Holiday transformed songs was by manipulating their rhythms. Her method of intentionally delaying the arrival of certain words and phrases is almost indistinguishable from rhythmic displacements used by trumpeter Louis Armstrong, one of her main influences. (Listen to her "She's Funny That Way" in *Smithsonian Collection of Classic Jazz*.) This caused an engaging syncopation and swing feeling. The combination of her bluesy inflections, jazzy accents, and improvising gave jazz flavor to her music.

Holiday toured and recorded with many of the top jazz musicians of the time, including Artie Shaw, Benny Goodman, and Count Basie. Her 1937 recording of "Carelessly" reached the #1 position on the popularity charts, and she had thirty-five other recordings reach the top twenty by 1945. She was prolific during the 1940s and 50s as well. Some listeners like her work of the 1930s the most. Others find her late recordings of the 1950s to be even more emotionally compelling. Not only did her life story inspire a popular movie (*Lady Sings the Blues*, 1972), but her recordings continue to sell today, fifty years after her death.

"Back in Your Own Back Yard" featuring Billie Holiday and Lester Young

((•—Listen on mysearchlab.com

Composed by Al Jolson; recorded January 12, 1938, by singer Billie Holiday, trumpeter Buck Clayton, tenor saxophonist Lester Young, pianist Teddy Wilson, bassist Walter Page, guitarist Freddie Green, and drummer Jo Jones.

Jazz instrumentalists have often made part of their living by accompanying singers. And to satisfy a segment of their audience, the practice of carrying at least one singer was common for leaders of jazz bands as recently as the 1950s. Appearing with singers sometimes produced results that had jazz value, though it was not usually as artistically fulfilling for instrumentalists as playing strictly instrumental music. Many jazz musicians consider it an imposition to have to accompany singers. They do it only to guarantee their livelihood. However, when asking musicians what music they themselves enjoy, one singer's name is often mentioned along with the names of instrumentalists—Billie Holiday.

This particular recording has more jazz in it than vocal features usually have. All the horn solos are outstanding. And if you listen carefully to Holiday's timing, you might even detect the influence of Louis Armstrong's rhythmic style. In other words, you might appreciate Holiday's part as jazz, too. Holiday did not scat sing or improvise in the manner of a jazz saxophonist. But she took liberties with the pitches and tone qualities of the notes in the song. And she took so much liberty with their timing that we might almost call her a jazz improviser. Those liberties were so creative, soulful, and swinging that she was held in high esteem even by musicians. Like Armstrong before her, Holiday in turn exerted considerable influence on other singers. And several of the tunes she recorded became standard repertory for jazz-oriented singers because her renditions were so stunning.

Pianist Teddy Wilson organized numerous recording sessions for Holiday and played tastefully on all of them. Wilson is also known for work with Benny Goodman, where his grace and swing feeling remain a marvel for other musicians to hear. In this particular recording, Wilson is joined by the Count Basie rhythm section, minus Basie.

0' 00" **Introduction** (32 beats)

Buck Clayton trumpet improvisation, accompanied by piano, guitar, bass, drums, and sustained tones on tenor sax.

0' 12" **Vocal Chorus** (A-A-B-A)

Holiday's singing is accompanied by muted trumpet and piano improvising counterlines while guitar, bass, and drums play time keeping rhythms.

0' 25" *Second A-section*

0' 38" *Bridge*

0' 50" *Final A-section*

1' 02" **Lester Young Tenor Sax Solo Improvisation** (A-A-B-A)

Young devises a smooth solo line in a very relaxed manner, using notes mostly from the low and the middle registers of his horn.

Accompaniment includes guitar and faint piano chords played in a simple and steady manner. A prominent accompaniment sound is the opening and closing high-hat played by the drummer.

1' 14"   *Second A-section*

1' 27"   *Bridge*

Notice the "kicks" and "bombs" from the drums, especially near the beginnings and endings of sections.

1' 38"   *Final A-section*

1' 47"   Cup-muted trumpet and tenor sax play a preset figure together during the final 8 beats of this section.

1' 50"   **Vocal Chorus** (A-A-B-A)

Holiday's singing is accompanied by improvised piano countermelodies.

2' 02"   *Second A-section*

2' 15"   *Bridge*

2' 28"   *Final A-section*

collectively improvised closing with lines coming from sax and unmuted trumpet

▶ Teddy Wilson, the pianist who organized many of Billie Holiday's best recording sessions. The sensitivity, grace, and intelligence of his improvisations were unmatched in the 1930s.

Courtesy of Frank Driggs

Ella Fitzgerald

Ella Fitzgerald (1918–1996) is considered by many to be the most outstanding non-operatic singer of the twentieth century. She had near-flawless technique. Listeners were impressed by her grace and lilt. Mastery of swing eighth notes and perfect timing of syncopations gave her singing the rhythmic effect achieved by the best swing era hornmen. Delivered with such bounce and lightness, her phrases actually swung more than those of some modern trumpeters and saxophonists.

First achieving prominence in the mid-1930s, Fitzgerald had a #1 hit in her 1938 rendition of "A-Tisket-A-Tasket" with the Chick Webb Band. With this group she recorded, toured, and, for several years after Webb died, served as leader. By 1955, thirty-four of her other records had risen to popularity positions within the top twenty. Albums of her concert appearances climbed to high positions on the popularity charts during the 1960s and again in the 1980s.

Ella Fitzgerald's tone was pure and supple. Her command spanned the unusually wide range of three and a half octaves. Singing in tune proves difficult for many singers, but not for Fitzgerald. Her pitch was accurate, no matter the register or tempo of the material. Her articulation was exquisite. A remarkable agility conveyed an effortless feeling. She gave every note a lift. Her overall manner achieved great presence and warmth. Her combination of spirit and ease imparted a bright touch even to ballads, as though she were never really sad. A youthful quality always pervaded her work, even when she was in her seventies.

Listen on **mysearchlab.com**
Listen to Ella Fitzgerald's scat singing on mysearchlab.com

Photo courtesy of Frank Driggs

◀ Ella Fitzgerald, the most outstanding non-operatic singer in the twentieth century and a leading popularizer of scat singing.

Recorded October 4, 1945, in New York by Ella Fitzgerald (voice), Vic Shoen (arranger), three trumpets, trombone, four saxophones, Moe Wechsler (piano), Hy White (guitar), Felix Giobbe (bass), and Irv Kluger (drums); composed by Benny Goodman and Lionel Hampton; originally issued by Decca Records.

This selection offers a very swinging performance by "The First Lady of Song." It also illustrates how the human voice can imitate a jazz horn.

The 1942 Lionel Hampton band's Decca recording of "Flying Home" was so rousing and melodic that Ella Fitzgerald learned Illinois Jacquet's saxophone improvisation from it. She also learned several of the band parts that had not been improvised. Then she began singing it without words at her own performances. The wordless vocal technique is known as **scat singing.** In 1945, Fitzgerald hired musicians for a studio session and recorded this arrangement of her scats. She was rewarded with high sales for this particular recording.

The "Flying Home" composition fits a 32-bar A-A-B-A form. As with instrumental jazz, Fitzgerald's vocal version cycles through several repetitions. A particular lift is provided when the arrangement moves the key from G to C at 1' 41".

On Fitzgerald's rendition, she entirely omits the "Flying Home" melody. But that does not mean there are no melodies in this performance. We can hear the melodic content of Jacquet's saxophone improvisation, beginning at 0' 30". Then, at the end of her first A-A-B-A chorus, about 1' 01", Fitzgerald borrows from the "Good Night Ladies" tune and sings the phrase "Merrily we roll along on a deep, deep, deep blue sea." In the bridge of her second chorus, about 1' 24", Fitzgerald scats the melody to "Yankee Doodle went to town riding on a pony."

There are other highlights that make our listening easy. Beginning at 1' 05", Fitzgerald repeats in a syncopated way the same note twelve times, as Jacquet did in his Hampton recording. In her third chorus, at about 2' 06", she ends the bridge with a quarter-note triplet just as Hampton had played on his vibraphone solo at that spot in the 1942 recording. In the final A-section, about 2' 08", Fitzgerald scat sings the same lick three times. This was the idea played by the Hampton saxophone section at about 0' 35" on their band recording.

Introduction

0' 00"	loud, big band ensemble statements
0' 02"	Band stops while Fitzgerald scat sings over the drummer who is improvising timekeeping patterns and accents with wire brushes on snare drum.

First Chorus (A-A-B-A)

0' 11"	Fitzgerald rests while pianist improvises a solo, paraphrasing the "Flying Home" melody, accompanied by walking bass. Drummer switches to stating every beat instead of varying his rhythms.
0' 18"	loud brass remarks
0' 20"	piano response, high-pitched Basie-style improvised line
0' 27"	brass interjections

Second Chorus (A-A-B-A)

0' 29"   A   Fitzgerald begins singing the melodic content of Jacquet's original saxophone improvisation.

                Pianist improvises concurrent line.

                Band plays chords in a punching manner.

0' 38"   A

0' 47"   Bridge

                Fitzgerald continues scatting Jacquet's sax solo.

0' 56"   A

1' 01"   Fitzgerald interpolates "Merrily we roll along on a deep, deep, deep blue sea."

Third Chorus (A-A-B-A)

           A

1' 05"   Fitzgerald sings the same note 12 times in a syncopated manner.

           A

1' 14"   Fitzgerald sings a new lick three times.

1' 23"   Bridge

                Fitzgerald scat sings melody to "Yankee Doodle went to town a riding on a pony."

1' 32"   A

Fourth Chorus (A-A-B-A) **in a new key**

           A

1' 41"   sings same lick three times

1' 48"   Fitzgerald sings melody of "Donkey Serenade" from Grofé's "Grand Canyon Suite" along with brass.

           A

1' 50'   Fitzgerald sings same lick three times.

           Bridge

1' 59"   Sustained saxophone tones accompany vocal. Improvised piano line runs concurrently.

2' 06"   Vocal ends the bridge with brass in a quarter-note triplet figure.

2' 08"   A

                Fitzgerald scat sings same lick twice, followed by brass response.

2' 15"   Final 2 Measures of **A**

                break for vocal, scat sings an ascending phrase

Ending Extension

                scat sings same phrase two more times, each time answered by band

2' 20"   comes down from third time, each stop in her descent being answered by drummer with wire brushes on snare drum

2' 23"   Fitzgerald sings "baaaaaaahhh—rip"

2' 24"   Loud band chord finalizes the piece as the drummer strikes snare drum loudly with brushes.

2' 27"   Bass drum "thud" concludes the piece.

Not inclined to the melodramatic attitude of so many other singers, Fitzgerald's effect is often called "cheerful," "exuberant," or "ebullient." Many consider her creative peak to be the 1950s and 60s, yet she was still giving remarkable performances during the 1970s and 80s.

Though she did not invent it, Fitzgerald was scat singing's best known practitioner. Among the modern scat singers who followed, almost all cite her work as their first inspiration. Contained within her scat devices were stock phrases from late swing and early bop improvisers. On some recordings she functions as a horn, using nonsense syllables exclusively, no lyrics. Fitzgerald was quite melodic in her scats. This was due in part to (1) basing portions of her passages on set routines rather than completely fresh improvisations in every performance and (2) improvising more around the melody of the original tune than from the chords of its accompaniment.

Scat singing Jazz improvisation using the human voice as an instrument, with nonsense syllables (dwee, ool, ya, bop, bam, etc.) instead of words

Despite her scat singing's historic visibility, that work represents only a small fraction of her output. Fitzgerald gets high marks from listeners who like a singer to stick to the melody as written. Some of the greatest pop tune composers were eager to have her perform their songs because her readings were so true to their original intent. So, in addition to her exalted position in jazz, she also had a large following among pop music listeners.

PIANISTS

Art Tatum

Art Tatum (1910–1956) is among the most widely admired pianists in jazz history. His music has survived his death by many years. With his impressive technical facility and unceasing energy, he still stands above all the very fast, imaginative pianists who have emerged since him.

Tatum's style combines a variety of techniques. He often employed stride-style in his left hand with horn-like lines in his right hand. Tatum's playing was quite flowery, with long, fast runs which sometimes overlapped

((•⊢ **Listen** on **mysearchlab.com**

Listen to Art Tatum's piano style on mysearchlab.com

▶ Art Tatum, the most widely admired piano virtuoso in jazz history.

Photo courtesy of Frank Driggs

each other. These runs seemed to throw showers of notes upon the listener. The rhythms in these showers were often odd combinations, not merely strings of eighth notes and sixteenth notes. But despite their complexity, Tatum's runs have been memorized by hundreds of pianists, and they have been used to decorate solos in performances by jazz pianists and popular pianists alike.

He was also a master at spontaneously adding and changing chords during his performance of pop tunes. This is termed chord *substitution*. Generations of jazz pianists have followed him and learned this technique. Sometimes Tatum changed keys several times within a phrase and still managed to resolve the harmonic motion gracefully. Tatum was very inventive and unpredictable rhythmically, too, and he frequently interrupted the direction of his own lines. He seemed to indulge his impulses and momentarily pursue musical tangents.

Art Tatum's impact on jazz history was enormous. The fast lines and added chords of Tatum were absorbed by saxophonists Don Byas and Charlie Parker. Tatum also influenced two pianists who were very important during the early days of modern jazz: Bud Powell and Lennie Tristano. Both Powell and Tristano, in turn, went on to influence numerous pianists of the 1950s, further extending the reach of Tatum's work.

Mary Lou Williams

Pianists have proven to be the most versatile musicians throughout music's history. **Mary Lou Williams** (1910–1981) exemplifies this tradition. She distinguished herself as a boogie-woogie player, a swing player in the style of Count Basie, a modern jazz stylist by the mid-1940s, and she even dueted with "free jazz" pioneer Cecil Taylor in 1977. No matter what style she played, her technique was stunning, and her improvisations were intelligently conceived. Williams penned arrangements for big bands led by

◄ Mary Lou Williams, pianist-composer-arranger who kept up with changing styles and continued effectively in the modern era.

Photo courtesy of Frank Driggs

Composed by the Original Dixieland Jazz Band; recorded March 21, 1933, by pianist Art Tatum.

This is the first solo record by Tatum to be issued, and it is one of the fastest jazz piano improvisations on record. It goes by at about 370 beats per minute. Tatum was legendary for his dazzling speed. He was also known for changing the mood and direction abruptly in the middle of his improvisations. A third virtue was his changing a piece's harmonies by substituting new chords for old and adding more. This third aspect was particularly inspiring to modern jazz musicians of the 1940s. His performance on "Tiger Rag" demonstrates all those talents, and it shows why Tatum's playing stood as a peak that hundreds of pianists aspired to.

0' 00" **Introduction**

Tatum made up his own opening to the piece, in the style of French composer Claude Debussy. He plays it in a free rhythmic style that does not depend on a steady tempo. Instead it slows and quickens according to its own internal drama.

0' 14" **First Theme** (A-A-B-A, each section having 8 groups of 4 beats)

Tempo begins at about 370 beats per minute. Tatum's left hand is playing bass notes on every other beat. His right hand plays melodic figures that cascade up and down the keyboard.

0' 24" *B-section* (two sections, each having 4 groups of 4 beats)

Tatum's right hand continues to improvise while his left-hand accompaniment pattern switches to short, stabbing chords.

0' 30" *A-section* (8 groups of 4 beats)

Left-hand accompaniment figure returns to bass notes on every other beat.

0' 35" **Second Theme** (4 groups of 4 beats, 4 more groups of 4 beats, 8 groups of 4 beats, and another 8 groups of 4 beats)

This theme is in a new key and a new style. Tatum plays the brief melody in a chordal style, followed by a torrid run that is not accompanied. Then he plays more chords and another unaccompanied run. This is like the stop-time method of a New Orleans jazz band.

0' 39" The theme continues with chorded melody played by the right hand and the stride-style accompaniment of bass notes alternating with chords played by the left hand.

Benny Goodman, Dizzy Gillespie, Woody Herman, and Duke Ellington. From 1929 to 1941, her arrangements set the pace for the band Andy Kirk and His Twelve Clouds of Joy, with which she was also the top soloist. She also wrote more than 250 original compositions. Her "Zodiac Suite" particularly impressed her contemporaries. (Though it contains some jazz passages, much of the suite was derived from her study of twentieth-century classical composers.) Her immense output as composer and arranger and the flair that she brought to her rendering of every new piano style is staggering.

0' 50" **Third Theme** (32 groups of 4 beats)

This new theme is in a new key and a new style. The melody is familiar to some listeners as the part of the song that repeats again and again the phrase "Hold that tiger!" Tatum takes liberties with that melody. Listen for the trill played by his left hand in the bass register of the piano.

0' 56" Second half of theme begins.

1' 00" Break in the middle of the theme permits Tatum to showcase his impressive left-hand skill.

1' 06" The theme concludes with some of the sounds Tatum used in the end of his introduction.

1' 11" **Repeat of the Third Theme** (32 groups of 4 beats)

Tatum improvises brilliantly with his right hand while his left hand plays stride-style accompaniment.

1' 21" A break is followed by a slightly different left-hand accompaniment style. Tatum uses his left hand to play a counter-melody while maintaining the stride-style accompaniment pattern at the same time.

1' 24" Second half of theme begins.

1' 30" As the theme ends Tatum builds his improvisation to a frenzy. An immense two-handed tremolo leads into the next rendition of the third theme.

1' 33" **Another Repeat of the Third Theme** (32 groups of 4 beats)

Tatum plays a riff by his right hand sounding chords. His left hand plays energetic walking bass lines. This gives the music a feeling of time units being composed of four pulses instead of two.

1' 42" A break midway through this theme is followed by more improvisation by Tatum's right hand. His left hand continues accompanying in the stride style.

1' 48" This theme ends with a 3-note riff played seven times.

1' 53" **Another Repeat of the Third Theme** (32 groups of 4 beats)

Tatum plays a descending run seven times. Then, over a stop-time break, that run is played an eighth time, but now it is stretched out to last longer.

2' 04" Second half of theme begins.

2' 10" This theme concludes with the 3-note riff that ended the previous time. Tatum plays another descending run, and ends the performance by arriving at a single note on the bottom end of the piano keyboard.

Partly because of her multitude of talents and genre switches, it has been difficult to identify a particular stamp of personal style in Mary Lou Williams' work. By the 1940s, she had begun what became the norm for young jazz musicians in the 1980s and 1990s, mastering the styles of different players in different eras and never sticking to any one of them. Williams continuously changed, assimilating more and more approaches. At various times during her career she sounded like Count Basie, Duke Ellington, Teddy Wilson, Art Tatum, Erroll Garner, Thelonious Monk, George Shearing, and Lennie Tristano.

LISTENING GUIDE

CD1—Track 14

"Walkin' and Swingin'" by Andy Kirk and His Twelve Clouds of Joy featuring Mary Lou Williams

((•—Listen on **mysearchlab.com**

Composed by Mary Lou Williams; recorded 1936 in NYC for Decca with three trumpets, one trombone, two alto saxophones, one tenor saxophone, piano (Williams), guitar, bass, and drums; reissued on *Andy Kirk & Mary Lou Williams: Mary's Idea*. (Decca Jazz: 622, c1993).

Sounds to learn from *Demo CD*: tenor saxophone (also heard at 1' 51" on "Walkin' and Swingin'"), alto saxophone, trombone (also heard at 2' 32" and 2' 36" on "Walkin' and Swingin'"). Terms to learn from Elements of Music Appendix: measure (bar), A-A-B-A form, mutes, syncopation.

Andy Kirk's 12-piece band was based in Kansas City during the 1930s, though they also played elsewhere, including extended engagements in New York and Pennsylvania. "Walkin' and Swingin'" is a composition and arrangement that pianist Mary Lou Williams prepared for it. The piece became a particular favorite of musicians who appreciate Williams' creativity. Its most outstanding feature is a line that Williams composed for trumpet and three saxophones to play on the second chorus, beginning at about 0' 46". The construction of this line hints at some of the melodic intricacies and syncopations that were used in the first modern jazz style, known as "bop," short for "bebop" (see Chapter 6). It is notable that Kirk shared Kansas City with several other excellent big bands, including a few that launched modern jazz: Count Basie's, which featured Lester Young, and Jay McShann's, which featured Charlie Parker. Like Lester Young and Charlie Parker, Mary Lou Williams was one of Kansas City's contributions to the roots of modern jazz.

Williams' piano remarks during this performance sound similar to those associated with Basie. This similarity could be a result of Williams imitating Basie and/or studying the same models that Basie had studied, including Fats Waller and Earl Hines. She certainly had plenty of opportunity to hear Basie up close while she and Basie were both based in Kansas City.

This recording also gives us a taste of tenor saxophonist Dick Wilson's playing at 1' 51". Wilson was one of the top Coleman Hawkins disciples on the 1930s jazz scene. Pay attention to his deep, dark tone, and his authoritative bearing. Listen to how logically he constructs his improvised lines.

The Kansas City style for big band arrangements is characterized by brief phrases called riffs; a few examples occur at 2' 37" and 2' 47".

The piece follows a 32-bar A-A-B-A construction, whose chord changes are similar to those of "I Got Rhythm," though the bridge is not. With no introduction at the beginning and no extra measures at the ending, the performance consists of four complete choruses of that A-A-B-A construction and a two-measure (8 quick beats) interlude between the end of the first chorus and the beginning of the second. In preparing this piece, Williams employed several arranging practices that were standard for big bands of the swing era: (1) assigning the theme to the saxophones and the punctuations to the brass instruments, as in the A-sections of the first chorus, (2) inventing an intricate, jazz improvisation-like line, as constitutes the second chorus that begins at 0' 46"; (3) delegating the improvised solo sections according to the song form, as she plays her own piano solo on the A-sections of the third chorus, beginning at 1' 32", and she gives the bridge to Dick Wilson for his tenor saxophone solo, beginning at 1' 50"; (4) call and response format (sequenced like a question and answer), as she gives the trumpets a brief riff as a question, at about 2' 37", and assigns the trombone an answer; then she gives the brass instruments a call and the saxophones a response, beginning at about 2' 47".

Though bass and drums play throughout the piece, their presence may be felt more than heard. You might detect them best at about 2' 32" during moments when horns pause.

This arrangement departs in a significant way from standard practices of the era. In selecting instruments to play the theme of the second chorus, Williams assigned one trumpet to play with three saxophones. In other words, she drew instruments from different sections of the band: the brass section and the saxophone section. Known as "cross-section voicing," this technique was unusual for arrangers of her time, though Duke Ellington was a notable exception.

First Chorus

0′ 00″	**A**	Saxophones play theme as brasses punctuate.
0′ 11″	**A**	Saxophones play theme as brasses punctuate.
0′ 22″	**B**	Brasses lead, sometimes mixed with saxes. Saxes respond.
0′ 33″	**A**	Saxophones play theme as brasses punctuate.

Two-Bar Interlude

0′ 44″	Brass and saxophones play a harmonized figure.

Second Chorus (same chords, different melody)

0′ 46″	**A**	One trumpet and three saxophones play boppish line.
0′ 57″	**A**	
1′ 10″	**B**	(note the valley-like contour of the moving pitches)
1′ 19″	**A**	

Third Chorus

1′ 30″	**A**	piano solo improvisation by Mary Lou Williams
1′ 41″	**A**	piano solo improvisation by Mary Lou Williams
1′ 51″	**B**	Dick Wilson tenor saxophone solo improvisation, accompanied by plunger-muted trumpets playing a syncopated countermelody
2′ 03″	**A**	piano solo improvisation by Mary Lou Williams
2″ 10″		final 2 measures: break for horns to play

Fourth Chorus

2′ 13″	**A**	Brass play highly syncopated riff, against a different saxophone riff, but one trumpet plays with saxophone part, and one trumpet plays with trombone part.
2′ 21″	**A**	Brass play highly syncopated line answered by saxes.
2′ 32″	**B**	Trumpets call and trombone responds, saxes playing underneath (drums and bass detectable as underpinning).
2′ 45″	**A**	Brass riff calls for saxes' answer.

Documenting her influence on other musicians is also difficult. Phrases of her tunes can be found in compositions credited to others, but she cannot be identified as the major source for the style of any other jazz pianist, or even a crucial part of any other pianist's concept. For instance, though several important musicians said they admired her work, and a number of luminaries in the bebop era were members of a study group that met at her home in the 1940s, no one has mentioned the particulars of her actual influence on their style. Thelonious Monk and Bud Powell were the most likely recipients of her ideas, yet they influenced her at least as much as she influenced them.

THE POPULARITY OF SWING

Certain jazz musicians were as well known to the general public during the swing era as rock stars are today. For example, Benny Goodman, Count Basie, and Duke Ellington were household names during the 1930s and 40s. The public knew them as leaders of dance bands more than as jazz musicians. Still, they were better known than the jazz giants of later eras. Even some of their soloists were well known and not just by jazz buffs. The big bands, famous and not so famous, employed hundreds of jazz musicians. This made it easier at that time for musicians to find work as performers. Unfortunately, however, most of the jobs with big bands did not permit much improvisation, except for a few star soloists, because these groups worked largely from written arrangements. Opportunities to improvise were generous in smaller combos, yet steady employment in jazz combos was difficult to find.

Though big bands went hand in hand with the swing era, *big band style does not necessarily mean swing style. There were also jazz-oriented big bands before and after the swing era.* Many of these sounded very different from swing bands. Big band style doesn't necessarily mean jazz style, either. In the 1930s and 40s, ten to sixteen musicians was the standard size of bands of all types. After that, the standard size decreased to about three to eight musicians.

Also during the swing era, journalists and musicians distinguished between bands that emphasized jazz improvisation and those that did not. For example, the very popular Glenn Miller big band was a swinging band. It had a handful of hit records that contained brief jazz improvisations. But the Miller band emphasized pretty arrangements and vocals more than improvised jazz solos. Therefore, despite its swinging qualities, the band was sometimes classified as a *sweet band*. This distinguished it from the *hot band* or *swing band* classification. Bands such as Count Basie's and Duke Ellington's fell into these categories because they had more solo improvisations.

Like rock combos since the 1950s, *one of the most important functions for swing bands of the 1930s and 40s was to provide dance music.* Jazz functioned as dance music more during the swing era than it ever did thereafter. Also like popular rock combos, swing era big bands usually used elaborate costumes and showy staging, and most of them routinely carried several singers. The visual appeal of the performance, including the personality and looks of the singers, was a primary attraction for a sizable portion of the audience. Most swing era hits contained vocals. Many that did not have singing were at least based on songs that listeners knew. This indicates that *jazz value was not the primary appeal of the pieces to the wider public. Such popularity simply reflects the same appeal that songs have had throughout history.* Only occasionally during the swing era were jazz musicians given paid opportunities to perform just for listening, as later became customary. In summary, the popular success of jazz bands during the swing era was partly a result of their appeal to the eyes and feet of fans instead of to the ears alone.

SUMMARY

1. Swing differs from early jazz in
    a. greater use of written arrangements
    b. less emphasis on ragtime-like pieces
    c. rejection of collective improvisation in favor of solo improvisation
    d. increased use of string bass instead of tuba
    e. greater swing feeling
    f. increased use of high-hat cymbals
    g. replacement of banjo with guitar
    h. emphasis on big band over small-group instrumentation
    i. saxophone becoming the predominant instrument

2. Important big bands were led by pianists Duke Ellington and Count Basie, and clarinetist Benny Goodman.

3. Ellington was the most creative and prolific composer-arranger in jazz history.

4. Basie's rhythm section played lightly and swung with great ease.

5. The most influential saxophonists were Coleman Hawkins and Lester Young.

6. Roy Eldridge paved the way for modern jazz trumpeter Dizzy Gillespie by improvising fiery, saxophone-like lines on trumpet.

7. Pianist Art Tatum possessed phenomenal speed. He was known for spontaneously changing and adding chords in pop tune accompaniments. He also introduced creative rhythmic surprises.

8. Mary Lou Williams was a versatile pianist who mastered many styles. She also created arrangements during the 30s and 40s for the bands of Andy Kirk, Benny Goodman, and Duke Ellington, among others.

KEY TERMS

break	rhythm guitar style	two-beat style
call and response	scat singing	walking style
head arrangement		

FURTHER RESOURCES

✓•—[**Study** and **Review** on **mysearchlab.com**

Features documentaries on Duke Ellington, Ella Fitzgerald, and Count Basie, and shows the makeup of a typical swing era big band.

You can also test your knowledge with the chapter quiz.

VIEW

The *Prentice Hall Jazz History DVD* (ISBN 0-13-602643-5) features performances by Count Basie, Duke Ellington, Artie Shaw, and Billie Holiday.

Tenor Titans (VAI) includes performances by Lester Young and Coleman Hawkins in addition to performances by modern performers.

Duke Ellington and His Orchestra: 1929–43 (Storyville Films): Historic film clips.

Duke Ellington: Live in '58 (Jazz Icons): European concert footage.

Count Basie: Live in '62 (Jazz Icons): European concert footage.

LISTEN

Ken Burns Jazz: The Story of America's Music. (Columbia/Legacy C5K 61432, 5 CD set) has Henderson, Basie, Ellington, Moten, Lunceford, Webb, Goodman, Holiday, Krupa, Shaw.

Smithsonian Collection of Classic Jazz (RJ 0010, 5 CD set, 1916–1981, c 1987) contains renditions of "Body and Soul" by Coleman Hawkins, "Willow Weep for Me" by Art Tatum, "Breakfast Feud" by Benny Goodman, "I Can't Believe That You're in Love with Me" by Roy Eldridge, "Lester Leaps In" by Lester Young and Count Basie, "Doggin' Around" by the Count Basie big band with Lester Young, "Ko-Ko" and "Concerto for Cootie" by Duke Ellington, plus other examples of swing era jazz.

Jazz Classics CDs for *Jazz Styles: History and Analysis* (ISBN 0–205–03686–4) contain Roy Eldridge's "After You're Gone," Benny Goodman's "Seven Come Eleven," three pieces by Duke Ellington: "Transblucency," "Cottontail," and "Prelude to a Kiss."

Prentice Hall Jazz Collection (ISBN 0–205–17896–4) has "Seven Come Eleven" by Benny Goodman, Lionel Hampton, and Charlie Christian.

Lester Young. *The "Kansas City" Sessions* (Commodore–402, 1938, 1944)

Count Basie. *The Complete Decca Recordings* (Decca Jazz GRD3–611, 3 CD set, 1937–1939)

Duke Ellington. *Never No Lament: The Blanton-Webster Band* (RCA Bluebird: 50857, 3 CD set, 1940–1942)

READ

Basie, Count. 1985. *Good Morning Blues* (autobiography). New York: Random House.

Büchmann-Møller, Frank. 1990. *You Just Fight for Your Life: The Story of Lester Young.* New York: Praeger.

Chilton, John. 1990. *Song of the Hawk: The Life and Recordings of Coleman Hawkins,* Ann Arbor: University of Michigan Press.

Chilton, John. 2002. *Roy Eldridge: Little Jazz Giant.* New York: Continuum.

Collier, James Lincoln. 1989. *Benny Goodman and the Swing Era.* New York: Oxford University Press.

Dahl, Linda. 2001. *Morning Glory: A Biography of Mary Lou Williams.* New York: Pantheon.

Dance, Stanley. 1970 (Da Capo reprint 1980). *The World of Duke Ellington,* New York: Scribner.

Dance, Stanley. 1974 (Da Capo reprint 1979). *The World of Swing.* New York: Scribner.

Dance, Stanley. 1981 (Da Capo reprint 1985). *The World of Count Basie.* New York: Scribner.

Driggs, Frank. 2005. *Kansas City Jazz: From Ragtime to Bebop—a History.* Oxford.

Ellington, Duke. 1973 (Da Capo reprint 1976). *Music Is My Mistress* (autobiography). New York: Doubleday.

Pearson, Nathan. 1987. *Goin' to Kansas City.* Urbana: University of Illinois Press.

Porter, Lewis. 2005. *Lester Young rev. ed.* Ann Arbor: University of Michigan Press.

Sandke, Randall. 2010. *Where the Dark and the Light Folks Meet: Race and the Mythology, Politics, and Business of Jazz.* Lanham, Massachusetts: Scarecrow.

Schuller, Gunther. 1989. *The Swing Era.* New York: Oxford University Press.

Stewart, Rex. 1972 (Da Capo reprint 1980). *Jazz Masters of the Thirties.* New York: Macmillan.

Tucker, Mark, ed. 1993. *The Duke Ellington Reader.* Oxford.

Charles Mingus (bass viol), Roy Haynes (drums), Thelonious Monk (piano), and Charlie Parker (alto sax).
Photo by Bob Parent, courtesy of Hulton Archive/Getty Images

THE BIRTH OF BEBOP

Modern jazz became a recognizable sound in the 1940s. It grew from roots laid down in the 1930s by saxophonists Coleman Hawkins and Lester Young, pianists Art Tatum and Nat Cole, trumpeter Roy Eldridge, and the Count Basie rhythm section. Early jazz and swing styles are often considered the "classic period." New styles which have emerged since 1940 are often classified as modern jazz. The first well-known modern jazz musicians were alto saxophonist Charlie Parker, pianist Thelonious Monk, and trumpeter Dizzy Gillespie. By the middle 1940s, they had inspired a legion of other creative musicians, including trumpeter Miles Davis and pianist Bud Powell. By the late 1940s, Parker and Gillespie had also influenced the music in several big bands.

◀ Charlie Parker and Miles Davis, 1947.

Photo by William P. Gottlieb

Modern jazz did not burst on the jazz scene suddenly. It developed gradually through the work of swing-era musicians. Parker and Gillespie themselves began their careers playing improvisations in a swing-era style. They expanded on swing styles and gradually developed new techniques. Their work eventually became a recognizably different style, though it was still linked to its roots in the swing era. Modern jazz improvisers were also inspired by contemporary classical music, particularly the work of Béla Bartók and Igor Stravinsky. Rather than being a reaction against swing styles, modern jazz developed smoothly *from* swing styles.

Bebop (or just "bop") is the name of the first modern jazz style. It was considerably less popular than swing, and it failed to attract dancers. However, it did contribute impressive soloists who gained followers for decades to come. The first bebop soloists created a new vocabulary of musical phrases and distinctive methods of matching improvisation to chord progressions. This became the standard jazz language for the next forty years. Even during the 1990s, musicians frequently evaluated new players according to their ability to play bebop. Mastery of this style was considered the foundation for competence as a jazz improviser.

HOW BEBOP DIFFERS FROM SWING STYLE

Bebop differed from swing in a number of performance aspects:

1. Preferred instrumentation for bebop was the small combo instead of big band.
2. Average tempo was faster in bebop.
3. Clarinet was rare in bebop.

4. Display of instrumental virtuosity was a higher priority for bebop players.

5. Rhythm guitar was rare.

6. Less emphasis was placed on arrangements in bebop.

Bebop differed from swing in a number of stylistic respects:

1. Melodies were more complex in bebop.

2. Harmonies were more complex in bebop.

3. Accompaniment rhythms were more varied in bebop.

4. Comping replaced stride style and simple, on-the-beat chording (*Demo CD* Tracks 20 and 38).

Demo CD Track 3 |
5. Drummers played their timekeeping rhythms primarily on suspended cymbal, rather than snare drum, high-hat, or bass drum.

6. Bebop musicians enjoyed leaving phrases in tunes suspended or unresolved.

7. Bebop was a more agitated style than swing was.

8. Bebop improvisation was more complex because it contained
   a. more themes per solo
   b. less similarity among themes
   c. more excursions outside the tune's original key
   d. a greater scope of rhythmic development

9. Surprise was more highly valued in bebop.

Bebop improvisations were composed mostly of melody lines that seemed jumpy, full of twists and turns. The contours of the lines were jagged. There were often large intervals between the notes and abrupt changes of direction. The rhythms in those lines were quick and unpredictable, with heavy emphasis on syncopation.

Bebop musicians did more than embellish the melody during their improvisations. They departed completely from the melodies and retained only the chord progressions of a song's accompaniment. Often they enriched a progression by adding new chords. Art Tatum had gotten in the habit of changing accompaniment harmonies for melodies that traditionally had been accompanied in only one particular way. He also had added chords to existing progressions. Coleman Hawkins had loved to improvise on complicated chord progressions and to add chords to the pieces he played. In these ways, Tatum and Hawkins prepared the way for the wide use of these techniques in bebop style (see Chapter 5).

Bebop players often wrote original tunes using the accompaniment chord progressions of popular tunes. Many of these new tunes went without names. The leader just called out the key and the name of the tune that provided the chord progression. In that way, members of the rhythm section could immediately play a tune they might never have previously heard. This technique was not new to bebop. It had been used in swing and early jazz. The chord progression for the 12-bar blues had been used in that way for decades. And Count Basie's recordings of the 1930s are filled

Photo by Lee Tanner

◄ Max Roach, the leading bebop drummer. Roach improvised more drum sounds than swing-style drummers used for timekeeping. This made bebop more spontaneous and exciting.

with loosely arranged performances in which riffs and improvisations are placed atop the accompaniments of such popular songs as "Lady Be Good," "Honeysuckle Rose," and "I Got Rhythm." This practice provided a common ground for jam sessions because all the participants knew the chord progressions to these popular songs. The practice merely became more common during the bebop era because the emphasis in bebop was on improvisation by small combos rather than set arrangements by big bands.

There were differences in drumming style, too. By comparison with swing-style, bebop drummers:

1. more frequently kicked and prodded the soloist, in addition to playing timekeeping sounds

| Demo CD Track 8

2. moved away from the heavy ways of timekeeping; for instance, the bebop drummer:
   a. feathered the bass drum instead of pounding it. Sometimes he did not use it for timekeeping at all.
   b. kept time primarily on the suspended ride cymbal.

| Demo CD Track 3

   c. snapped shut the high-hat crisply on every other beat.

| Demo CD Track 2

3. created an almost continuous "chatter" that increased the excitement of the performance. Much of this was generated on the snare drum, and it took the form of pops and crackles that seemed to provide a commentary on what else was happening in the band. Surprises came from the bass drum, too. This was called "dropping **bombs**."

Bomb A pronounced accent played by the drummer, often "dropped" in an unexpected place

CHARLIE PARKER

((•─Listen on **mysearchlab.com**

Listen to Charlie Parker's saxophone style on mysearchlab.com

The musician who contributed most to the development of bebop was alto saxophonist Charlie Parker (1920–1955), nicknamed "Bird." Jazz musicians and historians feel that he is the most important saxophonist in jazz history. Many musicologists consider Parker to be one of the most brilliant figures in twentieth-century music. Going beyond the advances made by Lester Young, Coleman Hawkins, and Art Tatum, he built an entire system by his improvisations and compositions. The system had new ways of selecting notes that fit around the notes in the accompaniment chords. It also had new ways of accenting notes so that the phrases have a highly syncopated, sometimes off-balance character.

Charlie Parker astonished other musicians with his tremendous fertility of melodic imagination, unprecedented mastery of the saxophone, and the dizzying pace with which he was able to improvise. By comparison with swing-style players, Parker sounded more hurried. He sounded like a modern composer who was improvising at lightning speed, not an easygoing romantic. Parker's solos were densely packed with ideas. During his improvisations, his mind seemed to be bubbling over with little melodies. It was as though he had so much energy and enthusiasm that he could barely contain himself. As a result he sprinkled his solos with double-time figures. Even in ballad renditions, he tended to ornament slow lines with double-time figures. Soon after Parker's mid-1940s recordings appeared, other musicians followed suit. There was an increase in the average tempo, the amount of double-timing, and the amount of melodic ideas in improvisations. This trend had begun during the swing era, but it was furthered by the example that Parker set.

CD1 Tracks 15 and 16: "Leap Frog" and "Parker's Mood"

Photo by Bob Parent, courtesy of Don Parent.

▶ Charlie Parker, the most significant saxophonist of the twentieth century and an inventor of bebop. His tunes and improvisations have been memorized and analyzed by thousands of modern jazz musicians.

Parker's tone quality departed from standard swing-era models. Rather than making it lush and sweet, Parker made his sound dry and biting. His tone fit his fast, serious attitude.

Charlie Parker's improvisations were inspired by many sources. He devised his lines by many of the same methods that classical composers use. He also drew phrases from such sources as the solos of Louis Armstrong and Lester Young, the melodies of blues singers and early jazz hornmen, pop tunes, and traditional themes from opera and classical music.

Parker wrote many tunes himself. Their character set the flavor for bebop as much as his improvisations did. Though not melody-like in the pop tune sense, they were catchy lines in a jazz vein. This was the musical language of bebop. Most were accompanied by chord progressions borrowed from popular songs. Many used accompaniments of the 12-bar blues chord progression. The phrases of Parker's tunes were memorized and analyzed by hundreds of jazz soloists. They were played at jam sessions for decades after he introduced them.

Parker had an immense impact on jazz. Bebop trumpeter Dizzy Gillespie cites Parker as a primary influence on his own style, and bebop pianist Bud Powell modeled some of his lines after Parker's. Methods of improvisation that Parker devised were adopted by numerous saxophonists during the 1940s and 50s. So many musicians imitated him that jazz journalists soon complained about a lack of originality and freshness among musicians at that time. As recently as 2013, musicians were still studying Parker's improvisations as a foundation for developing their own styles. Parker's work was treated by jazz musicians with as much respect as the works of Johann Sebastian Bach and Ludwig van Beethoven were treated among classical musicians. Jazz clubs were named for Parker—Birdland in New York and Birdhouse in Chicago. Parker's melodic inventiveness is so stunning that bebop singers performed his pieces with lyrics which had been written for his melodies as well as his improvisations. During the 1970s, a group called Supersax began using five saxes and rhythm section to play harmonized transcriptions of Parker's improvised solos. Supersax could treat his solos as compositions in their own right because Parker's work was so rich with catchy ideas.

DIZZY GILLESPIE

Louis Armstrong was the major jazz trumpet virtuoso of the late 1920s and early 30s. Roy Eldridge held a similar position after that. Then Dizzy Gillespie (1917–1993) appeared on the scene. His innovative melodic concepts and high-register playing were not only phenomenal for the 1940s, but have rarely been matched since. But Gillespie's awe-inspiring command of the trumpet accounts for only part of his impact. Much of his influence stems from his stirring musical ideas.

Dizzy Gillespie's harmonic skills were startling, and he flaunted them. His phrases were full of surprises and playful changes of direction. His work bristled with excitement. He would weave in and out of different keys within a single phrase, yet he always managed to resolve his line's logic to fit with the ways the chords changed in his accompaniment. He often zoomed up to the trumpet's high register during the middle of a phrase and

((●–Listen on **mysearchlab.com**
Listen to asymmetrical accenting by Charlie Parker on mysearchlab.com

((●–Listen on **mysearchlab.com**
Listen to Dizzy Gillespie's trumpet style on mysearchlab.com

((•[Listen on **mysearchlab.com**

Recorded September 18, 1948, in New York by Charlie Parker (alto saxophone), John Lewis (piano), Curley Russell (bass), and Max Roach (drums); composed by Charlie Parker; issued by the Savoy firm.

Terms to know from tracks on the *Demo CD:* 12-bar blues (19), walking bass (23), alto saxophone (72).

This performance remains one of the most identifiable sounds in jazz history. So it should be no surprise that it is even used as a theme song for a radio program. It is one of the best known 12-bar blues in modern jazz, probably because it contains a few singable improvisations and displays funky blues lines in a slow tempo. This improvisation is so melodic that the band Supersax treated Parker's improvisation as though conceived as a song. In 1972, they recorded it in harmonized form with five saxophones, piano, bass, and drums. It was even recorded (in 1962) with lyrics that singer Eddie Jefferson fitted to every note. The most memorable phrases in this recording are indeed singable, beginning with his stark, ringing sound for the opening introductory phrase. Parker's saxophone sounds almost like a blues singer in his beginnings for the second chorus at 0' 52" and the final chorus at 2' 06". His lyricism is especially apparent in the way he forms his first-chorus phrases. He poses a question at 0' 16' and answers it at 0' 19". Then he poses the same question again at 0' 22" with a new answer at 0' 26".

Though lyricism is this piece's strong suit, most of Parker's phrases on it demonstrate his taste for intricacy and decoration. Parker creates a tapestry, weaving extra twists and turns into almost every idea; he never leaves the main thread of any idea alone. It is as though a plain hamburger would never suffice, but with pickles, onions, lettuce, tomatoes, catsup, and mustard, he would have a good start toward satisfaction. He decorates his main notes with grace notes and his main ideas with afterthoughts. For instance, his flurry of notes at 0' 37" sounds like an afterthought following his main excursion from 0' 27" to 0' 34". Then at 0' 42" he generates a very ornate string of ideas. Despite the handful of songlike phrases, Parker's playing on "Parker's Mood" differs from his playing on other recordings only by being slowed down enough for us to follow his thinking. Such complexity is a prime component of bebop, and it was quite important to Art Tatum and Coleman Hawkins, who influenced Parker.

"Parker's Mood" also shows us Parker's fondness for accenting at odd instances, starting or reiterating phrases at unexpected times. This is exhibited at 0' 29" as soon as we get to the sixth and seventh measures of the main theme. Parker plays a figure comprised of 8 notes, the first 4 of which are bunched up together. He plays this figure four times in a row. The first time he starts it on the second beat of the measure. The second time he starts it on the fourth beat. The third time he starts it in the middle of the first beat. The fourth time he starts it on the third beat. Timekeeping remains in effect as before. Bass and drums are not restarting their counting with each accent of Parker's line. Yet the beginning of each rendition of this figure causes us to feel the beat beginning anew at that moment. So we lean toward restarting our counting as each repeat of the figure strikes our ears. Try beating yourfoot 1 2 3 4 1 2 3 4 from the time you first detect walking bass. Then notice what happens in the sixth and seventh measures, beginning at 0' 29". You will find Parker tugging against your pulse.

still managed to connect the melodic ideas logically. Sometimes he interspersed quotes from non-jazz pieces such as the opera *Carmen* or the pop tune "We're in the Money." He would use the quote as a point of departure

He might actually prevent you from landing accurately on the downbeat of the ninth measure at 0' 35". In other words, you could get turned around by his new accents.

This piece therefore showcases Parker's talent for generating patterns called **asymmetrical accents.** Symmetry is where there is a mirror image of one object opposite it. Balance is perfect when things are symmetrical. Asymmetry occurs where we are thrown off balance because something goes up but it does not come down where we would expect. The musical ways these practices throw us off balance is provocative. This is a prime characteristic of bebop. Jazz listeners delight in such surprises.

Introduction

0' 00"	alto sax intro over sustained piano chord
0' 05"	Piano improvises a melodic finish for intro. Bass is walking. Drummer is playing ride rhythms with brushes on snare drum.

First Chorus

0' 16"	Parker's melody poses a question, then an answer.
0' 22"	Parker poses same question, but gives new answer.
	Bass is walking. Drummer is keeping time with wire brushes on snare drum.

Fifth and Sixth Measures

0' 28"	one figure played four times, accenting different parts of the beat each time
0' 34"	Tension caused by reiterations is resolved.
0' 43"	Parker plays very ornate line.

Second Chorus

0' 52"	Parker makes a plaintive cry in the form of an octave leap.

Fourth, Fifth, and Sixth Measures

1' 02"	swinging line with a double-time feeling; Piano also doubles the time feeling. Bass only plays every other beat.
1' 07"	two fall-offs

Third Chorus

1' 29"	piano solo; light, delicate, resounding

Fourth Chorus

2' 06"	Parker returns, playing same note three times, as a blues singer.
2' 31"	Parker's line acknowledges each change in chord.
2' 46"	Parker restates introductory phrase.
2' 51"	Piano improvises a conclusion for Parker's phrase, leaves piece unresolved, but bass completes it and gets cut off.

for developing his own phrases. He sometimes increased tension by building a line higher and higher with staccato, syncopated notes and then released the tension by coming down with legato lines.

Asymmetrical accent An accent that falls in an unexpected place in the rhythmic scheme of a phrase

Improvised by Charlie Parker and Dizzy Gillespie; recorded June 1950 in New York by Parker (alto sax), Gillespie (trumpet), Thelonious Monk (piano), Curley Russell (bass), and Buddy Rich (drums), issued by the Verve firm.

"Leap Frog" displays the three inventors of bebop playing together in top form. The pace is very quick,which is typical of bebop. Also typical of Parker and Gillespie, the improvisations are densely packed with ideas that unfold in a continuous stream. Fertility of imagination is one attribute for which these giants were always known. Many nuggets of melody are here for the attentive listener to discover within this stream. The *entire* performance is improvised. There isn't even a written or memorized melody played at the beginning or end. Everything is invented and performed spontaneously atop the chord progression to "I Got Rhythm." Not only do trumpeter Gillespie and saxophonist Parker improvise complete choruses, they also alternate solo exchanges based on less than complete choruses, hence the title, "Leap Frog." "I Got Rhythm" is a 32-bar A-A-B-A song form, in which each section is 8 measures long, a total of 32 beats in duration.

After their complete solo choruses, Parker and Gillespie alternate improvisations based on successive halves of each 8-measure section. This practice is termed "trading fours" because each soloist improvises on 4 successive measures and gives up the next 4 to his partner. Then the horns alternate 4-measure sections with drummer Buddy Rich. This illustrates a common practice used at jam sessions for giving accompanists some solo exposure without losing the momentum of the piece. Note that Curley Russell was Parker's regular bassist, but Monk rarely performed with Parker or Gillespie, and Rich was not really a bebop drummer. Rich was a swing-era-style drummer hired by the session's producer, not by Parker and Gillespie.

0′ 00″	**Introduction** by drummer Buddy Rich	
	4 measures (16 beats): first on cymbals, then on snare drum	
0′ 04″	**First Chorus** (A-A-B-A) **Charlie Parker Alto Sax Solo**	
0′ 27″	**Second Chorus** (A-A-B-A) **Dizzy Gillespie Trumpet Solo**	
	Sax and Trumpet Trading Fours	
0′ 51″	Third Chorus (A-A-B-A)	
	A	Parker plays first 4 measures.
		Gillespie plays second 4 measures.
	A	Parker plays first 4 measures.
		Gillespie plays second 4 measures.
1′ 02″	**B**	Parker plays first 4 measures.
		Gillespie plays second 4 measures.

Gillespie exerted sweeping influence on modern jazz. His pet phrases became stock clichés for two generations of jazz trumpeters, pianists, guitarists, saxophonists, and trombonists. Several established trumpeters of the 1940s originally derived their styles from pre-modern sources. But when they heard

A Parker plays first 4 measures.
Gillespie plays second 4 measures.

1' 14" Fourth Chorus (A-A-B-A)

A Parker plays first 4 measures.
Gillespie plays second 4 measures.

A Parker plays first 4 measures.
Gillespie plays second 4 measures.

1' 27" **B** Parker plays first 4 measures.
Gillespie plays second 4 measures.

A Parker plays first 4 measures.
Gillespie plays second 4 measures.

Trading Fours with Drums

1' 38" Fifth Chorus (A-A-B-A)

A Buddy Rich drum solo first 4 measures
Parker plays second 4 measures.

A Buddy Rich drum solo first 4 measures
Gillespie plays second 4 measures.

1' 50" **B** Buddy Rich drum solo first 4 measures
Parker plays second 4 measures.

A Buddy Rich drum solo first 4 measures
Gillespie plays second 4 measures.

2' 02" Sixth Chorus (A-A-B-A)

A Buddy Rich drum solo first 4 measures
Parker plays second 4 measures.

A Buddy Rich drum solo first 4 measures
Gillespie plays second 4 measures.

2' 13" **B** Buddy Rich drum solo first 4 measures
Parker plays second 4 measures.

A Buddy Rich drum solo first 4 measures
Gillespie plays second 4 measures.

2' 25" **Ending**
Buddy Rich drum solo, 4 measures (16 beats)

Gillespie's approach, they began imitating him. He was only a year or two older, but he influenced them as a classic model rather than a contemporary.

Gillespie also made lasting contributions as a composer. His "Groovin' High" and "A Night in Tunisia" became jazz standards that are still played

The Dizzy Gillespie Big Band, with pianist John Lewis and bassist Ray Brown (who became founding members of the Modern Jazz Quartet) and Miles Davis (second trumpeter from the left).

Photo by William P. Gottlieb, courtesy of Library of Congress

frequently. After being recorded with lyrics, they gained wider audiences in the 1980s. Afro-Cuban music was one of Gillespie's special interests, and he explored it in his big band numbers "Manteca," "Cubano Be," and "Cubano Bop." These pieces are among the earliest appearances of Latin American music in modern jazz.

After co-leading a combo with Charlie Parker and leading a few small bands of his own, Gillespie began a series of bebop big bands. He kept his big bands going through most of the late 1940s, then formed others once in a while thereafter. His combos and big bands featured a number of powerful players. Many of them went on to lead significant groups of their own.

THELONIOUS MONK

Thelonious Monk (1917–1982) was a pianist who wrote compositions whose melodies were unorthodox and whose accompaniment chords severely challenged improvisers. His compositions influenced the flavor of much modern jazz. Several musicians have devoted entire albums to his music. A few touring bands have constructed their repertories primarily from his compositions. Like his compositional style, his approach to piano improvising was also influential. Many people consider Monk a creative genius responsible for significant directions taken by modern jazz.

Monk's tunes have a logic and symmetry all their own. Unlike the tunes of many popular composers, his are so perfectly structured that they cannot withstand tampering. Monk was expert at placing accents in irregular order. He was also especially skilled in ending phrases on the least expected notes, yet making the piece sound as though those phrase endings had been expected all along.

Photo by William P. Gottlieb, courtesy of Library of Congress

◀ Thelonious Monk, the first bebop composer and pianist. Monk's tunes became standard repertory for generations of jazz musicians who liked his unorthodox rhythms and harmonies.

As a pianist, Monk was a curious mixture. He used stride piano techniques, horn-like lines, and very dissonant chord voicings. He was famous for the blunt, strident way he struck the keyboard. As an accompanist, his work was not like conventional bebop comping style. Nor was it like the light and bouncing approach that evolved from Count Basie's methods. He would play a note here, a dissonant chord there. In addition to these irregularities, Monk often stopped comping for long passages, leaving the soloist to improvise with only bass and drums for accompaniment.

Monk's music conveys a sense of unsettling deliberation. He uses notes so sparingly that silence is almost as important as sound. The agonizing care he devotes to choosing each individual note and rhythm contrasts with the long, horn-like improvisations of most other pianists. His music is not smooth. His piano improvisations convey a sense that he is struggling to decide on every note, and then he reaches that decision just barely in time to play it. Nothing is produced casually or routinely. Each phrase is played very emphatically, and with much consideration for its maximum rhythmic effect. Monk's approach is very intense and percussive. He often strikes a note or chord several times in a row, as though knocking on a door. His music does not evoke the easy rise and fall of tensions associated with most jazz lines. Perhaps that's why listeners disagree about whether Monk's music swings.

Monk was one of the most original of all jazz improvisers. His lines often display jagged contours, and the construction of some of his improvisations is quite playful. In his harmonies, Monk is particularly known for combinations of tones that clash resoundingly with each other. It has been joked that Monk could make an in-tune piano sound out of tune. Combined with an uneven rhythmic style, these harmonic characteristics made his music quite jarring. But this is what he wanted.

Recorded February 1950 in New York by Bud Powell (piano), Curley Russell (bass), and Max Roach (drums); composed by Harold Arlen; reissued many times by Verve Records.

Terms to know from tracks on the *Demo CD:* scale steps and chord changes (16–18), left-hand chording (37), walking bass (23), A-A-B-A song form "I Got Rhythm" chord progression (33).

Bud Powell was the most influential bebop pianist. This bustling performance is typical of the high speed and densely packed lines that came out of the bebop era for soloists on all instruments, not just piano. This exuberant rendition of "Get Happy" is one of Powell's best showpieces. The fingers on Powell's right hand are racing through the chord changes, churning out idea after idea. A surging energy pervades the entire recording. Keep in mind that Powell himself chose this rapid tempo, and that pace best suited his creativity.

Powell's introduction is comprised of an intricate string of eighth notes in the upper register. His left hand inserts brief chords on the off-beats in the introduction and on the downbeats under the first theme statement. Sometimes his left hand seems to be rocking, playing a high note on the first of every 4 beats and a low note on the third.

Of all the composers associated with Broadway musicals, Harold Arlen seemed to have the greatest affinity for jazz. The construction of Arlen's "Get Happy" sounds as though it had been contributed by a bebop musician. The melody is loaded with syncopations that lend it internal swing. Its chords keep improvisers on their toes because they change so quickly.

"Get Happy" is not a 12-bar blues, and it does not strictly fit a 32-bar A-A-B-A form. The first strain is 8 bars long. The second strain bears the same melody as the first, but it is pitched four scale steps higher. In other words, the first two strains almost qualify for the "A-A" designation, but not quite. So we will designate the transposed A-section as A` (read "A-prime").

The 8-bar bridge of "Get Happy" is constructed of a 4-bar phrase played twice. In the accompaniment for this phrase, the chords change every 2 beats. Each chord is four scale-steps higher than the previous one. Musicians call this type of movement "going up in fourths," "going down in fifths," or "a circle of fifths progression." To understand how quick this speed is, consider the "I Got Rhythm" chord progression that is so popular among jazz improvisers. (It was borrowed for the "[Meet the] Flintstones Theme.") The chords in its bridge bear the same relation to each other as the chords in "Get Happy," but each chord in the bridge of "I Got Rhythm" lasts 8 beats before moving to the next. This means that the chords progress four times faster in the bridge of "Get Happy" than in the bridge of "I Got Rhythm." Understanding this becomes all the more significant for appreciating Bud Powell's rendition because the pianist has selected a very quick tempo. His tempo makes the rapidly changing chords change even faster. He has intentionally set a serious challenge for himself. You will hear how Powell rises to that challenge and makes the most of it.

Powell's lines usually are skittering over and past the chord changes such that their relation to the "Get Happy" melody and its accompaniment chords is difficult to detect. But during a few bridge sections, Powell actually plays the chord notes themselves to structure his improvised line. So, before trying to follow the improvisations, listen to 0' 19" where Powell emphatically plays the chords during his main theme statement. Then listen to 1' 09" where he uses important notes from those same chords to form his improvised line. His improvisation on the bridge at 1' 33" employs this technique. It allows us to hear the effects of the changing chords more clearly than elsewhere.

Though most passages in Powell's complicated streams of notes would be difficult to hum along with, there are hummable moments. You might detect a fragment of the Scottish Air "Comin'

Through the Rye" at 1′ 03″ and the children's game song "In and Out the Window" at 1′ 20″. But even if you cannot follow all the notes in his lines, or even just the contours, you will probably still be able to appreciate Powell's enthusiasm. (For example, at 1′ 39″ it sounds like the dam burst. His ideas are gushing forth more forcefully than ever before. The flow continues well into the next chorus.)

0′ 00″ **Introduction**
     improvised string of eighth notes

     First Chorus (Theme Statement: A-A`-B-A)
0′ 06″   A   first strain of "Get Happy" melody;
          bass walking, drummer keeping time by wire brushes on snare drum
0′ 13″   A` second strain of "Get Happy" melody
0′ 19″   Bridge of "Get Happy" melody
0′ 21″   second half of bridge
0′ 25″   A

     Second Chorus (A-A`-B-A)   Solo Improvisation
0′ 31″   A
0′ 37″   A`
0′ 43″   Bridge
          Powell's line sketches the chord progression.
0′ 50″   A
          Left hand is rocking bass notes.

     Third Chorus (A-A`-B-A)   Solo Improvisation
0′ 57″   A
1′ 03″   A`
          quotes "Comin' Through the Rye"
1′ 09″   Bridge
          Powell outlines the "circle of fifths" chord progression
1′ 15″   A

     Fourth Chorus (A-A`-B-A)   Solo Improvisation
1′ 20″   A
          quotes "In and Out the Window"
1′ 26″   A`
1′ 33″   Bridge
          outlines the "circle of fifths" chord progression
1′ 39″   A

     Fifth Chorus (A-A`-B-A)   Solo Improvisation
1′ 45″   A

1' 51"	A`
1' 57"	Bridge
2' 03"	A

Sixth Chorus (A-A`-B-A)   Solo Improvisation

2' 10"	A
	momentary return to "Get Happy" melody
2' 16"	A`
	departs melody, returns to improvising
2' 21"	Bridge
2' 28"	A return to "Get Happy" melody

Ending

2' 34"	Final phrase of melody is repeated but transposed up in pitch.
2' 35"	transposed up again
2' 37"	descending line
2' 40"	syncopated chords
2' 41"	rising progression of percussively stated chords
2' 43"	descending line
2' 44"	syncopated chords, sustained
2' 45"	same chord sounded five times
2' 47"	retard
2' 48"	ascending arpeggio

BUD POWELL

Bud Powell (1924–1966) is the most imitated of all bebop pianists. He crafted his approach from Art Tatum's, with other borrowings from the styles of Billy Kyle, Nat Cole, and Thelonious Monk. Atop these foundations, Powell incorporated the style and phrases of Charlie Parker and Dizzy Gillespie. The result was one of the first modern jazz piano styles.

Bebop pianists mastered comping. This is a technique of spontaneous chording that flexibly interacts with the improvised solo lines. This accompaniment technique had been used by Count Basie as early as the mid-1930s. Swing piano styles had begun to take advantage of the widening use of string bass. As a result, pianists placed less emphasis on the left hand for supplying chords under their own right-hand solo lines. They eventually phased out the practice of providing 1-note-at-a-time bass lines for themselves. By the time bebop was well underway, pianists had almost entirely abandoned the left hand's bass functions that were so common in the styles of stride, boogie-woogie, and swing piano players. A new left-hand style evolved which was to characterize jazz piano for several decades.

Powell de-emphasized the activity of the left hand, thereby departing from the stride tradition and the "chomp, chomp, chomp, chomp" style of

((•─[Listen on mysearchlab.com

Listen to Bud Powell's piano style on mysearchlab.com

◀ Bud Powell, the most influential bebop pianist. His approach combined piano styles of Art Tatum, Nat Cole, and Thelonious Monk with the horn styles of Charlie Parker and Dizzy Gillespie.

Photo by Bob Parent, courtesy of Don Parent.

chording used by many swing pianists. This served to lighten the way pianists had begun playing, even more than the streamlining introduced by Teddy Wilson and Nat Cole. In place of the striding left-hand figures, **Powell's left hand inserted brief, sporadically placed 2- and 3-note chords that reduced his statement of harmony to the barest minimum.** Sometimes the chords sustained for a few beats. Sometimes there was no left-hand sound at all. This comping style became standard for modern jazz pianists accompanying their own solo lines. This development was almost as significant within the history of solo piano as the emergence of comping had been for rhythm section pianists. In other words, **the breakthrough that Count Basie had made in lightening the manner in which a pianist supplied chords and support for an improvising soloist was paralleled by the way Powell lightened the manner in which a pianist accompanied his own solo lines.**

In his prime, Powell had the speed and dexterity to create piano solos that almost matched the high-powered inventions of Parker and Gillespie. He mastered the erratically syncopated rhythms of bebop and charged through his solos with terrific force. **Powell was the model for hundreds of pianists during the 1940s and 50s, as James P. Johnson had been during the 1920s and Earl Hines had been after Johnson.**

DEXTER GORDON

Dexter Gordon (1923–1990) was the first tenor saxophonist to be recognized as a bebop player. He was making important recordings in this new style as early as 1945. Though strongly influenced by Lester Young and Charlie Parker, Gordon used a tone that was deep and dark, not light or

Photo by *William E. (Bill) Smith*

▶ Dexter Gordon, the first bebop tenor saxophonist. Known for very logical and melodic solos, his style was widely imitated, especially among "hard bop" players of the 1950s. Gordon's approach provided a link between Lester Young's style of the 1930s and John Coltrane's style of the 1950s. Gordon remained an important figure on the jazz scene until his death in 1990. He was the saxophone-playing star of the movie *'Round Midnight.*

hollow like Young's. And his improvisations were not as unpredictable and jumpy as Parker's. Although Gordon's style was quite aggressive, his work conveyed great ease. There was a sense of authority and majesty in his playing. He used a large variety of melodic devices to create his lines. His phrase lengths and rhythms contained more variety than those of most other tenor saxophonists in bop. Gordon loved to quote from pop tunes and bugle calls. He was known for developing his solos by making firm statements and following through on them. His improvisations contained remarkable logic and continuity, a tendency that became even more conspicuous during the 1960s and 70s. He offered phrase after phrase of complete musical ideas, each of which was well rounded and meaty. Gordon influenced many tenor saxophonists whose styles in the 1950s were classified as "hard bop." He had a strong recording career from the 1940s into the 1980s, and his playing displayed depth of imagination and swing feeling all that time.

STAN GETZ

Stan Getz (1927–1991) was one of the most distinctive tenor saxophonists to emerge during the 1940s. He did not rely as heavily on Lester Young's ideas as most other bebop saxophonists did, and he used few of Charlie Parkers and Dizzy Gillespie's pet phrases. He developed an original melodic

Recorded December 22, 1947, in New York by Dexter Gordon (tenor saxophone), Fats Navarro (trumpet), Tadd Dameron (piano), Nelson Boyd (bass), and Art Mardigan (drums); composed by Dexter Gordon. It is available on several compilations of Gordon recordings for the Savoy firm.

Dexter Gordon is joined on this track by trumpeter Fats Navarro. Navarro refined Dizzy Gillespie's style and became the main model for Clifford Brown, who, in turn, became the most imitated trumpeter of the hard bop era that followed the bebop era. Navarro sported a somewhat smoother, larger tone than Gillespie. Navarro was not as harmonically or rhythmically daring in his exploits. Whereas Gillespie was full of surprises, Navarro codified the language that Gillespie invented. In his solo here, we can hear that he is relaxed and more careful than Gillespie. His first chorus of improvisation, beginning at about 1' 48", is quite graceful, and his execution of even the most involved lines is supple. In his second solo chorus, at about 2' 11", Navarro stresses a particularly odd note at 2' 17", as Gillespie was prone to do. In his third solo chorus, at about 2' 24", Navarro introduces some bluesy licks.

This piece is a 12-bar blues based on one phrase played three times. Such a formula was common for constructing springboards for jamming. According to convention, the line was played for two choruses before solo improvisations began. Gordon solos for four choruses. Fats Navarro solos for three choruses. Then, to end before the recording time ran out, they played the theme only once, instead of following convention whereby the blues themes are played twice after the solo passages.

First Chorus

0' 00"   Trumpet/tenor saxophone play the theme with piano comping, bass walking, drummer keeping time with drumstick on ride cymbal.

Second Chorus

0' 17"   same as first chorus

Third Chorus

0' 34"   improvised tenor saxophone solo by Gordon, much in the style of Lester Young

Fourth Chorus

0' 53"   saxophone continues

Fifth Chorus

1' 11"   saxophone continues

Sixth Chorus

1' 29"   saxophone continues

Seventh Chorus

1' 48"   improvised trumpet solo by Navarro

Eighth Chorus

2' 06"   trumpet solo continues

2' 11"   Gillespie licks in Navarro's solo

2' 17"   odd note choice in the style of Gillespie

Ninth Chorus

2' 25"   improvisation comprised of bluesy licks by Navarro

2' 43"   **Theme Statement**

▶ Stan Getz, the most popular jazz tenor saxophonist of the 1950s and 1960s. Though he first emerged during the bebop era of the 1940s, some listeners consider him a "cool jazz" or "bossa nova" player instead of a bebop stylist. But despite any resemblance to established trends, he really had his own style, and it was fresh and graceful.

Photo by Lee Tanner

and rhythmic vocabulary instead. His phrasing and accenting were less varied and syncopated than Parker's and Gillespie's. At times classical music seems to have influenced him more than bebop did. Some of his improvisations are quite pretty, and less like bebop than like classical music. That side of his style fit with his light, fluffy tone and graceful approach to playing the saxophone. Partly because of this, many listeners categorize the Getz style as "cool jazz," not bebop.

Getz was one of the few bebop musicians to become known outside a small circle of musicians and jazz fans. He could play hard-driving jazz that was envied by the best of his peers. But his greatest impact with the public was made with slow, pretty pieces. They showcased his sensitivity and tapped his talent for melody played with elegance and tenderness. His first hit came with a solo he played in a Woody Herman big band performance during the late 1940s: "Early Autumn." His other hits were in a similar vein. His 1952 "Moonlight in Vermont" with guitarist Johnny Smith was one of them. His 1962 "Desafinado" with guitarist Charlie Byrd was a major event in the popularization of bossa nova. This was a kind of music that combined jazz with Brazilian styles, and it had considerable popularity. During the mid-1960s almost every jazz musician recorded at least one piece in the style, and Getz recorded several albums of bossa novas. His 1964 recording of the bossa nova "Girl from Ipanema," with its vocal by Astrud Gilberto, outsold almost every previous modern jazz record.

LISTENING GUIDE

CD1—*Track 19*

"It Never Entered My Mind" by Stan Getz

((•-[Listen on **mysearchlab.com**

This selection was recorded during an October 25, 1957, performance at the Shrine Auditorium in Los Angeles with trombonist J. J. Johnson originally issued on an album called *Stan Getz & J. J. Johnson at the Opera House*. The piece was written by Broadway show tune composers Richard Rodgers and Lorenz Hart. The improvised introduction by pianist Oscar Peterson amounts to an original composition itself. Then, with his lightweight, fluffy tone, tenor saxophonist Stan Getz offers us a delicate, gentle manner for rendering the melody. Though some consider Getz to be a part of cool jazz, and some peg him in the bebop camp, he really is stylistically all his own.

If you don't already know the original tune, you may mistake Getz's entire line here for it. It might all sound fresh. Keep in mind, however, that even if you did know the original tune, you would not recognize all of it in this performance because Getz is paraphrasing most of the time. Getz's pacing and choice of notes for the paraphrase reflects the exquisite taste for which he is justly celebrated. No other tenor saxophonist in jazz ever matched the tenderness that Getz brought to his ballad playing. Few came close to his gift for melody, either. Getz has stated that he preferred playing ballads more than swinging numbers because slow ballad tempos gave him time to think. It is obvious here that he is thinking very carefully about what notes to play. Not only are his notes perfect, but so is their timing.

SARAH VAUGHAN

The best known singer to emerge from the bebop era was Sarah Vaughan (1924–1990). Recording with the top instrumentalists, including Dizzy Gillespie, Tadd Dameron, and Clifford Brown, she achieved a position of respect among musicians that sustained throughout her long career. Like Ella Fitzgerald, she also had a large following outside of the jazz audience. "Nature Boy" and "It's Magic" were hits for her in 1948; then her "Broken Hearted Melody" became a million-seller in 1959.

Vaughan's tone quality was darker and more richly textured than Billie Holiday's and Ella Fitzgerald's. As the years passed, her pitch range deepened into tenor and almost baritone range. (Listen to her "Body and Soul" on *Jazz Classics CD1* for *Jazz Styles, 11th Edition* and "My Funny Valentine" on *Smithsonian Collection of Classic Jazz*.)

Vaughan's voice control is a source of envy among singers. She showed none of the abruptness or lost tone quality and pitch control that typify most pop singers when they shift registers. She could glide through several octaves seamlessly. Like opera singers, she favored a quick and prominent vibrato, and she milked every note for its last vibration. Also as in opera, she emphasized the maximum drama that could be extracted from each phrase.

Vaughan, a professional pianist with a working knowledge of modern harmony, was an accomplished scat singer. But like other jazz singers, she rarely performed scat improvisations. Instead, she usually chose to sing the original words. The focus of her creativity was in recasting the rhythms and embellishing the pitches. These departures exceeded mere ornamentation, but they did not take the liberties that constitute scat singing.

Straight readings of tunes were not Vaughan's routine practice. She improvised extensively with the timing of words, as though the lyrics were

Photo by Popsie Randolf, courtesy of Frank Driggs

▶ Sarah Vaughan, the best-known singer associated with bebop. Noted for recasting melodies by seamlessly changing their pitches and rhythms, she extracted the maximum drama and sensuality from each phrase.

elastic and could be stretched to occur almost anywhere in relation to the passing beats. At the same time she also played with the enunciation of the words and their tone's pitch and timbre. The effect is exceedingly sensual. She drew us in by toying with almost every phrase. The result was that each of her renditions became an intimate experience. Ballad performances account for her greatest achievements. The slow-paced tunes were excellent vehicles for her mastery of nuance. She luxuriated in the depth and richness of her voice and took listeners along in this celebration of sound for its own sake.

Most singers lose tone and energy as they age. Yet Vaughan's tone quality, range, and technique actually increased over the years. Her performances were impeccable during all phases of her career, with her greatest virtuosity displayed during her final twenty years.

THE POPULARITY OF BEBOP

With the arrival of bebop, jazz began to achieve the status of classical chamber music more than that of American popular music. Its performance required highly sophisticated skills, and it was appreciated by a relatively small elite. Jazz had always required special skills because of its demand for so much spontaneous creativity. As far as American popular music went, it had long been an elite art form. Yet bebop crystallized those tendencies, removed jazz even further from most of American popular music, and turned it into fine art music.

Photo by David Redfern/Redferns/Getty Images

◀ The Modern Jazz Quartet, left to right: pianist John Lewis, bassist Percy Heath, drummer Connie Kay, vibraphonist Milt Jackson. This group was founded by bebop players but became associated with "cool jazz" because it played soft jazz that was polished and restrained.

Bebop was not nearly as popular as swing had been. When Charlie Parker died in 1955, he was an obscure figure compared to Benny Goodman, whose name was a household word. And yet Parker was musically a more significant force in jazz than Goodman. Several swing records sold more than a million copies. No bebop instrumentals ever came close to that. There are several possible explanations for this.

One reason why bebop was less popular than swing style is that it had **less visual appeal.** Most swing bands carried singers, and many also carried dancers and showy staging. Bop combos, on the other hand, rarely carried any of this. To appreciate modern jazz, people had to listen instead of watch.

Another factor is that, by comparison with swing, **bebop had a scarcity of singers.** The bebop listener was rarely offered song lyrics or the good looks and personality of the singer delivering them. More than ever before, jazz fans now had to follow melodies that had no words. This made jazz more abstract and less enjoyable to the casual listener. Singers have always been more popular than instrumentalists. Lyrics are in a language that is common to both the performer and the listener. Jazz instrumentals, on the other hand, are in a language that is known to only a tiny portion of the listening public. In addition, the human voice produces a sound that is far more familiar to listeners than that of any instrument.

Listeners have historically shown that they prefer relatively uncomplicated music. Furthermore, they like music to be fairly predictable. They especially like themes that they can sing along with, remember, and hum by themselves. **In comparison to swing, bebop is much more complicated and unpredictable. The written melodies in many bebop performances are difficult to follow.** A sizable percentage of bebop tunes are so complicated that, even if listeners know them, it is hard to sing along with them.

Another factor that made bebop more challenging to understand is **the change in ratio between written and improvised music.** Swing bands framed short improvisations inside extended arrangements. The arrangements included much repetition that made the music easy to digest. On the other hand, bebop combos featured improvisers who played long solos after a melody was stated. There was much less reference material. The listener was more on his own.

Remember, too, that the large amount of arranged material in a swing band performance stayed the same in every performance, recorded or live. This offered even more familiarity to the listener. Bebop performances, on the other hand, were created anew each time a tune was played. Again, this is because the emphasis was mostly on improvisation. The smaller amount of repetition in the bebop performance would therefore present a greater listening challenge.

Still, despite the lesser popularity of bebop, there were a few groups and a few records that did become commercial successes. That music had some of the same features as swing. Also note that Charlie Parker's best-selling records were those he made of well-known songs with written orchestral accompaniments.

It should be clear by now that a style's popularity is not based on its quality. Instead, **the degree of popularity of a style of music can largely be attributed to differences in performance practices and in the ways each style treats the basic elements of music.** In comparing bebop to swing, these performance practices are relevant: appearance, amount of improvisation, repetition, the amount of framing for improvisation, and presence of words in the music.

The musical elements of melody, harmony, and rhythm are also treated differently in the two styles. Bebop offered higher, faster, more complex playing. Bebop featured more variety in rhythms, in melody lines and in accompaniments. Bebop used richer chords, more chord changes, and a more elaborate relationship between the notes of the melody and the notes of the accompanying chords.

Modern jazz continued the jazz tradition of influencing American popular music and symphonic music. But it seemed to carve its own sturdy path for musicians and a small audience of nonmusicians. Bebop became the parent for a series of other fascinating modern styles, which were also less popular than swing. Jazz did not regain its popularity until the 1970s, when a jazz-rock fusion brought millions of new fans.

SUMMARY

1. Bebop differed from swing by using smaller bands; richer chords; more chord changes; more irregular rhythms; drier, more biting tone qualities; and faster playing with more surprises.

2. The originators of bebop were alto saxophonist Charlie Parker, trumpeter Dizzy Gillespie, and pianist Thelonious Monk.

3. Parker wrote numerous tunes based on the accompaniment harmonies for popular songs and 12-bar blues. These became standard repertory for generations of jazz musicians.

4. Gillespie devised an unorthodox trumpet style and led a string of outstanding combos and big bands.

5. Monk played piano in a very spare manner that was filled with unusual rhythms and harmonies. He wrote tunes that were difficult because of their odd accents and chord progressions.

6. The ideas of Art Tatum, Charlie Parker, Thelonious Monk, and Dizzy Gillespie appeared in the new piano style of Bud Powell. This new style was widely imitated, and Powell significantly influenced his followers by reducing the activity of the left hand.

7. Bebop drummers differed from swing drummers by increasing the frequency and spontaneity of kicks and prods, feathering the bass drum instead of pounding it, playing timekeeping rhythms on a suspended cymbal, and snapping the high-hat shut sharply on the second and fourth beats.

8. Bebop styles and their offshoots were less popular than swing styles because they used fewer popular tunes and singers. They also relied less on arrangements. Solos and accompaniments were more complicated. Consequently, there was less predictability in the music.

KEY TERMS

asymmetrical accent   bomb

FURTHER RESOURCES

✓•⌐Study and Review on mysearchlab.com

Watch documentaries on Charlie Parker and Dizzy Gillespie.

Test your knowledge with the chapter quiz.

VIEW

Prentice Hall Jazz History DVD (ISBN 0-13-602643-5)
    Features clips of Dizzy Gillespie and Charlie Parker, and Thelonious Monk.

Founding Fathers of Bebop (Stars of Jazz). Clips of Dizzy Gillespie and Charlie Parker.

Dizzy: The Life and Music of John Birks Gillespie (A&E). Documentary from the A&E television "Biography" series.

Thelonious Monk: Straight No Chaser (Warner Home Video). Documentary on Monk's life and music.

Thelonious Monk: Live in '66. Jazz Icons, c 2006. Quartet with Rouse in Norway.

Thelonious Monk: Live in France 1969. Jazz Icons, c 2011. Solo piano.

LISTEN

Bud Powell: Jazz Giant (Verve: 314 543 832–2, 1949–50, c 2011); *The Amazing Bud Powell, Vols. 1 & 2* (Blue Note: 32136/32137, 1949–53 c 2011).

Bud Powell's 1947 rendition of "Somebody Loves Me" is on *The Smithsonian Collection of Classic Jazz*. His 1951 rendition of "Night in Tunisia" is on *The Smithsonian Collection of Classic Jazz* (rev. ed.).

Thelonious Monk, *Genius of Modern Music, Vols. 1 & 2* (Blue Note: 32138/32139, 1947–52, c 2001).

Dexter Gordon. *Settin' the Pace* (Savoy 17027, 1945–47, c 1998).

Stan Getz is well represented on *The Complete Roost Recordings* (Blue Note: 59622, 3 CD set, 1950–54, c 1997); *Jazz Samba* (Verve: 521 413–2, 1962, c 1997); *Getz/Gilberto* (Verve: 521 413–2, 1964, c 1997); *At Storyville* (Roulette: 94507, 1951, c 1990); and *Stan Getz and J.J. Johnson at the Opera House* (Verve: 831 272–2, 1957, c 1986). *Prentice Hall Jazz Collection* has Woody Herman's "Four Brothers," which features Stan Getz.

Dizzy Gillespie. *The Complete RCA Victor Recordings* (RCA Bluebird: 66528, 2 CD set, 1937–49, c 1995) and *Groovin' High* (Savoy: 0152, 1945–46, c 1992). *Jazz Classics CD1 for Jazz Styles, 11th Edition* (ISBN 0-205-03686-4) has "Shaw' Nuff" and "Things to Come."

Many of Charlie Parker's most significant recordings are on *The Best of the Complete Savoy and Dial Studio Recordings* (Savoy 17120, 1944–48, c 2002). His "Groovin' High" with Dizzy Gillespie (1945) is on *Prentice Hall Jazz Collection* (ISBN 205-17896-0).

Original Recordings by Monk, Gillespie, Parker, Davis and other bebop players are on *The Smithsonian Collection of Classic Jazz* and *Ken Burns JAZZ* (Columbia/Legacy: C5K 61432, 5 CD set, 1917–92, c 2000). Thelonious Monk's "Round Midnight" and Dizzy Gillespie's "Groovin' High" are on *Prentice Hall Jazz Collection* (ISBN 0-205-17896-0).

READ

Gillespie, Dizzy. 1979. *To Be or Not to Bop* (autobiography). New York: Doubleday.

Gitler, Ira. 1966 (Da Capo reprint, 1983). *The Masters of Jazz: A Listener's Guide, Rev. edition, 2001.* New York: Macmillan.

Gourse, Leslie. 1997. *Straight, No Chaser: The Life and Genius of Thelonious Monk.* New York: Schirmer.

Kelley, Robin D.G. 2009. *Thelonious Monk: The Life and Times of an American Original.* New York: Free Press.

Maggin, Donald L. 1996. *Stan Getz: A Life in Jazz.* New York: William Morrow.

Mathieson, Kenny. 1999. *Giant Steps: Bebop and the Creators of Modern Jazz: 1945–65.* Edinburgh: Payback Press.

Owens, Thomas. 1995. *Bebop: The Music and the Players.* New York: Oxford University Press.

Paudras, Francis. 1998. *Dance of the Infidels: A Portrait of Bud Powell.* New York: Da Capo.

Reisner, Robert. 1962 (Da Capo reprint, 1975). *Bird: The Legend of Charlie Parker.* New York: Citadel.

Shipton, Alyn. 2001. *Groovin' High: The Life of Dizzy Gillespie.* New York: Oxford University Press.

Woideck, Carl. 1996. *Charlie Parker: His Music and Life.* Ann Arbor: University of Michigan Press.

Woideck, Carl. 1998. *The Charlie Parker Companion: Six Decades of Commentary.* New York: Schirmer.

Cool Jazz

Miles Davis, Lee Konitz, Gerry Mulligan. Photo by Popsie Randolf, courtesy of Frank Driggs

The term "cool jazz" refers to modern jazz that tends to be softer and easier than the bebop of Charlie Parker and Dizzy Gillespie. "Cool jazz" avoids roughness and brassiness. The term "cool" has been applied to the music of saxophonist Lester Young and some of the musicians whom he and Count Basie influenced. Though musicians inspired by Basie and Young were found in almost all regions of America, many of them were based in California during the 1950s. Because of this, **West Coast Jazz** came to designate soft bop and Basie-Young disciples who devised new styles there. New York, Chicago, and Boston were also centers of innovation in cool jazz.

LENNIE TRISTANO

Lennie Tristano (1919–1978) was a pianist, composer, and bandleader. He created a modern alternative to bebop during the 1940s in Chicago and New York. Tristano's music was just as complex as bebop, but it

Lennie Tristano, pianist-composer who invented a modern jazz alternative to the bebop style of Bud Powell. Though often considered part of "cool jazz," Tristano's playing conveys a surging intensity.

Photo by William P. Gottlieb, Courtesy of Library of Congress

West Coast Jazz The jazz style associated with Dave Brubeck, Paul Desmond, Gerry Mulligan, and Chet Baker during the 1950s, often applied to classify cool jazz by California-based white musicians

differed from it. He avoided the pet phrases of Charlie Parker and Dizzy Gillespie. Tristano preferred very long phrases, and his lines were smoother and less jumpy than those of Parker and Gillespie. Also, he did not swing his music in the customary bebop manner. Like bebop, his lines did not resemble popular songs: they had no easily "singable" quality to them.

In creating a style of his own, Lennie Tristano began by learning the work of the great masters. Art Tatum and Lester Young were particularly important influences. In developing mastery of piano playing, Tristano learned how to play Tatum's difficult and impressive runs. He also made himself and his students learn Lester Young's solo improvisations by carefully listening to recordings. The eighteenth-century composer Johann Sebastian Bach was also important to him. Tristano regarded Bach so highly that he required his students to practice Bach compositions and learn to improvise in that style.

LEE KONITZ

Tristano's most talented student during the 1940s was alto saxophonist Lee Konitz (b. 1927). Tristano joined Konitz and made recordings that still dazzle listeners today. By the late 1940s, Lee Konitz had developed a new jazz saxophone style. His speed and agility were very impressive and frequently compared to Parker's. Technically, these two alto saxophonists were in a class by themselves, outplaying all others. They were both masters

Photo courtesy of Frank Driggs

◀ Lee Konitz, the leading alto saxophonist in cool jazz. Inspired by Lennie Tristano's piano style, Konitz offered a modern jazz alternative to the bebop sax style of Charlie Parker.

of technique, but they played in different styles. This is an important point in jazz history: *Konitz's style was inspired by Tristano, while most other young alto saxophonists at that time were imitating Charlie Parker.*

Both Parker and Konitz steered away from the warm, syrupy lushness of older alto saxophonists Benny Carter and Johnny Hodges. But Konitz went further from swing era models than Parker: Konitz played with a light, dry, airy tone. He employed a slow vibrato and preferred the alto saxophone's upper register. His sound on the alto saxophone is comparable to Lester Young's on tenor. This represented a contrast with the biting, bittersweet sound of Charlie Parker. Also, Konitz did not like to sneak quotes from pop tunes into his playing the way Parker did. Konitz also differed from Parker in his rhythm and in the way he treated individual notes. He used less offbeat rhythm. Almost all the notes in his lines were slurred together, and he avoided hard, sudden attacks. The overall effect of the Konitz style typified "cool" jazz.

BIRTH OF THE COOL

In 1949 and 50, trumpeter Miles Davis organized recording sessions of a nine-piece band in New York. It became known as the Miles Davis Nonet or the "Birth of the Cool" band. The group was formed partly from members of the Claude Thornhill big band. The concept for the music was inspired

((•—Listen on **mysearchlab.com**
Listen to cool jazz alto sax on mysearchlab.com

Composed by Lee Konitz; recorded January 11, 1949, in New York City by Lee Konitz (alto sax), Billy Bauer (guitar), Lennie Tristano (piano), Arnold Fishkin (bass), and Shelly Manne (drums).

"Subconscious-Lee" was written by Lee Konitz in the style of Lennie Tristano, his teacher and the pianist on this recording. The piece follows the chord progression of the pop tune "What Is This Thing Called Love." The style of the melody and improvisations differs significantly from bebop in its pattern of accent, its extreme absence of space, its lack of variety in the lengths of notes, and its very quiet and smooth rhythm section sound. The tone of Konitz is lightweight, dry, and airy. The drummer uses brushes instead of sticks to play timekeeping rhythms. And he plays them on the snare drum in a smooth, slurred fashion, instead of on the cymbal in the more percussive manner of bebop drummers.

During the late 1940s and the early 1950s, many musicians liked this style more than they liked bebop. They were impressed by the comprehensive mastery Tristano's musicians had over their instruments. Many musicians were awed by the speed, precision, and grace with which they played. The sounds were more uniform, the articulation was cleaner, and the music was less brassy and explosive than in bebop. On the other hand, the choice of notes was often more adventuresome harmonically than in bebop, and the Tristano-inspired lines were less melodic than Charlie Parker's.

In this performance, there is no introduction. The theme occupies the entire first chorus of the "What Is This Thing Called Love" chord progression. Then each musician is featured for a complete chorus. The final chorus is broken into four parts. The first is a Tristano solo improvisation of 8 measures (termed 8 "bars" by musicians). The second is a Bauer solo improvisation of another 8 bars. (Musicians term such a sequence "trading eights.") The third is a Konitz improvisation and the fourth is a Tristano improvisation. The ending is a new 8-bar line played by sax and guitar.

0' 00"	**Theme** played in unison by alto and guitar, accompanied by walking bass, timekeeping rhythms played by wire brushes on snare drum, and piano comping.
0' 32"	**Piano Solo Improvisation** by Lennie Tristano
1' 03"	**Guitar Solo Improvisation** by Billy Bauer
1' 34"	**Alto Sax Solo** by Lee Konitz
2' 05"	**Piano Solo** by Lennie Tristano (First A-section of Form)
2' 13"	**Guitar Solo** by Billy Bauer (Second A-section of Form)
2' 21"	**Alto Sax Solo** by Lee Konitz (Bridge of Form)
2' 29"	**Piano Solo** by Lennie Tristano (Final A-section of Form)
2' 36"	**Ending:** New Line Played in Octaves by Alto Sax and Guitar

The "Birth of the Cool" band led by trumpeter Miles Davis (with alto saxophonist Lee Konitz and baritone saxophonist Gerry Mulligan at his left).

Photo by Popsie Randolf, courtesy of Frank Driggs

by the arranging style of Gil Evans, who had worked with Thornhill during the 1940s. In addition to Davis on trumpet, the nonet included Lee Konitz, who had played alto saxophone for Thornhill, and baritone saxophonist Gerry Mulligan, who had played and written for Thornhill. These three hornmen all employed lightweight tone qualities and preferred subdued effects. The nonet used a standard rhythm section of piano, bass, and drums. But Davis added something rather unusual. He added French horn and tuba along with a trombone, and he had no tenor saxophone or guitar. The overall effect was much more subdued than the sounds of big jazz bands had been. For this reason it was ultimately referred to as "cool jazz."

GERRY MULLIGAN

Gerry Mulligan (1927–1996) was Miles Davis' baritone saxophonist and primary composer-arranger on the Birth of the Cool recordings. He used a soft, dry, lightweight tone quality whose texture has been compared to tweed cloth. His approach was simpler and more direct than bebop. Rhythmically, Mulligan's improvisations were less jagged than those of Charlie Parker and Dizzy Gillespie. His choice of notes suggested great deliberation rather than wild exuberance. His phrases were coolly logical and systematically developed. He rarely squeezed a lot of notes into them. Mulligan's compositions were simpler than Tristano's and less intense than bebop

Photo by William Claxton/Courtesy of Demont Photo

▶ Baritone saxophonist Gerry Mulligan and trumpeter Chet Baker were distinguished for their dry, subdued approach to modern jazz.

Prentice Hall Jazz History DVD: "Avalon" by Gerry Mulligan

pieces. Some are quite song-like, and they share the same gentleness one hears in his improvisations. These features of his style combine with his subdued tone quality to place his music squarely in the "cool" category.

In 1952, Mulligan moved to California and launched a series of pianoless quartets. He played baritone saxophone, and was joined by another horn, bass, and drums. Let's take a moment to consider what it means to have a jazz group without a chording instrument. Normally a piano provides chords to the soloists. These chords act as a sort of an anchor, always reminding the horn players of where they are in the harmony that accompanies the tune. In some ways the piano chords direct the flow and texture of the music. A comping pianist complicates the sound considerably. Therefore the absence of piano in Mulligan's groups was partly responsible for the band's light, simple sound texture. It also highlighted the bass, which pianos often drown out. His drummers also contributed to this effect by playing conservatively, often using wire brushes instead of sticks to strike the drums and cymbals. All of these aspects together made Mulligan's band sound "cool." Though Mulligan was based on the West Coast for only about three years, his music came to stand for what journalists mean by the term **"West Coast Jazz."** Long after returning to the New York area, Mulligan maintained his piano-less format, and many listeners still considered him to be **"West Coast Cool"** style.

DAVE BRUBECK

Pianist Dave Brubeck (b. 1920) led the best known of all cool jazz groups. He performed in the San Francisco area during the 1940s and early 50s. He

Photo courtesy of Frank Driggs

◀ Alto saxophonist Paul Desmond, pianist Dave Brubeck, drummer Joe Morello, bassist Gene Wright.

achieved widespread international fame leading a quartet from 1951 to 1967 with California-born alto saxophonist Paul Desmond, a bassist, and a drummer.

The rhythmic feeling in a lot of Brubeck's playing has much in common with classical music. However, Brubeck never was a classical pianist. He simply stayed away from sounding like bebop players, either in his melody or his rhythm. This made him sound more "classical." In fact, sometimes he and Desmond improvised duets that sounded like the two-part inventions of J. S. Bach, accompanied by bass and drums. He is highly inventive, constantly making up his own improvised melodies. In other words, Brubeck is a modern jazz musician who does not use the bebop language, and who likes to play around with classical styles.

Brubeck's popularity may also be partly due to his "classical" sound. His compositions and improvisations are simple and tuneful. They are easier to follow than the jumpy and explosive phrases in bebop. His creations are orderly and clear, making the listener's job easy. In addition, most of Brubeck's pieces are pretty, and they convey a light and pleasant mood.

Brubeck was also an innovator with rhythm. His use of unusual meters brought him much publicity. It also influenced other jazz musicians. During the 1960s his quartet crafted a number of tunes and improvisations in odd meters such as 3, 5, and 7 beats to the measure, instead of the usual 4. His albums *Time Out* and *Time Further Out*, which explored those meters, were immensely popular. *Time Out* contained "Take Five," a funky and engaging little theme whose accompaniment was a simple, repeated rhythm in meter of five. During the 1990s, people were still asking jazz groups to play it.

In the period 1955 to 1985, Brubeck ranked second in record sales among all jazz recording artists. During the 1950s and 60s, his name became almost as synonymous with jazz as Louis Armstrong and Duke Ellington. His quartet's music provided an introduction to jazz for millions of new listeners, including a whole generation of college students.

Prentice Hall Jazz Collection: "Blue Rondo a la Turk" by Dave Brubeck

STAN KENTON

Stan Kenton (1912–1979) led the best known succession of big bands in modern jazz. He presented repertories that spanned several eras and featured numerous styles. His name first became well known during the 1940s while he was leading a big band in the swing era style. A number of cool style musicians played in his bands, and Kenton was based on the West Coast during the 1940s and 50s when it was linked with white musicians playing cool jazz. Kenton's music of the late 1940s and early 50s is also linked to cool jazz by arranging style. He was influenced by Claude Thornhill, after whom Miles Davis had modeled the "Birth of the Cool" band style. In addition, Kenton used a few arrangements by Gerry Mulligan, who had provided arrangements for the Davis band. Despite the connections with "cool" jazz, Kenton dubbed his music **"progressive jazz,"** and some have also called it "big band bop."

Kenton created a distinctive band style that is immediately recognizable. He turned out a large body of dance music. But the most impressive work he presented was non-swinging concert music that vividly exposed rich, modern harmonies. It was separate from the dance band tradition of big band jazz. The rhythmic feeling of classical music was common in his

Progressive jazz A term coined by Stan Kenton to describe his own music

▲ Stan Kenton's 1947 band, a platform for ambitious concert works, the most popular of all modern big bands, and a source for many "cool jazz" players. The five trumpets, five trombones instrumentation was popularized by Kenton and adopted by college "stage bands" thereafter. (A trumpeter closest to the drummer is mostly hidden in this photo of a rehearsal with Kenton seated at the piano.)

Photo by William P. Gottlieb

sound. The musicianship of his players was very high. The precision of his performances was almost equal to the sterling standards of symphony orchestras. Usually performed without vibrato, his brass and saxophone parts had a dry quality that some listeners call "transparent." Some pieces featured trumpet parts that were high-pitched, loud, and often included 5-note chords. These sounds were combined with saxophone lines written in long strings of rapid notes that came up from under the trumpet and trombone sounds like fountains.

Though Kenton's performances usually ranged from the softest to the loudest of sounds, Kenton earned a reputation for leading the loudest big band. This was partly due to the number of brass instruments. It was common to find five trumpets and five trombones in a Kenton band. Additionally, some Kenton trombonists doubled on tuba, and one version of his band carried four mellophoniums. These instruments were trumpet–French horn hybrids that were specially made for Kenton.

((•- Listen on **mysearchlab.com**
Listen to Kenton's powerful brass on mysearchlab.com

Another trademark of the Kenton band sound was its glossy trombone tones. The music frequently featured harmonized parts for five trombones that were performed very smoothly. Kenton's trombone soloists preferred high-register work, and they graced the beginnings of many tones with long, climbing smears. They used a meticulously controlled vibrato that started slow and then quickened dramatically near the tone's end. Their approach was extraverted, but in a well-manicured way rather than the rough, guttural way of earlier jazz trombonists.

To help put Kenton's sound in perspective, let's compare it with Basie's. While Basie's band conveyed an easygoing and swinging feeling, Kenton's conveyed a solemn and weighty feeling that is quite serious. Kenton's sound resembles twentieth-century concert music written for trumpets, trombones, and saxophones with rhythm section. Sometimes other instruments associated with symphony orchestras were added—strings, French horns, and tuba. Latin American percussion instruments were also added during a number of different phases in Kenton's career. The band's character is based more on elaborate arrangements than on the simplicity and swing feeling associated with Basie. The Kenton bands usually emphasized composition more than improvisation. Remember that the Basie band of the late 1930s functioned much as a big combo. Solo improvisation was primary, and many of the horn backgrounds were almost incidental to the music. Kenton's approach was sometimes the opposite. Solo improvisations could be almost incidental to the overall band sound. Arrangements were primary and solos were secondary. Kenton's sound contrasts with Basie's because its effect was frequently similar to a brass choir, not a big jazz combo.

((•- Listen on **mysearchlab.com**
Listen to glossy trombone playing by Bob Burgess on mysearchlab.com

Among Kenton's major contributions to jazz history were his skill at public relations and his motivation and talent for finding and leading creative modern musicians and composers. Lying behind this contribution is the fact that, because of his band's great popularity during the 1940s, Kenton became financially free enough to invest in musical experiments. He channeled this freedom into hiring relatively unknown writers and encouraging ambitious compositions that had little chance of realizing commercial success. Improvisers had enjoyed these kinds of opportunities throughout jazz history, but composers had not. He must also be credited

Recorded September 16, 1952, in Chicago by Stan Kenton band (five trumpets, five trombones, five saxophones, guitar, bass, and drums); composed by Bill Russo; originally released by Capitol Records on the album *New Concepts in Artistry in Rhythm.*

Terms to know from tracks on *Demo CD:* trumpet (59), trombone (78), alto saxophone (72), tenor saxophone (73), baritone saxophone (74), bowed bass (21), "straight" eighth notes vs. "swing" eighth notes (43), legato (44), wire brushes on snare drum (11), mutes (68).

The Stan Kenton band performance of Bill Russo's "Improvisation" illustrates how Kenton used the musicians of his big band to perform complicated concert music that was not intended for dancing. The harmonies, style, and depth of Russo's composition resemble what a symphony orchestra might play if it selected repertory from twentieth century composers. This is sometimes termed "modern classical music." The music on this selection differs, however, from most modern classical music because it contains improvisation and uses the instruments of a jazz band. It differs from most jazz because it does not swing. Therefore its classification remains in a netherworld because the music sounds much like classical music, but it is made by jazz musicians who bring their own point of view to their improvisations, even if none of the parts bear the rhythmic properties of swing feeling.

It is innovative, in part, because unlike many pieces played by jazz bands of the 1930s and 40s, "Improvisation" does not follow the chord progressions of a pop tune. It does not repeat a 12-bar blues or 32-bar A-A-B-A form again and again, either. With the exception of the progression of guitar chords from Sal Salvador underneath the alto sax solo from 3' 18" to 5' 03", it is continuously changing from beginning to end. This approach is termed "through composed."

There are a few other unique qualities worth trying to notice. The textures in this piece range from very loud and thick to very soft and lean. This band uses five trombones and five trumpets, unlike Duke Ellington, who carried three trombones and three trumpets during the 1930s and 40s, or Count Basie who carried only three trumpets and two trombones in the 1930s. The thickness of the sound here stems partly from that and partly from each brass instrument playing a different note, instead of the more common practice of doubling the same note.

The piece opens with a series of eighth notes slurred together. Unlike the eighth notes in most lines played by other jazz groups, these are not swing eighth notes. (Listen to *Demo CD* Track 43, and see Elements of Music Appendix for explanation.) Instead these show even duration and even emphasis. This is the type of eighth note associated with classical music.

More than any other band, Kenton's was known for glossy trombone tones. From about 0' 29" to 1' 14", we hear a high-pitched melody played by trombonist Bob Burgess. This manner defines the style associated with so many Kenton trombonists.

The main improvisations on this recording are by alto saxophonist Lee Konitz from 2' 03". Kenton had a number of interesting soloists throughout his career of band leading, but Konitz was undoubtedly his most original and creative improviser. By the time "Improvisation" was made, Konitz had already distinguished himself with the bands of Claude Thornhill, Miles Davis, and Lennie Tristano. Konitz would thereafter be known for leading small groups of his own. He was still active in 2012.

A secondary improvisation occurs from 2' 32" to 3' 07". No melody or chord changes were preset for this portion of the performance. It therefore qualifies as free jazz. This is historically significant because it was occurring several years before Ornette Coleman's and Cecil Taylor's first free jazz recordings and the wide acclaim they received. Note that Russo and Konitz had both studied under Lennie Tristano, who had recorded collectively improvised "free" improvisations as early as 1949. On

Russo's "Improvisation," alto sax (Lee Konitz), tenor sax (Bill Holman), trumpet (Buddy Childers), and trombone (Bill Russo) improvise around each other without accompaniment, except for drummer Stan Levey using wire brushes to keep time on snare drum, so softly it is almost undetectable. Konitz begins all by himself, then the trumpet answers Konitz's idea by echoing it at 2′ 35″. Trombone enters at 2′ 37″. By 2′ 42″ four horn parts are moving slowly. The meditative mood is shattered at 3′ 08″ by a series of extremely loud figures from the full band played in staccato fashion. Then it is followed by a descending run, first by alto saxophones, then joined by tenor and finished by baritone sax and string bass played with a bow.

0′ 00″   Trumpets play series of descending eighth notes in 5-part harmony.

0′ 10″   Saxophones continue the series, joined by two muted trumpets.

0′ 23″   written trombone solo, slurred, high-pitched; Saxophones accompany with a counter-line.

0′ 55″   Very loud, full-band chords begin.

1′ 14″   Muted trumpets and trombones create slow, rocking motion. Texture thickens.

1′ 44″   Saxophones call.

1′ 47″   Trombones respond.

1′ 48″   Saxophones call.

1′ 50″   Trombones respond.

1′ 51″   Saxophones call.

1′ 53″   Trumpets in 5-part harmony play a complex ascending run to a very loud high note, joined at the end by trombones.

Lee Konitz Alto Saxophone Improvisation

2′ 03″   Screaming high brass cease; soft alto sax solo improvisation begins, accompanied by low trombones, guitar, bass, and snare drum played with wire brushes.

2′ 18″   prominent slurred trombones climbing up a scale underneath Konitz solo

2′ 25″   accompanied by written sax part moving with notes slurred together (legato)

Free-Form Improvisation by Five Musicians

2′ 29″   unaccompanied Konitz improvisation

2′ 34″   Trumpet answers by echoing Konitz's idea.

2′ 37″   Trombone enters with its own improvisation.
         Tenor sax and snare drum are almost inaudible.

2′ 42″   Four horn parts are moving slowly in collective improvisation.

Full Band Passage

3′ 08″   shattered by extremely loud, full-band staccato figures
         descending run by alto saxes, then joined by tenor, finished by baritone

3′ 15″   sustained bass note by bowed bass viol

3′ 17″   guitar chording

Lee Konitz Alto Saxophone Improvisation

3' 21"	accompanied by guitar chording and drummer playing snare drum with wire brushes
5' 00"	Guitar stops.
5' 14"	Bass trombone begins slurred tones.
5' 24"	Three trombones join in slow moving line, slurred.
5' 35"	triangle rings
5' 46"	extremely loud band chord
5' 51"	break in which Konitz echoes himself in improvised solo line

Full Band Passage

5' 55"	clashing, extremely loud band chord
5' 59"	bombastic full-band, marching chords
6' 10"	high-pitched, loud trumpets
6' 15"	trombones marching chords
6' 19"	Brasses play emphatic short notes for ending.

with tenacity and durability. Kenton began leading bands in 1941, when the big band era was still flourishing. Significantly, he then continued into the 1960s and 70s, when big bands were out of fashion. Moreover, he was one of the founders of the college stage band movement which is today the enormous jazz education establishment represented by Kenton-sized jazz bands in almost every high school and college. This movement in schools continued the big band tradition in jazz long after regularly touring big bands disappeared.

THE POPULARITY OF COOL JAZZ

A few players in the "cool" category are the most popular musicians in modern jazz. Trumpeter Miles Davis and saxophonist Stan Getz could pack nightclubs and concert halls. The Dave Brubeck Quartet was among the first groups in jazz that were sufficiently popular to tour regularly as concert artists. They appeared on college campuses and in recital halls that before them had presented only classical musicians. But only a few non-vocal cool jazz groups were this popular. For instance, Lennie Tristano and Lee Konitz were not known outside of well-informed jazz fans.

SUMMARY

1. Cool jazz is a term for modern styles that sound more subdued than the bebop of Charlie Parker and Dizzy Gillespie.
2. Count Basie and Lester Young were important influences on the cool jazz styles.
3. Pianist Lennie Tristano, alto saxophonist Lee Konitz, and trumpeter Miles Davis were among the first jazz musicians to devise styles that came to be called "cool."
4. The nine-piece band that Miles Davis recorded in 1949 and 1950 became known as the "Birth of the Cool" band.
5. Lee Konitz and baritone saxophonist Gerry Mulligan played in the "Birth of the Cool Band" with Miles Davis.
6. While in California, Mulligan began leading a series of quartets that did not use piano. Because of their location and sound, he is still identified with the label "West Coast Jazz" or "cool jazz."
7. Pianist Dave Brubeck was the most famous cool jazz musician. His quartet performed and recorded from 1951 to 1967.
8. Stan Kenton led the best known string of modern jazz big bands. Many of his musicians were associated with cool jazz.

KEY TERMS

progressive jazz **West Coast Jazz**

FURTHER RESOURCES

Study and **Review** on **mysearchlab.com**

Test your knowledge with the chapter quiz.

VIEW

Prentice Hall Jazz History DVD (ISBN 0-13-602643-5) features a clip of Gerry Mulligan performing "Avalon."

Dave Brubeck Live in '64 & '66. (Jazz Icons). Features Paul Desmond with the Brubeck quartet.

Lennie Tristano: The Copenhagen Concert (Storyville Films). 1965 solo performance.

LISTEN

Miles Davis—*Birth of the Cool* (Capitol 30117, 1949, 1950)

Stan Kenton—*New Concepts of Artistry in Rhythm* (Capitol 92865, 1952)

———, *Kenton Showcase* (Capitol 25244, 1952–1954)

Jazz Classics CD2 for *Jazz Styles, 11th Edition* (ISBN 0-250-03686-4) has Stan Kenton/ Lee Konitz's "My Lady."

Lennie Tristano—*Intuition* (Blue Note 52771, 1949)

Lee Konitz—*Subconscious-Lee* (Fantasy OJC–186) has excellent recordings of Lee Konitz and Lennie Tristano from 1949.

————, *Konitz Meets Mulligan* (Pacific Jazz 46847, 1953)

Smithsonian Collection of Classic Jazz contains one piece by Lennie Tristano with Lee Konitz and one piece by the Miles Davis Nonet with Konitz and Gerry Mulligan.

The Best of the Gerry Mulligan Quartet with Chet Baker (Pacific Jazz 95481; 1952–1953)

Two Dave Brubeck Quartet albums that contain representative material are: *Jazz at Oberlin* (Fantasy 31991, 1953) and *Time Out* (CBS CK65122, 1959) *Prentice Hall Jazz Collection* (ISBN 0-250-17896-0) has "Blue Rondo a la Turk."

READ

Gioia, Ted. 1992. *West Coast Jazz*. New York: Oxford University Press.

Gitler, Ira. 1962 (Da Capo reprint, 1983). *Jazz Masters of the Forties* (contains a discussion of Lennie Tristano and Lee Konitz). New York: Macmillan.

Goldberg, Joe. 1965 (Da Capo reprint, 1983). *Jazz Masters of the Fifties* (contains a discussion of Gerry Mulligan and Miles Davis). New York: Macmillan.

Gordon, Robert. 1986. *Jazz West Coast*. New York: Quartet.

Hall, Fred. 1996. *It's About Time: The Dave Brubeck Story*. Fayetteville: University of Arkansas Press.

Hamilton, Andy. 2007. *Lee Konitz: Conversations on the Improviser's Art*. Ann Arbor: University of Michigan Press.

Klinkowitz, Jerome. 1991. *Listen: Gerry Mulligan*. New York: Schirmer, 1991.

Lee, William F. 1980. *Stan Kenton: Artistry in Rhythm*. Los Angeles: Creative Press.

Shim, Eumni. 2007. *Lennie Tristano: His Life in Music*. Ann Arbor: University of Michigan Press.

Sparkes, Michael. 2010. *Stan Kenton: This is an Orchestra*. Denton, Texas: University of North Texas.

Stein Crease, Stephanie. 2002. *Gil Evans: Out of the Cool—His Life and Music*. Chicago: A Cappella.

Hard Bop 8

CHAPTER

Nat Adderley, Cannonball Adderley, and Charles Lloyd. Photo by Lee Tanner

CHAPTER OUTLINE

Horace Silver

Miles Davis

Clifford Brown

Freddie Hubbard

Cannonball Adderley

Sonny Rollins

John Coltrane

Wes Montgomery

The Popularity of Hard Bop

Summary

Further Resources

A number of jazz styles emerged during the 1950s and 60s. Most of them, including many of the "cool" styles, were variants on bebop. Though musicians tended to refer to all these styles as simply "bop" or "bebop," journalists and publicists coined new names such as hard bop, funky jazz, mainstream, post-bop, and soul jazz. The label "funky jazz" was attached most frequently to earthy, blues-drenched, gospelish pieces by Horace Silver, Cannonball Adderley, and others. The bluesy quality influenced a number of players who were popular in the 1960s and 70s. The proportion of their music called "funky jazz" was more popular than almost any other segment of modern jazz.

Let's look at several styles that coexisted with "funky jazz" and were sometimes performed by the same musicians who included funky pieces in their repertory. This stream of styles has no single, widely accepted name. "Hard bop" is the designation we use in this textbook. The sounds of most styles within this stream differ little from the

Listen on mysearchlab.com
Listen to hard bop drumming style on mysearchlab.com

sounds of bebop. But when they do differ, these trends frequently can be observed:

1. Drummers play with more activity.
2. Tone colors are darker, weightier, and rougher.
3. Chord progressions in the accompaniment are less frequently identical to those of pop tunes.
4. There is somewhat less of the start-and-stop quality that leaves the listener off balance.
5. There is a hard-driving feeling that pushes relentlessly, with an emphasis on consistent swinging.
6. Piano comping has more variety in rhythms and chord voicings.

These traits first appeared during the early 1950s in the work of trumpeter Clifford Brown and the bands led by drummer Art Blakey. Later they persisted in the music of other bands that included those same musicians. They also survived in the music of their associates and followers. The musicians playing with Horace Silver worked within this style into the 1990s.

The sounds of hard bop were not found in only one particular geographic region. For example, forerunners of hard bop tenor sax styles included Los Angeles–based as well as New York–based players. In addition, Philadelphia and Detroit contributed many vital players, and so did Indianapolis.

The hard bop category also includes a second wave of players. This wave went beyond hard bop in creating its own stream of styles. These players made their mark in the 1960s and derived their approaches even less directly from bebop than did those players mentioned above. Much of their music draws upon sources outside hard bop. With the notable exception of saxophonist John Coltrane, who died in 1967, the most prominent

► Art Blakey, hard bop drummer and bandleader. Blakey's groups played with hard-driving, unrelenting force, always swinging with supercharged energy. For four decades Blakey continued to hire the top players, including Clifford Brown, Wayne Shorter, Freddie Hubbard, and others.

Photo by Lee Tanner

in this wave were still active in the 1990s. They remained models for aspiring jazz musicians to imitate. The outstanding tenor saxophonists in this category are Joe Henderson and Wayne Shorter. The top trumpeter is Freddie Hubbard. The pianists are McCoy Tyner, Herbie Hancock, Chick Corea, and Keith Jarrett. The drummers are Tony Williams and Elvin Jones. You may know some of these names because of other styles they developed later. Such versatility is common to jazz giants. For example, Herbie Hancock contributed significantly to hard bop during the early 1960s and then created new styles in jazz-rock fusion of the 1970s and 80s.

HORACE SILVER

Horace Silver (b. 1928) is one of the biggest names in hard bop, a reputation derived mostly from his work as a composer and bandleader. But he also developed an original and substantial piano style. By the 1960s, he had replaced bebop's emphasis on long, bobbing lines with his own brief, catchy phrases. Virtuosity is not essential to Silver's style. He almost never plays fast for long stretches. Compactness and clarity are far higher priorities in his playing than speed and agility. His ideas unfold with a logic that is clear even to the inexperienced listener. Silver made considerable use of silence and was very clever in timing the starting and stopping points of his phrases. His solos are like his tunes—filled with simple ideas that are hummable and easy to remember. Each melodic segment is played in a forceful, percussive way. It is as though, while improvising, Silver keeps on composing at the same level of creativity and clarity that he maintains in his writing.

Photo by Jan Persson, courtesy of JazzSign/Lebrecht Music & Arts

((◉ Listen on **mysearchlab.com**
Listen to Horace Silver's solo piano style on mysearchlab.com

◀ Horace Silver, the leading pianist-composer-bandleader in hard bop. Prolific and versatile, Silver composed catchy themes and arranged them for his quintets. His music swung with an appealing crispness and bounce.

Recorded May 15, 1964, in Englewood Cliffs, New Jersey, by Lee Morgan (trumpet), Wayne Shorter (tenor saxophone), Curtis Fuller (trombone), Cedar Walton (piano), Jymie Merritt (bass), and Art Blakey (drums); composed by Curtis Fuller; originally issued by the Blue Note firm on the album *Indestructible*.

Terms to know from tracks on *Demo CD*: piano comping (20), trombone (78), tenor saxophone (73), walking bass (23).

If you like this piece, you might like other selections on Art Blakey's *Indestructible* album because most of them share the same style, energy, and outstanding solos and ensemble playing that this piece has. The music provides a prime example of the solemn power and drive associated with the Art Blakey groups of the 1950s, 60s, and 70s. It conveys the sense of urgency and intensity for which these bands were known. These bands were a major part of the jazz landscape at that time, made many recordings and were widely revered by musicians and dedicated fans.

Art Blakey (1919–1991) was a swing and bebop drummer who continued to incorporate African elements in his drumming. In fact, the first 14 seconds of the performance are devoted solely to Blakey roaming from one drum to another, in descending pitch, with his drumsticks striking snare drum in a pulse of "123456 123456." Blakey also does this in answer to each horn phrase in the bridge of the piece, particularly at 1' 05" and 1' 08". Emphasizing the different pitches and tone qualities of drums is an African tradition.

The mood of the music on "The Egyptian" derives partly from sustained chords played here by Cedar Walton and high-pitched, repeating figures played by bassist Jymie Merritt. The construction of trombonist Curtis Fuller's melody reflects practices that became especially common in jazz of the 1960s: maintaining just one main chord sound for long stretches. "Modal" became the term for passages in which only one chord's harmonies remain in effect. Instead of resounding tones stating each beat, the bass part in these sections consists of high-pitched embellishments. Only the tune's bridge is typical of bebop. In these ways, this piece samples both the tail end of hard bop's development and the influence of a new approach that followed it. The music on this selection is heavy, hard driving, and soulful, but also modal.

The line-up of soloists for this band is stellar. Trumpeter Lee Morgan (1938–1972) shows roots in Clifford Brown, but had his own originality as well. Along with Freddie Hubbard and Donald Byrd, Morgan was the most prominent trumpeter in hard bop during the late 1950s and early 1960s. Curtis Fuller was a prominent trombonist in hard bop, and still is. He is also the composer of "The Egyptian." Cedar Walton was one of the most in-demand pianists of the idiom and remains sought after as accompanist, soloist, and bandleader.

The melodic continuity and logic in each musician's solo on "The Egyptian" should be easy to follow because the hornmen devise hummable ideas and develop them systematically. As listeners, we also have the advantage in detecting the composition's form because the rhythm section outlines it in rising and falling patterns. The composition follows an A-A-B-B-A construction in which the A-sections contain long passages with just one harmony. In addition, there are moments along the way that we can come to expect because the arrangement uses simple horn figures that anchor the parts under soloists during A-sections within the flow of improvisation. The B-sections resume standard accompaniment practices in which piano comping is joined by walking bass, and Blakey no longer distributes triplets across his drum set. He returns to conventional timekeeping patterns. This provides relief from the tension accumulated in the A-section by assorted bass figures, sustained piano chords, horn trills, and by Blakey's 6's. Instead of sounding like carpenters building a garage, Blakey settles down when the B-sections occur.

The introduction has 8 measures of Blakey playing alone. Then he is joined for 16 measures by piano repeating a sustained chord in the rhythm that will set the mood for the A-sections, and by bass doubling the piano rhythm.

TIME ELAPSED

Introduction

0' 00"	Blakey is striking different drums in succession, distributing triplets across his snare drum.
0' 12"	Piano repeats sustained chord in rhythm.

First Chorus (Theme Statement)

0' 35"	A-section
	Horns state the first phrase of the melody (4 measures).
0' 40"	Horns repeat first phrase of the melody (4 measures).
0' 45"	A-section repeats
0' 56"	Bridge
	Horns state the first phrase of bridge, answered by Blakey.
0' 59"	Horns state the second phrase of bridge, answered by Blakey.
1' 08"	Repeat of Bridge
1' 19"	A-section repeats

Second Chorus (Curtis Fuller Trombone Solo)

1' 29"	trumpet/sax trill underneath
	Piano, bass and drums provide ocean of activity, heaving and swelling.
	Piano repeats opening figure, keeping same harmonies in effect.
1' 52"	Bridge
	Bass walks. Piano comps. Drums stop 6-pulse feeling.
2' 14"	Trumpet/sax trills; 6-pulse returns in drums.
2' 48"	Repeat of Bridge
	6-pulse in drums stops.
3' 10"	A-section
	6-pulse returns; piano chords sustain.

Third Chorus (Wayne Shorter Tenor Saxophone Solo)

3' 23"	Introduced by press-roll on snare drum. Solo is emotionally evocative, filled with wailing sounds.
3' 43"	Bridge
4' 05"	A-section
	Shorter "worries" a high note.
4' 16"	trumpet/trombone back-up figures
4' 28"	Shorter plays staccato figures.

4' 38"	Bridge
	Shorter plays a high note emphatically 17 times, as a gut-wrenching cry.
4' 59"	trumpet/trombone back-up figures
5' 02"	A-section

Fourth Chorus (Lee Morgan Trumpet Solo)

5' 13"	Lee Morgan trumpet solo; using upper register; creating exhilarating, expansive feeling.
5' 33"	Bridge
5' 45"	quadruple-timing in the style of trumpeter Clifford Brown
5' 56"	A-section
6' 06"	trills from trombone/sax
	Bridge
6' 29"	Morgan works over the same motif seven times, building tension.
6' 53"	Morgan works over one idea using pinched tones, answering himself.

7' 03" Fifth Chorus (Cedar Walton Piano Solo)

	Bridge
7' 24"	Walton plays around a Middle Eastern scale to 7' 36".
7' 44"	A-section
7' 56"	Horns sustain under piano solo.
8' 06"	Walton repeats a funky line.
8' 18"	Bridge
	Walton uses block chording for his solo line.
8' 39"	A-section
	Horns trill under piano solo.
	Walton reiterates a mordant-based idea.

8' 51" Sixth Chorus (Theme Returns)

9' 12"	Bridge
9' 21"	Blakey striking high-hat cymbals
9' 29"	Blakey roams from snare drum to tom-toms.
9' 34"	A-section
9' 45"	Vamp
	6-pulse feeling
	Trombone/saxophone call, trumpet responds, four times.
10' 15"	Fade Out

As an accompanist, Horace Silver initially drew from bebop style. By the late 1950s, however, he had perfected a new style of accompaniment. His accompaniment patterns sounded like structured setups for his soloists. This differed from the normal practice of spontaneous chording that responded to the twists and turns of solo improvisations. In this way, the soloists in Silver's bands were supported by backgrounds similar to those in big bands. Remember that big bands use written arrangements to supply the same accompaniment figures each time the soloist improvises on a piece. This gave Silver's music more continuity than was common in most modern groups. These accompaniments also posed a restriction, however, since they limited the range of moods an improvising soloist could create. But Silver's accompaniments gave listeners something easier to hear, and this may account for his greater popularity.

Horace Silver was hard bop's most prolific composer. For the Blue Note record company alone, he composed almost all the tunes on over twenty-five years' worth of his bands' albums. Silver put together arrangements that were generally more elaborate than those of other hard bop groups. They often contained written melodies in the middle of a piece, as well as Latin American rhythms and hints of gospel music. Silver often assigned notes to trumpet and tenor saxophone, creating harmony that made it sound as though his quintet contained more than five musicians. In addition to using this technique, Silver often wrote bass figures and played them on the piano in unison with his bassist. These figures had an engaging quality that expanded the limited scope of bebop bass lines. It is partly for these reasons that his quintet was easily distinguishable from other bebop or hard bop groups.

Horace Silver's quintet performances were consistently swinging and polished, and they featured many of the best musicians of the 1950s and 60s. Silver continued to tour and record in his original style until retiring in 2003.

MILES DAVIS

Jazz trumpeter and bandleader Miles Davis (1926–1991) played a pivotal role in the history of modern jazz. For fifty years he showed the foresight to anticipate trends in jazz styles well before they became widespread. During this period Davis created a very diverse body of music, which defined jazz for three different generations of listeners. His recordings won the near universal admiration of fellow jazz musicians. A significant slice of modern jazz history is documented in Davis-led recording sessions because he picked out the key innovators of each period for his bands and let them direct the course of his music in ever-changing ways.

Unlike most artists, Davis never became limited to one particular band style. Among his most important contributions are

1. Creating an original and substantial **trumpet style.** This was first evident in recordings he made with Charlie Parker's group in the mid-1940s. It influenced many trumpeters of the cool jazz and hard bop styles.

2. Producing a large body of recordings with many distinctive, **high-quality performances.** His recordings served as textbooks for modern musicians in the way that recordings of Louis Armstrong and Lester Young had served earlier generations.

Recorded November 10, 1972, in Englewood Cliffs, New Jersey, by Michael Brecker (tenor saxophone), Randy Brecker (fluegelhorn), Horace Silver (piano), Bob Cranshaw (bass guitar), and Mickey Roker (drums); composed by Horace Silver; originally released by the Blue Note firm on the Horace Silver album *In Pursuit of the 27th Man*.

Terms to know from tracks on *Demo CD*: double-timing (35), tenor saxophone (73), fluegelhorn (60). This recording was selected to accompany the *Concise Guide to Jazz* for two reasons:

1. It contains Michael Brecker's most talked-about tenor saxophone solo. Since Brecker is discussed in Chapter 11, a particularly well-constructed illustration of his work was sought. The best happened to be this early-period example, rather than anything from his better known pop recordings of later periods. Brecker's solo contains his typically raw, soulful, biting approach. It also features some of his quadruple-timing virtuosity at 1′ 46″ and 2′ 25″. It is drawn from an album that has been a staple in the record collections of modern jazz musicians ever since it first came out, Horace Silver's *In Pursuit of the 27th Man*. The album's quality is consistent from track to track. So if you like this piece, you probably would enjoy others on it, too.

2. It offers a sample of Horace Silver's capacity for establishing and maintaining a catchy groove. This is but one of many Silver recordings that succeed at achieving a cheerful feeling, funky flavor, and remarkable continuity at the same time as outstanding solo improvisations. Though known best for his work during the 1950s and 60s, Silver continued to record and tour with excellent bands as recently as the 1990s. He did not retire until 2003.

   The piece is not unified by any standard bebop or swing rhythm. A Latin American rhythm drives a repeating accompaniment figure by Silver on piano. Together with a highly syncopated bass guitar part and drumming, this piano figure ties together the performance.

   The form of the composition contains an A-section of 16 bars that repeats, followed by a bridge of 8 bars, then a return to the A-section. After the theme is played, each soloist takes an entire chorus. Then the band skips the A-A sequence and jumps to the bridge, followed by one more rendition of the A-section before a tacked-on ending passage, known as a "tag." The melody for the first 4 bars is stated in unison by fluegelhorn and tenor sax. Then a countermelody is played under the fluegelhorn by tenor sax and piano. The three improvisations contrast markedly with each other. Michael Brecker's tenor saxophone solo is very hot and funky. It displays the raw, biting manner that Brecker learned from Junior Walker. This quality made him very much in-demand for pop music in which a soulful jazz solo was sought to spice up the vocal recording. His solo here is bursting with so much energy that many of his ideas are played two times as fast as the tempo of the tune ("double-timing"). Brother Randy Brecker's fluegelhorn solo is mellow like the naturally soft tone of his instrument. (See photo on page 60.) He swings his phrases in a relaxed way. He double-times only during the bridge and final A-section, but never so intensely as Michael.

   Horace Silver's piano solo is extremely economical and logical. In fact, his first line merely restates a brief idea six times, each rendering at a higher pitch. Then he comes back down again. Unlike describing Michael Brecker's attitude here, "unrestrained exuberance" is not the way you would characterize Silver's manner.

TIME ELAPSED

First Chorus (A-A-B-A)

0′ 00″	**A**	fluegelhorn/saxophone unison; piano repeating syncopated chording
0′ 14″		Fluegelhorn continues melody. Saxophone and piano play countermelody.

0' 25"	**A** same as first A-section
0' 49"	**Bridge**
	fluegelhorn/saxophone unison
1' 00"	**A**

Second Chorus (A-A-B-A) **Michael Brecker Tenor Sax Solo**

1' 24"	tenor sax solo
1' 31"	Saxophone improvisation is double-timing.
1' 51"	Saxophone improvisation is double-timing to 1' 57".

2' 10"	**Bridge**
	Saxophone improvises swinging melodic figures.
2' 20"	continues swinging figures
2' 25"	Saxophone improvisation is double-timing to 2' 27".
2' 28"	Saxophone improvises swinging melodic figures.
2' 39"	Saxophone improvises double-timing figures to 2' 43".

Third Chorus (A-A-B-A) **Randy Brecker Fluegelhorn Solo**

2' 44"	Fluegelhorn solo begins relaxed improvisation.
3' 08"	fluegelhorn improvising double-time figures to 3' 11"
3' 15"	fluegelhorn improvising syncopated, swinging, melodic figures

3' 29"	**Bridge**
	fluegelhorn improvising swinging melodic lines in relaxed manner
3' 37"	double-timing

| 3' 41" | **A** |
| 3' 48" | double-timing |

Fourth Chorus (A-A-B-A) **Horace Silver Piano Solo**

| 4' 03" | piano solo |
| | rising figure played six times, each time a higher pitch, then in falling pitches |

| 4' 25" | **A** |
| | single, brief phrase repeated in different pitches |

| 4' 47" | **Bridge** |
| | Piano improvises question and answer. |

| 4' 59" | **A** |
| | Improvised melody line is chorded. |

Out Chorus (B-A + Tag)
Bridge

| 5' 21" | Fluegelhorn/saxophone return. |

| 5' 32" | **A** |
| 5' 55" | Ending |

Recorded in 1958 by Miles Davis (trumpet; no solo), Cannonball Adderley (alto sax), John Coltrane (tenor sax), Red Garland (piano), Paul Chambers (bass), and Philly Joe Jones (drums). From *Milestones* album (Columbia 40837)

The material for this performance was adapted from a composition originally written in the 1940s by pianist John Lewis for the Dizzy Gillespie big band. The title is a play on words. It refers to the presence of two bassists in Gillespie's band as well as baseball terminology. Lewis recorded other versions of this piece under the title "La Ronde."

This recording was selected for several reasons:

1. to demonstrate hard bop drumming as exemplified by Philly Joe Jones, illustrating particularly well his

    a. super-charged, highly interactive manner

    b. crisp use of sticks on snare drum, especially at 4' 32"

    c. melodically conceived fills that are woven into breaks occurring between phrases of theme statements by the horns, especially at 43" to 57"

    d. coordination with accompaniment rhythms of the pianist, especially at 2' 01" and 3' 03"

    e. running commentary on the sax solos (this seems to pop and crackle, thereby increasing the excitement of Coltrane's and Adderley's work)

2. to demonstrate the mid-1950s style of tenor saxophonist John Coltrane, captured in a hard-swinging context. This particular style preceded a string of innovative approaches that Coltrane began developing after this recording session.

3. to demonstrate the alto saxophone style of Cannonball Adderley with one of his best solos on record.

4. to offer a sample of what many musicians consider to be one of the best Miles Davis albums: *Milestones*.

TIME ELAPSED

0' 00"   **Introduction** (32 beats)

   Unison statements by trumpet, alto sax, tenor sax, piano, and bass alternate with drumming statements.

   Melody

0' 07"   *A-section* (4 groups of 4 beats)

   Horns play a phrase, and piano echoes it. Bass is walking.

0' 10"   *A-section repeats with variations*

0' 14"   *B-section* (8 groups of 4 beats)

   Unison statements by trumpet, alto sax, tenor sax, piano, and bass alternate with drums.

0' 21"   *A-section, with variations*

0' 25"   *A-section, with variations*

0' 28"   *C-section* (8 groups of 4 beats)

   Horns and piano play in unison.

0' 36"	*D-section* (8 groups of 4 beats)
	Horns play in unison. Piano accents.
0' 43"	*E-section* (16 groups of 4 beats)
	Horns, piano, and bass play stop-times under drum solo.

John Coltrane Tenor Sax Improvisation

0' 57"	**1st Chorus** (Form Switches to 12-bar blues)
	Accompaniment includes: piano comping, walking bass, high-hat snapping shut sharply on every other beat, "chatter" made by drumsticks striking the snare drum, ride rhythms played by a drumstick striking the ride cymbal.
1' 07"	*2nd Chorus*
1' 18"	*3rd Chorus*
1' 29"	*4th Chorus*
1' 39"	*5th Chorus*
	Piano drops out.
1' 50"	*6th Chorus*
2' 01"	*7th Chorus*
	Piano returns, punctuating in unison with drums.
2' 12"	*8th Chorus*

Cannonball Adderley Alto Sax Improvisation

Notice the new sax's brighter tone quality and higher pitch.

2' 23"	*1st Chorus*
	Accompaniment has piano and drums coordinated to begin this new solo. Walking bass continues.
2' 33"	*2nd Chorus*
2' 43"	*3rd Chorus*
	Piano drops out.
2' 53"	*4th Chorus*
3' 03"	*5th Chorus*
	Piano returns, punctuating in unison with drums.
3' 14"	*6th Chorus*
	Piano plays preset rhythms with drums.
3' 25"	*7th Chorus*
3' 37"	*8th Chorus*
3' 48"	*9th Chorus*
	Piano begins this chorus by playing four strokes in unison with the drummer, then piano stops playing.
3' 59"	*10th Chorus*
4' 10"	*11th Chorus*

Trumpet plays descending scale to accompany sax solo.

4' 22"   *12th Chorus*
Trumpet plays descending scale to accompany sax solo.
Drumming becomes highly active.

4' 32"   **Philly Joe Jones Drum Solo** (32 beats)

4' 39"   **Horns Play Melody**
Horns play a phrase, and piano echoes it (8 bars).
4' 50"   Horns and bass sustain tones while drums continue.

4' 57"   **Drum Solo** (32 beats)

5' 05"   **Horns Return**
Horns play the same note three times in unison.

5' 10"   **End**
Drums and cymbals end the piece.

A written transcription of Coltrane's solo is available from Andrew's Music, 4830 South Dakota Avenue N.E., Washington, D.C. 20017: phone 202-526-3666.

3. Making a **significant change** during the 1960s in his original trumpet style. In the 1980s, this variation became the basis for trumpet styles of Wynton Marsalis, Terence Blanchard, Wallace Roney, Dave Douglas, and others.

4. Being part of the "Birth of the Cool" recording sessions of 1949 and 1950 that combined Claude Thornhill's and Gil Evans' styles of orchestration with the subdued approaches of Gerry Mulligan, Lee Konitz, and himself: **"cool jazz."**

5. Pioneering **"modal jazz"** on the *Kind of Blue* album in 1959.

6. Pioneering the predominant group approaches and individual instrumental **styles of the 1980s and 1990s** (such as Marsalis and Wallace Roney) with his quintet of 1965–68.

7. Pioneering **jazz-rock fusion** styles with an original mixture of elements from "modal jazz," rock, and funk music on his *Bitches Brew* album of 1969.

Miles Davis did not invent entire jazz idioms himself. He organized bands of key innovators at early moments in the development of bop, cool jazz, modal jazz, and jazz-rock fusion. Davis' musicians often produced the best work of their careers while in his bands. They speak highly about his help in their own development and his wise editing of their music. There is a feeling of intelligent, well-measured musical creation in most Davis recordings.

THE CLASSIC MILES DAVIS QUINTET

Miles Davis made many of his historically significant recordings as a bandleader for the Prestige record company. Musicians tend to prefer *Steamin'*, *Cookin'*, *Workin'*, and *Relaxin'*, all recorded in 1956 with tenor saxophonist John Coltrane, pianist Red Garland, bassist Paul Chambers, and drummer "Philly Joe" Jones. The style and energy of those recording sessions were particularly evident again in *Milestones*, an album he made for Columbia record company in 1958, with the same musicians plus alto saxophonist Cannonball Adderley (see previous page).

Though Miles Davis had long been linked with cool jazz, the band on these recordings sounds more like hard bop and later styles. The musicians play with blistering intensity. Their work has an unusual freshness and excitement that combined to make these among the most striking jazz performances since the groundbreaking Parker-Gillespie records of the previous decade.

These recordings signaled the first time that many jazz fans heard John Coltrane's tenor saxophone. His work with Davis was so original that he would still qualify as a jazz giant if he had never done anything else. Still, some journalists considered these early recordings to be merely a development stage for Coltrane.

The classic quintet, with the addition of Cannonball Adderley, was responsible for a landmark event in jazz history. With their recording of the tune "Milestones" in 1958, they broke away from the practice of guiding improvisations solely by chord progressions. Most of the tunes Davis had recorded before 1958 were pop tunes or bebop compositions with frequently changing chords in their accompaniment. But instead of using frequently changing chords to guide their improvisations on "Milestones," the musicians used different scales. The first was in effect for 64 beats, the

Cannonball Adderley (alto sax), Paul Chambers (bass), Miles Davis (trumpet), and John Coltrane (tenor sax). Each man was a modern jazz giant on his respective instrument, and all were present on the historic *Milestones* and *Kind of Blue* recording sessions. Pictured here at the 1958 Newport Jazz Festival.

Photo courtesy of Frank Driggs

second for another 64 beats, followed by a return to the first for the final 32 beats. Basing a tune on scales allowed improvisers new types of freedom. They had fewer demands placed on their attention, so they could more easily concentrate on piecing together interesting melodies and rhythms. After the *Milestones* album (containing "Milestones") was released, this approach—the absence of changing chords—became popular among modern jazz musicians. This trend became especially popular following the release of Davis' very modal album *Kind of Blue,* recorded in 1959.

THE MILES DAVIS TRUMPET STYLE

Miles Davis created an unmistakable sound with his trumpet. It is so distinctive that we can instantly pick it out, even in the crowded mix of a rock record or the background music for a movie. He was such a uniquely creative thinker that he altered what listeners came to expect from jazz trumpet. His personal sound seems almost independent of the instrument. It is so much his own that to call it "Miles Davis" might be more accurate than to call it "jazz trumpet."

The uniqueness of the Davis style can be divided into at least seven components. The first two are manners of handling the trumpet sound. The most obvious is his expressively toying with pitch and tone quality at the beginnings and ends of notes.

A second component of Davis' highly personal style comes from using a Harmon mute. This resulted in a wispy sound that is delicate and intimate. He used this mute much more than other trumpeters used it. (See the illustrations below and on page 282.)

Demo CD Track 65 and Jazz Classics CD2 Track 2

Listen on **mysearchlab.com**
Listen to Harmon-muted trumpet on mysearchlab.com

Photo by William E. (Bill) Smith

▶ Miles Davis playing trumpet with Harmon mute. The sound that Davis produced when playing into this mute was so personal he might as well have patented it.

A third component of the Davis style is an unusually skillful timing and dramatic construction of melodic figures. Davis was a master of self-restraint. His placement of silence is at least as significant as his choice of notes, and he often let several beats pass without playing. (Listen to *Jazz Classics CD2* Track 9.) During the moments he was not sounding his own notes, the sound of bass, drums, and piano came through clearly, further establishing the mood. The success of this very lean approach depends on the steadiness of swing feeling and overall musicality of the rhythm section. The silences in his own solos were filled in a highly musical, well-paced manner because Davis always hired the best accompanists.

More than most improvisers, Davis gave the impression that he was editing his solos very carefully while performing them, clarifying his ideas in his mind before letting them go through his horn. As Lester Young did on the tenor saxophone, Davis pared his thinking down to a bare core of melodic material; and like Young's solos, the best Davis improvisations seem to "tell a story."

A fourth component of the Davis style can be identified by comparing rhythmic concepts. Most modern trumpeters play swinging lines staying close to a strict tempo and swing feeling, even when they play slow tunes. These players practice a very precise subdivision of each beat. Miles Davis, on the other hand, not only improvised swinging melodic figures, but he also sometimes played outside of strict tempo and away from the swing feeling. This introduced a further element of rhythmic freedom.

A fifth component is an acute sensitivity in paraphrasing. The Davis paraphrases of popular songs were constructed in such fresh ways that the finished products were like new melodies.

A sixth component is Davis' simplicity. He could play with bebop-style complexity. But, instead, he often constructed solos of brief, simple phrases. Many of his improvisations on blues and slow pieces consist of only a few notes. These notes were chosen and timed so well and played so expressively that the effect is dramatic.

A seventh component is his handling of tone quality and pitch range. During the 1940s and 50s, Davis played with a tone quality that was lighter, softer, and less brassy than that of most other trumpeters. He used almost no vibrato; he favored the trumpet's middle register over its flashier high register; and he rarely double-timed. His style was gentle by comparison with the styles of most other modern trumpeters.

CLIFFORD BROWN

The modern styles of trumpet playing began in the 1940s with Dizzy Gillespie, who influenced Miles Davis and Fats Navarro. However, it was the successor to these men who had the greatest impact on hard bop. His name was Clifford Brown (1930–1956), and he drew his style largely from Navarro. Among musicians, Brown is probably the most widely admired trumpeter since the swing era. However he is not widely known outside the inner circles of modern jazz musicians, and he recorded only from 1952 to 56.

((•— **Listen** on **mysearchlab.com**
Listen to Miles Davis' mid-1960s trumpet style on mysearchlab.com

((•— **Listen** on **mysearchlab.com**
Listen to Clifford Brown's trumpet style on mysearchlab.com

LISTENING GUIDE

"Blue in Green" featuring Miles Davis and Bill Evans

((•-Listen on mysearchlab.com

Composed by Bill Evans, though often mistakenly credited to Miles Davis; recorded in 1959 by Miles Davis (Harmon-muted trumpet), John Coltrane (tenor sax), Bill Evans (piano), Paul Chambers (bass), and Jimmy Cobb (drums); originally released on *Kind of Blue* (Columbia PC 8163)

This selection demonstrates

1. the chord voicing and ballad style of pianist Bill Evans

2. the unique tone qualities and musical character achieved by trumpeter Miles Davis playing through a Harmon mute

3. the very personal manner that Miles Davis originated for playing slow pieces and generating calm, reflective moods

4. the unique touch that tenor saxophonist John Coltrane used for treating slow, meditative pieces

5. a sample of *Kind of Blue*, the album that is most frequently cited by jazz musicians and critics in lists of all-time favorites.

TIME ELAPSED

Introduction

0' 00"   Bill Evans plays gently on piano, accompanied by the bassist sounding one note on each chord. Each chord lasts 2 beats.

0' 17"   **First Chorus**

Miles Davis plays the melody on Harmon-muted trumpet. The harmonic pace shifts to one chord for every 4 beats. Davis' manner is very relaxed, almost lagging behind the beat on purpose. The drummer is dragging wire brushes around the surface of the snare drum (achieving an almost continuous "shhhhhhss" effect).

1' 00"   **Second Chorus**

Davis takes more liberties with the melody. Bass improvises counterlines.

1' 43"   **Third Chorus**

Improvised piano solo by Bill Evans. He doubles the harmonic pace so that each chord lasts for 2 beats.

2' 04"   **Fourth Chorus**

Piano solo continues.

Brown used a wider, more deliberate vibrato than either Gillespie or Davis. Brown's slow vibrato may be responsible for its renewed use by jazz trumpeters in the 1950s and 60s. Another distinguishing mark of Brown's style is the overall contour of his solos. Brown tended to jump into the high register less often than Gillespie. The contours of Brown's lines are also usually smoother than Gillespie's, and he did not tend to make as many peculiar note choices as Gillespie. His improvisations were more melodic and pretty.

2' 25" **Fifth Chorus**

John Coltrane tenor sax improvisation. He begins in the high register and plays a solo that uses very few notes. This is one of the most elegant Coltrane improvisations on record.

2' 47" **Sixth Chorus**

Sax solo continues.

3' 07" **Seventh Chorus**

New piano solo by Evans. Original melody is played almost verbatim. But the pace has doubled so each chord lasts only one beat.

3' 17" **Eighth Chorus**

Piano solo continues with Evans improvising upon the melody.

3' 27" **Ninth Chorus**

Improvised trumpet solo, with the pace of chord movement so slow that each chord lasts 4 beats.

4' 09" **Tenth Chorus**

Davis continues soloing, and Evans punctuates and complements the solo with improvised piano chords. Bass plays only a few notes instead of a regular pattern.

4' 49" **Eleventh Chorus**

Evans plays the melody on piano at four times the pace of the preceding chorus; that is, each chord lasts one beat.

4' 54"   Drummer rubs his brushes on the snare drum then drops out. Bass drops out.

5' 01"   Bass returns, now bowing instead of plucking his strings.

5' 04" **Twelfth Chorus**

5' 16" **Conclusion**

Bowed bass concludes Evans' phrase.

A written transcription of Coltrane's solo is available from Andrew's Music, 4830 South Dakota Avenue N.E., Washington, D.C. 20017; phone 202-526-3666. Transcriptions of all solos on the *Kind of Blue* album are available from Hal Leonard Publications, *www.halleonard.com*.

Let's consider several reasons why musicians were so impressed with Clifford Brown's playing. Most important was that Brown managed to convey relaxation in his playing, even when playing complicated melodic figures. This has at least two possible causes: his masterful control over the trumpet and his attempt to refine bebop instead of blazing new trails as Parker and Gillespie had. Brown also preferred to swing rather than to try to throw off his listeners with surprise after surprise, as bebop soloists often did. Brown developed a repertory of his own phrases that led him

Recorded June 22, 1953, in New York by Clifford Brown (trumpet), J. J. Johnson (trombone), Jimmy Heath (tenor saxophone), John Lewis (piano), Percy Heath (bass), and Kenny Clarke (drums); composed by Harold Arlen; issued by Blue Note Records several times, recently on the album *The Eminent J. J. Johnson, Vol. 1.*

Clifford Brown was the most influential hard bop trumpeter and extended the tradition of Fats Navarro, heard on Dexter Gordon's "Index," on *Jazz Classics CD1.* This is one of Brown's earliest and most impressive recordings. He uses more notes per phrase than anyone else at this session. With his pretty tone, Brown swings gracefully and articulates with a bounce and evenness that distinguished him from all other bebop trumpeters.

J. J. Johnson was the most influential modern trombonist, and his playing on this piece is typical of the high standards he set for his own musicianship. His improvisation here is extremely concise, well organized, filled with tuneful ideas.

Tenor saxophonist Jimmy Heath has always been an outstanding, though neglected, figure in modern jazz. He emerged from the Philadelphia jazz scene of the 1940s at the same time as John Coltrane. Both men played in the big band of Dizzy Gillespie and the combos of Miles Davis. Both also contributed compositions that were played by hundreds of musicians during the 1960s and 70s. Heath was still touring and recording with his own band in 2012. On "Get Happy," he takes one of his typically robust and well-developed solos. It is hard swinging and packed with crystal clear, bebop phrases. Beginning at 2′ 13″, he outlines the chord progression of the tune's bridge by playing the same idea six times, transposed accordingly for each chord. Then at 2′ 20″, he fills the final A-section by quoting the pop song "And the Angels Sing."

The rhythm section here is the Modern Jazz Quartet minus vibraphonist Milt Jackson. Pianist John Lewis was one of the top composers in modern jazz and a very thoughtful improviser. His playing is also available on *Jazz Classics CD1* in Charlie Parker's "Parker's Mood." Kenny Clarke is often considered the first bebop drummer. We hear his crackling fills on snare drum throughout the piece, a solo on the bridge of the final chorus, and a tie-it-up figure to conclude the performance.

Though hard bop musicians were distinguished for writing their own original compositions instead of relying on pop tunes, this arrangement of Harold Arlen's "Get Happy" sounds so firmly in the hard bop style that it might as well have been written by one of the musicians here. (See the description of its form in the listening guide for Bud Powell's rendition on page 110 of the bebop chapter.)

gracefully through the chord progressions. These techniques, his fluid manner, and easy swing feeling influenced numerous other trumpeters. Brown's contributions then became a stock vocabulary for other hard bop players.

Clifford Brown's music projected a joyful spirit. This, together with the lilt and bounce in his lines, was contagious. He could generate long,

0' 00" **Introduction**
       Piano plays quick bebop line.

       First Chorus
0' 04"   melody played by horns in harmony, with snare drum filling pauses

       Second Chorus
0' 33"   J. J. Johnson trombone solo
       piano comping, walking bass, ride rhythms on ride cymbal, kicks on snare drum

       Third Chorus
1' 01"   Trombone solo continues.

       Fourth Chorus
1' 30"   Jimmy Heath tenor saxophone solo

       Fifth Chorus
1' 58"   Tenor sax solo continues.

       Sixth Chorus
2' 27"   Clifford Brown trumpet solo

       Seventh Chorus
2' 54"   Trumpet solo continues.

       Eighth Chorus
3' 23"   piano solo by John Lewis

       Ninth Chorus
3' 51"   Piano solo continues.

       Tenth Chorus
4' 19"   Melody (A-A')
       Horns state theme in harmony.
4' 33"   Bridge
       Kenny Clarke drum solo
4' 40"   Final A-section
       Full band returns.
4' 46"   sustained chord from horns
4' 48"   Drums play a tie-it-up figure.

flowing lines at furious tempos and still maintain the warmth and ease of his wide, glowing tone. Most other trumpeters were amazed at Brown's dazzling speed and agility. Also, he did what is almost impossible at those frantic speeds: he kept very accurate pitch, what musicians call "playing in tune." He also kept his swing feeling relaxed. His firm command of accurate articulation was unparalleled in modern jazz. The result was

▶ Clifford Brown, the favorite trumpeter for most jazz musicians of the 1950s. An exceptionally melodic improviser, Brown had a pretty tone and unprecedented playing speed and agility. Shown here with saxophonist Lou Donaldson.

Photo courtesy of Metronome/Archive Photos/Getty Images.

that meaty phrases came tumbling from his horn, chorus after chorus after chorus. This happy feeling, along with his pretty sound and fertile imagination, strongly influenced an entire generation of modern trumpeters.

FREDDIE HUBBARD

Miles Davis and Clifford Brown remained models for aspiring trumpeters to imitate long after they first became known among musicians. But by the

▶ Freddie Hubbard, the most imitated trumpeter of the 1970s. He followed Miles Davis and Clifford Brown by devising an original style that was compatible with hard bop and jazz-rock.

Photo courtesy of Frank Driggs

1970s, the majority of young trumpeters were imitating another model: Freddie Hubbard. Though his early playing drew from Clifford Brown and Miles Davis, Hubbard (b. 1938) had developed his own original approach by the early 1960s. His playing style departed from bebop and was compatible with "free jazz" approaches of the 1960s and "jazz-rock" approaches of the 1970s.

A number of characteristics can help us distinguish Hubbard from Brown and Davis. Although he incorporated some Davis techniques of altering his tone quality and pitch, Hubbard refused to stray from the beat the way Davis liked to. Instead, Hubbard stuck close to the beat and liked to double-time. Also, in contrast to the more solemn and methodical manner of Davis, much of Hubbard's work sounds offhanded and playful. There is a looseness to his approach that implies great creative freedom and flexibility. Instead of following through on every idea, he does not hesitate to interrupt himself to pursue a new one. His style bristles with excitement; even his ballad renditions reveal great verve. Like saxophonist John Coltrane, he avoids stock bebop phrases. Instead he will spontaneously construct and rework figures from odd combinations of notes and rhythms. In this way he was daring and impulsive. The richness and range of his imagination combined with his free manner to build a new vocabulary for jazz trumpet style.

Freddie Hubbard is almost universally envied among trumpeters for his outstanding mastery of the instrument. His tone is clear and well focused. His intonation is excellent. His articulation is crisp. He can improvise coherently at brisk tempos and sound as though he still has plenty of strength and agility in reserve. Like Brown's, Hubbard's sense of time is very precise.

CANNONBALL ADDERLEY

Cannonball Adderley (1928–1975) was one of the best improvisers to play alto saxophone after Charlie Parker died. In a few respects, Adderley's style is like Parker's: very flowing, supercharged with energy, and unpredictable. But Adderley's first inspiration was not Parker but the swing era styles of Pete Brown and Benny Carter.

Cannonball Adderley's tone quality on the alto saxophone was so deep and full that listeners sometimes mistook it for a tenor saxophone. Together with the vibrato Adderley used, the effect of his tone was warm and glowing. He colored this huge tone with blue notes and wails. The result was an earthy, legato style that has been called "blues drenched." In contrast to the serious urgency of most hard bop, Adderley's playing suggests fun. He loved to double-time, and he often put snippets of pop tunes into his improvised lines. Often he dug into an improvisation and spun inspired lines, with a dense rush of activity and zigzagging directions (*Jazz Classics CD1* Track 23). But Adderley was not always bouncy and lighthearted. He could also be calm and meditative. For instance, his solos on the Davis

((•– Listen on **mysearchlab.com**

Listen to Cannonball Adderley's saxophone style on mysearchlab.com

Photo by Jan Persson Archives/Redferns, courtesy of Getty Images

◀ Cannonball Adderley, hard bop alto saxophonist-bandleader-composer. One of the top improvisers in the 1950s and 60s, Adderley also became an important figure in funky jazz. The bands he co-led with his brother Nat Adderley (also pictured here) had a number of hit records that helped define the bluesy, soulful, gospelish approach.

album *Kind of Blue* sound very reflective. They are among the most original improvisations he recorded.

On and off during the 1950s, 60s, and 70s, Cannonball Adderley co-led a series of bands with his brother, cornetist Nat Adderley. The groups enjoyed a large following and continued until Cannonball's death in 1975. Many pieces in the band's repertory were categorized "funky jazz": "Jive Samba," "Work Song," "Sack o' Woe," "Walk Tall," "Country Preacher," and their biggest hit, "Mercy, Mercy, Mercy." Though most of its repertory was swinging music in the bebop style, the group was best known for its funk hits. These tunes, their style and feeling, anticipated jazz-rock fusion.

SONNY ROLLINS

There were many excellent tenor saxophonists who played hard bop. Although an entire book could be written about them, we will consider two stand-outs—John Coltrane and Sonny Rollins. Coltrane created an original hard bop style that was documented in recordings he made in the 1950s while with the combo of Miles Davis. Rollins had his creative peak during the 1950s and remains the favorite jazz tenor of many musicians.

Sonny Rollins (b. 1930) began recording in 1949 and was second only to Stan Getz as the most popular tenor saxophonist of the 1950s. Though he is known today for his originality, Rollins was among the first group of musicians to use Charlie Parker's alto sax style on tenor saxophone. His name is often mentioned along with Charlie Parker and John Coltrane when saxophonists themselves list their favorites.

People admired Rollins for the way he started with simple melodic ideas and then developed them. In this way he produced solos that drew a listener in and told a musical story. He has such a powerful musical mind that he avoids musical clichés, even at high speeds. When playing fast,

Photo by Chuck Stewart

◄ Clifford Brown (left) and Sonny Rollins (right), the top hornmen in hard bop of the 1950s.

most jazz musicians tend to use easily fingered patterns instead of original melodic ideas. Not Rollins.

During the 1950s, the Rollins tone quality was hard, rough, and dry. Some listeners called it "brittle." His vibrato was slow and very deliberate. While most bebop tenor saxophonists used a smooth *legato* style phrasing, Rollins frequently used a choppy *staccato* style phrasing. Often he would attack bluntly, move to legato and back again to staccato. He delivered his phrases without ornamentation or any other kind of softening. The over-all effect of his playing was brusque and aggressive, though not necessarily explosive or blistering.

Sonny Rollins is a giant in the history of improvisers. He mastered the rhythmic devices necessary to swing, and he swung whenever he wished. But he also purposely deviated from the tempo at times, as if he were inside the beat one moment and ignoring it the next. Rollins treated a piece as though its tempo, chord progressions, and melody were mere toys to be played with. He redesigned them from moment to moment without necessarily respecting their original flavor.

Some listeners feel that Rollins' career reached its peak during the 1950s. They feel he did his most lyrical playing with Miles Davis and his most swinging playing with Clifford Brown. There is no question that his recordings in the 1950s stand as landmarks in the history of tenor saxophone style.

During the 1960s, Rollins streamlined his style and explored less conventional approaches to improvisation. During the 1970s and 80s, Rollins played in ways that differed significantly from his style of the 1950s and 60s. He adopted a sound that was broader, coarser, and more guttural. In addition, he played with less speed and crispness. In contrast to his earlier style, his playing became simpler and funkier. Rollins kept the singing quality in his playing, but now his roots in Charlie Parker were barely detectable.

The tunes he performed in the 1970s and 80s were simpler, too, and their accompaniments sounded like disco, funk, and Latin American dance styles. Although Rollins occasionally returned to more bebop-like playing, he now preferred to play in his new style. In fact, it was so gutsy and so much like popular music that it fit perfectly with the style of the Rolling Stones. That popular blues-oriented rock and roll group used him on one of their recordings. So twenty years after being the top hard bop tenor player, Sonny Rollins had mastered a new style, gained a broader audience, and is still going strong.

JOHN COLTRANE

John Coltrane (1926–1967) is among the ten most important figures in jazz history. He had profound impact as a tenor and soprano saxophonist, composer, and bandleader. Hundreds of Coltrane imitators could be found among saxophonists of the 1960s, 70s, 80s, and 90s. His improvisational concepts and compositions were used not only by saxophonists but also by pianists, trumpeters, and guitarists. The combo sound that his quartet perfected became a major force during the few years the quartet toured, and it has remained an influential model ever since the group disbanded. The immense force of Coltrane's music has inspired poetry, sculpture, and modern dance. Even a church was founded in Coltrane's name.

▶ John Coltrane, the most influential saxophonist since Charlie Parker.

Photo courtesy Michael Ochs Archive/Getty Images

Coltrane had developed a very individual style by 1955, when he first recorded with Miles Davis. By then, his roots were far less evident than his own fresh ideas. His approach was unusually vigorous. His tone was rough-textured and biting, huge and dark. Coltrane gave it a massive core and a searing intensity. It was full and penetrating in every register, from the lowest notes to the highest. He played with remarkable speed and agility, possibly as much as any other saxophonist in jazz history. Coltrane's impressive command over the tenor saxophone inspired hundreds of other saxophonists to work very hard on instrumental proficiency. Like Charlie Parker before him, Coltrane stimulated a taste for rapid, densely packed solo improvisations among young players.

Coltrane's pre-1960s playing showed a fascination for chord changes. His system involved putting chords together that sounded odd next to each other. Then, when he improvised solos, Coltrane devoured the chord changes. He tried to play every note in every chord and every scale that might be compatible with it. This was a historically significant contribution to the evolution of jazz styles. Journalist Ira Gitler described Coltrane's furiously paced streams of notes as "sheets of sound" (*Jazz Classics CD1* Track 23).

((•–[Listen on mysearchlab.com

Listen to John Coltrane's hard bop saxophone style on mysearchlab.com

The classic example of Coltrane's rapid playing over frequently changing chords was the title track on his *Giant Steps* album, recorded in 1959. Chords in it seldom last more than two fleeting beats, and each chord stakes out new territory. Coltrane originally wrote "Giant Steps" as an exercise to gain mastery over a difficult and unconventional situation for an improviser.

Coltrane exerted a striking effect on his listeners. People who hated his music argued in print with those who were impressed by it. Some felt that jazz history ended with Coltrane, whereas today many feel it only just started with him. So many saxophonists in the 1970s and 80s were imitating him that journalists of this period were complaining about a general lack of originality just as they had done with the wave of Charlie Parker followers that rose during the 1950s. Saxophonist Andrew White was so inspired by Coltrane's music that he listened very carefully to more than seven hundred recorded Coltrane solos and wrote down every note in each one.

Each of Coltrane's style periods caused many musicians to try out the techniques that Coltrane had used. First it was multi-noted playing and difficult chord progressions. Coltrane's way of replacing the chord changes from standard tunes was widely imitated. Musicians wrote tunes in which chords moved in ways similar to Coltrane's. Then it was modal style, as discussed in the next chapter. After that, it was simultaneous collective improvisation and the creation of frantic turbulence that emphasized textures more than the development of melody-like lines. Sometimes it appeared as though an entire community of jazz musicians had decided that Coltrane was their guide, and they waited to see what he was going to do next before they acted on their own. Even important musicians who were already known for considerable originality felt the impact of Coltrane's work.

Recorded January 26, 1960, in New York by Wes Montgomery (guitar), Tommy Flanagan (piano), Percy Heath (bass), and Albert Heath (drums); composed by Wes Montgomery; originally released by the Riverside firm on the album The Incredible Jazz Guitar of Wes Montgomery.

Terms to know from tracks on the *Demo CD*: octave-voiced piano lines (41), guitar in octaves (87), guitar plucked with thumb (86), double-time (35), staccato (45), syncopation (20), high-hat (2), piano comping (20), guitar comping (89).

The song form is 32-bar A-A-B-A. After the improvised solos at 3' 53", however, the band skips the A-A sequence and returns to the bridge. Then they play a final A-section at 4' 07" before repeating one chord again and again to a fade-out.

The opening theme is stated in unison by octave-voiced guitar, bass, and piano. The drummer does not enter until 0' 08". Piano echoes the opening phrase, accompanied by guitar playing chords in a staccato manner with syncopated rhythms from 0' 09" to 0' 13".

Montgomery's solo is played by plucking the strings of his guitar with his thumb instead of using a pick. The result is a soft, round tone quality. Sometimes he plays his lines 2 notes at a time, separated by the interval of an octave. This is the way he makes his melody statement during the first nine seconds of "Mr. Walker." This technique adds body to the sound. Though he was not the first to do it, he is the guitarist best known for such octave voicing. Additionally, he created a sensual effect in part by prefacing his main notes with a slide up from a slightly lower pitch. This is called using "grace notes" because the lower pitches "grace" the main notes. By combining his soft, round tone, octave voicing, grace notes, and a gentle manner, Montgomery achieved a warm effect in his guitar playing.

Montgomery opens his solo improvisation at 0' 58" with a very melodic figure and follows with simple ideas comprised of quarter notes and eighth notes. Some of his phrases amount to improvised melodies. They are so catchy they almost sound familiar, and if they don't, they soon will. They might stay with you all day. It sounds like the band is having a good time, smiling through their music. After this string of ideas, Montgomery moves to double-timing the rest of them. It is as though he has so much creative energy that he must go twice as fast to get it all out.

Montgomery sometimes harmonizes his line and executes it in staccato manner with crisp syncopations, as in his second chorus, beginning at 1' 56". On the bridge of his second solo chorus, 2' 25" to 2' 46", Montgomery improvises his melodic line at the same time as he harmonizes it by complete chords. The highest pitch of each chord carries the melody.

Montgomery's sense of melodic pacing and swing feeling is unsurpassed. The development of a solo is Montgomery's forte. For instance, in the second A-section, at about 1' 27" to about 1' 35", he plays the same phrase three times, as though to develop the plot of the "story" he is telling, before going on to making his next point.

Montgomery had a knack for establishing a groove, then creating swinging improvisations that never disturbed it. On "Mr. Walker," his accompanists are also impeccable in following that example. A relaxed, earthy feeling is conveyed, and such an effect typifies a "soft," "smooth" branch of hard bop.

The rhythmic style of the performance here is a cross between hard bop and Latin American pop music. Through much of the piece, the drummer is striking his closed high-hat in a rhythm of steadily repeating eighth notes (twice on every beat as "ding, ding, ding, ding") instead of the bebop practice of striking the ride cymbal and using a "ching chick a ching chick a ching" rhythm.

Time Elapsed

Theme Statement

First Chorus (A-A-B-A)

0'00"	**A**	octave-voiced guitar and bass
0' 08"		Drummer enters. Piano echoes guitar phrase.
0' 09"		Guitar accompanies piano crisply with syncopated chords.
0' 15"	**A**	
0' 30"	**Bridge**	(New Theme Played by Guitar, Piano and Bass)
0' 41"		Drummer reinforces melodic rhythms on tom-tom and snare drum.
0' 43"	**A**	

Guitar Solo

Second Chorus (A-A-B-A)

0' 58"	**A**	Montgomery improvises a guitar solo.
1' 10"		Montgomery starts double-timing.
1' 12"	**A**	
1' 23"		Montgomery stops double-timing and forms very melodic lines.
1' 27"	**Bridge**	
		Montgomery continues inventing clear, melodic lines.
1' 41"	**A**	
		Montgomery returns to double-timing.

Third Chorus (A-A-B-A)

1' 56"	**A**	chorded solo, very syncopated, staccato guitar playing
2' 11"	**A**	
2' 25"	**Bridge**	
		harmonized solo line, lots of grace notes
2' 40"	**A**	
		harmonized solo line
2' 47"		chromatic chord progression like the James Bond Theme

Piano Solo

Fourth Chorus (A-A-B-A)

2' 54"	**A**	Improvised piano line begins, voiced in octaves, then moves to single-note-at-a-time manner.
3' 05"		octave-voiced piano lines
3' 09"	**A**	
3' 11"		single-note lines

| 3' 24" | **Bridge** |
| 3' 38" | **A** |

Ending Theme Statement

Fifth Half Chorus (B-A)

3' 53"	Bridge (Theme Statement by Piano, Guitar and Bass)
4' 07"	Final A-section (Theme Statement by Octave-Voiced Guitar and Bass)
4' 16"	Guitar gives syncopated, staccato repeating of same chord while piano improvises lines voiced in octaves.
4' 22"	Measures 9, 10, and 11 fade out as piano improvises.

WES MONTGOMERY

Wes Montgomery (1925–1968) was the most influential guitarist in modern jazz. Not only did he invent a graceful style inspired by bebop horn lines, but he also refined it with such flair that his work became the model for George Benson and numerous guitarists who rose to prominence during the 1970s. Those he influenced have been heard on "smooth jazz" radio broadcasts ever since the 1980s.

((•–[Listen on **mysearchlab.com**
Listen to guitar played in octaves by Wes Montgomery on mysearchlab.com

▶ Wes Montgomery, the most influential guitarist in modern jazz. He specialized in voicing his lines in octaves. Using a soft, smooth sound, he invented well-paced solos that were crisply swinging and very melodic.

Photo by Chuck Stewart

THE POPULARITY OF HARD BOP

Like bebop musicians, hard bop musicians found that the public tended to neglect their music. Only a few managed to make steady livelihoods from performing jazz. The historically significant bands of Clifford Brown were unknown except to musicians and a small population of fans. During the 1950s, Sonny Rollins and John Coltrane were well known by jazz fans but almost unknown otherwise. The few hard bop pieces that found their way onto jukeboxes were mostly simple, funky compositions arranged with lots of very repetitive accompaniment rhythms and less improvisation than was found in most hard bop performances. Some of these accounted for brief periods of success enjoyed by Cannonball Adderley and Horace Silver, especially during the 1960s and 70s. But the highest record sales went to the organ-guitar-drums groups of Jimmy Smith and the piano-bass-drums group of Ramsey Lewis. These are groups whose music is much simpler and helps define funky jazz. Musicians and critics do not ordinarily consider their music to be as serious as that of the other players we have discussed.

SUMMARY

1. Hard bop evolved directly from bebop during the 1950s, mainly among East Coast and Midwest musicians.

2. When hard bop differs from bebop, it is simpler; has more variety in accompaniment patterns; fewer pop tune chord progressions; darker, weightier tone qualities; and more emphasis on hard swinging.

3. Funky jazz is a subcategory of hard bop. It is characterized by bluesy inflections of pitch and gospel-type harmonies. Several pieces performed by the bands of Horace Silver and Cannonball Adderley were popular because of their funky qualities and simple, catchy melodies.

4. The most prominent figures in hard bop were drummer-bandleader Art Blakey; pianist-composer Horace Silver; trumpeters Clifford Brown, Miles Davis, and Freddie Hubbard; alto saxophonist-bandleader Cannonball Adderley; and tenor saxophonists Sonny Rollins and John Coltrane.

5. Miles Davis was a pivotal bandleader in bebop, cool jazz, modal jazz, and jazz-rock fusion. His trumpet style is very distinctive in many ways that are widely admired.

6. John Coltrane was the most influential saxophonist in jazz after Charlie Parker. He was also important for several styles of composing.

FURTHER RESOURCES

✓●—[Study and **Review** on **mysearchlab.com**

Test your knowledge with the chapter quiz.

VIEW

The Prentice Hall Jazz History DVD (ISBN 0-13-602643-5)
features "So What" performed by Miles Davis and John Coltrane and "Directions" performed by the Miles Davis Quintet from 1968 (featuring Chick Corea, Dave Holland, Wayne Shorter, and Tony Williams).

Horace Silver: Live at the Umbria Jazz Festival. Arthaus Musik, c 2009. Recorded live in Europe in 1976.

Jazz Casual—Cannonball Adderley and The Modern Jazz Quartet. Idem Home Video. 50s-era TV clips.

John Coltrane Live in' 60,' 61 & '65. Jazz Icons. Live footage featuring Coltrane with Miles Davis Quintet (1960) and as a group leader.

The World According to John Coltrane. Medici/Euroarts, c 2010. Documentary from 1993.

Saxophone Colossus: Sonny Rollins. Acorn Media, c 2008. Documentary film featuring 2 concerts from 1995.

Wes Montgomery Live in'65. Jazz Icons. Three European TV shows filmed "live" in the studio.

Cannonball Adderley: Live in '63. Jazz Icons, c 2008. Sextet in Germany and Switzerland with Nat Adderley, Yusef Lateef, Joe Zawinul, Sam Jones, and Louis Hayes.

Art Blakey & the Jazz Messengers: Live in '58. Jazz Icons, c 2006. Quintet in Belgium with Lee Morgan, Benny Golson, Bobby Timmons, and Jymmie Meritt.

Art Blakey Jazz Messengers: Live in France 1959. Jazz Icons, c 2011. Quintet with Lee Morgan, Wayne Shorter, Walter Davis, and Jymie Merritt.

Freddie Hubbard: Live in France 1973. Jazz Icons, c 2011. With Junior Cook, George Cables.

Sonny Rollins: Live in '65 & '68. Jazz Icons, c 2008. Trio and quartet in Denmark.

John Coltrane: Live in France 1965. Jazz Icons, c 2011. Quartet with Tyner, Garrison, and Jones.

LISTEN

Smithsonian Collection of Classic Jazz has renditions of "Pent-Up House" by Sonny Rollins and Clifford Brown, "Blue Seven" by Sonny Rollins, and "So What" by Miles Davis, John Coltrane, and Cannonball Adderley.

Cannonball Adderley—*Quintet in Chicago* with John Coltrane (Mercury 559770, 1959) and *Mercy, Mercy, Mercy* (Capitol 29915, 1966)

The *Jazz Classics Compact Discs* for *Jazz Styles: History and Analysis* (ISBN 0-205-03686-4) phone 800–947–7700) contain the 1959 recording of "Flamenco Sketches" by Miles Davis, John Coltrane, Cannonball Adderley, and Bill Evans; 1967 recording of "Masqualero" by Miles Davis, Wayne Shorter, and Herbie Hancock; 1964 "Maiden Voyage" by Herbie Hancock and Freddie Hubbard; 1957 "Cranky Spanky" by Art Blakey; and 1956 "Señor Blues" by Horace Silver.

Freddie Hubbard is well represented on Herbie Hancock's albums *Empyrean Isles* (Blue Note 98796, from 1964) and *Maiden Voyage* (Blue Note 95331, from 1965).

Horace Silver is well represented by his own albums *Horace-Scope* (Blue Note 84042, from 1960) and *Cape Verdean Blues* (Blue Note 90839, from 1965).

Art Blakey recordings that typify his hard bop bands include: *A Night at Birdland* (Blue Note 32146/7, from 1954) and *Mosaic* (Blue Note 46523, from 1961).

Sonny Rollins and Clifford Brown recorded some of their best work on *Sonny Rollins Plus Four* (Prestige 30159, from 1956).

READ

Alkyer, Frank. 2007. *The Miles Davis Reader: Interviews and Features from Down Beat Magazine.* New York: Hal Leonard.

Blancq, Charles. 1983. *Sonny Rollins, the Journey of a Jazzman.* Boston: Twayne.

Blumenthal, Bob. 2010. *Saxophone Colossus: A Portrait of Sonny Rollins.* New York: Abrams.

Carr, Ian. 1999. *Miles Davis: The Definitive Biography.* New York: Thunder's Mouth.

Catalano, Nick. 2000. *Clifford Brown: The Life and Art of the Legendary Jazz Trumpeter.* New York: Oxford University Press.

Chambers, Jack. 1998. *Milestones* (biography of Miles Davis). New York: Da Capo.

Cook, Richard. 2007. *It's About That Time: Miles Davis On and Off Record.* New York: Oxford University Press.

Davis, Miles. 1989. *Miles Davis: The Autobiography.* New York: Simon & Schuster.

Goldberg, Joe. 1965 (Da Capo reprints, 1980, 1983). *Jazz Masters of the Fifties.* New York: Macmillan.

Kahn, Ashley. 2001. *Kind of Blue: The Making of the Miles Davis Masterpiece.* New York: Da Capo Press.

Mathieson, Kenny. 2002. *Cookin': Hard Bop and Soul Jazz, 1954–65.* Edinburgh: Cannongate.

Porter, Lewis. 2000. *John Coltrane: His Life and Music.* Ann Arbor University of Michigan.

Porter, Lewis, et al. 2007. *The John Coltrane Reference.* New York: Routledge.

Silver, Horace. 2007. *Let's Get to the Nitty Gritty: The Autobiography of Horace Silver.* Berkeley: University of California Press.

Swed, John. 2002. *So What: The Life of Miles Davis.* New York: Simon & Schuster.

Thomas, J.C. 1975 (Da Capo reprint, 1976). *Chasin' the Trane* (biography of John Coltrane). New York: Doubleday.

Woideck, Carl. 1998. *The Coltrane Companion: Five Decades of Commentary.* New York: Schirmer.

9 Avant-Garde of the 1960s and 70s

The John Coltrane Quartet, left to right: Elvin Jones, Coltrane, Reggie Workman, McCoy Tyner.
Photo courtesy of Michael Ochs Archives/Getty Images

The term "avant-garde" refers to the advance group of creators in any field of art or music. It designates individuals who are ahead of everybody else in developing the newest, freshest styles. All of the style chapters in this book are about innovators rather than imitators. So all the chapters could justify having "avant-garde" in their title; yet this is the only chapter titled "avant-garde." There are two reasons for this. First, the term has been applied in recent writing about jazz history as though it was a style by itself. New kinds of jazz in the 1960s and 70s were classified by a single term such as "avant-garde" or "the new thing," instead of original names such as Dixieland, swing, or bebop. Second, this textbook needs a chapter to discuss several significant modern styles that don't really fit in the other chapters. So the full title for this chapter ought to be "avant-garde jazz musicians of the 1960s and 70s not treated elsewhere." Keep in mind that, as in the rest of the book, we are only looking at a few of the most prominent

Photo by David Redfern. Courtesy of Redferns/Getty Images

◀ Cecil Taylor.

musicians of the period. There were other outstanding players during this period we don't have the space to discuss.

"Free jazz" is a classification that is sometimes applied to a few avant-garde jazz styles of the 1960s. It is most closely associated with **Ornette Coleman** and **Cecil Taylor. "Free jazz"** *gets its name from the fact that the musicians are improvising jazz that is free from preset chord progressions.* The term has also been applied to improvisation that is free from conventional practices of any kind, not just preset chord progressions. But the term can be deceiving because very little of the music is entirely free of tempo or key. It is rarely free of distinctions between soloists and accompanists. Moreover, a lot of the so-called "free" music does contain preset aspects such as a written or memorized melody, a definite order for soloists, and so forth.

A model for this music is a 1960 album by Ornette Coleman called *Free Jazz.* This recording contains music by two bands of musicians who are all playing at the same time and trying to improvise without following preset key, melody, or chord progressions. During the 1960s and 70s, a number of other modern jazz musicians tried collective free improvisation. Much of it was high-energy, high-density playing that contained no bebop phrasing or swing feeling. Similar styles appeared during the 1970s and 80s. Some of the inspiration for this also came from John Coltrane because he was the most prominent bandleader to try this approach.

Most free jazz groups omitted piano. There are several reasons for this. Historically the jazz pianist had assumed a role of providing chord progressions. Yet the restrictions created by preset chord progressions were exactly what free players were trying to free themselves from. Another reason is that few pianists were comfortable improvising without the suggestion of chords or key. It was as though, having been the harmonic gatekeepers for so long, they did not want to function when preset chord progressions were removed.

Free jazz An approach associated with Ornette Coleman and Cecil Taylor, in which the music contains improvised solos which are free of preset chord progressions, and sometimes also free of preset meter

The role of the drummer in a free jazz group was significantly different from that in more conventional groups. *Instead of functioning as a timekeeper, sometimes the drummer provided only an undercurrent of drum sounds.* He used all the different instruments of the drum set to create a continuous variety of shadings. All four limbs were devoted to generating textures that popped and crackled. Free jazz drummers produced sound patterns that were less predictable than those of their counterparts in swing and bebop. *This was a major departure from the drumming traditions of marching band and dance band.*

Three qualities associated with free jazz have nothing to do with the absence of chord progressions:

1. **More extensive manipulations of pitch and tone quality.** Ultra-high-register playing was common, with the addition of shrieks, squawks, wails, gurgles, and squeals. Rough, hoarse tone qualities were also common.

2. **The creation of textures often seemed more important than the development of melodies. The "free jazz" label was often applied to music of high energy and dense textures which maintained turbulent activity for long periods.** In fact, high-energy, dense-textured playing was sometimes dubbed "free jazz" even when the music was not free of key, set chord progression, or steady tempo.

3. **The free players' concept of melody displayed a loosening of bebop melodic and rhythmic practices that had been standard for jazz musicians since the 1940s.** Phrasing was often more fragmented. Sustained tones were alternated with screeches and moans. There was more of an unfinished quality in free style than in bebop style performances.

((•Listen on
mysearchlab.com

Listen to free-form collective improvisation on mysearchlab.com

((•Listen on
mysearchlab.com

Listen to Ornette Coleman's saxophone style on mysearchlab.com

Some avant-garde jazz players of the 1960s and 70s pursued **non-European musical approaches which don't rely much on chord progressions. This includes some types of music from Africa, Indonesia, China, the Middle East, and India.** Like free jazz, many of these non-European forms of music did not use chord instruments. So it was logical for such development to have occurred with free players who also stayed away from piano and guitar. This interest led to combining jazz with music of non-European cultures, sometimes termed **Third World music** or **World music.** This resulted in kinds of music that are simpler than bebop.

You can see from this discussion that free jazz players have developed new ways of playing their instrument as well as playing in a group. Free jazz players also opened themselves to music from other cultures.

ORNETTE COLEMAN

Alto saxophonist Ornette Coleman (b. 1930) was one of the most influential forces in jazz of the 1960s and 70s. Some consider him to have been as historically significant as Charlie Parker. In addition to being an important improviser, Coleman is also one of the freshest, most prolific post-bebop composers. His style is quite original, and he has an exceptional gift for melody. Some of his tunes are quite catchy, despite their unusual rhythmic and harmonic qualities. A few are strikingly playful.

Though Coleman's music is known for its freedom from preset accompaniment chords, that's about all it's free of. The music actually has quite a

Photo by Bob Parent, courtesy of Don Parent.

◄ Ornette Coleman, the
best-known of the so-
called "free jazz" musicians
who improvised without
following preset chord
progressions. His sax style
influenced numerous
avant-garde musicians of
the 1960s, 70s, and 80s.
Pictured here in 1960,
playing a white plastic alto
saxophone because he
could not afford to buy a
more expensive instrument
made out of brass (though
he began to like the difference in sound afforded by
this plastic instrument).

bit of self-imposed structure. The musicians usually play at the same tempo throughout a given piece. They use written and memorized tunes during some portion of each performance. Though Coleman freely changes keys while he is improvising, he usually stays in each one long enough for us to hear that he is indeed in a particular key. And there is nothing haphazard about the freedoms with which Coleman and his musicians play. They are limited by their decision to listen to each other carefully, and they plan out their music while they improvise. Coleman's brand of free jazz also uses instruments in conventional solo and accompaniment roles. In his trio, for instance, there is interaction between saxophonist, bassist, and drummer, but there is little doubt that Coleman is the soloist.

Coleman attempts a difficult task when he rejects preset chord changes and the supportive sound of a pianist's comping. Without the rise and fall of musical tension indicated by chord changes, Coleman has little to support and inspire his creations. Every moment is taxing his imagination, call-ing upon him to fill it with an interesting line. He brought us an especially abstract form of musical experience by doing away with chord patterns that repeat again and again in cycles.

Recorded in 1965, live at the Golden Circle in Stockholm, Sweden, by Ornette Coleman (alto saxophone), David Izenzon (bass), and Charles Moffett (drums); composed by Ornette Coleman; originally issued by Blue Note Records on the album *Ornette Coleman at the Golden Circle, Vol. 1*.

Though "Dee Dee" represents "free jazz" on your *Jazz Classics CD2*, it is important to keep in mind that, contrary to the reputation for non-swinging, chaotic, ultra-high intensity music that has been acquired by much "free jazz," (a) this example is quite melodic and relatively relaxed. (b) It evokes a flowing, swing feeling. (c) Though they dispense with his original theme and its implied chords, Ornette Coleman's newly improvised lines possess their own integrity and often suggest their own progression of chords. In other words, (d) Coleman goes his own way, but his solo flows continuously, and nuggets of fresh melody emerge frequently. The result differs from previous styles only by not following a repeating chorus structure.

Despite Coleman's music ordinarily being classified as "free jazz" and that label's association with complexity, the sounds on "Dee Dee" are less complicated and more hummable than most bebop. What is avant-garde about this improvisation is that Coleman changes keys whenever inspired. (He does this 13 times in five minutes.) Remember that in conventional jazz a given chord's pitches remain in effect only for a set number of beats. By contrast, (a) each one of Coleman's tone centers remains in effect as long as he wishes, (b) his lines can imply any set of chord progressions he wishes, and (c) they can change at any moment. Such freedom is unusual. On his improvisation here it seems as though Coleman likes using a set theme, its rhythms, and implied harmonies as a jumping off point. His solo often repeats the original theme's melodic rhythms but uses different pitches. It is as though he is generating variations on a theme. No matter how fresh, most of his inventions adhere to the original theme's flow and its light-hearted feeling. He recruits the "Dee Dee" tune structure whenever it suits him. He dispenses with it whenever it doesn't.

TIME ELAPSED

Theme

0' 00"   A-section
      alto saxophone melody, melodic rhythms underscored by snare drum and string bass
      staccato saxophone phrases answered by drums and cymbals
0' 09"   Bridge
0' 14"   A-section
      saxophone melody, bass synchronized with certain phrases
      Bassist runs hand up and down fingerboard to warp pitch in a humorous way.
0' 23"   Bridge
      Sticks on snare drum accentuate and underscore saxophone melody.

CECIL TAYLOR

Cecil Taylor (b. 1929) is a pianist, composer, and bandleader who developed a unique and specialized style of modern jazz during the late 1950s and early 60s. His style is not merely different, innovative, or

0' 27"	**Saxophone Solo Improvisation**
	bass walking, drummer keeping time with ride rhythms on ride cymbal, high-hat closing on every other beat
1' 25"	Original melody's rhythm is used for playing new pitches.
1' 44"	key change
1' 59"	key change
2' 07"	Saxophone paraphrases first part of original melody.
2' 14"	staccato articulation
2' 23"	key change
	more paraphrase of original melody
2' 30"	Saxophone plays same melody four times, each transposed downward.
2' 47"	drummer striking wood shell of drum
2' 54"	key change
3' 18"	key change
3' 20"	quotes original melody
3' 34"	key change
3' 40"	key change
3' 49"	key change
4' 06"	Bass responds to saxophone figures.
4' 10"	Saxophone quotes the opening melody phrase.
4' 14"	key change
4' 32"	key change
4' 38"	key change
4' 40"	Saxophone devises self-imposed question and answer sequence.
4' 54"	sounds like a chord progression-based sequence of same phrase transposed down several times
4' 56"	key change
5' 08"	opening phrase of original theme
5' 15"	key change
5' 30"	key change
5' 37"	drum fill
5' 39"	fade-out to bass solo, not heard on this excerpt

unconventional. Rather, it is **a major alternative to the dominant modern jazz styles.**

Taylor does not play with modern jazz swing feeling. His music is too tense to swing, and he does not try to swing. **He frequently emphasizes complex musical textures rather than musical lines.** Taylor often generates

Pianist Cecil Taylor with bassist Buell Neidlinger pictured here in 1956 as Taylor was beginning to devise the most unorthodox style of piano improvisation ever to emerge from the jazz tradition. It was a nonswinging, densely textured sound.

Photo by Bob Parent, courtesy of Don Parent.

notes in layered groups rather than singable phrases. The resulting textures are rich in internal movement. They shimmer and explode. In fact, much of Taylor's music is percussive and violent, with few moments of serenity. Many of his performances seem to draw on a continuous source of high energy. They maintain a feverish intensity for long periods.

During the late 1950s, Taylor based his improvisations on tunes and chord changes, and he employed bebop-style bassists and drummers. Then during the 1960s he began playing without preset chord progressions or constant tempo. He preplanned only what he called "unit structures." These were phrases and overall concepts about the architecture that the piece should assume. His preparation for performance does involve extensive rehearsal, and he does provide his musicians with pitches and rhythms to play. However, he does not specify the exact order of themes or a synchronization of them, their timing, or tempo. In addition, he requires his musicians to improvise some passages completely freely. These improvisations are not guided by preset themes or chord progressions. In other words, Taylor's music is not entirely free-form, but it is free of the preset forms that most jazz musicians use.

Taylor plays a very unconventional role as pianist in his groups. His comping is jagged and dense. It does not provide the springboard for soloists that other styles of comping provide. Instead it often sounds more like a separate and contrasting activity. It increases the density of the group sound more than it complements, mimics, or anticipates the rhythms of the soloist in a particularly obvious way.

Listeners who enjoy Taylor find that his playing is a spiritually uplifting experience. They do not listen to him to relax. Listening to him requires a different kind of mental openness. A listener must be ready to be carried along by the energy without being put off by dissonance or lack of swing. To enjoy Taylor's playing takes a special effort, but there is real reward for those who bother.

MODAL JAZZ

During the late 1950s, Miles Davis recorded improvisations guided by the notes in scales. He did this to get away from improvising in ways that are guided by the notes in progressions of chords. In chord progression-based improvisation, whenever a chord changes, there are new notes that the improviser becomes restricted to playing. In bebop styles, the chords changed rapidly, and improvisers were confronted with a dizzying string of decisions. This did not allow them to relax. Davis reasoned that the character of the improvisation would change if a single chord were in effect for a long time or if improvisers could choose their notes from those in a single scale (known as a mode) that was in effect for a long time. The most famous example of this music is the Miles Davis album *Kind of Blue* with tenor saxophonist John Coltrane and pianist Bill Evans. This approach was dubbed **"modal jazz,"** and it proved to be highly influential.

Modal jazz Jazz improvisation based on a mode (or scale) rather than on chord changes

Scale-based pieces by John Coltrane and his disciples were even more influential than those by Miles Davis. One of Coltrane's most famous "modal" performances can be heard on the title track of his 1960 album *My Favorite Things*. The strategies Coltrane used to construct his performance of "My Favorite Things" became a model format. First he played the

Photo by William E. (Bill) Smith

((•◦ **Listen** on **mysearchlab.com**

Listen to soprano saxophone on mysearchlab.com

◄ John Coltrane, pictured here playing soprano sax, the instrument he popularized during the 1960s.

"Your Lady" Jazz Classics CD2
Track 6 is modal

Prentice Hall Jazz History DVD:
"So What" with Miles Davis and
John Coltrane

melody while his pianist and bassist used the tune's original chords as accompaniment. Then Coltrane abandoned the original chords and based his solo improvisation on a two-chord repeating pattern played by the piano. Those two chords together contained all the notes in the scale that guided his improvisation. It was much easier than "Giant Steps," with its ever-changing accompaniment chords. This new approach became popular with improvising musicians. In fact, many prominent modern jazz combos played only this kind of jazz between the late 1960s and the mid-1970s.

Some jazz of this period was turbulent and not swinging. It featured several musicians improvising different lines at the same time by playing densely packed, rough-textured streams of notes that swirled around. Though it was loosely guided by preset scales, some listeners considered it "free jazz." One of the most widely discussed and most influential examples of this style is the *Ascension* album that John Coltrane recorded in 1965. Inspired by Ornette Coleman's 1960 album *Free Jazz*, Coltrane hired four other saxophonists, two trumpeters, and rhythm section to maintain feverish activity through most of the performance. The results did not sound like most music that uses preset organization even though Coltrane had preset a series of four scales to guide the improvisations. After this, Coltrane recorded other albums using similar approaches with smaller bands. Because of these works, Coltrane's name became associated specifically with free jazz, though he never played entirely free from any preset arrangement of harmonies. Coltrane's work was clearly "avant-garde," but not really "free" jazz.

"Jitney #2" on Jazz Classics CD2
Track 7 is free of meter and
chord progression

BILL EVANS

The most influential pianist in jazz after Bud Powell was Bill Evans (1929–1980). His style is not rough and wild like most avant-garde jazz styles of the 1960s.

▶ Bill Evans, the most influential pianist of the 1960s and 70s. He popularized the jazz use of harmonies based on modes and adapted the chords of French composers Claude Debussy and Maurice Ravel. Evans was also known for rhythmic practices in which he often avoided accenting the most obvious beats.

Photo by Chuck Stewart

((•‒[Listen on mysearchlab.com

Composed by John Coltrane; recorded November 18, 1963, by John Coltrane (soprano saxophone), McCoy Tyner (piano), Jimmy Garrison (bass), and Elvin Jones (drums); issued by Impulse Records on the album *Live at Birdland* but was not actually recorded there, but rather in a New Jersey studio.

This recording is included for several reasons. The style of accompaniment provided by this rhythm section constituted a new approach in jazz. The combination of unusual parts was particularly unique. The very active playing of drummer Elvin Jones often dispensed with regularly repeating patterns. On the other hand, the bass part was a very simple pattern that repeated almost continuously. The bassist plays the same note again and again. This is termed a "pedal point" or "drone." The chords used here by pianist McCoy Tyner became the main sound preferred by pianists of the 1970s. The piece illustrates basing jazz improvisation on the notes in a single scale instead of a progression of different chords. It is an example of modal jazz. The pivot of that harmony was reiterated continuously by the bass. Coltrane's soprano saxophone playing here became a model for hundreds of musicians in the three decades that followed. By the 1990s, his impact had not let up at all. Many saxophonists bought soprano saxophones because they heard Coltrane's playing. His influence could be heard on thousands of records by jazz bands and jazz-rock fusion bands.

TIME ELAPSED

0' 00" **Introduction**

Bassist plays repeating rhythmic figure that anchors the piece's basic unit of three pulses. Drums and cymbals generate complex patterns around it.

0' 13" Pianist begins syncopated chording.

Theme Statement

0' 28" Melody is played by soprano sax, without piano accompaniment.

0' 49" Rhythm section plays accompaniment patterns without sax.

1' 04" Melody played again by soprano sax, without piano accompaniment.

Soprano Sax Improvisation

1' 26" Piano returns and sax improvisation begins.

2' 11" Drumming becomes particularly full under sax solo. Bassist continues repeating its pedal point.

2' 14" Piano drops out.

Theme Statement

4' 30" Sax plays melody again.

4' 49" Piano returns. Sax begins another improvisation.

5' 30" Sax plays melody again without piano.

5' 54" Piano returns. Sax stops.

Ending

6' 20" Piano stops.

6' 35" Bass and drums end the piece.

A written transcription of Coltrane's solo is available from Andrew's Music, 5830 South Dakota Avenue N.E., Washington, D.C. 20017; phone 202-526-3666.

LISTENING GUIDE

"Jitney #2" by Cecil Taylor

((•●-[Listen on **mysearchlab.com**

Recorded July 2, 1974 at the Montreux Jazz Festival in Montreux, Switzerland. Originally available on the album titled *Silent Tongues,* manufactured by Freedom records, reissued by Arista records, out of print, but available as a download from the firm called 1201 Music, using the catalog number: 9017.

This is a highly spirited, free-form improvisation by pianist Cecil Taylor. It was spontaneously created and performed at a jazz festival. You may enjoy the performance by merely letting its sounds take you on their own journey as they wash over you. There is nothing wrong with that strategy. Some listeners, however, might be puzzled by the way the improvisation is organized. For such listeners it may be instructive to recognize that Taylor's approach differs in several respects from the approaches used for most other music on the *Jazz Classics* CDs for this book. (1) Instead of long lines of tones slurred together in a way that musicians call "legato," this piece has many sounds that are short and separated, which is what musicians call "staccato." (2) Instead of coming at us within an obvious tempo and bouncy swing feeling, the sounds in this music come in short bursts. The notes in these bursts are percussively executed with great force. The sounds emerge abruptly. (3) Taylor's improvisation is not divided into an introduction, A-section, B-section, or any chorus structures that you can easily latch onto. He does not adhere to a preset song form, such as a twelve-bar blues or a piece with thirty-two-bar A-A-B-A construction. Instead, "Jitney #2" follows its own spontaneous organization. Instead of using traditional organizing principles for his improvisation, Taylor offers us what he calls "unit structures," which are what musicologists call "cells." We can hear these at various moments during the piece, and we can hear numerous transformations of them. Sometimes it seems as though the cells and their transformations are talking to each other. At the beginning, for example, the pianist plays two bass notes, each of which he harmonized. He uses them much like a question, and he follows them with a chorded answer that is comprised of tones pitched slightly higher. Then when he reiterates that opening statement he sometimes repeats the pattern almost intact, and sometimes adds one or two notes to it. You might be able to recognize its recurrences among Taylor's more complicated inventions. Listen for transformations of it that are faster or slower and pitched higher. Keep in mind, however, that often the pianist does not refer to this unit structure at all. Much of his playing constitutes cascading sounds and jarring clusters of tones that seem to be jangling in the air almost as a stream of conscious.

Terms to learn from *Elements of Music Appendix* and *Demonstration CD:* chord, tremolo

Elapsed Time	Musical Events
00′ 00″	Opening statement of two harmonized bass tones, followed by rocking motion of four, successive, harmonized tones in low-pitch range, then echoed by a lower-pitched figure
00′ 04″	mid-register chords
00′ 10″	opening statement again, echoed by various transformations played in higher registers
00′ 17″	opening statement, followed by broken chords
00′ 19″	more variations of the opening idea, leading to rapidly-played, broken chords and a return to that same idea

0' 26"	opening idea again, followed by chords
0' 31"	rapid, broken chords that paraphrase the opening idea
0' 37"	a new idea and its development
0' 44"	Taylor reaches the upper register of the keyboard.
0' 46"	return to opening statement, developed rapidly
0' 48"	a series of repeated, broken chords played as though trembling ("tremolo") by two hands in the middle of the keyboard, then scattered across the keyboard
0' 57"	switch to single notes instead of chords and offers a new idea
0' 58"	develops new idea
1' 02"	new idea
1' 06"	return to the opening idea
1' 08"	opening idea again
1' 10"	opening idea again
1' 12"	opening idea again
1' 13"	new idea
1' 15"	development of the new idea
1' 17"	further development of the new idea
1' 20"	further development of the new idea
1' 21"	new idea
1' 23"	Intensity increases.
1' 26"	notes scattered all over the keyboard
1' 33"	tremolos scattered all over the keyboard
1' 40"	notes scattered all over the keyboard
1' 47" to 1' 55"	variations of the opening idea
1' 50"	Intensity further increases as heavy chords are played at a slower pace.
1' 54"	a new idea
2' 04"	a new idea
2' 05"	very rapid sprinkling of notes, lasting until 2' 39"
2' 13"	cascades of notes, variations of the idea, in different keys
2' 27"	bass-range answering of the treble–range idea
2' 36"	bass-range answering of the treble–range idea
2' 43"	Intensity starts increasing again, in preparation of the last climax, with briefly repeated runs.
	High pitched ideas occur with chorded responses in bass range.
2' 45"	Taylor is briefly melody-like until 2' 53".

2' 53"	resumes turbulence
3' 10"	Quick trills are exchanged in different registers of keyboard.
3' 15"	Taylor plays tone clusters alternately in low register, then high registers.
3' 17"	Taylor pounds out a string of tone clusters, ending in the low register.
3' 10"	series of tremolos
3' 15"	high-pitched clusters answering bass figures
3' 17"	extremely forceful chords from high pitch to low pitch range
3' 21"	Taylor concludes abruptly with a restatement of his opening idea.
3' 23"	abrupt ending

Much of Evans' music is smooth and pretty, despite its highly explorative nature. Because of this, many people do not consider it avant-garde. The playing is too polished, and the innovations are too subtle to jar them. However, Miles Davis hired Evans in 1958 precisely because Evans was avant-garde, and Davis wanted to change the style of his music in directions that Evans was taking. Davis knew that Evans was devising ways of constructing harmonies around the flavors of certain scales called modes. Evans was showing the jazz world how improvisations could be developed in terms of scales. To do this he used harmonies that sounded quite different from bebop. He did this with popular songs as well as bebop tunes. Evans had built this jazz system from harmonies used by Claude Debussy and Maurice Ravel, who were French composers of piano music and symphonic music during the first part of the twentieth century. His unique combination of these methods influenced many pianists. Such well-known pianists as Herbie Hancock, Chick Corea, and Keith Jarrett all derived important aspects of their harmonic approaches from the model that Evans provided. Davis got what he sought from Evans, and the character of Davis' subsequent music reflected this. The music on the 1959 Davis-Evans album *Kind of Blue* became a textbook for the new approach. The melodies, harmonies, and concepts in that album were still being imitated by other musicians during the 1990s.

Bill Evans was not only avant-garde in a harmonic way. He was also avant-garde in a rhythmic way. Evans perfected a very involved manner of phrasing his improvisations without stressing notes that land on the most obvious beats. Instead of frequently accenting notes at times where we tend to clap our hands or tap our feet, Evans accented at other moments. Moreover, he often began a phrase in a way that was staggered across a series of beats. He could displace his phrases for entire passages

See *Prentice Hall Jazz History DVD*: "Up with the Lark" by Bill Evans. Also available on mysearchlab.com.

((◉ **Listen** on
mysearchlab.com
Listen to Bill Evans' rhythmic displacements on mysearchlab.com

and never land resoundingly on a strong beat. When he was doing this, his rhythms did not directly state the pulse, though he always kept it in mind while he was improvising. This means that you might not be able to hear the beat unless you pay close attention to the notes of the bassist or drummer accompanying Evans. This style was called *non-obvious pulse* or **floating pulse.** Though this kind of thinking was evident in his 1950s recordings, Evans developed it most in the 1960s and 70s. He could play in the bebop manner, and he occasionally did. And he could swing conventionally. But he frequently chose not to. Instead he often played in a way in which he floated across the beats very subtly. His rhythmic manner departed from bebop. But, because his manner was so highly organized and subtle, most listeners were not aware of how avant-garde it was.

Another aspect of the Bill Evans style is also relatively unique in the history of jazz piano playing. His tone and conception often sound delicate without being fragile. On slow pieces he often created a harp-like effect by sounding single tones and letting them ring, as though to savor each vibration before proceeding to the next note. Though he possessed considerable dexterity, his work was never flashy, and he steered clear of conveying an aggressively percussive manner.

Evans crafted his improvisations with exacting deliberation. Often he would take a phrase or a rhythmic idea and then develop several choruses of lines from that single idea. During his performances, an unheard, continuous self-editing was going on. This resulted in sparing the listener his false starts and discarded ideas. Though he had a creative imagination, he never improvised solos that merely strung together ideas at the same rate that they popped into his head. The results of these deliberations could be an exhilarating experience for the listener. However, they reflected the well-honed craftsmanship of a performer working in the manner of a classical composer more than the carefree abandon and rush of ideas that we associate with jazz improvisation. Because of this his music was sometimes called "brooding" or "introspective" instead of "swinging" or "light-hearted."

Floating pulse A method of improvising that avoids stressing the most obvious beats, while extending phrases across several beats, pioneered by Bill Evans; also called **non-obvious pulse**

(((•─[Listen on
mysearchlab.com
Listen to Bill Evans' contemplative style on mysearchlab.com

(((•─[Listen on
mysearchlab.com
Listen to a solo piano line voiced in octaves on mysearchlab.com

MILES DAVIS MID-'60s QUINTET

The Miles Davis Quintet of 1964 to 1968 was one of the best combos in jazz history. They displayed stunning musicianship, unceasing originality, extraordinary energy, and significant breakthroughs in melody, harmony, and rhythm. Key to the group's success was its talented personnel: Ron Carter on bass, Wayne Shorter on tenor saxophone, Herbie Hancock on piano, and Tony Williams on drums. Shorter and Hancock were both talented composers and helped bring a new repertory and style to Davis music. All of these musicians have gone on to have their own distinguished and varied careers in jazz.

Recorded June 25, 1961, at the Village Vanguard in New York City by Bill Evans (piano), Scott LaFaro (bass), and Paul Motian (drums); composed by Chuck Wayne; originally issued by Riverside Records as *Sunday at the Village Vanguard.*

Terms to know from tracks on *Demo CD:* high-hat (2), ride cymbal (3), snare drum (5), piano comping (20), walking bass (23), embellished walking (24), horn-like pizzicato bass (27), non-repetitive bass style (28), half-time (36), left-hand comping, right-hand lines (37), octave-voiced piano lines (41). Terms to know from Chapter 2 and Elements of Music appendix: chorus, turnaround, chord changes, walking bass, comping, ride rhythm, high-hat, ride cymbal, snare drum, octave, triplet, and eighth note (particularly the explanation of syncopation by accenting the "ands" which are also known as "up-beats").

This selection is drawn from one of the most pivotal albums in post-bebop. It has become a "desert island choice" for many musicians. The recording brought together three unorthodox thinkers who worked tirelessly to realize their goals of formulating jazz of depth and substance that was stylistically fresh. Though not routinely mentioned as avant-garde in the sense of Ornette Coleman's and Cecil Taylor's albums, *Sunday at the Village Vanguard* certainly was avant-garde because it dispensed with important conventions, and it succeeded esthetically while doing that.

Bill Evans had several different stylistic phases in his career. The *Jazz Classics* CD set samples two of them. His piano voicings, modal thinking, and very spare solo style affected the sound of "Blue in Green," on *CD1,* a selection taken from the Miles Davis album *Kind of Blue* of 1959. "Solar" was selected for *CD2* to (a) give the clearest example of the unique approach that Evans and bassist Scott LaFaro developed for playing together and (b) illustrate LaFaro's revolutionary solo style. Unlike traditional bass playing that provides a very predictable foundation for the soloists, LaFaro does not walk. Moreover, his rhythms contain very little repetition. LaFaro's role here can be likened to an ever-changing counter-activity. Sometimes it is not clearly subordinate to Evans but instead seems to go its own way. For example, in the first few choruses (from 0′ 11″ to 0′ 56″), **concurrent with Evans, LaFaro improvises melody lines of his own, in the character of the "Solar" melody.** Some listeners have construed it as an almost continuous musical conversation with Evans. In the first four choruses, two interweaving melodies are offered instead of the usual format in which piano melody is accompanied by walking bass. Both melodies come in and out of the foreground. Though LaFaro's lines are usually somewhat subordinate to Evans's, they are denser, more varied, and closer to the foreground than bass parts had traditionally been. For instance, LaFaro only occasionally plays downbeats in the first eight measures of the second from last rendition of the theme at 8′ 06″ to 8′ 12″. Then at 8′ 17″ LaFaro uses his high register and a triplet feeling to paraphrase an echo of the theme and does it again at 8′ 31″. **LaFaro's accompaniment does not resemble the ways bassists had traditionally accompanied jazz pianists.**

This performance of "Solar" also illustrates subtle ways of phrasing that came to characterize more and more Evans solos after the 1950s. Termed **"non-obvious pulse"** or **"phrasing across the bar line,"** these approaches are particularly evident in the fifth chorus (beginning at 0′ 56″) and the seventh chorus (beginning at 1′ 22″). In the fifth chorus, almost all the accents in Evans' line are on the offbeat, and all three of his phrases are staggered across several measures. They are rhythmically displaced, never starting or clearly resolving on a strong beat, for example, the moments when we usually tap our feet or click our fingers. (If you are counting "1234 1234," Evans makes it difficult for you to know where "1" is.) He achieves this again, even more thoroughly, in the thirty-sixth chorus (beginning at 7′ 17″). Occasionally **Evans seems to stretch figures out so they sound half-time.** For example, at the end of the thirty-fourth chorus (at 7′ 01″), he creates a half-time effect with a triplet feeling.

The rhythms that Evans uses are so subtle in their relationship to the underlying pulse that we may have difficulty verifying the passage of beats and the beginnings of choruses if we ignore the drummer's timekeeping rhythms. Even then it is challenging on this recording because drummer Paul Motian's timekeeping style itself draws upon such a diverse collection of rhythms. In other words, Evans intentionally blurs conventional landmarks in the composition so thoroughly that **this recording represents a significant departure from a jazz tradition of rhythmic obviousness.**

Evans also achieved a significant departure from jazz tradition by moving away from harmonic obviousness when he transcended the positions in his phrases relative to the chord progression where we expect pauses. This means that he did what Ornette Coleman tried to do but without entirely abandoning chorus structure or chord progressions. This was a new kind of jazz piano style. By comparison with swing style and bebop style improvisers, chorus beginnings and endings are much less obvious. Both Evans and LaFaro demonstrate such a sense of continuity in their solos here that often we are not reminded at all of where one chorus ends and another begins. It is as though Evans and LaFaro conceived their lines in units that were longer than previously customary. Paul Motian also contributes to the blurring of chorus beginnings by omitting typical drum figures (known as "fills") in the final measure of each chorus that we would expect to end on the downbeat of the next chorus. To obscure the effect of the turnarounds is a considerable achievement. **So, with Evans hardly ever indicating an obvious pulse and rarely playing chords, and with drummer Paul Motian playing displaced, fragmented patterns, we have an extremely complicated two-part invention, improvised by piano and bass, that remains unified only by the collective genius of these extraordinary musicians.**

The "Solar" recording on *Jazz Classics CD2* gives us a full-length example of the solo style originated by Scott LaFaro. His energy seemed unquenchable, and the attitude conveyed by his work here is sheer impetuosity. As a melodic improviser, he is richly inventive, executing fluid, horn-like lines, chorus after chorus after chorus. (He solos for 15 choruses!) But it was primarily his speed and dexterity that astounded musicians when they first encountered this solo (at 3′ 33″). Incidentally, prior to LaFaro, most jazz bassists had plucked their strings with just their forefinger or used two fingers at a time to pull the string with great force. LaFaro innovated by alternating several different fingers in sequence, thereby expanding the potential for speed and fluency almost as a classical guitarist. This recording is a landmark in the history of jazz bass playing.

Evans uses four different ways for playing melody in this performance: He (a) plays the melody in harmony for the first two choruses, (b) improvises his solo line voiced in octaves from the third chorus (0′ 30″) to the eleventh chorus (2′ 13″), (c) solos with single-note-at-a-time lines from the middle of the eleventh chorus (2′ 18″) until the sixteenth chorus (3′ 15″), (d) voices his solo lines in locked-hands block chording at the thirty-sixth chorus (7′ 17″) and thirty-eighth chorus (7′ 41″).

The composition was written by guitarist Chuck Wayne, though it has always been mistakenly credited to Miles Davis. It is 12 measures long, but it does not follow the chord progression of a typical blues. In fact, the first 8 measures were inspired by the chord progression of "How High the Moon." This form is not as easy to follow as 12-bar blues and 32-bar A-A-B-A forms. It may be even more difficult to keep your place on this particular recording because (a) in creating their complex rhythmic displacements, the musicians mask chorus beginnings and endings, (b) Evans blurs the movement of chords in the tune's structure, thereby removing some of the chord progression cues that we ordinarily expect, (c) Evans goes for long stretches without comping, thereby omitting chord change cues that we would otherwise use for keeping our place, and (d) the melodic continuity in the solos by Evans and LaFaro often spills across chorus endings, making it challenging to detect the beginning of a new chorus. The solution is to follow the timings provided below.

TIME ELAPSED

0' 00" First Chorus

Melody Statement by Evans on Piano

Evans plays the first 4 measures alone in octaves, then the second 4 measures in harmony.

0' 11" LaFaro plays the melody's last 4 measures with Evans, accompanied by Motian's ride cymbal, accents on snare drum, and high-hat cymbals, then devises other counter-lines.

0' 15" Second Chorus

Evans Restates the Melody

Evans harmonizes his piano phrases. LaFaro echoes "Solar" melody in his low register, then contrives countermelodies. Motian plays ride rhythms on ride cymbal, closes high-hat cymbals every other beat, accents on snare drum.

0' 30" Third Chorus

Evans starts his solo improvisation, voicing all his lines in octaves. His right-hand melody is doubled by his left hand, separated by the interval of an octave. He is not comping for himself. No harmony is stated until 2' 18". LaFaro paraphrases the melody.

0' 43" Fourth Chorus

Evans and LaFaro continue to improvise counter-lines to each other, LaFaro occasionally quoting the melody.

0' 56" Fifth Chorus

LaFaro moves to a less melodic and more rhythmic role. Evans phrases his own improvisational ideas in rhythmic ways that do not convey the pulse of the piece in a particularly obvious manner.

1' 09" Sixth Chorus

Evans continues to voice his improvisations in octaves and not comp for himself.

1' 22" Seventh Chorus

Piano solo filled with rhythmic displacements. Evans places most phrases on offbeats, shifting entire ideas later than when we would expect them to fall, stretching the tension by not landing on a first of 4 beats.

1' 36" Eighth Chorus

1' 47" Ninth Chorus

1' 50" Beginning in the fourth measure of this chorus, Evans constructs about 12 measures worth of lines from quarter-note triplet figures. LaFaro continuously varies the rhythm of his timekeeping figures.

1' 60" Tenth Chorus

2' 13"   **Eleventh Chorus**

LaFaro plays the same low note 11 times, letting each ring.

2' 18"   After the fourth measure of this chorus, Evans stops voicing his lines in octaves and begins to play 1 note at a time instead. He generates solo lines with his right hand and comps lightly and infrequently with his left hand. The character of his lines is more relaxed, and Evans takes more chances now. This pattern persists until the sixteenth chorus. Bass plays resounding low notes (to 2' 23").

2' 25"   LaFaro plays same note five times ("pedals") for 16 beats, then another note, four times, for another 16 beats (to 2' 31").

2' 25"   **Twelfth Chorus**

2' 38"   **Thirteenth Chorus**

2' 50"   **Fourteenth Chorus**

Meter of 3 is implied here by LaFaro instead of the tune's meter of 4 that Evans and Motian are in.

3' 01"   Obvious piano-bass communication: As Evans increases the density of his improvisation, so does LaFaro. Bass actually rises to similar pitch range. Together they increase the intensity of the music.

3' 04"   **Fifteenth Chorus**

LaFaro's accompaniment rhythms are extremely varied.

3' 15"   **Sixteenth Chorus**

Evans paraphrases the melody, harmonizing thicker and thicker as the chorus unfolds.

3' 28"   **Seventeenth Chorus**

Evans fades out.

3' 33"   **SCOTT LAFARO BASS SOLO**

LaFaro begins his bass solo with an ascending scale during the sixth measure of the chorus.

3' 40"   **Eighteenth Chorus**

LaFaro hints at the original melody. Fluid, horn-like lines come from the bass in a facile manner.

3' 48"   Piano's comping chords are intentionally delayed in relation to the beat.

3' 53"   **Nineteenth Chorus**

Evans stops playing piano until 32nd chorus. LaFaro's lines are packed with fresh ideas, composed almost entirely of eighth notes.

4' 04"   **Twentieth Chorus**

LaFaro is emphatically reiterating two-note figures. Then he comes out of that motif with scale-like lines that spill seamlessly into the next chorus.

4' 18"   **Twenty-First Chorus**

LaFaro's improvisation is composed of scale-like lines.

4' 29" **Twenty-Second Chorus**
LaFaro designs sporadically connected lines of almost continuous eighth notes.

4' 41" **Twenty-Third Chorus**
LaFaro's lines reach into high register then descend to low register and return again to high register.

4' 52" **Twenty-Fourth Chorus**
LaFaro alludes to the original melody.

5' 04" **Twenty-Fifth Chorus**
It temporarily sounds like LaFaro is ending his solo, but then he gets a second wind and forges ahead for several more choruses.

5' 17" **Twenty-Sixth Chorus**

5' 29" **Twenty-Seventh Chorus**
LaFaro's solo is constructed of almost continuous eighth notes.

5' 42" **Twenty-Eighth Chorus**
At 5' 46" LaFaro plays a five-note pattern five times that runs against the grain of the meter.

5' 54" **Twenty-Ninth Chorus**

6' 06" **Thirtieth Chorus**

6' 17" **Thirty-First Chorus**

6' 31" **Thirty-Second Chorus**
Evans returns with improvisation voiced in octaves.

DRUMS TRADING CHORUSES WITH PIANO

6' 43" **Thirty-Third Chorus** (Paul Motian begins trading choruses with Bill Evans)
Paul Motian's drum solo for entire chorus. Bass continues to play.

6' 54" **Thirty-Fourth Chorus**
Evans improvises a chorus voiced in octaves.

7' 01" Evans is ending his chorus with half-note triplet displacements.

7' 05" **Thirty-Fifth Chorus**
Paul Motian's drum solo for entire chorus. For the first 8 measures, LaFaro paraphrases the melody at same time.

7' 17" **Thirty-Sixth Chorus**
Evans improvises entire chorus in locked-hands block chording, sustaining each chord after using starting points that are all staggered in relation to the beat.

7' 30" **Thirty-Seventh Chorus**
Drum solo for entire chorus. LaFaro interjects sporadically.

7' 41" **Thirty-Eighth Chorus**
Evans improvises entire chorus in locked-hands block chording, using much rhythmic displacement.

7' 53"   **Thirty-Ninth Chorus**

> Drum solo for entire chorus. Motian uses much rhythmic displacement.

RETURN TO MELODY

8' 05"   **Fortieth Chorus**

> *Evans Restates the Melody*
>> Evans plays the melody harmonized and changes its rhythms at the end.

8' 17"   **Forty-First Chorus**

> *Evans Restates the Melody*
>> Evans toys with the rhythms of harmonized melody. LaFaro echoes it in high register, playing triplets.

8' 30"   **Vamp for Ending** formed over repeating sequence of 2 chords

> Motian is crafting varied rhythms on closed high-hat while Evans is playing harmonized line of quarter-note triplets, implying a meter of 3, creating a rocking motion.

8' 34"   LaFaro is repeating a 7-note figure in a meter of 4 against the triple meter implied by Evans.

8' 36"   Evans is gently sounding very high-pitched piano keys, chosen higher and higher, letting them ring, as though plucking harp strings.

8' 44"   Ending Vamp to fade-out with unaccompanied bass repeating his 7-note figure.

THE POPULARITY OF AVANT-GARDE JAZZ

The styles of Ornette Coleman and Cecil Taylor are among the most exciting and challenging styles in history. From their earliest years, their groups had a devoted following. However, their music was not wanted by most jazz clubs or record companies. Their following was just too small. No album by Ornette Coleman or Cecil Taylor ever made the "top 200" best-selling albums in any year. Though very little modern jazz of any kind is played on the radio, the situation is especially unfortunate for free jazz. Some major cities never heard more than a few samples of free jazz during the entire decade of the 1960s. In fact, there are jazz stations that have never played any of Cecil Taylor's music. The problem is that most listeners find free jazz recordings unswinging, difficult to follow, and chaotic. Yet these musicians do occasionally play to large crowds at concerts. So even if people do not buy many of their records, the avant-garde musicians' names are famous enough to occasionally attract fans to jazz festivals. John Coltrane and Bill Evans were more popular. Coltrane's music was not played on the radio very often during the 1950s or 60s. But his records did sell, and night clubs were almost guaranteed a full house when they booked him.

Recorded in 1967 in New York by Miles Davis (trumpet), Wayne Shorter (tenor saxophone), Herbie Hancock (piano), Ron Carter (bass), and Tony Williams (drums); composed by Wayne Shorter; first issued on the Columbia album *Sorcerer*.

Terms to know from tracks on *Demo CD*: high-hat (2), ride cymbal (3), tom-tom (6), piano comping (20), trumpet (59), tenor saxophone (73), non-repetitive bass (28), staccato (45).

The music on "Prince of Darkness" was avant-garde for its period, though it was not "free jazz." Less jarring than the music of either Ornette Coleman or Cecil Taylor, this Davis Quintet rendition used fixed chorus lengths and steady tempo, and it stayed in the same key for the entire performance. But that is about all that is conventional. Neither the composition nor its execution imparts the character of hard bop or cool jazz. It offered a relatively abstract product, instead. In fact, you can tell the influence of free jazz in its departure from a more controlled rhythm section and its greater freedom of improvisation. The solos show considerable flexibility in rhythm, rather than following the easy rise and fall of swinging figures that are common to earlier styles.

There are other reasons that this recording is avant-garde. The melody does not bear the jagged twists and turns of bebop. It has smooth contours instead. The bass part and the drum part are continuously varying in their rhythms instead of carrying the patterns established in bebop. Like the music of Ornette Coleman, this piece uses hardly any piano chording. Mostly it has just horns, bass, and drums. Therefore you cannot depend on recurring chord sounds of piano comping to guide you. The horn solos are entirely original in style. They contain none of Charlie Parker's or Dizzy Gillespie's phrases. (This recording demonstrates how both trumpeter Miles Davis and tenor saxophonist Wayne Shorter invented new ways of improvising.) None of the phrases in the piano solo are derived from standard bebop vocabulary, either.

Herbie Hancock "Prince of Darkness" was chosen partly to showcase the intelligence and originality of Herbie Hancock's improvisational thinking. He improvises as the distinctive composer he is. In this way Hancock proves that he is a true original.

For starters, you might notice that he departs from the bebop practice of feeding chords with his left hand to accompany melodic lines played by his right hand. His solo line is treated as a horn line. In fact, he rarely injects any comping chords.

Observe how systematically Hancock develops his solo. For example, he opens his solo at 4' 04" with four sets of two different tones, one high, the other low. He allows each to ring. It is as though he is taking his time and testing the water before entering the turbulent ocean of activity that surrounds him. At 4' 19" he takes just one idea and expresses it into four phrases. At about 4' 28" Hancock takes an idea and plays it three times, each of which is placed at a lower pitch. Yet another idea is begun at about 4' 38" and played five times, each one transposed down in pitch. At about 4' 58" he comes up with still another idea and reiterates it five times in different pitches. At 5' 11" he begins a string of repetitions for the same rhythm played six times in descending pitches. (This technique is called "isorhythmic" because "iso" means "same," and Hancock is using the same rhythm to play different pitches.) At 5' 19" Hancock plays five sets of two different tones, each of which is allowed to ring before going to the next. He followed this same formula when he opened his solo, at about 4' 04".

Tony Williams The quite substantial ideas of Hancock are skittering over a carpet of popping and crashing sounds from drummer Tony Williams. Nothing conventional is occurring in any of the band parts, not in the solos and definitely not in their accompaniments. The result is possibly the most original approach of its era that swings.

The drumming on this recording is unmatched for variety of sounds and rhythms. Williams is the most imaginative drummer in jazz history, and he certainly proves his genius here. There are passages in which high-hat is snapping shut every other beat. But this is far from continuous. There is also the driving feeling of ride cymbal rhythms. These rhythms, however, do not follow the usual "ching chick a ching" pattern that repeats over and over. They are highly varied instead.

Williams is an exceedingly fertile source of ideas that are bubbling with energy and excitement here. Listen, for example, for sounds resembling cannon fire and explosions from 1' 19" to 1' 26", booms from his tom toms at 1' 34", his snare drum popping like gunfire from 1' 54" to 1' 59", cymbal crashes at 2' 11". Williams increased the density of drumming activity that had become common in hard bop with Art Blakey and Philly Joe Jones. (Listen to Blakey on "The Egyptian" on *Jazz Classics CD2* and to Jones on "Two Bass Hit" on *Jazz Classics CD1*.)

Though the accompaniment devised by Williams and bassist Ron Carter resembles Brazilian samba, to call it "a modified samba" would be a disservice to the brilliant originality shown here. *Some musicians consider Williams' playing on this selection to be a turning point in the evolution of jazz drumming. It demonstrated a way to have a single drummer take the rhythms of a multi-member Latin American drum ensemble and combine them with the freedom of swinging modern jazz.*

Ron Carter This selection is notable for the richness of nontraditional accompaniment devices invented spontaneously by bassist Ron Carter. His bass parts on "Prince of Darkness" are possibly the most complicated of any on jazz recordings that keep time. The lack of repetition within these parts is very unusual for jazz that keeps steady tempo. Careful listening will reveal a stop-start, push-pull character to the generation of accompaniment rhythms that heightens the excitement and adds depth. It is as though Carter and drummer Tony Williams are continuously turning their work inside out, then upside down and back again. They never lose continuity or momentum, however. In fact, their playing carries a lot of the momentum for the entire band. Also notice the bassist's sleek tone. His pitches use this tone, slurring one from the other, to propel the band by stating the leading edge of each beat.

Wayne Shorter Thoughtfulness and drive are married here in every solo improvisation, especially Wayne Shorter's. Always original, saxophonist Shorter never truly fit any style category. Never conventional in any respect, he did not even fit the "hard bop" designation when playing with the prototypic hard bop group of Art Blakey. (Listen to "The Egyptian" on *Jazz Classics CD2* for a sample of that work.) As an improviser, saxophonist Shorter was one of those extremely rare musicians who did not depend upon a fixed bag of tricks to be used again and again. Instead, his every idea was new, and most led logically one from the other. Note that he could still devote this much focus and originality to his playing in later years. He actually toured with pianist Herbie Hancock in 1997 as half of a duo in which he continued thoughtful explorations of the sort heard on "Prince of Darkness." (See Chapter 11 for more about Wayne Shorter.)

Miles Davis The trumpeter on this recording had invented a new style for this period of his career. (See Chapter 8 for more about Davis.) It responded to the open, airy feeling of Shorter's tunes with their absence of pop tune chord progressions. This was the Miles Davis style imitated by "neo-classicists" Wallace Roney, Terrence Blanchard, Wynton Marsalis, and Dave Douglas during the 1980s and 90s. Incidentally, one of the reasons for including "Prince of Darkness" on *Jazz Classics CD2* is to demonstrate origins for many of the so-called "neo-classicists" of recent years. Another reason for including this selection is to help readers understand what broadcasters, marketers, and journalists were calling "traditional jazz" or "mainstream jazz" during the beginning of the twenty-first century. (See "Celebrating the Past" on page 257 in Chapter 11 for further discussion.)

How to Listen The form of the piece is not derived from a pop song. It does not fit a 12-bar blues or a 32-bar A-A-B-A construction. It is 16 bars long. Like much of Wayne Shorter's composing, it is thoroughly original.

The "Prince of Darkness" melody is so logical and easy to follow that you may wish to memorize it. Then hum it silently to yourself, over and over again, throughout the quintet performance. You will come to appreciate that jazz improvisation is far from random or haphazard. The solos of trumpeter Davis and saxophonist Shorter often include quotes and paraphrases of the piece's theme. Their solos are so obviously linked to the theme that our job of reconciling improvisation with the underlying song form is made easy. It is also unusual to find improvisations that hang together as well as these solos do.

Rehearings are always beneficial with any jazz, and they are particularly useful for complex examples such as this. After a first hearing, you may extract the most from this recording if you focus solely on drums and cymbals the next time you listen. After that, you might listen just to the sound of the bass viol. Finally, you could return to easier aspects such as horn lines. Ultimately, you might be able to detect ways that the parts are linked.

TIME ELAPSED

0' 00"   **Theme Statement**
trumpet/saxophone unison. Bass is not walking, just decorating every other beat. The rhythm on the ride cymbal is not the ordinary ride rhythm, though high-hat is closing on every other beat.

0' 16"   **Second Theme Statement**
Saxophone continues original line while trumpet paraphrases it.

0' 23"   Trumpet goes higher.

0' 31"   **Miles Davis Solo Improvisation** begins 8 beats before next chorus starts

0' 33"   Bass is playing quarter-note triplets (3 tones for every 4 beats).

0' 34"   First complete chorus of improvisation begins; Davis solo paraphrases original tune.

0' 49"   second chorus of Davis solo

1' 04"   third chorus of Davis solo

1' 13"   high-pitched descending bass line during pauses in trumpet solo

1' 20"   fourth chorus of solo. Trumpet paraphrases/quotes the original melody.

1' 21"   drummer plays small tom-tom

1' 30"   Drummer is closing high-hat on every other beat; adding rim shots.

1' 34"   fifth chorus of Davis solo

1' 50"   sixth chorus of Davis solo

1' 53"   Open high-hat cymbals ring. Williams strikes snare drum and its rim.

2' 05"   seventh chorus of Davis solo

2' 11"   cymbals crashing

2' 18"   eighth chorus: Davis ends his solo by playing original theme's opening phrase.

2' 21"   **Wayne Shorter Saxophone Solo** starts after first phrase of chorus where Davis leaves off.
opens with very loose, rhythmically flexible manner, as though spilling notes, not necessarily even 8th, 16th, or 32nd notes

2' 26"	double-stop on bass
2' 35"	second chorus of saxophone solo
2' 38"	Shorter paraphrases the original melody.
2' 49"	third chorus of saxophone solo
	Shorter states the original theme, but now in his high register.
2' 52"	More paraphrase forms question and answer routine using the tune's phrases.
3' 04"	fourth chorus of saxophone solo
	galloping, jumps in pitch, riding same rhythm up-down, up-down
3' 11"	Shorter quotes the original melody.
3' 18"	fifth chorus; quotes, paraphrases, quotes in staccato
3' 24"	Shorter poses questions and provides answers himself, using the original theme.
3' 34"	sixth chorus; flurries of notes
3' 48"	**Return to Theme** by unison trumpet and saxophone
4' 04"	**Herbie Hancock Solo**
	Piano Improvisation opens with carefully chosen, sustained tones, then the logical development of just one idea expressed into four phrases.
	Hancock rarely injects any comping.
4' 18"	second piano solo chorus; Hancock paraphrases the original theme.
	Bass is playing modified 2-beat rhythm; drummer using sticks on opening and closing high-hat
4' 26"	Hancock generates another idea and plays it three times, each of which is pitched lower.
4' 34"	third piano solo chorus; break, another idea expressed into three cells
4' 39"	a new idea reiterated four times, transposed down each time
4' 47"	Solo line blurs chorus ending.
4' 49"	fourth piano solo chorus
4' 51"	densely packed but logical new ideas
4' 58"	a new idea, reiterated three times in different pitches
5' 08"	descending pitch repetitions of one idea in same rhythm (isorhythm)
5' 11"	new idea played six times
5' 31"	**Return to Theme** by unison trumpet and saxophone
5' 45"	repeat of theme
6' 00"	last phrase played five more times
6' 21"	Bass replies. Open high-hat cymbals ring.

▶ Ornette Coleman's band without Coleman: Don Cherry (pocket trumpet), Charlie Haden (bass), Eddie Blackwell (drums), and Dewey Redman (tenor sax). During the mid-1970s, this personnel went by the name of "Old and New Dreams."

Photo by William E. (Bill) Smith

The most avant-garde of Bill Evans' records, including the classic *Sunday at the Village Vanguard*, with "Solar," did not sell well when they were first released. His reception improved over the years that followed, though he was never as widely known as three pianists he influenced: Herbie Hancock, Chick Corea, and Keith Jarrett. The most avant-garde of Miles Davis Quintet albums, particularly the one providing his "Prince of Darkness," heard on *Jazz Classics CD2*, were the lowest selling of his recording career.

SUMMARY

1. Free jazz improvisation doesn't use preset progressions of chords. In some cases it also dispenses with preset melody and steady timekeeping.

2. By comparison with bebop, free jazz uses a wider variation in pitch and tone quality.

3. Some free jazz involves lengthy collective improvisations that are loud and frenzied.

4. Free jazz drummers often generate an ever-changing undercurrent of activity instead of playing standard time-keeping patterns.

5. Prominent free musicians are saxophonist Ornette Coleman and pianist Cecil Taylor.

6. "Modal jazz" is the term applied to long improvisations accompanied only by two-chord, continuously repeating patterns and guided by notes in a scale called a mode, rather than by notes in accompaniment chords.

7. Much modal jazz, especially that of John Coltrane, was as frenzied sounding as free jazz. Many listeners therefore classified it with free jazz despite its preset, un-"free" arrangement.

8. The biggest names in modal jazz were Miles Davis and John Coltrane.

9. Pianist Bill Evans was pivotal in moving the Miles Davis repertory to a modal approach, and his piano style influenced Herbie Hancock, Chick Corea, and Keith Jarrett. He also perfected a rhythmic approach that did not make the beat as obvious as previous jazz piano styles did.

KEY TERMS

floating pulse   free jazz   modal jazz

FURTHER RESOURCES

✓●─[Study and **Review** on **mysearchlab.com**

Test your knowledge with the chapter quiz.

VIEW

Prentice Hall Jazz History DVD (ISBN 0-13-602643-5)
"So What" with Miles Davis and John Coltrane; "Up with the Lark" with Bill Evans; and "Connections" with Miles Davis, Wayne Shorter, and Chick Corea.

John Coltrane Live in '60, '61 & '65. Jazz Icons. Live footage featuring Coltrane with Miles Davis' Quintet (1960) and as a group leader.

The World According to John Coltrane. Medici/Euroarts, c 2010. Documentary from 1993.

Sound: Ornette Coleman Trio. Rhapsody Films. 1966 29-minute film of the saxophonist's trio.

Bill Evans Trio: The Oslo Concerts. Shanachie Home Video. Two concerts from 1966 and 1980.

LISTEN

Smithsonian Collection of Classic Jazz contains excerpts from Cecil Taylor's album *Unit Structures* and Ornette Coleman's album *Free Jazz*. It also contains Coleman's "Lonely Woman."

Jazz Classics Compact Discs for *Jazz Styles: History and Analysis, 11th Edition* (ISBN 0-205-03686-4; phone 800–947–7700) contain Albert Ayler's 1964 "Ghosts: First Variation," mode-based improvisations on Miles Davis' 1959 "Flamenco Sketches" (with Bill Evans and John Coltrane) and John Coltrane's 1963 "Afro Blue."

Ornette Coleman—*Free Jazz*, 1960 (Atlantic 1364)

Ornette Coleman—*The Shape of Jazz to Come*, 1959 (Atlantic 1317)

Coleman's "Civilization Day" (1971) is on *Prentice Hall Jazz Collection* (ISBN 0-205-17896-0).

Bill Evans—*Sunday at the Village Vanguard*, 1961 (Riverside 30509)

John Coltrane—*My Favorite Things*, 1960 (Atlantic/Rhino 75204)

John Coltrane—*A Love Supreme*, 1964 (Impulse B0010970-02)

John Coltrane—*Interstellar Space*, 1967 (Impulse 314 543415)

Cecil Taylor—*Silent Tongues*, 1974 (1201 Music 9017)

READ

Anderson, Iain. 2007. *This Is Our Music: Free Jazz, the Sixties, and American Culture*. Philadelphia: University of Pennsylvania Press.

Jenkins, Todd. 2004. *Free Jazz and Free Improvisation: An Encyclopedia*. Westport, CT: Greenwood Press.

Jost, Ekkehard. 1974, 1981, 1994. *Free Jazz* (chapters on Miles Davis, John Coltrane, Ornette Coleman, Cecil Taylor, and other avant-garde musicians of the 1960s). New York: Universal, Da Capo.

LaFaro-Hernandez, Helene. 2009. *Jade Visions: The Life and Music of Scott LaFaro.* Austin, TX: University of Texas.

Lee, David. 2006. *The Battle of the Five Spot: Ornette Coleman and the New York Jazz Field.* Toronto, ON: Mercury Press.

Litweiler, John. 1992. *Ornette Coleman: A Harmolodic Life.* New York: Morrow.

Pettinger, Peter. 2002. *Bill Evans: How My Heart Sings.* New Haven, CT: Yale University Press.

Porter, Lewis. 1997. *John Coltrane: His Life and Music.* Ann Arbor: University of Michigan.

Spellman, A.B. 1966 (Limelight reprint, 1966; University of Michigan reprint, 2004). *Black Music: Four Lives* (long interviews with Ornette Coleman and Cecil Taylor). New York: Shocken.

Such, David. 1993. *Avant-Garde Jazz Musicians.* Iowa City: University of Iowa Press.

Thomas, J.C. 1975 (Da Capo reprint 1976. *Chasin' the Trane* (biography of Coltrane). New York: Doubleday.

Wilmer, Valerie. 1980. *As Serious as Your Life: The Story of the New Jazz* (covers Cecil Taylor, Ornette Coleman, and other avant-garde musicians of the 1960s). Westport, CT: L. Hill.

Woideck, Carl. 1998. *The Coltrane Companion: Five Decades of Commentary.* New York: Schirmer.

Yudkin, Jeremy. 2007. *Miles Davis, Miles Smiles, and the Invention of Post Bop.* Bloomington: Indiana University Press.

For discussion about the role of politics in the emergence of free jazz, see "Misconceptions in Linking Free Jazz with the Civil Rights Movement." *College Music Symposium*, Vol. 47, 2008, pages 139-155; available at http://www.jazzstyles.net/illusory.html.

For in-depth discussion of emotion in John Coltrane's playing, see "Perception of Emotion in Jazz Improvisation" in *Advances in Psychology Research*, Vol. 62, edited by Alexandra M. Columbus (Nova Science Publishers, 2010), pages 163-184; available at http://www.jazzstyles.net/Emotion.html

Fusion

Chick Corea and John Patitucci, 1990. Photo by Dan Morgan

FUSION

Jazz-rock fusion is a stream of styles that emerged during the late 1960s. It became the most popular jazz for the next thirty years and the first to have widespread popularity after the swing era.

Jazz, rock, and funk music share similar roots in (1) gospel music, (2) work songs, and (3) the blues. But they represent the products of two different lines of musical evolution. For example, jazz (1) employs aspects of formal European concert music and (2) steers away from vocals. It is primarily instrumental music that is almost as complicated as twentieth-century symphonic music. Rock and funk music, on the other hand, (1) emphasize vocals and (2) stick largely to simple compositional forms such as (a) the 4-chord, 12-bar blues and (b) other brief chord progressions that repeat continuously.

Rock and funk music became a main stream in popular music. Jazz, meanwhile, attracted only a small and specialized audience. While it is true that blues singers from the first part of the twentieth century are

((•● Listen on
mysearchlab.com

*Listen to audio-visual
demonstration of electric bass
guitar on mysearchlab.com*

▶ Bass guitar (also known
loosely as "Fender" bass),
the key element in jazz-
rock rhythm sections.

Jazz-rock A variety of styles
beginning in the late 1960s that
use jazz improvisation, electric
instruments, funk rhythm
section accompaniments; also
known as fusion music

routinely cited in jazz history texts, they are usually mentioned in discussions of the origins of jazz rather than the dominant course of jazz itself. The stream of evolving styles that runs from the earliest blues singers through B.B. King to Jimi Hendrix was already essentially separate from jazz by the 1920s.

Prior to the 1950s, blues and gospel music performed by black performers were popular with black audiences. Ranging from Bessie Smith in the 1920s to Louis Jordan in the 40s, these performers made music which marketers called "race records." In 1949, this category acquired a new name: rhythm and blues (R&B). From that time on, it strongly influenced another style of popular music called rock and roll. Besides its R&B roots, much rock also reflects the predominantly white musical streams of country music. Rock is distinctly separate from jazz, and it is further removed than R&B. Despite differences in racial and ethnic origins, however, rock and R&B remain similar because they both use (1) extremely simple melody lines, (2) repeated bass patterns, (3) very steady tempo, and singers as well as instrumentalists who (4) bend the pitches of their notes extensively in a highly stylized manner.

Some R&B in the 1960s contained accompaniment rhythms that are more complicated than the rhythms in rock. During the late 1960s, some black styles that extended R&B became the source for intricately syncopated drum patterns and complementary bass figures. Some of the rhythm section musicians working for Motown recording artists and for singer James Brown, for example, devised accompaniment patterns that were more complicated than the patterns used at that time by rock groups. The work of accompanists for Sly Stone during the early 1970s was especially complex, having built upon the Motown and James Brown techniques (*Demo CD* Track 30). By this time, more people began referring to this music as "funk" and "soul" rather than calling it R&B. It was this funk-soul category, more than rock, which influenced a number of jazz musicians during the 1970s.

By the mid-1960s, the dominant jazz and rock styles had evolved into uniquely separate idioms with little in common. Then, during the late 1960s, a partial blending of the soul-funk stream and the jazz stream occurred, and was labeled "jazz-rock fusion." Some jazz musicians were not affected by funk, and many funk groups were not affected by jazz. But much of the jazz played during the 1970s and 80s was heavily influenced by funk, and some funk groups incorporated more of the improvisation and advanced harmonies found in jazz.

DISTINGUISHING JAZZ FROM ROCK

Jazz of almost any period can be distinguished from rock and funk music in that rock and funk typically have:

1. shorter phrase lengths
2. less frequent chord changes
3. less complexity of melody
4. less complexity of harmony
5. less use of improvisation, especially in accompaniments
6. much more repetition of melodic phrases
7. more repetition of brief chord progressions
8. simpler, more repetitive drumming patterns
9. more pronounced repetition of bass figures
10. More is preset in rock and funk performances than in jazz performances. Jazz ordinarily requires both solos and accompaniments to be improvised fresh each time they occur.
11. Where jazz places emphasis on rhythmic flexibility and relaxation, rock stresses intensity and firmness. Jazz projects a shuffling or loping kind of feeling. Where jazz attempts to project a lilting, bouncy feeling that seems to pull each beat along, rock and funk music seem to sit on each beat. Jazz musicians characterize the time sense of rock and funk musicians as "straight up and down."

12. Jazz musicians tend to choose non-electronic instruments, while their rock and funk counterparts rely heavily on electronic instruments and high amplification of ordinary instruments.

HOW DID JAZZ AND ROCK MERGE?

Jazz-rock fusion mixed jazz improvisation with the instrumentation and rhythms of R&B. This mixture was very popular, both with young musicians coming up and with older established players. Rhythm sections changed instrumentation by replacing piano with electric piano and synthesizer and by replacing acoustic bass viol ("string bass") with electric bass guitar ("Fender") (see page 196). Pianists and guitarists often adopted repeating accompanying riffs in place of the spontaneous comping which had been customary since the 1940s. Bassists began collecting the strongly rhythmic, syncopated and staccato bass patterns in the style of James Brown and Motown funk bands of the late 1960s and the back-up groups for Sly Stone of the early 1970s. Just as some swing-era bassists had to switch from brass bass (tuba) to string bass, early fusion bassists often had to switch from string bass ("acoustic") to bass guitar ("electric" or "Fender").

Demo CD Tracks 30 and 98 |

Drummers learned new timekeeping patterns that resembled those of R&B as well as Latin American styles. Jazz-rock drumming style was very full and active. Following the lead of Tony Williams, the high-hat was snapped shut sharply on every beat instead of every other beat. There was more emphasis on the bass drum, and less on cymbals for timekeeping. The rhythms were stated insistently and repeatedly, and not in the more subtle, highly varied manner of jazz. The jazz-rock style maintained a high level of tension for long periods. There was considerably less bounce and lilt than

▶ Tony Williams, the drummer who invented a style that set the pace for jazz-rock fusion. He was also a prime force in the innovative band of Miles Davis during the mid-1960s.

Photo by Jan Persson, courtesy of JazzSign/Lebrecht Music & Arts

in jazz of the 1950s, and timekeeping was more strictly stated than during the exploratory years of jazz in the 1960s.

The more jazz-oriented soloists in jazz-rock fusion tended to draw upon John Coltrane's early-1960s style as a model if they were saxophonists, Freddie Hubbard if they were trumpeters, and Herbie Hancock, McCoy Tyner, and Chick Corea if they were pianists. Bebop melodic rhythms were not compatible with most funk accompaniment patterns, but the lines of Coltrane and Tyner were. The less jazz-oriented pianists in fusion devised their own simpler styles or imitated players who leaned more toward the rock side of the jazz-rock mix. The less jazz-oriented saxophonists in fusion used models from R&B and R&B-oriented jazz such as King Curtis, Junior Walker, Wilton Felder, Hank Crawford, and Grover Washington, Jr. Additionally, David Sanborn and Michael Brecker, who had themselves absorbed the R&B styles, became major influences during the 1980s. Wilton Felder had been a strong influence on Kenny G. Then Kenny G, in turn, became an influence on many saxophonists of the 1990s.

MILES DAVIS AND FUSION

Besides pioneering work in a number of jazz styles, the Miles Davis Quintet of 1964–68 was one of the first established jazz groups to mix rock and funk with jazz. Rhythmic styles other than bouncy, swinging jazz patterns appear on some of their records. But it didn't happen all at once. Little by little Davis' rhythm section players introduced elements that sounded more like rock than jazz. Drummer Tony Williams began playing straight, repeating eighth notes on the ride cymbal, and occasionally stated each beat by sharply snapping closed the high-hat. Bassist Ron Carter sometimes complemented those drumming patterns with simple, repeating bass figures that did not resemble walking bass style. Beginning in 1968, Davis also used electric piano and electric bass guitar. All of this was similar to rock.

Two Davis albums became particularly significant in directing modern jazz of the 1970s. These albums were *In a Silent Way* and *Bitches Brew*, both made in 1969. They contained a variety of musical approaches, but their dominant style was a combination of jazz and rock.

Instrumentation

The post-1968 music of Davis differed in several ways from his 1963–68 style. For example, instrumentation was altered as follows:

1. Electric piano and organ replaced conventional piano. Davis often employed two or more electric keyboard instruments at once. (Listen to *Demo CD* Track 98 for Fender Rhodes electric piano. Listen to Track 31 to compare bebop style rhythm section using acoustic instruments with funk style rhythm section using electric instruments.)

2. Electric bass guitar replaced acoustic bass viol. (Listen to *Demo CD* Track 30 to compare walking style by acoustic bass with three different samples of funk style by electric bass guitar.)

3. Davis used electric guitarists. At one time, he had three in a single band.

4. The Davis saxophonists of this period spent more time playing soprano sax than any other instrument. The high-pitched soprano could make its sound be heard over drums and electric instruments, where a tenor might not cut through. (Listen to *Demo CD* Track 70 for soprano saxophone. Listen to Track 77 to compare tenor saxophone with soprano saxophone.)

5. Davis usually employed two or more drummers. By the early 1970s, he had settled into the pattern of using one player on conventional drum set and another playing auxiliary percussion such as conga drums, shakers, rattles, gongs, whistles, and a large number of instruments from Africa, South America, and India.

The rhythm section concept was another way in which Davis' post-1968 groups differed from his 1963–68 groups. The later groups created elaborate colors and textures, and rhythm section members played with a very high level of activity. The beat was easily detectable, but it was surrounded by a mass of constantly changing sounds. Complexity was now concentrated in the accompaniments rather than the melodies. These ranged from delicate to turbulent sounds. Textures often seemed to be created for their own sake rather than what would ordinarily be construed as accompaniments. The "accompaniment" textures on *In a Silent Way* and *Bitches Brew* are as much in the forefront as the written melodies and improvised solo lines. These textures were generated by several electric keyboard instruments (piano and organ), guitar, basses, and several drummers. Bass lines blended rock formulas, a freely improvised non-walking style, and accompaniment figures borrowed from Latin American music. Most post-1968 Davis music centered around a simple idea. This could consist of a few repeated chords, a repeating bass figure, or a mode.

Performance Format

The ways that soloists improvised in this new style followed techniques that John Coltrane and his pianist McCoy Tyner had developed for improvising on mode-based forms and repeating bass figures. These techniques replaced the bebop concepts of jazz phrasing. Charlie Parker's and Dizzy Gillespie's pet phrases were not used. In fact, much of the lyricism that had been associated with bebop was not evident in this new style. Improvisers seemed more intent on creating moods than melodies.

In the jazz-rock works of Miles Davis, the mood was usually very outgoing and full of unrelenting tension. The level of musicianship was very high, and the complexity of the music set it apart from rock. Its energy, however, was at the level of many rock bands of the late 1960s and 70s. Davis' music reflected his admiration for such non-jazz musicians as Jimi Hendrix and Billy Preston. The post-1968 Davis recordings displayed a blend of the jazz tradition, 1960s and 70s funk music, and the music of India and South America. It was infused with the spirit of Coltrane, but the tone colors were those of rock.

The mid- and late-1980s recordings of Davis emphasized preset accompaniments that were produced for him. Davis added his trumpet sound over funk vamps, some of which had been prepared for him by computerized synthesizers. His formula for much of the 1980s was to employ a Jimi Hendrix-style player on guitar and a John Coltrane-style player on saxophone. Both could play hot, funky solos on demand. This was placed atop thick layers of sounds from electronic keyboards, all underpinned by a drummer and a bassist playing in the funk style. Davis rarely allowed his keyboardists to solo. His music of this period was highly arranged and not as freewheeling or daring as before. It was energetic, however, and its sound remained distinct from most pop music of the period.

JOHN MCLAUGHLIN

John McLaughlin (b. 1942) is important to jazz history as a fusion guitarist, bandleader, and composer. He was born in England and was active in British rock bands and jazz groups since the late 1950s. He first became known to American musicians during the period 1969–71 when he started recording with Miles Davis and began playing with Lifetime, the fusion band of Davis's drummer Tony Williams.

Despite his status as a jazz musician, McLaughlin uses a tone that is unlike traditional jazz guitar quality. It is hard, not soft; cutting, not smooth; and metallic, not warm. In short, it has the color and texture preferred by rock guitarists, not jazz guitarists. Also, he frequently alters the size and shape of his tone by use of a wah-wah pedal and a phase shifter. (The phase shifter produces a subtle swirling of the sound.) Also, most of his improvisations contain little of the pronounced syncopation and the easy, relaxed swing feeling that had previously typified jazz. The syncopations in McLaughlin's lines are more typical of rock than of jazz. His solos are often composed of long strings of sixteenth notes periodically interrupted by held tones that McLaughlin expressively distorts in waveform and pitch. The inflections he prefers are refinements of those found in rock and blues guitar playing.

McLaughlin's work in Lifetime and in his own Mahavishnu Orchestra conveyed a very high level of energy. This was due to high amplifier settings; rapid-fire, intricate themes; and extremely busy accompaniment.

◀ John McLaughlin, virtuoso guitarist and leader of the premier fusion band, The Mahavishnu Orchestra.

Photo by John Sobczak

McLaughlin is notable for his phenomenally high level of instrumental proficiency, and he likes to play dazzlingly fast strings of notes with razor sharp precision. There is a quick-paced interaction and intense determination on his Mahavishnu Orchestra albums. Many listeners consider his 1971 *Inner Mounting Flame* and his 1972 *Birds of Fire* recordings to be models of group cohesion and inspired jazz-rock improvisation. Feeling for this music was so high that in 1973 *Birds of Fire* reached the very high position of number 15 on the *Billboard* record sales chart. Most jazz albums never even reach position number 200 on that chart. These two Mahavishnu albums are also distinctive for their use of irregular meters—time signatures that had previously been rare in jazz and rock. Many listeners consider this to have been the greatest of all fusion bands.

Not all of McLaughlin's 1970s output consisted of high-intensity electronic music. He also recorded on acoustic guitar, as on his 1970 album *My Goal's Beyond.* McLaughlin abandoned the non-electric approach for a few years right after this album, but he returned to it when touring and recording with Shakti, a band specializing in Indian music and instruments. During the 1990s he again employed Indian musicians while touring and recording. He innovatively combined rock, classical, and Indian music in many different ways, all the while retaining the attitude of jazz improvisation.

WEATHER REPORT

In 1971 pianist **Joe Zawinul** (1932–2007) joined saxophonist Wayne Shorter and founded a new band called Weather Report. Shorter had composed extensively for the bands of Art Blakey and Miles Davis during the 1960s.

▶ Joe Zawinul.

Photo by Jeff Forman

Similarly, Zawinul's pieces had been central to the bands of Cannonball Adderley and Miles Davis. In their new group, Zawinul and Shorter were accompanied by a bassist and two drummers. One drummer played a conventional drum set, and one played exotic percussion instruments. Though they used a number of different bassists and drummers over the years, Zawinul and Shorter stayed together until 1985. Some people consider them mainly a funk and fusion band, but Weather Report actually created its own idiom and performed a broad range of musical styles.

In the context of Weather Report's first three albums, Zawinul, Shorter, and their colleagues presented a new concept. Though they had the standard instrumentation of saxophone, piano, bass, and drums, Weather Report did not use it in standard ways. For instance, their bassist rarely played walking lines. Their drummer rarely played standard ride rhythms. Zawinul usually did not comp for Shorter. Instead of being played in the usual bebop ways, the instruments in Weather Report were used in a variety of different ways. Spurts of melody might come from any member, not just the saxophone. Rhythmic figures and fills could come from any member, not just a bassist or drummer. For example, **Miroslav Vitous,** Weather Report's first bassist, improvised melodies on bass. (To hear acoustic bass improvising melodies, listen to *Demo CD* Track 27.) He knew how to engage his bass in musical conversations with other group members. Vitous' contributions included fragmented melody statements, bowed sustained tones, and syncopated interjections. He could just as easily bow melody in unison with saxophone as feed rock-style bass figures into the group texture. He could play timekeeping rhythms coordinated with the drummer, or he could coordinate with a rhythm of the pianist. He could quickly go back and forth, too. There was often no distinction between soloist and accompanist. Each member's work contributed to the prevailing mood and color rather than to a solo. Weather Report had exchanged the long solos of conventional jazz for a greater variety of moods and sound textures. With only a few exceptions, they retained this practice thereafter.

Prentice Hall Jazz History DVD: "Boogie Woogie Waltz" by Weather Report

((•— **Listen** on **mysearchlab.com**
Listen to theme from Weather Report's "Birdland" on mysearchlab.com

Photo by William E. (Bill) Smith

◀ Wayne Shorter (soprano sax), Miroslav Vitous (bass), and Joe Zawinul (piano), co-founders of the innovative band called Weather Report. They presented collective improvisation in ways that often steered clear of conventional jazz roles for their instruments. Some of their music mixed popular funk styles with jazz improvisation and wide-ranging electronically synthesized sounds with exotic rhythms.

Composed by Joe Zawinul; recorded in 1977 on piano, Arp 2600 synthesizer, and Oberheim polyphonic synthesizer (Zawinul), tenor and soprano saxophones (Wayne Shorter), bass guitar (Jaco Pastorius), drums (Alex Acuna), and tambourine (Manolo Badrena); originally issued on the album *Heavy Weather* (Columbia 34418; reissued on CD with same number).

"Birdland" is Weather Report's most popular piece. It has been set to lyrics, sung by the vocal group Manhattan Transfer, performed by large jazz groups, marching bands, and lounge acts. It was a hit at discotheques.

Though originally known for freely conceived group improvisations, Weather Report preset everything heard here except Wayne Shorter's tenor sax solo and a few bass guitar and piano remarks. Using set figures is a common practice in rock and funk bands. It has not been as common in jazz, where the emphasis traditionally has been on spontaneity instead. But the swing era and the fusion era attained wide popularity when their music was made of short, repeating riffs of the sort heard on "Birdland." In fact, Zawinul composed his fusion-style "Birdland" as a recollection of hearing the riff-style band of Count Basie play at the New York City nightclub Birdland.

There are many unusual sounds on this recording. Tones made by the electronic synthesizers of Zawinul and the electric bass guitar of Jaco Pastorius are the most prominent. The overtones of the bass guitar were used by Pastorius to play high-pitched notes that sound like an entirely different instrument. His very smooth, slurred manner contributes to his unique effect. The second theme of the piece is carried by those unusual sounds, beginning at 19 seconds into the recording. Within the second theme we also hear tambourine playing steady eighth notes (two pulses per beat), and an open high-hat cymbal struck with stick on upbeats and snapped shut on downbeats.

TIME ELAPSED

0' 00"   **First Theme** (2 phrases) played 3 times by bass notes on the Arp 2600 electronic synthesizer

0' 20"   **Second Theme** played 4 times by bass guitar overtones, piano harmonizing the melody, accompanied by Arp synthesizer repeating the first theme, tambourine playing steady eighth notes, open high-hat cymbal struck with stick on upbeats and snapped shut on downbeats

0' 43"   **Third Theme** played by piano, tenor sax, and Oberheim synthesizer, accompanied by bass guitar playing a different phrase

0' 56"   **Interlude**

1' 03"   **Fourth Theme** played in unison by Oberheim synthesizer and piano 4 times. Arp is sustaining its low note.

1' 20"   Bass notes on the Arp stretch the opening theme underneath repeats of the fourth theme.

1' 32"   **Fifth Theme** played by tenor sax in upper register and Oberheim synthesizer, accompanied by sustained tones in bass guitar and piano chords

1' 46"   Bass guitarist plays by himself.
         brief exchanges between bass guitar playing harmonized remarks and piano playing funk licks

2' 00"   **Main Theme**

       First Rendition

          voice, piano, soprano sax

2' 06"   *Second Rendition*

          voice, piano, soprano sax

2' 12"   *Third Rendition*

          Oberheim synthesizer joins them.

2' 18"   *Fourth Rendition*

          same as third rendition

2' 25"   *Fifth Rendition*

          Oberheim plays harmonized melody with them.

2' 31"   *Sixth Rendition*

          same as fifth rendition

      Interlude

2' 38"   Bass guitar, voice, Arp 2600 synthesizer and high-hat cymbals play over a single sustained pedal tone, as though to cool down before more action begins again.

2' 49"   Synthesizer plays a new theme three times in the bass register.

3' 08"   a sequence of eight descending chords is played seven times by piano, bass guitar, and Oberheim synthesizer, answered each time by tenor sax improvisations, piano improvising punctuations that are high pitched and staccato

3' 29"   a passage occurs here that sounds like the opportunity to cool down before getting hot again

3' 36"   **Second Theme** sounded by bass guitar overtones,
                      while tenor sax talks back

3' 48"   Arp begins repeating first theme under bass guitar's melody.

3' 54"   Synthesizer and tenor sax play second theme in harmony, accompanied by Arp playing first theme.

4' 00"   **Third Theme** played loudly, as though a big band

4' 13"   **Fourth Theme** played by piano and Oberheim synthesizer

4' 24"   **Main Theme** played by sax, piano, and synthesizer, accompanied by bass guitar decorations,
                hand claps on every other beat, tambourine playing steady eighth notes,
              high-hat struck on upbeats, snapped shut on downbeats

4' 36"   voice countermelody

4' 49"   Voice joins repeating theme.

5' 01"   Arp 2600 improvisation over top of repeating theme
repeats to fade-out.

An essential aspect of Weather Report's sound after 1972 was the rich combination of orchestral sounds produced by Zawinul's mastery of electronic synthesizers. Among jazz musicians, Zawinul is held in high esteem for his command of electronic instruments, his taste in their use, and his fertile imagination.

An important ingredient in Weather Report's idiom was the sound of **Wayne Shorter's** saxophone playing. It was frequently added to the bubbling layers of colorful sounds made by Zawinul's electronic synthesizers. Sometimes Shorter carried the melody. Sometimes he played brief fragments of a line. Shorter's work was soulful at the same time as it was mysterious and otherworldly. Sometimes he held a single tone, as though taking a paint brush and applying one long stroke to a canvas that was busy with other patterns. In this way Shorter's playing functioned in the manner of an orchestral composer instead of an accompanied jazz soloist. Especially significant is that his playing frequently softened the effect of the synthesizer and percussion sounds. Shorter's notes could immediately touch a listener's emotions. And his style was instantly recognizable. It would be hard to mistake for the style of Lester Young, Charlie Parker, or Ornette Coleman.

Weather Report's career had two main phases, their emphasis on collective improvisation of textures and their funk band emphasis. Though they did not entirely abandon collective approaches, much of their work after their 1973 *Sweetnighter* album left collectively improvised approaches in favor of approaches using extensively repeated, written themes and

▶ Jaco Pastorius, bass guitarist with Weather Report from 1976–1982. His sleek tone and the singing quality of his lines introduced a new style for the bass in jazz-rock fusion.

Photo by Tom Copi, courtesy of Frank Driggs

preset rhythm section figures. With *Sweetnighter*, Weather Report began using more repetition. In its new style, compositions were constructed of brief phrases repeated continually and accompanied by a funk rhythm section style. With this new emphasis on repetition and funk, Zawinul sought a larger audience for his band. Their 1977 hit piece "Birdland" culminated that trend.

Weather Report's role was larger in American popular music as a whole than in jazz. Though some jazz groups were touched by their methods, most of the bands that learned from Weather Report played music that was not closely related to swinging jazz. They did not closely follow methods of improvisation used by swing era and bebop models. Some of the styles were closer to new age and funk music. The musicians in Weather Report all had previously achieved considerable reputations in the field of jazz. But their work in Weather Report and their influence on American music was with a group of musical styles that were not necessarily jazz.

HERBIE HANCOCK

Pianist Herbie Hancock (b. 1940) is best known to the public as a leader of jazz-rock fusion bands. However, Hancock is best known to musicians as a tremendously original and versatile jazz pianist and composer. He played with Miles Davis from 1963 to 1969 and became the most sought-after band pianist of the 1960s. Hancock's freshest work is the soloing and accompanying he did with Davis. Hancock comped in a brisk manner and used a gentle, even touch. He managed to sound light and airy, yet muscular and firm, all at the same time. (See "Prince of Darkness" listening guide on pages 188–191 for more about his solo style.)

((•–Listen on
mysearchlab.com
Listen to Herbie Hancock's piano style on mysearchlab.com

Photo by Rob Lacey, courtesy of vividstock.net/Alamy

◄ Herbie Hancock, composer-pianist-bandleader, shown here in 2009. His hit records *Head Hunters*, *Thrust*, and "Rockit" all featured use of electronically synthesized sounds in a funk style.

Though known for his originality, Hancock absorbed several influences while he was developing his style during the late 1950s and early 60s. Some of his playing has funky, bluesy figures and a contagious rhythmic bounce that recall styles within the hard bop idiom. But Bill Evans was the most significant influence on Hancock. Evans' use of harp-like, ringing tones surrounded by silence can be heard in Hancock's playing on slow pieces. And he was also influenced by Evans' harmonies and mode-based thinking. He displayed more bebop than Evans did, however. Hancock also drew from the ideas of twentieth-century classical composers. But he did not merely imitate the music of his models. He extended their methods and added so many original ideas that his style became instantly recognizable.

Another side to Hancock's creativity is his productivity and originality as a composer and arranger. By the early 1970s, he had written every tune on eight of his own albums, and he had written or coauthored many of the tunes on seven more. His "Dolphin Dance" has become a modern classic among jazz compositions. Musicians praise its beauty and the clever progression of chords and pedal points that are intertwined with its delightful melody. His "Maiden Voyage" became a staple for young musicians of the 1960s and 70s, especially because of its modal construction. His funky, bluesy piece "Watermelon Man" also became very popular. Many bands played their own arrangements of it, and it was performed by almost every wedding band in America to satisfy dancers' demands for a funk piece.

Hancock enjoyed immense success for styles that he devised from a type of popular music known as *funk music*. His first big hit came when he imitated the style of Sly Stone's accompanists by creating the *Head Hunters* album, which sold a million copies. His follow-up album, *Thrust,* was almost as popular. Most of his funk music since the mid-1970s has featured electronic keyboard instruments instead of conventional ("acoustic") piano. Much of his bandleading and recording has been with groups containing funk style bass guitar playing and funk style drumming.

Between the mid-1970s and the mid-80s, his most popular music had less and less jazz improvisation in it, and more and more dance rhythms that were highly syncopated and very repetitive. Melodies were simple and heavily rhythmic. As of this writing, his widest recognition has come from a 1983 work called "Rockit." The recording is a light-hearted construction of novel sound effects in an engaging funk rhythm, all tightly arranged with Hancock's usual sense of balance and completeness. It was included in *Future Shock,* an album that went gold and stayed on the popularity charts for more than a year. As a single, "Rockit" remained in the popularity charts for nine weeks, and as a video it was one of the fifteen most popular of the year. Though much of the public routinely places it in the jazz category, Hancock himself does not consider this music to be jazz. By the 1980s, Hancock's funk music had captured a slice of the market for dance music and youthful party music.

Photo by Takehiko Tokiwa

◀ Chick Corea, pianist-
composer-bandleader, a
major force in acoustic
and jazz-rock fusion styles.
Shown here in 2006.

CHICK COREA

Like Herbie Hancock, pianist Chick Corea (b. 1941) is better known to the
public as a bandleader in the jazz-rock fusion style than as a jazz pianist.
However, Corea followed Herbie Hancock as pianist in the Miles Davis
Quintet of 1968 and soon became one of the most prominent pianists in
jazz. Like Bud Powell and Bill Evans before him, Corea created a harmonic
and melodic vocabulary that fostered a new stream of jazz piano styles (*Jazz
Classics CD2* Track 11). Yet his approach to piano improvising was only one
of several contributions Corea made to jazz history. He also introduced fresh
and compelling styles as a composer and bandleader. These styles became
almost as widely imitated as his piano playing.

Corea's piano style started with aspects from the approaches of Bud
Powell, Horace Silver, Bill Evans, and McCoy Tyner. He also drew from the
classical pieces of twentieth-century composers Paul Hindemith and Béla
Bartók. Latin American and Spanish music also inspired Corea's style. His
playing often bears the rhythmic feeling and some of the melodic flavor of
Latin American music. In addition, his crisp, percussive touch enhances the
Latin feeling. This fits with his bright, spirited style of comping.

Corea's work was already important in jazz history prior to his association
with jazz-rock fusion. There are several reasons for this. His music was played
with a stunning level of musicianship. Its style was not really bebop or hard bop.
His manner of choosing notes for his lines was fresh. The way that he related
his lines to the accompaniment chords was fresh, too. The rhythms in Corea's
compositions and his improvised lines also differ considerably from bebop. They
don't have the same patterns of accent that we hear in most bebop style playing.
He made his music dance with a snap and lightness that are not conveyed by

Prentice Hall Jazz History DVD:
"Children's Songs" by Chick
Corea and Gary Burton.

bebop piano styles. Some of Corea's playing also has the ring of classical music. The sparkling touch of Corea and the bright tone quality he extracts from the piano also remind us of classical music.

Corea led a number of different bands. Each played in a unique style. His group of the early 1970s had considerable impact on jazz-rock fusion styles. For this band, Corea chose to play Fender Rhodes electric piano (*Demo CD* Track 98), an instrument that produces a light, vibraphone-like tone. Stanley Clarke played bass viol and electric bass guitar. Airto Moreira played drums, and Flora Purim sang. The group's music sounded light and happy, full of Latin American rhythms and Spanish themes. The name for the band and its first album was *Return to Forever*. Their second album was titled *Light as a Feather* (*Jazz Classics CD2* Track 11). These two albums became favorites among young musicians of that period. Within a few years, the influence of this sound was evident in a number of jazz-rock fusion bands.

A band that Corea carried through the middle 1970s was influenced by rock and funk music. Corea employed rock-influenced electric guitarists—first Bill Connors, then Al Dimeola. Bassist Stanley Clarke remained from the earlier band, now playing electric bass guitar more than acoustic bass viol. Lenny White played drums with the group. White's style was a very full, active approach which combined aspects of modern jazz and funk drumming styles with the techniques of Latin American percussionists. In addition to playing the piano, Corea used a diverse assortment of electronic keyboard synthesizers. In fact, he became widely known for his synthesizer playing and continued to master new electronic instruments during the 1990s. Corea's records from this period sold well, and independent recording careers soon resulted for Clarke and Dimeola. White and Dimeola left Corea in 1976, but the Return to Forever group name was retained for a number of Corea's subsequent projects. Thereafter, Corea appeared in a wide assortment of contexts. Al Dimeola, Stanley Clarke, and Lenny White went on to lead jazz-rock fusion bands of their own, occasionally regrouping with Corea for touring and recording as they did in 2008.

Corea was widely influential among jazz musicians as a composer in addition to his influence as a pianist. For instance, during the 1970s, his "Windows" and "Crystal Silence" became jazz standards. His "Spain" was so well known among musicians that it became a vocal piece. Singer Al Jarreau's rendition of it became a hit record in the 1980s. Though Corea's acoustic, non-fusion music of the 1960s and 70s appealed to many musicians, it did not gain a particularly large public. On the other hand, his jazz-rock fusion music acquired a mass following. Corea continued to write and perform in that more popular style long after he made his first fusion recordings of the mid-1970s. The Chick Corea Elektric Band of the 1980s and 90s was quite successful.

SMOOTH JAZZ

By the 1980s hardly any jazz of any style could be heard on the radio. Station managers and their advisers realized that if they were going to broadcast jazz and still earn a profit for their stations they would have to play recordings that would appeal to the largest number of listeners. Market testing could determine the selections that would serve this function. So they pursued the testing. The result was a repertory that began in 1986. It was initially termed "The Wave" format and additionally termed "Smooth Jazz." The repertory contained music that was intentionally less challenging to hear than other forms of modern jazz. It emphasized refinement instead of exploration. Smooth jazz was not adventurous but was intended instead for easy listening. Much of it was soft and pleasant, thereby serving as jazzy background music with a beat. The themes in the melodies and the improvisations were neither intricate nor elaborate. Melodies and improvisations in smooth jazz were more melodic than in other modern jazz. Phrases in improvisations were shorter and their melodic development was limited.

Accompaniments in smooth jazz were more predictable and less jarring than in previous jazz styles. They had far fewer chord changes than had been customary in hard bop. Accompaniment rhythms resembled those common to the repeating patterns of accompaniments in Latin American pop music and American country music. They were not the spontaneously shifting improvisations that had evolved during the swing era and bebop era for comping. The continuous commentary of drumming "chatter" that characterized bebop was replaced by continuously repeating patterns.

Freddie Hubbard and Miles Davis were the main models imitated by smooth jazz trumpeters, the best known of whom were Rick Braun and Chris Botti. Saxophonists imitated Grover Washington, Jr., and David Sanborn. (See Chapter 11 for more about the "soul saxes" and their influence on smooth jazz.) Among the most heard saxophonists were Kenny G, Dave Koz and Boney James. Guitarists imitated Wes Montgomery and George Benson. Among the top smooth jazz pianists were musicians who had already created some of the most popular watered-down forms of jazz-rock fusion: Joe Sample of The Jazz Crusaders and Bob James of Four Play.

Ultimately, the smooth jazz format attracted the largest new adult radio audience of the 1990s. By 2006, the only commercial radio stations that broadcast any type of jazz in the U.S. were dedicated to smooth jazz. Almost every major American city had a smooth jazz station. Whereas only a handful of college and National Public Radio stations featured other types of jazz, and they offered it only a few hours per week, there were more than one hundred smooth jazz stations available around the clock. Unlike other kinds of modern jazz, this sound was not relegated to small nightclubs and limited-range radio stations. It was heard frequently in airports and shopping malls, auditoriums and arenas. Concert tours became commonplace for the musicians heard on these broadcasts.

Broadcasters and journalists slotted smooth jazz in the category of "contemporary jazz," by which they distinguished it from what they termed "traditional jazz." That term was used to designate hard bop and such imitators of the mid-1960s Miles Davis bands as the Marsalis Brothers. Smooth jazz and contemporary jazz, in turn, fell under the broadcasting umbrella category of "New Adult Contemporary." Though insiders often resisted including smooth jazz in the "jazz" category, there was a considerable amount of jazz improvisation in the recordings that were broadcast by smooth jazz radio stations. Therefore, despite purist jazz fans' disdain for the music, the extent of improvisation qualified smooth jazz for the "jazz" label and distinguished it from merely continuing a pop radio tradition of instrumental background music. Note also that during the first few years

Recorded April 10, 1970 at the Fillmore West, San Francisco, California by Miles Davis (trumpet), Steve Grossman (soprano saxophone, not heard on this excerpt), Chick Corea (Fender Rhodes electric piano), Dave Holland (bass guitar), Jack DeJohnette (drums), Airto Moreira (auxiliary percussion). Available on the album *Black Beauty: Miles Davis at Fillmore West* (Columbia C2K 65138).

This recording excerpts the final five minutes from a very intense concert performance of "Spanish Key" by the Miles Davis electric band. It showcases the work of pianist Chick Corea. Previously known as a pace-setting improviser playing on acoustic piano, Corea plays the Fender Rhodes electric piano here. Using electronic attachments, he produces an edgy sound to convey some highly explorative excursions. In their hot execution and raspy tone quality these excursions fit perfectly with this jazz rock-fusion setting. In the background, sometimes moving into the foreground, we hear the highly active drumming of Jack DeJohnette, the colorful sounds of auxiliary percussionist Airto Moreira, and some continuously changing figures by bassist Dave Holland. All these elements sizzle and pop.

Instruments. Beginning in 1968 Miles Davis began asking his pianists to play electronic keyboard instruments. In 1969 he began asking his bassists to substitute the electric bass guitar for the acoustic bass viol. His drummers began using timekeeping rhythms that incorporated elements from funk music and rock music.

Frequent distorting of the electric piano's tone quality can be heard here. These effects were intentional. They were achieved by channeling the piano's electric signal through electronic attachments literally known as "distortion effects" and "wah-wah" pedals, as used by electric guitarists in rock music. Near the performance's ending, from 11′ 14″ (4′ 38″ in this excerpt) to 11′ 42″, we hear the effect of running the piano's signal through a distortion device called a ring modulator. Its effect may remind you of extra-terrestrial sounds in science fiction movies.

Colorful percussion sounds occasionally emerge from the accompaniment. For example, the sound of a tambourine is particularly apparent from 8′ 41″. Then, near the end of the piece, there is a metallic waver of pitches at 11′ 15″ (4′ 30″ in this excerpt). This was created by Airto Moriera playing an instrument called a frigideira, which is also known as a Flextone when manufactured in the United States by the Latin Percussion company. This sound is similar to those of Corea's ring modulator, and it coincides in this performance with distortions of the electric piano's tones. Therefore, you might not be able to distinguish sounds created by Moreira from sounds created by Corea.

Part of what qualifies this performance for the jazz-rock fusion label is Jack DeJohnette's drumming on it, especially during the first two minutes. His patterns derive from a steady subdivision of each beat, such that an even four pulses sound for each beat. (Musicians call this a "sixteenth-note feel.") He played this instead of the typical ride rhythm's "ding dickta ding dickta ding" pattern. A further contrast with earlier styles is that the timekeeping patterns were sounded primarily on drums, particularly the snare drum, not just on cymbals. This was another departure from bebop-derived styles. Note, however, that the patterns in DeJohnette's playing are extremely varied here, not repetitious in the manner of the pop music styles that inspired the shift from jazz to jazz-rock. In fact, in this particular passage it is almost as though DeJohnette is soloing at the same time as Corea, instead of providing an accompaniment rhythm. This facet is no surprise because DeJohnette is among the most imaginative of all drummers. In fact, among jazz musicians, DeJohnette is among the most widely revered post-bop drummers.

Tips for Listening. At first, especially from 8′ 51″ (2′ 04″ of this excerpt), the speed and density of piano sounds may prove to be a bewildering jumble. Sometimes Corea's flurries of notes may seem like a blur. But if you listen from 8′ 51″ to 9′ 57″ (3′ 13″ in this excerpt) again and again, individual phrases will begin to stand out. Little by little, individual notes in the phrases will no longer remain a blur. They will become distinct. You will begin to notice germs of melody that are repeated and varied. With more listening experience, your hearing will speed up, and the music will not seem to be going by as fast. Once in a while you could focus solely on the drumming. At other times, try to follow just the tones of the bassist. Ultimately, your appreciation for this excerpt will be rewarded by repeated listenings.

Organization of Harmonies. The improvisations in this performance do not follow a progression of changing chords as was common to most previous jazz. In fact, you will not even be able to hear chords to use as points of reference, except in a few transitional passages. The pianist rarely plays any chords, either with his left hand, which usually comps underneath solo lines played by his right hand, or with both hands together, as when comping for horn soloists. Instead, most of his work is one note at a time, producing lines similar to those that a jazz saxophonist or trumpeter might play.

The harmonic guide for the solo is the type of repeating chord and bass line that musicians ordinarily call a "vamp." In this case, it is primarily just one chord. (Technically, it is what musicians call "a D seven sharp nine," which specifies the notes D, F#, A, C and F.) Some listeners feel that the harmonic character for the piano improvisations seems to waver between what musicians call "major" and what they call "minor." (See Elements of Music Appendix page 271 for explanation of "major" and "minor." Play Track 55 on *Demonstration CD* to hear a narrated illustration.) Some listeners feel that the harmonic character of Corea's lines leans more toward the minor during his first two minutes and more toward the major during his final minute. But you may find it more useful to perceive the harmonic character in terms of an exotic scale. This may be better than pegging the solo line's character as "major" or "minor." (Try to detect this character yourself by playing D-Eb-F#-G#-A-C-D.) A slightly Spanish flavor is evoked by that scale, and this may have led to the piece's title "Spanish Key."

The band sticks with the same harmonies from 6′ 45″ until about 8′ 48″ when Corea begins transitioning. He then arrives resoundingly on a new harmony at 8′ 51″. The basis of this section is one scale step higher than what preceded it. (Technically, the first two minutes were played off what musicians call "a D pedal" whereas lines during the final minute of the solo were played off what musicians call "an E pedal.") You may feel a corresponding lift in mood because this harmony is pitched a step up from the previous passage. (Technically, the basis for Corea's solo has moved from a D chord, in its first two minutes, to what musicians call "an E seven sharp nine chord," in its final minute. You can play this chord yourself by depressing all of these keys on a keyboard: E, G#, B, D and G.). As with the previous passage, the music's harmonic character might best be illustrated by a scale. (Try E, F, G, G#, A#, B, D, E.)

Usually we can detect the harmonic basis of a passage by focusing on the tones that the bassist plays, especially when the bassist continuously repeats a brief figure. But the pitches in Dave Holland's bass lines are so varied under the piano solo that his playing does not offer a consistently reliable indication for the harmonic basis of the passage. Sometimes it is almost as though Holland is playing melodies of his own.

The pianist was free to play almost whatever came to mind and whenever it came to mind. Phrases in this setting could be any length and separated by as much time as desired. Making any generalizations about particular harmonies directing the solo lines may be misleading here because Corea often makes up his own chords as he goes along. He makes chords to fit his lines instead of making lines to fit the piece's chords. Any chords that he is making up to direct his solo still remain in his mind, not in our ears.

Some listeners perceive one overall harmonic feeling from about 8′ 51″ until 10′ 10″. A return to the piece's original harmonic organization occurs when trumpeter Miles Davis joins the band to state the first phrase of the piece, which is a simple, riff-like theme (F, F, B, C, D, Eb) and then its second phrase (A, B, C, B, A).

Improvisational Strategy. Corea's solo is freewheeling, and the pianist infused this improvisation with extraordinary energy. Unlike the construction of many conventional jazz solos, individual elements here are not necessarily essential elements in an overall plan. Sometimes Corea spins flurries of notes (as at 7′ 10″, 7′ 17″ and 7′ 22″) as though an artist flinging paint onto his canvas instead of constructing a recognizable figure. Few of his phrases create an entire picture. The apparent spontaneity of the action can be deceiving, however. These flurries are not random. Each of these gestures was precisely crafted, and Corea knew exactly what he had in mind for every note in them. The point here is merely that the method and its effect contrast with practices that were common to solo improvisations for previous styles that followed a chord progression. Note, however, that with extensive use of repetition and variation, there is order that may be obvious in passages where each subsequent rendition of an idea has evolved from its predecessor. Between 7′ 32″ and 7′ 41″, for instance, Corea repeats one figure thirteen times with variations. He uses this strategy again between 8′ 13″ and 8′ 43″ in which he varies one gesture seven times, resting momentarily on a "wah-wah" dirtied tone at 8′ 31″ before using the same idea again at 8′ 36″, 8′ 38″, 8′ 40″, 8′ 41″ and 8′ 43″. Beginning at 9′ 04″ Corea takes the kernel of one gesture and uses it with variations and different pitch ranges eleven different times before 9′ 20″.

It is important to keep in mind that Corea originated a fresh vocabulary all his own. The overall construction of his solo and the content of its phrases are not very similar to previous jazz traditions. Incidentally, this music does not qualify as free jazz because the band does keep time, and the music remains within a given key for long stretches. Corea's solo does sometimes suggest the abandon of free jazz, however, and it sometimes suggests moments in the wildest twentieth century concert music, such as that of European composer Karlheinz Stockhausen. The music in this performance qualifies as avant-garde because it was not exactly like anything else that preceded it, and it combined aspects of free jazz, modal jazz, funk music, and modern classical music in a very original way.

Ending the Piece. Davis abruptly tacked on a new phrase at 11′ 09″. He borrowed the ending from a piece that his other bands had used for many years to close their sets when performing in night clubs. This set closer had been labeled "The Theme" on several issues of previous albums.

Elapsed Time in Original Recording	Elapsed Time in Excerpt	Musical Events
6:45	0:00	Piano solo begins by quoting second phrase of "Spanish Key" melody: A-B-C-B-A, as end of piece's form, cueing to beginning of piece's form and new key
6:48	0:03	Band begins piece's form, in new key. Piano invents fragment of a melodic idea, altered in five ways.
7:09	0:24	rapid sequence of piano notes
7:12	0:27	new melodic idea
7:15	0:31	rapid sequence of piano notes
7:20	0:35	Tambourine becomes evident here and continues to end.
7:22	0:37	rapid sequence of piano notes
7:24	0:39	ascending passage of quick piano notes, as though up and down a staircase
7:26	0:41	descending gesture that does not strictly adhere to the scale
7:32	0:47	a figure of clashing effect by alternate piano tones, repeated five times, by right hand, interspersed with jagged, two-note combinations by left hand
7:47	1:03	Progression of intricate figures rests on a trill.
7:51	1:07	An intricate figure rests momentarily, altering loudness, on the verge of distorting the tone, is then developed into a melody with a Spanish tinge.
8:00	1:16	new solo phrases
8:13	1:27	one melodic figure played seven times to 8:43 (1:57 in this excerpt); Drumming gets louder.
8:31	1:46	resting on "wah-wah"
8:39	1:54	raspy tone quality
8:43	1:57	slow descent through held pitches, leading to new harmonic basis at 8:51 (at 2:07 of this excerpt)
8:50	2:04	new melodic idea played in octaves
8:55	2:11	melodic idea continued, but not in octaves or tone distortions

9:04	2:19	Piano plays same gesture 11 times, with variations and in different pitch ranges before 9:20 (at 2:36 of excerpt).
9:30	2:46	piano trills
9:34	2:50	Piano plays same descending figure six times.
9:49	3:05	Sustained chords begin transition out of solo.
9:53	3:09	Chorded melody line forecasts new passage.
9:57	3:13	Ascending sequence of distorted-tone chords ends the piano solo.
10:03	3:18	A resounding new piano chord signals trumpet's entrance.
10:08	3:23	Trumpet repeatedly plays first phrase of "Spanish Key" melody.
10:24	3:39	Piano quotes the accompaniment pattern for Lee Morgan's "Sidewinder."
10:40	3:55	Trumpet punches staccato tones.
10:47	4:03	Trumpet plays second phrase of "Spanish Key" melody, echoed by piano.
10:51	4:06	Trumpet trills.
10:54	4:10	Bass begins repeating a brief funk figure.
10:58	4:14	Trumpet punches out staccato tones.
		return to the piece's starting chord
11:03	4:20	Bass plays brief repeating figure.
11:08	4:24	Trumpet plays ending strain from different piece: "The Theme."
11:12	4:27	cymbal crash
11:15	4:30	A percussion sound by Flextone mimics an electronic instrument.
11:18	4:33	drum roll on tom-tom
11:20	4:37	Piano signal is driven through Ring modulator and feedback.
11:22	4:38	cymbal crash
11:26	4:41	Ring modulator is making science-fiction movie sounds.
11:30	4:45	tom-tom and tambourine struck slower and slower
11:38	4:54	Ring modulator sounds fade out.

of the twenty-first century, smooth jazz broadcasters added vocals to their playlists. Market surveys had shown that their listeners would like such vocalists as Stevie Wonder, Luther Vandross, and Anita Baker, even though their music did not draw much from jazz traditions. While this broader fare satisfied more customers it also risked confusing listeners who might be trying to learn what "jazz" meant by tuning into their local "smooth jazz" radio station. Over subsequent years, broadcasters continued increasing the proportion of vocal recordings in their programming.

ACID JAZZ

The term **"acid jazz"** was coined during the late 1980s by English disc jockeys Gilles Peterson and Chris Bangs at a weekend-long party in England where each room provided a different kind of music. One was a type of dance music originating in Detroit and Chicago called "house music." Some of it was intended to accompany the effects of taking the drugs called "ecstasy" and LSD, nicknamed "acid." So it became known as "acid house music." Announcing the availability of jazz in one of the rooms, Peterson reportedly remarked to the partiers, "Now that you've had your fill of 'acid house,' we're going to give you acid jazz." Though originally offered as a joke, the term was soon applied whenever disc jockeys combined current pop dance music with excerpts from old jazz albums. Gilles Peterson and other British disc jockeys particularly liked funky hard bop recordings of the 1960s from the Blue Note and Prestige firms, sometimes by Art Blakey, Horace Silver, Lou Donaldson, Herbie Hancock, and Grant Green. Gilles Peterson's firm, in turn, founded a subsidiary called Acid Jazz, and some of the groups they hired thereby defined the genre. Like the swing style of the 1930s and 40s, acid style functioned primarily as dance music.

At the same time, rap groups were beginning to borrow jazz sounds. They had at least two reasons. First, they needed a new way to get accompaniments cheaply. So they were excerpting the introductions, during which the pace and feeling of the original selections were established. At first they borrowed accompaniment riffs from the funkiest of jazz records because it helped provide a continuous pattern of repeating rhythms to play under their rap. Second, some rappers believed that their performance would gain a jazz flavor if any element associated with jazz were incorporated. This might consist of a very brief part of a trumpet or saxophone improvisation, a few piano chords that typified jazz of the 1960s or 70s, a walking bass pattern, or a jazz drummer's ride rhythm. Some rappers felt that just naming famous jazz musicians within the rap itself would make their product more hip.

Within some acid jazz selections, even those without rap, jazz horn work is **overdubbed** in a way that merely decorates whatever else is happening. It is not the main focus of attention. For example, in some selections, horn sounds provided only minor coloration, while the drum beat remained the most prominent aspect of the sound. This reversed the roles traditionally occupied in most jazz. Drums were background, while horns were foreground. *Though using jazz solos as decoration reversed the trend for jazz, it continued a long tradition in popular music.* "Hot solos," as they were

Acid jazz Usually the creation of a disc jockey who takes funky accompaniments that have been synthesized electronically and/or sampled from jazz recordings, then repeats them continuously with raps and/or jazz improvisations superimposed atop them

Overdub A new recording placed on top of an earlier source, such as adding a bass part to a pre-existing track

called, had been added to otherwise non-jazz pieces as early as the 1920s. They were commonly included in performances by rhythm and blues singers of the 1940s and 50s. Early rock bands frequently carried a saxophonist for this purpose. Soul bands of the 1960s and 70s had occasionally used brief jazz improvisations, too.

Sampling

Much of acid jazz depends upon electronically excerpting portions of old albums. This procedure is called **"sampling"**. Among producers, the term is used in two slightly different ways. The older meaning refers to recording samples of a given instrument's tone from each pitch range. The result remains stored in a computer to be altered according to the programmer's wishes. Entire melodies and accompaniments can be pasted together by electronically changing the pitch and rhythms of that tone. The synthesizers can even determine the ways that tones begin and end. The programmer can thereby give them the character of a live hornman or human voice, for instance. This had been common in pop music products since at least the early 1980s.

The newer meaning for "sampling" is the one that applies more to acid jazz. Entire phrases from an old album are recorded into a computer. Then they are re-synthesized into another recording apparatus if a new album is being created. Or they are re-synthesized into playback facilities if a disc jockey is using them spontaneously at a dance party. In some of the earliest acid jazz mixtures, disc jockeys sampled more than just accompaniment phrases. They excerpted a few moments of intact music from an old jazz album. The particular way the phrases were mixed was determined by the creativity of the disc jockey. Performing these procedures became a career for disc jockeys who termed themselves **"mixers"**. When devised during a dance party, the resulting mixtures were not usually saved. When devised in the studio, however, the mixtures often became part of CDs that the disc jockey copyrighted and marketed as new material.

Sampling In acid jazz, lifting an entire part from an earlier recording to form the basis of a new creation

Mixer The title for the disc jockey who blends excepts of various recordings and adds scratching sounds from wiggling the turntable underneath an album while the needle is connected to the loudspeaker

▶ DJ with one hand on turntable, other on mixing board.

Photo by Randy Norfus

Looping

In many acid jazz selections, the instrumental phrase that was sampled came from the accompaniment portion of an old recording. It was then repeated continuously by a process called **"looping"**. This produced an accompaniment groove. On top of this was placed an assortment of additional sounds from samples or electronically synthesized sources. Often the additions included a loud snare drum sound on every other beat. This is known as a "back beat" if it happens on the second and fourth of every group of four beats. Sometimes the addition was a closed high-hat cymbal struck twice for each beat, thereby providing a continuous pulse. A strong bass drum rhythm was also added in some mixes. Usually all these elements were added. Then a collection of new raps and jazz improvisations were placed on top of that foundation. In other words, *acid jazz was not invented by musicians. It was invented by disc jockeys and rap artists.*

Looping A recording technique in which a short musical phrase is repeated

Overdubbing

The methods for creating acid jazz were not entirely new. For instance, overdubbing had been used already for several decades in pop music. But among most jazz musicians and purist fans, it was considered cheating. Though it was uncommon in jazz until the 1970s, guitarist Wes Montgomery's popular recordings of the 1960s had expanded the practice. By the 1980s, most of Miles Davis' albums used at least some overdubbing. Also for more than a decade, disc jockeys had been devising original mixtures by adding sound effects to recordings and by taking sounds from one recording and adding them to another.

Sampling was not new, either. For example, *by the mid-1980s, composer-arrangers owned electronic samples of most musical instrument sounds.* This conveniently allowed composers to excerpt and reprocess sounds to create complete performances without hiring musicians. **Producers had assumed the role of performers several years before the emergence of acid jazz.**

What was new with acid jazz was the extent to which disc jockeys became involved in making the music themselves, instead of only playing the work of others. Musicians were hired by disc jockeys to record fresh improvisations on top of accompaniments prepared by synthesizer, drum machine, and loops. Occasionally a disc jockey actually toured, as though a bandleader. He would plug in his playback equipment and allow one or two musicians to perform live music over the recorded sounds.

Turntablists

The converse of this situation was presented by jazz musician Herbie Hancock when he added a disc jockey to his touring band to contribute his own original sounds. Some of these sounds were made by scratching records with the stylus while the system was connected to loudspeakers. This technique became so popular that its practitioners acquired the name of **"turntablists,"** later subsumed under "DJ," not to be confused with people who merely play recordings intact for parties and radio broadcasts. The new role of DJ also mixes music by running records on two separate turntables at the same time, changing its music's meter, tempo, and pitch, and in

Turntablist A disc jockey who usually operates two turntables simultaneously, mixing and altering the source material to form new sounds

DJ Logic, one of the best known turntablists. Treated as a musician for his interactive role with strong musical sense, he appeared on albums by jazz bandleaders such as Steve Coleman, Dave Douglas, Medeski, Martin & Wood, and he occasionally acted as a bandleader himself. Shown here in 2004 at the Beachland Ballroom in Cleveland.

Photo by Jeff Forman

some cases, creating new melodies from old materials to actually create new music. The modern DJ's signature is derived from what he does with his selection of materials. DJ Logic and Grandmaster Flash are among the best known. (Hancock's hit recording "Rockit" had incorporated such sounds.) Some work by turntablists contributed to the rhythm section or background sound effects. Other work took a melodic lead. By 2005, the technique had become so common in pop music that competitions were being held for turntablists, and college courses were offered in "turntable," just as they had traditionally been offered for "trumpet," "percussion," "piano," etc. In jazz bands of this period it was not unusual to see a turntablist treated as an instrumentalist. In fact, among some audiences for the newest forms of jazz, the top turntablists were better known than jazz musicians. Note that at this time in pop music there were groups comprised entirely of rappers and turntablists, no musical instruments at all. (See above for photo of DJ Logic in action, and see page 218 for close-up of a turntablist with one hand on the mixing board and the other on the turntable.)

From selection to selection, the amount of improvised jazz that could be found in "acid jazz" varied widely. The term eventually became applied to hip-hop music that was only slightly jazzy and usually did not have fresh jazz improvisation. In the mid-1990s, "Acid Jazz" appeared on the labels of some recordings that contained only rap music.

Categories of Acid Jazz

In summary, acid jazz can be divided into three categories:

1. **Fusions devised by disc jockeys of jazz elements with various pop dance music styles** current from the mid-1980s into the 1990s, such as hip hop, techno, trip hop, and rap. Medleys were devised spontaneously by disc jockeys during parties in England. Some

medleys and mixtures were prepared in studios and issued for sale. Some of their mixture incorporated excerpts from the funkiest hard bop albums of the 1960s and 70s, particularly the selections that maintained a groove and had tempos similar enough to loop into the continuous medleys. Selections featuring organ and guitar were particularly welcome. Though most music in this category is described above, a slice of their programming somewhat overlapped the format that American radio stations of that period called "smooth jazz." This music contained improvisation but rarely swung in the jazz manner. Rhythmic feeling in some smooth jazz was less stiff than in most acid jazz, however. It was more elastic because a group of musicians, as live performers in smooth jazz, do not keep absolutely perfect time, whereas machine-made rhythms that typify acid jazz are perfectly constant. Though many listeners don't realize when they are hearing a drum machine, real drumming has an organic quality not conveyed by electronic imitations. A drum machine supplies neither the richness of tone qualities nor the spontaneous variations in rhythms. The most important part missing is the subtle ebb and flow of tensions. Of course, smooth jazz recordings that used drum machines resembled acid jazz in rhythmic feeling.

2. **Fresh music** made specifically for this audience by bands based in cities all over the world, not just England and America. Their music exhibited a wide range of styles.

3. **Renamed music from earlier recordings.** A commercial enterprise in America and England during the mid-1990s applied the "acid jazz" designation to their old recordings and resold them. This succeeded as long as the selections were sufficiently funky and sustained a groove. Record companies reclassified several of their previous recording artists, for example Ahmad Jamal, Roy Ayers, Houston Person, and Don Patterson, as "legends of acid jazz." Some companies used the term "roots of acid jazz" to designate their old music by Wes Montgomery and Jimmy Smith. They sold it in different combinations of selections, with new album covers and new commentary. In other words, "acid jazz" served more as a marketing term than a musical style. But it was so loosely applied in music stores that a customer might have to seek the "rap music" bins to locate it.

Dominant Aspects of Acid Jazz

Despite the diversity of sounds that have been called "acid jazz," at least three aspects of acid jazz make all but category 3 something more than a mere marketing term:

1. The most dominant aspect is the accompaniment rhythm and the way it feels. This is termed "the groove." It is very important because the music serves to stimulate dancing.

2. Another distinguishing aspect is that few chord changes occur. Often an entire selection revolves around two chords that continuously alternate with each other. Much of it borrows the introduction from some other funky recording, for instance, soul music, disco, or

boogaloo. Then the selection repeats that introduction continuously, with occasional variations. Based almost entirely upon an introduction, the harmonic content of most acid jazz selections is understandably limited because the function of an introduction is to set the pace, not offer harmonic development.

3. Melodic development is less elaborate than in any other style of jazz. In fact, many acid jazz selections have no melody at all.

In these three respects, acid jazz is more African than any other kind of jazz because much African folk music is focused primarily on rhythm and tone quality, not melodic or harmonic development. It is no coincidence that one category of pop music from the mid-1990s that was being incorporated into British acid jazz around 1996 was called "jungle music."

BUT IS IT JAZZ?

After fusion had arrived, many musicians and jazz fans did not consider it to be a form of jazz. Most of them eventually softened in their view, but some still consider fusion styles to be separate from the descendants of dixieland, swing, and bebop. Keep in mind, however, that before fusion, many reacted to the avant-garde of Ornette Coleman and Cecil Taylor by saying that it was not "jazz," either. But despite the views of some musicians and purist jazz fans, both the avant-garde of Coleman and Taylor and the fusion of Miles Davis, Weather Report, and Kenny G continue to be found in the jazz bins of music stores, not in the classical or rock bins. This indicates that—at least to the outsider—these styles sound more like jazz than like anything else. Were the outsiders missing the distinctions? Or were the insiders missing the commonalities? Incidentally, big band swing had been classified as non-jazz by many dixieland fans during the 1930s and 40s. They felt that it was not true jazz, partly because it represented a dilution of jazz traits. Collective improvisation did not occupy as much of each performance as it did in early jazz, for instance. Swing big bands emphasized refinement more than spontaneity.

▶ The Mahavishnu Orchestra of 1970: Jerry Goodman (violin), John McLaughlin (guitar), Billy Cobham (drums), Rick Laird (bass guitar), Jan Hammer (keyboards), the premier fusion band.

Photo by David Redfern, courtesy of Getty Images

Different people use different criteria for deciding whether a given performance is jazz. For those whose definition requires both improvisation and jazz swing feeling, much music by Weather Report fails to qualify because its rhythmic properties do not resemble the swing era or bebop grooves, though they do achieve their own infectious groove. Music stores, on the other hand, use much looser criteria and display Weather Report in their jazz bins.

Let us examine three other labeling dilemmas:

1. For those who find jazzness in music whenever it uses saxophones and a particular accompaniment style, music by Kenny G qualifies as jazz, even though it would not qualify by a strict definition that requires swing era or bebop rhythmic properties. Musicians might be more specific, though, and call music of Kenny G **"jazzy pop."**

Jazzy pop Pop music that has certain jazz elements—such as instrumentation or improvisation—but is not viewed as "real" jazz by purist listeners

2. Classification procedures are so loose that jazz journalists once contemplated including rap in the jazz category. Perhaps this was suggested by the African American origins they share. However, (a) most rap does not have melody. It is poetry recited atop a repeating funk rhythm. Though rhythmically compelling, (b) most rap does not swing in the jazz sense, and (c) not much of it is freshly improvised for each performance.

3. If a personal perception of jazzness increases with the number and obviousness of aspects that remind a person of jazz, then acid jazz performances would qualify to the extent that they featured instruments and harmonies associated with jazz, even without improvisation or swing feeling. If any passages conveyed swing feeling, for instance, they would bear more jazzness.

There is another motive for saying something is not jazz despite its roots in the jazz tradition: rejection of pop jazz. By saying a style is not jazz, some fans imply that (1) improvisation does not occupy as much of each performance as in more serious jazz and/or that improvisations in it are not (2) as elaborate or (3) as well-crafted or (4) as rhythmically compelling as in other styles. Or it is a way these fans say (5) they do not like it and are

Photo by Mark Vinci

◀ The electric jazz-funk band that ended a five-year retirement for trumpeter Miles Davis in 1981: (left to right) soprano saxophonist Bill Evans (his tenor sax is sitting to his right), bass guitarist Marcus Miller, Miles Davis (wearing hat, holding trumpet), Mino Cinelu (playing conga drum), Al Foster (playing full drum set). Guitarist Mike Stern, a regular member of this group, is not shown.

refusing to give it their stamp of approval by calling it "jazz." Some dislike it because of reasons 1–4. Some dislike it for other reasons. *There has long been reluctance among musicians and purist fans to include within the jazz category any watered-down variants of a style that derive from the jazz tradition.* This was why distinctions were made between swing bands and sweet bands during the 1940s. Count Basie fit the former category, and Glenn Miller fit the latter, for instance. Some did not even consider Glenn Miller's to be primarily a jazz band. During the 1990s, the same distinctions could be made between saxophonists Michael Brecker and Kenny G. To be fair in classifying styles, we need to consider the actual characteristics of the music, not just the reactions of listeners. When one listener dislikes a style, this does not necessarily mean that another listener will also consider it bad music. We have also learned that if one listener does not consider a musical style to be jazz, this does not necessarily mean the style will not qualify as jazz for another listener.

THE APPEAL OF FUSION

By 2000, rock had maintained a high level of popularity three times as long as swing's popularity. Jazz-rock fusion itself had been popular for three decades. It became the first jazz style since the swing era to gain anywhere near as much popularity.

By incorporating elements of R&B and rock into their music, several established jazz figures achieved popular success as great as that of any jazz player since the end of the swing era. Though jazz instrumentals ordinarily sold fewer than 10,000 to 20,000 copies, jazz-rock albums of the 1970s and 80s frequently sold more than 100,000 copies. This music was so popular that it also came to be referred to as **"crossover"** music because sales of the records crossed over from the jazz market into the popular music market.

Crossover Music that "crosses over" from appealing only to jazz fans to also appealing to fans of popular music

This new success for jazz musicians did not depend so much on their music's jazz character as on its *jazz-rock* character. As with swing era big band recordings, those pieces with the least improvisation tended to receive the most popular acclaim. And, as with the hits of the swing era, jazz-rock hits were identifiable by simple, repeating riffs syncopated in a catchy way. Much of what went by the jazz-rock label consisted of little more than funky rhythm vamps, simple chord progressions, and an improvised solo riding on top.

There are several possible explanations for the new popularity of jazz and jazz-rock in particular:

1. Rock had already been popular for more than fifteen years by the time that Herbie Hancock's *Head Hunters* was released. So perhaps when jazz adopted the electric instruments and the accompaniment rhythms associated with rock, listeners found it more familiar and therefore easier to listen to.

2. The increased prominence of drums was more inviting to dancers.

3. The relative simplicity of chord progressions found in jazz-rock. The new music was more complex than rock had been before, but it was harmonically less complex than other jazz styles.

4. The extensive use of repetition for a single accompaniment pattern. Technically this is known as *ostinato*, which means that a particular rhythm or brief melodic figure is repeated continuously. It was basic to most of the jazz-rock hits of the 1970s. Many of the largest-selling recordings in every category of music, not just jazz, are simple, rhythmically striking, and very repetitive. This combination of features could also account for much of jazz-rock's commercial success.

SUMMARY

1. Jazz and rock represent different streams in African American music, but they have occasionally overlapped.

2. Jazz differs from rock in its (a) smaller amount of repetition, (b) larger amount of improvisation, (c) greater complexity, and (d) higher level of musicianship.

3. Guitarist John McLaughlin led several innovative bands containing musicians who were themselves important jazz-rock bandleaders.

4. Herbie Hancock and Chick Corea were important jazz pianists during the 1960s who became better known as composers and bandleaders during the 1970s and 80s because of the fusion styles they created.

5. Joe Zawinul's compositions and arrangements formed the basis for the important Miles Davis jazz-rock albums of 1969 *Bitches Brew* and *In a Silent Way* and for Weather Report, an innovative fusion band which lasted from 1971 until 1985 with saxophonist Wayne Shorter.

6. Weather Report originally began with much collective improvisation but eventually adopted approaches employing extensive preset repetition and the feeling of soul music. This culminated in Zawinul's riff-based hit "Birdland."

7. The post-1968 work of Miles Davis displayed a blend of the jazz tradition, funk music, and the music of India and South America.

8. Smooth jazz became the easy listening variant of jazz-rock fusion, with Kenny G as its best known practitioner.

9. Acid jazz emerged during the late 1980s as a blend of hip hop and rap music with jazz improvisations added as decoration.

10. Acid jazz was devised by disc jockeys mixing excerpts from old recordings with the sounds of drum machines and repeating loops of accompaniment sounds.

KEY TERMS

acid jazz	jazzy pop	overdub
crossover	looping	sampling
jazz-rock	mixer	turntablist

FURTHER RESOURCES

✓•⌐**Study** and **Review** on **mysearchlab.com**

View the documentary on Herbie Hancock.

Take the online quiz to test your understanding of this material.

VIEW

Prentice-Hall Jazz History DVD. (ISBN 0-13-602643-5) features Weather Report's "Boogie Woogie Waltz" and Gary Burton's and Chick Corea's "Children's Songs."

John McLaughlin and Mahavishnu Orchestra: Live at Montreux 1974/1984. Eagle Rock Entertainment. Video of 1974 performance along with audio tracks of appearance from a decade later.

Weather Report: Live at Montreux Jazz Festival 1976. Eagle Rock Entertainment, c 2007.

Joe Zawinul: A Musical Portrait. Arthaus Musik, c 2007. Documentary with extensive interviews and performance clips.

LISTEN

Miles Davis—*Bitches Brew,* 1969 (Columbia 54519, 2CD + DVD set)

Miles Davis—*Filles de Kilimanjaro,* 1968 (Columbia 86555)

Weather Report—*Weather Report,* 1971 (Columbia 48824)

Weather Report—*Heavy Weather,* 1977 (has "Birdland") (Columbia 65108)

Weather Report—*I Sing the Body Electric,* 1971–72 (has "Surucucu") (Columbia 46107)

Tony Williams/John McLaughlin/Larry Young—*Emergency!,* 1969 (Verve 314539 117)

Mahavishnu Orchestra (John McLaughlin, 1971) *The Inner Mounting Flame* (Columbia 65523)

Mahavishnu Orchestra—*Birds of Fire,* 1972 (CBS 66081)

Return to Forever (Chick Corea)—*Light as a Feather,* 1972 (Polydor 827148-2 or Verve 557 115)

Return to Forever—*Return to Forever,* 1971 (ECM 1022)

Return to Forever—*Hymn of the Seventh Galaxy,* 1973 (Verve 825 336–2)

Herbie Hancock—*Future Shock,* 1983 (Columbia 65962) (has "Rockit")

Herbie Hancock—*Head Hunters,* 1974 (Columbia 65123)

Herbie Hancock—*Maiden Voyage,* 1964 (Blue Note 95331) (has "Dolphin Dance")

US3—*Hand on the Torch,* 1993 (Blue Note 80883) (has acid jazz)

Miles Davis—*doo-Bop,* 1991 (Warner Bros. 26938) (has acid jazz)

Note: *Jazz Classics Compact Disc 3* for *Jazz Styles: History and Analysis, 11th Edition* (ISBN 0-205-03686-4; phone 800-947-7700) has "Surucucu" from 1972 by Weather Report, Herbie Hancock playing piano with Miles Davis on the 1967 recording of "Masqualero," Chick Corea playing "Steps" in an acoustic trio format from 1968, and Hancock's "Chameleon" from the 1974 *Headhunter* album.

READ

Chambers, Jack. 1985. *Milestones 2.* Toronto: University of Toronto Press, DaCapo, 1998. (discusses the Miles Davis fusion period).

Coryell, Julie, and Laura Friedman. 2000. *Jazz-Rock Fusion.* New York: Hal Leonard.

Cotgrove, Mark. 2009. *Acid Jazz: From Jazz, Funk, and Fusion to the History of the UK Jazz Dance Scene.* London: Author House/Chaser Publications.

Davis, Miles. 1989. *Miles: The Autobiography.* New York: Simon & Schuster.

DeCurtis, Anthony, et al., eds. 1992, *The Rolling Stone Illustrated History of Rock and Roll.* New York: Random House.

Fellezs, Kevin. 2011. *Birds of Fire: Jazz, Rock, Funk, and the Creation of Fusion.* Durham, North Carolina: Duke University.

Nicholson, Stuart. 1998. *Jazz-Rock.* New York: Schirmer.

Tingen, Paul. 2001. *Miles Beyond: The Electric Explorations of Miles Davis, 1967–1991.* New York: Billboard.

The Maria Schneider Orchestra of 2005. Photo by Takehiko Tokiwa.

Curious about what was happening in jazz after the mid-1980s? This chapter outlines a few of the most visible trends.

SOUL SAXES AND "CONTEMPORARY JAZZ"

The 1980s and 90s saw the wide acceptance of a long tradition in funky, soulful saxophone styles. Jazz that emphasized grit more than melodic or harmonic complexity became immensely popular. These styles emulated blues singing and gospel singing by using short, simple phrases and voice-like cries, wails, and moans. The tone qualities were not lightweight, dry, or pale, as for cool jazz saxophonists Stan Getz and Lee Konitz. Nor were they rich, lush, or smooth, as for swing-era saxophonist Johnny Hodges. Instead, they were coarse, and were delivered with a hard-edged insistence. Their accompaniment sounds were rough, too, stressing granite stability, not the elasticity, variety, and surprises that typified bebop-influenced approaches. They established a groove and stuck with it. Usually electric instruments supplied these back-ups—organ, bass guitar, electric piano were common—and drummers played patterns more common to funk and soul music than bebop traditions. Their models were Latin American music and accompanists for singers James Brown and Sly Stone. (For an example of the soul sax style, though not performed by a player commonly identified with it, listen to Herbie Hancock's solo on "Chameleon" on *mysearchlab.com*.)

The most-used models for the big names of the 1990s became available during the 1950s and 60s in the playing of several other saxophonists from the American south, particularly Texas. Most had roots in bebop, though they simplified their improvisations so much that bebop character was barely detectable in this pop style. (1) A prototype for this style was Fort Worth-born King Curtis (1934–1971), a tenor saxophonist on many New York recording sessions and a regular with the rock group called The Coasters, the singer Aretha Franklin, and the rock band led by Duane Eddy. (2) Another was Arkansas-born Junior Walker (1931–1995), the tenor saxophonist on Motown recordings with his own band, The All-Stars. (3) A number of these saxophonists had been with the band of singer Ray Charles during the 1950s and 60s: Memphis-born Hank Crawford, Dallas-born David "Fathead" Newman, and Dallas-born James Clay. (4) Houston-born Wilton Felder achieved considerable exposure when recording with pianist Joe Sample and the Jazz Crusaders, later known merely as The Crusaders. (5) The style of North Carolina–born alto saxophonist Maceo Parker personifies the searing tone, insistent delivery, short, clipped phrases, and gospel singing-like exclamations that became popular through David Sanborn and his disciples. Parker was heard often with singer James Brown.

In all the sounds of these saxophonists there was a "twang" that had not been present in the traditional jazz saxophone styles, even those coming from the American Southwest. We can distinguish the style from most hard bop and cool sax styles by a quicker, steadier vibrato and an extra emphasis on scoops of pitch beginning important notes. These characteristics, in addition to the striving for simplicity, set the soul saxophonists apart from the main stream of jazz saxophone sounds.

Not all of the important roots for the soul saxophones of the 1980s and 90s came from the American south. (6) Pittsburgh-born Stanley Turrentine (1934–2000) had pioneered these traits during the 1960s. He had begun his career in hard bop. Later he crafted an individual approach that emphasized simplicity and a very funky flavor. He devised an exceptionally melodic manner, far more concise than other hard bop styles. Quite significant in Turrentine's sound is a characteristic "twang" that was not common to hard bop but became essential to the soul saxophonists heard on "smooth jazz" radio broadcasts from the late 1980s and as recently as 2012. Turrentine preceded the more influential (7) Buffalo-born Grover Washington, Jr. (1943–2001). Turrentine may well be the stylistic grandfather of many soul saxophonists who are now classified as part of the "smooth jazz" idiom described next.

To understand vibrato and scoops of pitch, see *Demo CD* Tracks 46–53.

During the 1980s, these soul/funk influences were manifested in at least three different branches: (1) a refined **"smooth jazz"** style, (2) a rough, raw style, and (3) a more complicated, jazz-oriented style. During the 1990s and as recently as 2012, the first two of these categories were routinely being classified as "Contemporary Jazz." Though the so-called "smooth" variant still had the edginess of its models' sound and retained the insistent, shouting quality that characterized its roots, this variant serenaded more than it exhorted. The style drew partly from the alto saxophone and soprano saxophone playing of Grover Washington, Jr., whose *Winelight* album sold over a million copies during the 1980s. Washington was not only an influence but also a successful example himself until his death in 2001. Washington was more widely known than his models Hank Crawford and David "Fathead" Newman (Newman's "Hard Times" recording significantly influenced Washington). Then Najee, Boney James, Dave Koz, Kirk Whalum, Richard Eliot, and others crafted their own variations of this approach and attained prominence during the 1990s. As the twenty-first century arrived, James and Koz were immensely popular and influencing disciples of their own. Koz even had his own radio show. Their style of music occupied the largest share of the entire jazz market.

The biggest seller among the smooth variant of soul saxophonists was **Kenny G** (b. 1959). By the mid-1980s he had already attained top-seller status. Building upon the 1960s style of Wilton Felder and 1970s style of Grover Washington, Jr., Kenny G softened their manners and simplified their tendencies toward melodic development. He stressed ornamentation more than generating new melodic ideas. The instrument heard most on his hits is the soprano saxophone, but he also plays the other saxophones. For example, his alto and tenor playing are prominent on the *Silhouette* album, allowing us to better detect his Washington and Felder roots, respectively. The music does not swing in the manner of 1930s jazz or the bebop patterns of subsequent styles, but Kenny G does improvise. Moreover he derives his music from the jazz tradition, which is obvious in his work with the Jeff Lorber Fusion band of the 1970s. No matter how they are classified by most jazz musicians or purist jazz fans, his CDs remain in the jazz racks of music stores, not in the rock, pop, or classical racks. Furthermore his music is heard primarily on "jazz" radio, not on "classical" or "rock" radio. Radio broadcasters and music journalists included this style in the category called "contemporary jazz."

To put Kenny G's success in perspective, we need to keep in mind that (a) selling 7,000 copies would be deemed a successful sales run for albums by most non-smooth jazz musicians, but (b) most failed to surpass 3,000, and (c) many excellent jazz albums sell in the hundreds, not the thousands. (By 2003, the average sales run for a good jazz album produced by an independent label, not by one of the big four conglomerates, was 500–800 copies.) Charlie Parker never had a gold record (500,000 copies), and John Coltrane only had one (*A Love Supreme*). By contrast, however, Kenny G's albums not only went gold, but usually multi-platinum (several million copies). His *Silhouette* sold more than four million copies, his *Duotones* album with the hit "Songbird" had sold more than six million copies, and his *Breathless* sold more than twelve million copies. A pervasive part of the

Smooth jazz Music played on radio stations subscribing to "The Wave" format of the 1980s and 90s: Kenny G is the most successful performer in this style

Alto saxophonist David Sanborn.

Photo by Jan Persson, courtesy of Redferns/Getty Images.

auditory landscape for about twenty years, his music is so common that millions of people hear it all the time, recognize that it is familiar, but don't know that it is Kenny G making the sound. With sales surpassing fifty million albums, he is the most popular saxophonist in jazz history and the top selling instrumentalist in the history of recording, not just jazz.

(2) A second branch of the third generation of soul saxophonists is the rough, raw style that is extremely aggressive, almost scorching in its intensity. It is exemplified by alto saxophonist **David Sanborn** (b. 1945) and his disciples. Influenced in part by Maceo Parker and Hank Crawford, his alto sax presence was popular with a broad base of listeners for its very hot brand of funky playing. Almost untouched by bebop, his style was fluent, bursting with energy, and densely packed with soulful phrases. It is distinguished by the immediate, emotional cry that characterized Hank Crawford's manner. Having toured with the Paul Butterfield Blues Band and Motown singer Stevie Wonder during the 1970s, Sanborn was already an established voice in the hard-edged, soulful blues approach by the time he achieved the widest exposure during the 1980s on his own television series, *Night Music*, and in appearances on *Late Night with David Letterman* and *Saturday Night Live*. His sound was also heard with such pop singing groups as the Rolling Stones, The Eagles, and David Bowie, among others. Sanborn was second only to Kenny G as the most widely heard saxophonist of this period. By 2002, he had sold about seven million albums worldwide. Seven of his albums sold more than 500,000 copies a piece. Though hardly smooth, his playing could be heard frequently on "smooth jazz" radio broadcasts during the 1990s and the beginnings of the twenty-first

Photo by Leon Morris, courtesy of Redferns/Getty Images.

◀ Michael Brecker, shown here at the New Orleans Jazz Festival, 1995

century. His music was ordinarily placed in the "contemporary jazz" category. Sanborn continued to have significant influence on young, still-developing saxophonists, such as Dave Koz.

(3) A more complicated, more jazz-oriented branch of the soul sax tree emerged in the style of **Michael Brecker** (1949–2007). Beginning in 1970, he became a major force in saxophone styles. Brecker invented a new approach by mixing the methods of John Coltrane, Wayne Shorter, and Stanley Turrentine with his own original ideas and the King Curtis/ Junior Walker funky styles. Brecker's approach had its own vocabulary and became the most imitated jazz tenor sax style of the 1970s and 80s. He emphasized virtuosity. Impressive speed and agility are hallmarks of his style; Brecker filled almost every space with rapid-fire, multi-noted exclamations. It is was though he were racing all the time. His lines were packed with his own original patterns, often played in double-time, and all delivered with very hot, funky expression. He played with an intensity that never let up, even for a moment.

Brecker, like King Curtis, was known primarily as a sideman, though he was also involved as co-leader in bands called Dreams, The Brecker Brothers, and Steps Ahead. Hundreds of recording sessions employed him when a hot, fluid, funky flavoring was desired. His sound was heard on

((•─[Listen on **mysearchlab.com**
Listen to Michael Brecker's saxophone style on mysearchlab.com

recordings by Paul Simon, James Taylor, Joni Mitchell, Richard Tee, and Steely Dan, to name just a few of the pop stars he accompanied. Not limited to the commercial funk role, Brecker also had been in demand for more straight-ahead, post-hard bop situations, as when he toured with Horace Silver and Herbie Hancock or recorded with McCoy Tyner. During the late 1980s, when he began making a new string of albums as a leader, he became better known than when he had served primarily as a sideman. By 2001, he had six albums out as a bandleader for the same company and had mounted several tours fronting his own groups. (Listen to his most-acclaimed solo, available on Horace Silver's "Gregory Is Here" on *Jazz Classics CD2* Track 1.)

CONTINUING LEGACIES

The 1990s and beginnings of the twenty-first century marked continued vitality in the careers of modern jazz giants who had become established in prior decades: Cecil Taylor, Sonny Rollins, McCoy Tyner, Herbie Hancock, Keith Jarrett, Lee Konitz, Jim Hall, Freddie Hubbard, Chick Corea, John McLaughlin, Ornette Coleman, and Joe Zawinul.

Other developments included the perpetuation of methods devised by Ornette Coleman, Albert Ayler, Cecil Taylor, and John Coltrane in the hands of second- and third-generation free jazz players. Many hailed from Chicago, but pockets of free jazz also remained in Los Angeles (Bobby Bradford and Horace Tapscott, for instance) and New York jazz communities (Charles Gayle, Billy Bang, David S. Ware, Matthew Shipp, for example), and a steady stream continued to emerge from Europe (Peter Brotzmann, for example). Some of these musicians had played during the 1960s and 70s with Cecil Taylor (Ken McIntyre and William Parker, for example) or the Chicago avant-garde (Fred Anderson and Anthony Braxton, for instance).

Pianist-composer-bandleader **Keith Jarrett** (b. 1945) has been a major figure on the jazz scene of the 1980s and 90s. He started attracting attention during the late 1960s in the bands of drummer Art Blakey, saxophonist Charles Lloyd, and trumpeter Miles Davis. His style combined many sources. He drew from both the fields of classical music and jazz. His most obvious inspirations were pianist Bill Evans, pianist Paul Bley, and saxophonist-composer Ornette Coleman. (Jarrett's attraction to Ornette Coleman is evident in the melody and piano improvisations on "The Wind-Up" on *Jazz Classics CD2*, Track 12).

▶ Keith Jarrett, shown here during the early 1970s.

Photo courtesy of Michael Ochs Archives/ Getty Images.

By the end of the 1960s, Jarrett was already an impressive soloist known for striking originality, but his greatest contributions were still to come. These can be grouped as conceptual, compositional and pianistic.

Jarrett's best-known breakthrough came with the concept of improvising unaccompanied piano solos that had little or no planning. Many such performances constitute joyous excursions into whatever Jarrett fancied during the heat of creating. (We get a sample of this in "The Wind-Up" on *Jazz Classics CD2* because the content of Jarrett's solo break at about 1' 55" is not really guided by any preset progression of chords.) The style on these pieces ranged through several extremes. Some moments sounded like he was excerpting from a wide assortment of twentieth-century European piano music. Often Jarrett explored the sonorities of just one or two chords, repeating the sound continuously for many minutes. (Listen to "Sundial, Part 1" on *Jazz Classics CD3* for *Jazz Styles, 11th Edition*.) Most of his extended solo improvisations displayed outstanding continuity, and his transitions were seamless. The character of impassioned singing often pervades Jarrett's improvisations. Some of his solo improvisations sounded like the twangy piano style of country and western music. Other moments sounded like African American gospel music. ("The Wind-Up" recording illustrates Jarrett's attraction to gospel music in the catchy rhythm and chords that drive the introduction.)

By the 1990s, Jarrett had put out more than eighty albums. His unaccompanied solo piano concept filled a library of discs. *Facing You*, his first album in this style, and *Staircase*, his most adventuresome, are favorites among musicians. His *Köln Concert* found its way into the record collections of listeners with very diverse tastes, not just jazz fans. In fact, by 1995 it had sold 2.5 million copies. This put him in a market size that no previous jazz pianist had ever reached. As recently as 2006, it was still selling more than 100,000 copies each year, and Jarrett was still performing solo concerts and releasing albums in this style. Vijay Iyer garnered considerable media attention by playing in a style inspired by this facet of Jarrett's approaches, particularly by the music on the *Köln Concert*.

During the 1970s, Jarrett wrote and played for two important quartets. He composed mounds of new material for both groups. One is the group we hear on "The Wind-Up." This has been termed Jarrett's "European Quartet" because the remaining three members are from Scandinavia. The other is his "American Quartet" with Bill Evans' former drummer Paul Motian and two musicians associated with Ornette Coleman: saxophonist Dewey Redman and bassist Charlie Haden. The music of his American Quartet was inspired in part by the Paul Bley Quartet of 1964 that included saxophonist John Gilmore, bassist Gary Peacock and drummer Paul Motian. It also drew from the music of Ornette Coleman's Quartet of 1968 that had included Dewey Redman. The music of the Middle East and Latin America was also incorporated. Neither band produced music that was the least bit conventional. Almost all their pieces were original compositions, and their rhythmic character as well as melodic character diverted drastically from hard bop and cool jazz. Additionally, a parallel career existed for Jarrett. He wrote classical music

Recorded in 1974 in Norway by Jan Garbarek (soprano saxophone), Keith Jarrett (piano), Palle Danielsson (bass), and Jon Christensen (drums); originally issued by the ECM firm, on the album *Belonging*; composed by Keith Jarrett.

This selection samples Keith Jarrett's composing style, piano improvising style, and one of his best collaborations with Norwegian saxophonist Jan Garbarek. We get a taste of his attraction to African American gospel music in the catchy rhythm and some chords he uses to drive the introduction. Jarrett's interest in Ornette Coleman's style of composing is evident in the melody that Jarrett wrote for this recording. Coleman's style is also apparent in many phrases of Jarrett's piano improvisation and saxophonist Jan Garbarek's improvisation. Both of these men have their own styles, but they chose to make their affinity to Coleman prominent here. One of the main reasons for including this piece on *Jazz Classics CD2* for *Concise Guide to Jazz* is because Jarrett's improvisatory excursion here is so inspired that musicians rank it among his most exciting melodic inventions on record.

After the introduction and theme statement, Jarrett jumps into his solo improvisation at 1' 55" as Ornette Coleman might, throwing twists and turns at us and never letting up. (Listen to "Dee Dee" on *Jazz Classics CD2* to sample Coleman's style.) Jarrett unfurls idea-rich lines with his right hand on the piano keyboard and almost entirely omits left-hand comping. Like Coleman, Jarrett's solo line here is not really guided by any preset progression of chords. Even when joined by bass and drums at 2' 31", Jarrett goes his own way harmonically instead of adhering to the form of the opening theme or its harmonies. Omitting comping makes sense if Jarrett is not following chord progressions, and that is exactly what we associate with Coleman.

"The Wind-Up" qualifies as "swinging" for listeners who designate as "swinging" any music that has steady tempo, lots of syncopation, and gets "hot." Certainly this performance swings in its own elastic kind of way. But this selection does not consistently show swing era or bebop traditions for timekeeping or comping. Only rarely does the bassist really walk for very long, and it is more often under Garbarek's saxophone than under Jarrett's piano. Only rarely does the drummer offer steadily repeating rhythms that state the pulse, and they occur more often under Garbarek than under Jarrett. Instead, he continuously varies them. Though not usually included within the "avant-garde" classification, these rhythmic properties, the peculiar melodic style, and the improvisations' lack of adherence to preset chord progressions make the music avant-garde. To be fair, perhaps these Jarrett-Garbarek creations should be classified as "second generation avant-garde" because they arrived more than fifteen years after the most radical departures from bebop were made by John Coltrane, Ornette Coleman, and Cecil Taylor. The Jarrett-Garbarek music is nowhere near as raw. In fact, there is a considerable amount of refinement.

Note that Garbarek's playing here does not typify the flavor he is best known for, even though it is at a very high level of creativity. His solo is atypical because he usually plays tenor saxophone, not soprano saxophone, and because this solo is so busy. He usually plays more sustained tones in a dreamy manner that some listeners find haunting. There is usually an otherworldly quality in Garbarek's sound. Incidentally, musicians generally consider him to be within the small handful of truly original saxophone improvisers to appear after John Coltrane. "The Wind-Up" samples just one facet of the work that Jarrett wrote for the saxophonist. To examine Garbarek's career exceeds the scope of *Concise Guide to Jazz*, but you are encouraged to track down his recordings because a large body of original music is present in them, and you might find it quite satisfying.

Introduction

0' 00"	funky, gospelish piano figure
0' 04"	Bass and drums join piano.

First Theme Statement (Unison Piano and Soprano Sax)

0' 39"	**A-section**
0' 47"	**A-section**
0' 54"	**B-section**
1' 00"	**A-section**
1' 05"	**C-section**
1' 09"	**C-section**
1' 13"	**Introduction** (funky, gospelish piano figure)
1' 21"	**Repeat of Theme Statement**

Keith Jarrett Piano Improvisation

1' 55"	solo break for piano improvisation (right hand only)
2' 18"	Jarrett uses a Persian scale in his line.
2' 30"	Bass and drums join piano; bass is irregularly walking; drums imitating melody.
3' 03"	funky line by piano
3' 12"	bass ascending line then descending
3' 31"	Piano is quadruple-timing.
3' 48"	Bass is almost walking.
4' 10"	Drums echo piano.
4' 18"	New idea is developed over three occasions.
4' 40"	**Introduction**
4' 42"	**Theme Statement (Saxophone Joins Piano)**

Jan Garbarek Soprano Sax Improvisation

4' 54"	solo break for saxophone improvisation
5' 09"	Saxophone solo uses Ornette Coleman-like cries.
5' 31"	Bass and drums rejoin saxophone.
5' 42"	walking bass; drummer playing ride cymbal
6' 04"	funky remark; piano chord
6' 24"	piano chord
6' 30"	Piano responds to saxophone improvisations. Bass is walking.
6' 34"	Saxophone begins excerpting from "The Wind-Up" melody and paraphrasing it.
6' 54"	hint of a chord progression to 7' 07"
7' 00"	Saxophone repeats same idea five times. Jarrett injects piano chords suggested by the sax line.

7' 06"	Jarrett injects piano chords suggested by the sax line.
7' 08"	Jarrett injects piano chords suggested by the sax line.
7' 10"	Sax quotes and paraphrases original theme.

Main Theme

7' 24"	Return to A-A
7' 41"	**Introduction**
7' 48"	**A-section** by sax and piano
8' 02"	**Bridge**
8' 10"	**A-section**

for a variety of instruments, and he performed recitals of classical piano music by composers of several different centuries.

A fourth phase of Jarrett's contributions is found in collaborations with bassist **Gary Peacock** (b. 1935) and drummer **Jack DeJohnette** (b. 1942). Gary Peacock had begun receiving wide attention in the early 1960s, partly as a result of his astounding technical facility and his ground-breaking avant-garde explorations with the innovative saxophonist Albert Ayler. He had also played with Jarrett's main influences, Bill Evans and Paul Bley. DeJohnette had played alongside Jarrett in the innovative Charles Lloyd band of the late 1960s, then with Miles Davis. Musicians generally rank DeJohnette as among the most musical of all jazz drummers and one of the top to emerge after Tony Williams and Elvin Jones. He has played with a wide assortment of great jazz musicians and led numerous groups of his own that produced distinctive music that was unlike any other music genres of the time.

Jarrett's collaborations with Peacock and DeJohnette are among the most conventional of Jarrett's efforts. Their repertory is primarily pop tunes and jazz standards, though they sometimes play avant-garde improvisations without planning, and occasionally they play their own original compositions. Their most important albums were *Standards Vol. 1 & 2*, and *Standards Live*. Musicians also particularly favor their renditions of standards on the albums *Tribute* and *The Cure*. Understandably, then, this group has become known as Jarrett's "Standards Trio." They sometimes feature straight-ahead swinging in the style of trios led during the 1950s and 60s by Wynton Kelly and Ahmad Jamal. Much of their music is also inspired by the 1950s and 60s trio music of Bill Evans. Jarrett's trio has been recording for more than thirty years, and is still performing in concert halls and night clubs. During the 1990s and the beginning of the twenty-first century, Brad Mehldau attained considerable attention for his own trio recordings inspired in part by the music of Jarrett and Jarrett's Standards Trio.

It is ironic that despite his penchant for unfettered experimentation, Jarrett was known more during the 1990s for looking to the past stylistically. To be fair, note that looking to previous styles for inspiration was a widespread trend at this time, and the quality of achievements when Jarrett played in this earlier style far exceeded the quality of improvisations by other musicians of the 1980s and 90s who borrowed earlier styles. In fact, many musicians found the numerous recordings of the Standards Trio to be the most consistently satisfying jazz of the 1980s and 90s. They eagerly awaited each new release. The amount of substance in Jarrett's improvisations and the sensitivity, good taste, and musicianship of Peacock and DeJohnette were a pinnacle to which other musicians strived.

Pianistic contributions mark every stage in Jarrett's career. His speed and agility remain unsurpassed. Moreover, almost all his lines, even the fastest, are loaded with rich ideas. What may be even more significant is that, especially in slow passages, Jarrett manages to extract the prettiest sound ever associated with jazz piano. Though Bill Evans and Herbie Hancock were strongly influenced by the way that fellow pianist George Shearing could celebrate the beauties of tone, Jarrett triumphed most consistently in this regard. Jarrett's touch and his careful attention to the arrival time for every note let each vibration of the piano sing. His tone, timing, and choice of chord voicings convey a remarkable tenderness, particularly in the ballad renditions on each album by his Standards Trio.

Though influential among noncommercial musicians and known to well-informed jazz fans for a long time before this period, saxophonists Wayne Shorter and Joe Henderson enjoyed their widest media recognition during the 1990s. Newly invigorated careers for these two men made them more visible. Tenor saxophonist **Joe Henderson** (1937–2001) had been appreciated by fellow musicians and knowledgeable jazz fans since the early 1960s. He had played uncompromising, fresh variants on hard bop, going beyond Sonny Rollins and Stan Getz, two of his inspirations. He had toured with the bands of Horace Silver, Miles Davis, and Herbie Hancock, as well as leading his own all-star groups. His largest album sales and widest media exposure, however, did not occur until the 1990s with a series of "concept" albums and effective marketing. When he devoted albums to the music of better known figures, such as Antonio Carlos Jobim, George Gershwin, Miles Davis, and Billy Strayhorn, he reached a larger audience and finally attained the broad recognition he had long deserved. Despite the more familiar repertory, Henderson's improvisations were still rich with invention and daring. His ideas were highly syncopated in endless variations. He used a vocabulary all his own and threw clusters of notes at us, swirling and falling in fragments that were connected loosely by his own unorthodox continuities. His was an extremely loose manner, but organic and speech-like, executed with razor-like tone and exquisite command of the instrument. Henderson displayed a highly developed sense of melody, and he could logically place unexpected textural effects at his least whim. Like Sonny Rollins, he could swing conventionally or intentionally play

▶ Tenor saxophonist Joe Henderson, shown here at the Copenhagen Jazzhouse, Copenhagen, Denmark, 1992

Photo by Jan Persson. Courtesy of Lebrecht Music & Arts.

free of the tempo by developing melodic figures that do not fit neatly with the beats beneath them. He invented swinging fragments inside a sense of tempo that was surgical in its precision. Phrases spilled out of Henderson's tenor saxophone with elasticity, going up and down and around, separate from anything we might expect, yet neither really so haphazard-sounding nor as jarring as the phrases of the free jazz style. They somehow sounded highly logical yet spontaneous at the same time. Few clichés are ever heard in his music. Henderson displayed a seemingly complete freedom. The amount of originality he brought to each solo represents a stunning accomplishment, and it reflects musical intelligence of the highest order.

The contributions of saxophonist-composer **Wayne Shorter** (b. 1933) to jazz history boast four different careers, and he is still going strong and capable of adding a fifth. As the twenty-first century began, his fourth career found him touring with a band of cutting-edge young modernists: Danilo Perez, possibly the most original piano stylist to emerge during the 1990s; John Patitucci, virtuoso bassist who had become known in the previous decade with Chick Corea (see photo on page 195); and Brian Blade, a drummer of uncanny responsiveness and imagination who could make even the most original nonrepetitive rhythms swing in a compelling way. The sounds of this quartet were abstract, sometimes obscuring any reference to an underlying tune or beat. They flitted in and out of funk and fusion styles. They also contained many moments of suspension that featured colors and textures floating together for their own sake. Like some of the earliest Weather Report creations, many passages discarded solo playing. Instead, Shorter's musicians demonstrated group improvisation propelled by a unity

((•–Listen on **mysearchlab.com**
Listen to tenor saxophone by Wayne Shorter on mysearchlab.com

◀ Tenor saxophonist Wayne Shorter, shown here at the 2002 Tri-C Jazzfest in Cleveland.

Photo by Jeff Forman.

that depended on a nearly impossible-to-conceive exchange of complementary ideas. In addition, like a kaleidoscope, they changed continuously.

Before his breakthrough band of 2001, Shorter had three significant careers: (1) As a strikingly original tenor saxophone soloist with Art Blakey's Jazz Messengers (1959–1964), as illustrated on "The Egyptian" on *Jazz Classics CD1*, Track 22. Shorter also changed the character of the Blakey sound with many new pieces, each composition offering forms and sounds that did not imitate any previous models. (2) His fresh new style of improvising on tenor sax and radically new style of compositions drastically altered the concept of the Miles Davis Quintet sound (1964–1969), as illustrated on "Prince of Darkness" on *Jazz Classics CD2*, Track 9. (3) He co-led and wrote for Weather Report (1970–1985), a band with pianist Joe Zawinul, fusing widely assorted styles together with funk rhythms and combinations of sounds that seemed almost orchestral. They set the pace for an entire branch of jazz-rock fusion. Above all, Shorter's historical significance is achieved partly by the unusual ways he makes chords move within his compositions. Shorter is regarded as one of the most important of all post-bebop writers. His pieces are widely performed, and they have become the subject of much study by musicians and scholars.

As a saxophonist Shorter has always been a true original. Though some listeners think they detect hints of John Coltrane or Sonny Rollins, whatever remnant there is from those styles is so thoroughly transformed it makes discussion unwarranted. A heavyweight, broad-textured, gray tone, with only a touch of vibrato, characterized his style of the first twenty years. It was a hard tone with soft edges. He quickened his vibrato thereafter and lessened the density of his tone somewhat. His work was fluid and extremely intense. It projected a rawness that came to be identified with hard bop, though without the burning associated with funk and fusion sax styles that threatened to singe every listener's ears. Shorter's playing also exhibited a highly logical, often tuneful quality, though he became more and more impulsive as the 1990s unfolded. The quality of improvisation in many of his solos is on a par with written melodies. In his most recent period he sometimes spun showers of notes at the listener in a plaintive way. Often the way he organized the showers seemed to be around the beat but not within it. Many of his solo statements seemed somehow ferocious and graceful at the same time. Some listeners detect a bittersweet quality in his playing. Many perceive a sense of mystery. He contradicted what jazz listeners had come to expect from tenor saxophone players. Shorter had such extremely high standards for originality that he usually managed to improvise solos that were free of patterns. He tried to create something entirely new upon each opportunity to improvise, and he usually succeeded. Also note that, beginning in 1969, he began concentrating on the soprano instead of the tenor saxophone. His own peculiar sound on this instrument influenced a number of prominent jazz players, and he continued with this new sound in the twenty-first century.

FRESH APPROACHES

Acid jazz continued during the 1990s (see Chapter 10 for overview), but it also spawned an interesting offshoot that ran concurrently on the jazz and avant-garde pop music scenes. Drummers and bassists imitated the acid jazz sounds of the drum machines, scratching rhythms of disc jockey/"mixers," as well as the sampling and the loops thereof. With this they made live music that bore the groove previously achieved only by the mixers. They also added their own ideas. As a source of originality, they could chop up the samples, fuse them together, and phrase them across larger units of time than they had come from. Mixers had actually doubled the speed of some samples, and this served as an additional example to the drummers. Combining different elements offered endless variations. Some musicians were attracted to this source of fresh sounds because they felt it offered a richness not offered by swing rhythms. It provided the desired manic esthetic that was sufficiently spastic and hyper-complex to satisfy their tastes and inspire new concepts in solo improvisations. The approach was dubbed **"Drum 'n' Bass."** Not all bands that offered this used it all the time. Most bands merely added it to an already varied palate. Albums by these musicians usually collected a taste of each different groove they were exploring during that phase in their evolution. The Drum 'n' Bass groove was just one within an assortment. Their work often resembled Herbie Hancock's "Rockit" and Miles Davis' *Bitches Brew* and *On the Corner*. Note that most of these groups were not in the jazz idiom. They were more clearly within avant-garde pop, variants on what was termed "techno" or "electronica." But a few were jazz groups with highly explorative, earnestly improvising soloists, such as saxophonists Chris Speed and Josh Smith.

Note that emergence of the Drum 'n' Bass genre came after the interest a few jazz musicians had focused on superimposing jazz improvisation atop the accompaniments for rap music, better known as **"hip-hop."** Saxophonists Greg Osby and Steve Coleman were among the musicians who pursued this during the 1980s. Saxophonist Branford Marsalis formed the band Buckshot Lefonque to try this during the 1990s. All these musicians had careers in other styles of jazz, but they decided to experiment with this for a while, and their interest produced a body of music with a decidedly different feeling from bebop and bebop-derived jazz. To further place the Drum 'n' Bass genre in historical perspective, remember that the incorporation of pop music accompaniment styles into jazz reflects a long tradition. Jazz originated by musicians who were hired to play music for such dances as the quadrille and the schottische. Later they were called upon to accompany the stomp and the slow drag, for which they obliged by creating what is today known as swing style and slow blues, respectively. They adapted marches and rags to satisfy the dancers, too, and ended up inventing Dixieland out of that. Then during the 1960s, Brazilian samba was so popular with jazz musicians that a soft, gentle version of it was tried by many jazz improvisers and called "bossa nova" (Portuguese for "new beat"). During the 1970s, the music for the dance known as "boogaloo" was tried by a number of jazz musicians, and their funkiest playing was set atop it.

During the 1970s and 80s there was also a burgeoning interest in Eastern European Jewish music, such as that of Romania, Croatia, Serbia,

Hip-hop The general term that covers a wide range of artistic expression, from rap music to graffiti art and fashion

◀ Trumpeter Dave Douglas at the Venice Jazz Festival, 2003

Photo by David Redfern, courtesy of Redferns/Getty Images.

and Bulgaria. A number of musicians reproduced variations that had been developed upon it in twentieth-century America. (A nationally occurring revival occurred in Yiddish Klezmer music among musicians of varied backgrounds, not just jazz.) Though the term represents a broad spectrum of traditions and repertory, **Klezmer** music is most easily described as traditional dance music for Jewish weddings. (Some of its character is indicated in the Broadway musical *Fiddler on the Roof*.) This interest inspired clarinetist Don Byron to spend much of the 1980s investigating the possibilities of blending it with jazz. Byron and saxophonist-clarinetist Chris Speed pursued both traditional and original variations on this music. They appeared in widely varied contexts, often joined by alto saxophonist John Zorn and trumpeter Dave Douglas. (Listen to "Red Emma" on *Jazz Classics CD3* for *Jazz Styles, 10th Edition*.)

Klezmer Eastern European Jewish instrumental music for weddings

In addition to fusing Klezmer music with jazz, other trends are historically significant for the same men who became distinguished for their Klezmer-inspired jazz. (1) Many of Byron, Zorn, and Douglas' explorations had nothing to do with jazz or Klezmer music. For instance, cartoon sound track music, movie music, and classical music are just a few of the non-jazz attractions they explored. Classification of their output is challenging because of this. Though Zorn's classical music managed to get cataloged with classical music, the other non-jazz projects of these musicians often appeared in the jazz bins of music stores primarily because the musicians had a reputation for jazz and marketers did not make appropriate distinctions. (Perhaps they did not have separate bins for such other kinds of music.) (2) A larger trend also emerged during this period of jazz history. Versatility and the pursuit of numerous unrelated projects characterized the activities for many of the most talented new musicians of the 1980s and 90s, not just Byron, Zorn, Douglas, and Speed.

John Zorn (b. 1953), saxophonist-composer-bandleader, is probably the most versatile and hard working figure associated with Klezmer jazz in the 1990s. Originally a rock musician, he became interested in Lee Konitz and Paul Desmond. He mastered bebop styles by the end of his teen years, and he can still offer a passable imitation of Phil Woods, the Charlie Parker-disciple on whom Zorn modeled his early playing. Moreover, he reveals an understanding of the Ornette Coleman Trio concept whenever he wishes. (Listen to "Dee Dee" on *Jazz Classics CD2* Track 5 for the Coleman Trio concept.) Zorn's most distinctive contributions were the more than 250 works collectively termed *Masada*. In these, Zorn absorbed Yiddish folk music and combined it with the methods of Ornette Coleman and Phil Woods. With his collaborators trumpeter Dave Douglas, bassist Greg Cohen, and drummer Joey Baron, Zorn created impassioned improvisations with virtuosic execution that had a groove all their own. They swung infectiously without following bebop traditions for accompaniment rhythms.

Jazz is just one of Zorn's interests. He is a musical force of immense scope and energy. One of the leading innovators in the 1990s, he tackled twentieth-century classical music so successfully that his string quartet recordings now reside in libraries around the world. His symphonic writing is known even to music scholars who specialize in the traditional big names

Photo by Takehiko Tokiwa.

◀ Masada, the klezmer jazz band of John Zorn (alto saxophone), Dave Douglas (trumpet), Joey Baron (drums) and Greg Cohen (bass). Shown here in 1977.

of twentieth-century "serious" orchestral music: Bartók, Stravinsky, Berg, Stockhausen, and Varèse. He also mounted numerous projects in improvised music in which chance is systematically incorporated. (Zorn hired some of the same musicians from his jazz bands when he pursued these projects.) He also prepared interpretations of movie music and had his own rock band at this time.

The other musician most closely identified with Klezmer jazz is trumpeter **Dave Douglas** (b. 1963). With enviable command over the trumpet and swaggering confidence, he has performed improvisations in conventional hard bop, as with Horace Silver (1987–1990), and in mid-1960s Miles Davis style. He has also recorded sterling examples of classical trumpet playing (as on non-jazz albums by John Zorn and Uri Cain). In fact, the influence of modern classical music gives his jazz trumpet improvisations part of their unique flavor. For instance, the music on his *Parallel Worlds* album is influenced by twentieth-century classical composers Anton Webern and Igor Stravinsky. But he shows himself to be a truly fresh voice in Zorn's *Masada* jams and Douglas' own Tiny Bell Trio. There he composed new frameworks from varied traditions for Eastern-European folk music. He combined aspects from the jazz trumpet styles of Miles Davis, Don Cherry, and Lester Bowie with his own original ideas to improvise solos within the fresh frameworks he had composed. (Listen to "Prince of Darkness" on *Jazz Classics CD2* Track 9 to sample the Davis style he imitated and "Civilization Day" on *Prentice Hall Jazz Collection* for the Cherry style he imitated.) As a composer and bandleader, Douglas has proven endlessly explorative. Employing instruments rarely found in jazz such as violin and accordion, he mixed jazz improvisation with rhythms and melodic styles in the folk traditions of Hungary, Romania, Macedonia, Serbia, and Croatia and came up with fresh music, again and again.

LATIN JAZZ

Caribbean music had played a major role in the origins of ragtime during the 1800s, and it had been influencing jazz before the 1920s. Jelly Roll Morton wrote several pieces that used Latin American rhythms and recorded them during the 1920s. Duke Ellington had recorded pieces with Latin American flavor during the 1930s and 40s. The Cuban mambo was popular in New York during the 1940s, and Latino bandleaders mixed their rhythms and percussion instruments with improvisation and harmony of concurrent modern jazz styles. By the end of that decade, bandleaders Dizzy Gillespie and Stan Kenton were carrying auxiliary percussionists on tour with them to play the portions of their repertory devoted to Latin American styles. In the 1950s and 60s, Cal Tjader and George Shearing did the same. Saxophonist-bandleader Stan Getz enjoyed tremendous popularity when he embraced Brazilian repertory that combined North American cool jazz with samba. His 1962 and 1963 recordings lent impetus to a bossa nova craze in the U.S. In fact, bossa nova repertory became standard fare for jazz musicians thereafter.

In the 1980s and 90s, combinations of jazz improvisation with Caribbean and South American music seemed to get more recognition than ever before. **Afro-Cuban** musicians landed contracts with major North American recording firms, and they were featured in newspapers, magazines, televised awards programs, and movies. Cuba contributed several exciting jazz instrumentalists to the U.S. jazz community. Jazz festivals around the U.S. were routinely presenting **"Latin jazz"** groups. The genre was even canonized in 2004 when the Lincoln Center for the Performing Arts founded a resident repertory band there for Latin jazz: The Afro-Latin Jazz Orchestra with Arturo O'Farrill. Lincoln Center was home to the New York Philharmonic Orchestra and the Metropolitan Opera. Adding a Latin jazz band represented serious recognition of the music's value.

Latin jazz's ascendance to broad media attention in the 1980s and 90s belies a long tradition. Cuban bands were including jazz improvisation at least as early as the 1920s, and some of them appeared in New York at that time. Cuban dance music had influenced the development of ragtime during the 1800s, and the influence of Cuban musicians has been almost continuous since then. The rhumba in the 1930s and the mambo in the 1940s saw so much popularity in North America that at East Coast balls attended by wealthy society people, it was not unusual to have three different bands alternating: a swing band (perhaps in the style of Benny Goodman), a sweet band (perhaps in the style of Guy Lombardo or Wayne King), and a Latin band. This persisted at least as recently as the 1960s.

Two of the best "Latin bands" that gained prominence in the 1980s and 90s had also been around long before this new recognition. They were led by **Tito Puente** (1923–2000) and Eddie Palmieri. Both leaders were New York–born of parents who had Puerto Rican heritage. Prior to the 1980s, their bands had been termed "mambo bands" and "salsa bands." Now they were also being promoted as "Latin jazz bands."

A bandleader since the 1940s, Puente played marimba, vibraphone, and percussion. Among the percussion instruments he played, the timbales

Afro-Cuban Music developed in Cuba that shows the influence of African and Hispanic immigrants

Latin jazz Jazz that incorporates rhythms and instruments from Latin America

Photo by John Sobczak

Tito Puente playing timbales. Notice the two cowbells suspended in front of the timbales. Shown here at the 1990 Detroit-Montreux Jazz Festival.

received the most emphasis. This Cuban instrument consists of two short, metal drums without drumheads on the bottom. It is a descendent of the timpani (kettle drum) used by Cubans to play their high-society music called danzon. They are positioned on a waist-high rack that also has cowbells attached, as well as a splash cymbal. The cowbells have their clangers removed and are played with a drumstick. The rhythms played on these percussion instruments have African origins that have been retained in Caribbean culture from the time of slavery. North American drumming rudiments were added to the repertory by Puente, and he featured timbale solos in band performances. Puente brought the timbales greater recognition.

Unlike the pulse in jazz for swing dancing, in which we have high-hat sounding on 2 and 4, ride cymbal sounding on 1, 2, 3, and 4, there is a rhythmic pattern in Latin American music called clavé, around which each type of dance is centered. The clavé rhythm is different for each dance and essential to the feeling evoked by the dance band. For example, mambo and rhumba each have their own distinct clavé rhythm.

In the Puente bands, the leader's timbale playing is joined by one musician playing conga drum and one playing bongo drums. Sometimes the timbale player or the bongo player plays cowbell. One or two singers are also common. The singers also play cowbell, clavés, maracas, and guiro (scraper). This function is essential because the rhythm they play evokes the particular feeling appropriate for that dance. Sometimes the hornmen also play percussion instruments when not blowing their horns. Piano plays both a harmonic and a percussive role by repeating an eight-beat pattern in the improvisation section called the *montuno*. In this way the piano links the harmonic structure to the rhythmic structure. The rhythms coming from these percussionists are packed with syncopations that represent African retentions. They provide layers of accompaniment that lend

Afro-Cuban music its essence. Together, these musicians create a very busy and exciting sonic texture.

In most jazz performances, the bass supplies a steady pulse while syncopation results from the soloists' improvised notes tugging against it. The jazz practice of walking bass, however, is not followed in Afro-Cuban music. A more complicated pattern called the *tumbao* is played by the bassist. This pattern accents the "and" of the second beat and accents the fourth beat to produce an effect analogous to a swinging hammock. Because the bassist does not emphasize the first and third of every four beats, it is often difficult for jazz listeners to discern the organization of beats in the music. The first beat of any four is not even sounded. This means that in Afro-Cuban music, the offbeat is actually used as an accompaniment.

Significant as a composer-arranger, Puente's arrangements in the 1950s used big band jazz instrumentation. He even had a "Latin Jazz" album at that time, thereby anticipating the way his mambo bands would be billed thirty years later. Puente blended North American jazz harmony, instrumentation, and improvisations with Cuban rhythms and percussion instruments. During the 1980s and 90s, not only did Puente maintain a large dance band, but he also toured with a smaller band that emphasized jazz solo improvisations.

Eddie Palmieri (b. 1936) has been a significant pianist, composer, and leader of Afro-Cuban style dance bands since the early 1960s. He has been carrying hornmen who were already established in non-Latin jazz. A subset of his repertory and recordings since the late 1970s has been classified with "Latin Jazz." As a pianist Palmieri distinguished himself as a master at devising cross rhythms. During his comping and soloing, he displaced the positions of his phrases in seemingly endless new ways relative to the underlying beat and still managed to make sense and evoke dancing. During the late 1970s and early 80s, Palmieri exhibited the influence of John Coltrane's jazz pianist McCoy Tyner, who himself had assimilated African and Latin American rhythms. As in jazz of all periods, once again the lines of influence were running in both directions: Latin American rhythms influencing jazz, and jazz improvisations and harmonies influencing musicians in Latin bands.

The most eminent Cuban jazz musicians to become known to North American audiences during the 1970s and 80s were initially part of a Cuban band called Irakere. The leader of Irakere was pianist **Chucho Valdés** (b. 1941). Widely respected in jazz circles for his pianistic power and virtuosity, he is also very eclectic. He chose material as stylistically far flung as Thelonious Monk and Bill Evans, as well as standard repertory from Cuban popular music. His imagination for inventing compelling rhythms impressed many musicians. Two members of the band ultimately relocated to the U.S.: alto saxophonist **Paquito D'Rivera** (b. 1948) and trumpeter **Arturo Sandoval** (b. 1949). They became mainstays on the North American jazz scene of the 1990s. Quite accomplished as musicians in classical music, not just jazz, both were impressive instrumentalists. Sandoval, for instance, occasionally played the intricate phrases of Dizzy Gillespie's improvisations that were situated in a stratospherically high register. A huge tone and majestic manner characterized Sandoval's work.

D'Rivera also had command of the altissimo register and exhibited crisp articulation. He developed his own jazz vocabulary such that his playing became instantly recognizable. The improvisations of D'Rivera conveyed a very confident, exuberant attitude, and the effect was highly animated and light-hearted. Though both could handle non-Latin musical contexts, neither Sandoval's nor D'Rivera's improvisational vocabulary was entirely bebop-derived. In other words, one of the main contributions of Sandoval and D'Rivera was a unique fusion of modern jazz phrasing with Afro-Cuban style phrasing.

The Afro-Cuban music of Irakere and many other Latin Jazz groups showed more African characteristics than any other kind of jazz. Afro-Cuban music was far more polyrhythmic than swing or bop-style because it contained (a) more layers of accompaniment rhythm, (b) more complicated rhythms in those layers, and (c) more extensive repetition of those rhythms. In fact, it may be that what jazz fans perceive in Afro-Cuban music as accompaniment or predominately background is actually the foreground.

CONTEMPORARY BIG BANDS

Carla Bley (b. 1936) is a composer and bandleader who has written a wide assortment of compositions that cumulatively fit no conventional jazz category. The distinctiveness and originality of her accomplishments is so wide that we might consider Bley to have predated what commentators in the twenty-first century have awkwardly termed "poly-stylistic post-modernism." The term has been applied to characterize the careers of John Zorn, Dave Douglas, and Don Byron, and it fits the entire career of Charles Mingus. Bley has been continuously active since the 1960s and always remained avant-garde, no matter what decade she was living in. Spearheading the cutting edge Jazz Composer's Orchestra, she was initially part of the free jazz movement. Her stature is indicated partly by the sizable number of eminent musicians who have recorded her compositions.

The character of Bley's pieces spans a range than runs from a lush ballad ("Fleur Carnivore") to works for big band that are loud and swinging (such as "Floater," "Birds of Paradise," and "On the Stage in Cages"). Some employ unusual chord progressions (as in "Strange Arrangement"). Her writing is always well edited, strikingly melodic, and never muddy. Her sources range from English music hall to Thelonious Monk ("On the Stage in Cages," "Strange Arrangement," "Batteriewoman") to tango ("Reactionary Tango") and Anglo-American church music (*The Carla Bley Big Band Goes to Church*). She mixes and matches these sources in odd combinations that end up sounding perfectly natural. Standouts among her most ambitious works include her opera "Escalator Over the Hill," her suite "A Genuine Tong Funeral" (with vibraphonist Gary Burton), and her writing for bassist Charlie Haden's Liberation Music Orchestra.

Bley was one of the first jazz writers whose work says, in effect, "There are no rules." It is as though she starts from point zero for each piece. If the sounds are pleasing, the piece doesn't have to be a set form. It can be just notes. It could be merely a springboard for improvisation. Her arrangements are very open, not fitting the big band tradition of densely packed, busy figures. Instead, the band usually functions as a big small group, with plenty of time for soloists to stretch out with little interruption. She considers a number of her pieces just to be frameworks for jazz musicians, with a snippet of music at the beginning and end, but huge holes in the middle for free improvisation. A prime characteristic of her work is extreme economy. Her arrangements are so spare that we might call her a minimalist, in the tradition of non-jazz composers Erik Satie and John Cage, though occasionally she might remind us of jazz composers Thelonious Monk and Duke Ellington as well.

A sense of playfulness is more prominent than any other characteristic in Bley's music. Her irreverent sense of humor is striking, and it recurs in both the construction of her pieces and her choice of tune titles (for instance, "On the Stages in Cages," "The Girl Who Cried Champagne," and "Song to Anything That Moves"). She even wrote a spoof on baseball stadium organ playing ("Baseball"), and a comic reworking of national anthems ("Spangled Banner Minor and Other Patriotic Songs"). Sometimes we might conclude that she hardly takes anything seriously, though her craft is unquestionable. In fact, she subscribes to the idea that avant-garde saxophonist Albert Ayler's music gave her the license to be maudlin. Some of her pieces are so exaggerated in their effects that she has certainly succeeded in following his lead. Much of her work sounds like music for the theater because it is intentionally so melodramatic.

▶ Carla Bley, at the 1996 Chicago Jazz Festival.

Photo by Michael Jackson.

◄ Maria Schneider, 2005.

Photo by Takehiko Tokiwa.

Maria Schneider (b. 1960) is a composer and bandleader who became prominent in the 1990s. She was first appreciated and given exposure in Europe more than the United States. Several features of her writing stand out:

1. Unlike standard formats for band arrangements such as a 32-bar chorus structure that repeats continuously with variations, Schneider's formats sport much longer sections and much less repetition (for instance, "Wrygly"). Most don't cycle at all. They are composed freshly throughout with their own original form, thereby fitting the "through-composed" designation.

2. Schneider's pieces can run from 8 to 20 minutes and often don't begin solo improvisation until more than three minutes into the piece (for instance, "Concert in the Garden" and "Choro Dançado"). Though previously used by Duke Ellington, long stretches without improvisation are unusual in jazz writing (for instance, "Gush").

3. Schneider uses improvising soloists; but when she calls upon them, their role is almost like that of an actor in a play. The solo becomes integral to the feeling of overall development and fabric of the piece instead of a display for the player's virtuosity as in conventional big band jazz.

4. Tone color is another respect in which Schneider's music departs from common practices. She favors flutes, clarinets, muted trumpets, and trombones more often than saxophones and unmuted brass. In fact, it may be accurate to describe the effect of much music by Schneider as pastel and delicate. This departs from most big band jazz with its bright tone colors.

Composed by Carla Bley; recorded in 1999 in Oslo, Norway, for Watt by Lew Soloff (trumpet), Wolfgang Puschnig (alto saxophone), Andy Shepard (tenor saxophone), Gary Valente (trombone), Larry Goldings (organ), Carla Bley (piano), Steve Swallow (bass), and Victor Lewis (drums); available on *4x4* Watt/ECM: 30, 1999, c2000); reissued on Bley, *rarum xv Selected Recordings* (ECM B 0001795, ©2004).

Carla Bley's "Baseball" is inspired by the sounds that we often hear from an organist at a big city baseball game. In the music you will hear those trademark phrases, but you will also hear Bley moving their pitch up a few times. This shows how Bley can cleverly make music out of the simplest elements. Unlike much modern jazz that is serious and very intricate, Bley's music is fun and not nearly as complicated. But don't mistake the fun and simplicity for lack of originality. Bley is strikingly fresh in her creativity, and the result swings, too.

Bley creatively varies the presentation of parts in her music. In this way, she takes us on an adventure in which we are not likely to get bored. Sometimes, for instance, she changes accompaniment rhythm or meter, as when she switches from a modified New Orleans street beat to a waltz. Drummers in New Orleans parade bands invented this particular street beat, and it is also found in pop music from New Orleans, such as that of the Meters. The passage at 2' 55" is in waltz meter, which is a dramatic contrast from the rhythm of the New Orleans street beat that precedes it. During a few moments, the street beat rhythm is actually played in waltz meter. Other times it is played against waltz meter.

The melody of "Baseball" consists primarily of just two phrases: a 3-note phrase and a 4-note version of the same phrase. The chords in the progression that accompany it move in very small steps, not the usual pitch ranges of most tunes. Sometimes the effect of the alternating chords is mysterious. The two alternating chords lend the music a Spanish flavor, especially during the trombone solo. It is as though bull-fight music meets baseball music.

The sections that organize the main portions of the piece follow an A-A-B-A structure. The bridge (B-section) consists of two two-note phrases that could be construed as a "call," followed by the 4-note phrase that opened recording's beginning. In this location, that 4-note phrase could be construed as a "response." Incidentally, the A-sections are 8 measures long, whereas the bridge is only 6 measures long. This makes the ending of the bridge feel premature and abrupt.

Despite the 8-8-6-8 construction of sections for statements of the main melody, the improvised sections of "Baseball" use an 8-measure bridge. This accommodation makes the solos easy to follow because 8-measure sections are typical of songs in A-A-B-A form, whereas 6-measure sections are rare.

The piano solo paces the passage of chords so that each chord lasts twice as long as it did for the organ solo that preceded it. The trombone solo follows a somewhat different set of chord changes. Instead of A-A-B-A, the chords are arranged A-A-A'-A'-B-A-A, in which A' (pronounced "aay PRIME") designates the transposition of the chord's pitch up a half a scale step.

TIME ELAPSED

	Musical Events
	Introduction (6 measures)
0' 00"	Unaccompanied organist plays the first phrase of "Baseball" three times at successively higher pitch levels.
0' 06"	the "Charge" fanfare

Theme Statement (8-8-6-8 measures)

First Four Measures

0' 08"	**A**	Saxes, trumpet, and organ play the melody's 3-note and 4-note phrase,
0' 10"		then play it again in harmony.

Second Four Measures

0' 12"	Organ and rhythm section play waltz rhythm over modified New Orleans street beat.

First Four Measures

0' 17"	**A**	Saxes, trumpet, and organ play in unison the melody's 3-note and 4-note phrase, then
0' 19"		they play same phrase in harmony.

Second Four Measures

0' 22"	Organ and rhythm section play waltz over modified New Orleans street beat.

Bridge

0' 26"	**B**	Trumpet and trombone play two 2-note phrases.
0' 28"		Saxophones respond with the original 4-note phrase in harmony.
0' 30"		Trumpet and trombone play two 2-note phrases at a lower pitch level.
0' 32"		Saxophones respond with the original 4-note phrase in harmony.

First 4 Measures

0' 34"	**A**	Saxes, trumpet, and organ play in unison the melody's 3-note and 4-note phrases,
0' 36"		then play them again in harmony.

Second 4 Measures

0' 38"	Organ and rhythm section play waltz over modified New Orleans street beat.

Organ Solo Improvisation (Larry Goldings)

A-Section (8 measures)

0' 42"	**A**	Solo logically takes brief idea and transforms it several times. accompanied by drummer playing modified New Orleans street beat on snare drum

A-Section (8 measures)

0' 51"	**A**	particularly melodic solo line

B-Section (8 measures)

1' 00"	**B**	Solo employs a brief melodic idea and logically transforms it several times, at lower pitches that correspond to the chord changes. Drummer switches timekeeping from snare drum to cymbal.

A-Section (8 measures)

1' 09"	**A**	Organ uses brief, funky lick for solo line. Drummer returns to snare drum. Brief phrases echo each other.

Second Chorus of Organ Solo

1' 18"	**A**	Chorded solo line; accompaniment chords move by small steps.

1' 27"	**A**	Organ returns to unharmonized melody.
1' 36"	**B**	One brief musical idea is transposed to lower and lower pitches, transformed over several repetitions.
1' 45"	**A**	Densely packed flourishes comprise the foreground.

Third Solo Chorus for Organ

1' 54"	**A**	New phrase gives solo a different character. Organ repeats brief phrase at successively lower pitches; accompanied by sustained chords from saxes and brasses.
2' 03"	**A**	Solo uses whole-tone scales, lines successively lower in pitch.
2' 14"	**B**	Organ harmonizes the melody line in chord form.
2' 21"	**A**	Funky chords comprise solo line.

Interlude 1

2' 30"	**A**	With halting accompaniment, guttural trombone-call alternates with saxophone response.
2' 40"	**A′**	Trombone call alternates with trumpet-saxophone response, this time pitched a half a scale-step lower.
2' 50"	**B**	Horns launch four-measure-long excerpt of waltz meter "Take Me Out to the Ballgame" ("For it's one, two, three strikes, you're out in the …").
2' 54"		Original 4-note phrase causes premature conclusion of interlude.

Improvised Piano Solo by Carla Bley

Throughout Bley's improvisation, note the chord changes cycling in left hand, dreamy melody in right hand, using stretched-out waltz meter atop drummer playing modified New Orleans street beat on snare drum.

2' 57"	**A**	**16-bar section** (deceptive note choices as though secretly changing keys, wandering cleverly through unlikely chord changes)
3' 19"	**A**	**16-bar section**
3' 33"	**B**	**16-bar section** (particularly melodic solo ideas)
3' 51"	**A**	**16-bar section** (organ joins accompaniment)
3' 55"		new melodic idea

Interlude 2

4' 10"		4-note phrase by organ
4' 14"		the "Charge" fanfare by organ using discordant pitches
4' 16"		drum rolls
4' 26"		cymbal crash

Trombone Solo Improvisation (Gary Valente)

sound quality: raucous tones achieved by over-blowing

accompanying chords: alternating pair of chords, not exactly the previous chord progression; lends a Spanish flavor

4' 29"	**A**	**8 bars**
4' 38"	**A**	**8 bars**
4' 47"	**A′**	Harmony is raised a step.

4' 56"	**A'**	**8 bars**	
5' 05"	**B**	**8 bars (new harmonies and several changes)**	
5' 14"	**A**	**8 bars**	
5' 23"	**A**	**8 bars**	

Second Chorus of Trombone Solo

5' 32"	**A**	**8 bars**	
		particularly melodic new phrase	
5' 41"	**A**	**8 bars**	
5' 50"	**A'**	harmonies move up a half a scale-step	
6' 00"	**A'**		
6' 09"	**B**	**8 bars (new harmonies and several changes)**	
6' 18"	**A**	short figure introduced, then transformed four times	
6' 27"	**A**	new melodic idea	

Theme Statement (8-8-6-8 measures)

Ending

7' 11"	Horns suggest a reprise of "One, two, three strikes …" in waltz meter.
7' 16"	Band plays one note, then leaves trombone alone to solo.
7' 23"	Band plays one note, then leaves trombone alone to solo.
7' 31"	Organ begins reprising "Charge" fanfare.
7' 38"	Three-note phrase and four-note phrase, followed by drum figure and one loud band note featuring trombone in foreground and high-pitched trumpet.

5. Schneider emphasizes soft sounds and uses shifts in volume quite subtly. ("Gush," for example, is a long, very gradual crescendo all the way to the end.) This practice differs from such tendencies of big band jazz as prolonged loud passages and intentionally blunt pronouncements.

6. We rarely find bluesy feeling or bebop character in her music.

7. By contrast with traditional big band jazz, much of Schneider's work recalls the albums that Gil Evans scored for Miles Davis, such as *Quiet Nights* and *Sketches of Spain*. Her later music even carries the influence of Brazilian and flamenco music ("Choro Dançado" and "Bulería, Soleá y Rumba") that one hears on these Gil Evans recordings.

8. In addition to the presence of South American and Spanish rhythms, some of her work evokes the floating feeling achieved by pseudo-rubato passages in recordings of Bill Evans and Keith Jarrett. In other words, it is not hard driving, and the beat is not routinely made obvious. Whereas much big band jazz elicits images of swing dancers in the 1930s, Schneider's music tends to elicit images of ballet.

9. Much writing for jazz groups is inspired by self-imposed technical puzzles and technical exercises. By contrast, many of Schneider's pieces are largely autobiographical, evoking her own experiences, such as sailing ("Coming About") and flying ("Hang Gliding"). This fits what at the beginning of the twentieth century became known as "Impressionism." French orchestral composers Claude Debussy and Maurice Ravel exemplify this style. Not entirely coincidental is that Schneider borrows harmonies from these same composers and the jazz arrangers who favored them.

The nine characteristics identified here cumulatively lead some listeners to feel that Maria Schneider is creating her own idiom in the jazz world.

CELEBRATING THE PAST

During the 1980s and 90s there was a proliferation of "ghost bands" that continued the music of deceased bandleaders. These groups were often led by musicians who had played with the former bandleaders whose names they now borrowed as banners for their own bands. Many musicians enjoyed successful tours by booking under slogans such as "The Count Basie Orchestra under the leadership of Grover Mitchell," "The Woody Herman Band under the leadership of Frank Tiberi," "The Mingus Dynasty," Sphere (Thelonious Monk's music), "The Art Blakey Legacy Band," "The Dizzy Gillespie Alumni All-Stars," etc. There was also a proliferation of repertory bands that provided opportunities analogous to theatrical companies in which actors become very good at playing different roles, putting on different plays they had mastered, perhaps a collection of William Shakespeare or George Bernard Shaw, for example. Some cities had "jazz orchestras" for this purpose, such as the Lincoln Center Jazz Orchestra and the Carnegie Hall Jazz Orchestra in New York.

During the same period there was also a renewed popularity of swing dancing, which in turn revived the music of the 1930s and 40s big bands and their imitators. Classes in almost every major city were devoted to teaching the jitterbug and the Lindy hop. The movie *Swing Kids* sparked some of the ensuing popularity. The public was also reminded of these pop jazz styles by the touring musical revue about Louis Jordan called *Five Guys Named Moe*. Because of the swing dance craze many jazz musicians found employment in the "neo-swing" bands playing for these dancers, even though this work involved playing styles quite unlike their preferred jazz approaches. Remarkable sales sometimes accompanied new albums by young musicians imitating the late 1940s/early 1950s "jump bands" of Louis Jordan and Louis Prima, and the hottest of the 1930s swing bands, such as Cab Calloway's and Fats Waller's. Some of their repertory also drew upon early 1950s rockabilly. For instance, Brian Setzer's *Dirty Boogie* sold more than two million copies. The Royal Crown Revue and the Squirrel Nut Zippers were also successful.

In the history of jazz, imitation has traditionally been a first step toward developing a young musician's understanding of the intricacies in serious improvisation. This usually involved deep study of at least one significant style and learning how to play like a particular master. Dizzy Gillespie, for instance, learned the complicated style of Roy Eldridge. The next step was practicing long and hard to arrive at a fresh contribution. This process was called "finding your own voice." Referring again to our example of Gillespie, recall that he used Eldridge's approach as a foundation from which to devise an even more complicated style that was comprised mostly of Gillespie's own original ideas. Sometimes a young musician would study two or more different styles and combine them in a distinctive way. For example, Charlie Parker combined elements of Buster Smith's and Art Tatum's styles with a wide assortment of other sources such as Lester Young, blues, and classical music. Miles Davis combined elements from the styles of Freddie Webster, Dizzy Gillespie, and Charlie Parker. During the 1950s, John Coltrane drew from Sonny Stitt's style, then during the 1960s from John Gilmore's and Albert Ayler's. Keith Jarrett combined approaches of Bill Evans, Ornette Coleman, and Paul Bley.

Though the great innovators all came up with something new, the majority of jazz musicians either remained imitators or they offered a twist to an existing style that made their own playing distinguishable from it. The improvisers who came up with distinctive twists are known by insiders, but their names are not recognized by most jazz fans today because they have not interested historians enough to write about them or include them in compilations of historic recordings. For example, many of the best young trumpeters of the 1930s and 40s did not go beyond Louis Armstrong or Bix Beiderbecke. Most trumpeters of the 1950s did not go substantially beyond the 1940s style of Fats Navarro or the early 1950s style of Miles Davis. Similarly, numerous saxophonists of the 1940s and 50s were content to learn the phrases of Lester Young and piece their own solos together with them. Once they learned his phrases, they continued playing in that style throughout their career. They played well but did not receive much attention from jazz historians because they were not original.

Concurrent with the rise of ghost bands and repertory bands during the 1980s and 90s was wider publicity for a number of talented young musicians who rotated among various historic styles. A trend emerged in which a number of the most talented newcomers stopped at the imitation stage, and some did not stop after learning just one model. They went from style to style. The mastery of their instruments and the immense worked they devoted to learning other styles is impressive. It became common for a young pianist to begin by learning Herbie Hancock's or Chick Corea's approach. The pianist might record and tour in that style and subsequently learn another style, such as Thelonious Monk's or Oscar Peterson's, then tour and record in it. Some pianists of the 1980s and 90s even went on to learn a third style. For instance, a few eventually specialized in stride-style or ragtime for a while. It was not unusual for young saxophonists to first learn one style period of John Coltrane, then tour and record in that style. Almost as often, they then moved to learning another style. Sometimes it was from an earlier era. For instance, a few learned Ben Webster's approach of the 1940s after first learning Coltrane's of the 1960s. A few began with Ornette Coleman's and then went back in history to learn a different style. A number of trumpeters moved back and forth between the mid-1960s styles of Miles Davis and Freddie Hubbard and then went back to learn the 1950s style of Clifford Brown. In other words, the new breed of jazz musicians never developed substantially new approaches of their own. They alternately took on the character of different historic figures.

Dixieland and swing styles had been revived periodically ever since first appearing. A similar phenomenon was now evident. For example, in 2005 there were young bands playing in the styles of the 1965 bands of Miles Davis and Art Blakey. This recalls the forty-year interval that separated young musicians in the 1960s from the 1920s-style Dixieland they played. The infatuation with the past occurring during the 1980s and 90s was nothing new. In fact it represents a familiar pattern. But four attitudes about it were new: The wide availability, press coverage, and lionization of the revivers accidentally conveyed the impression that (1) the revived music was actually new and (2) that the improvisations in it were almost as substantial as those of the models they imitated. Some listeners who had limited access to major recordings by previous innovators mistakenly assumed the newcomers were originators and that they were improvising as well as the jazz giants. (3) This was also coinciding with a tendency for more musicians than ever before, both young lions and old veterans, to be looking backward for sources of inspiration instead of inventing fresh approaches. These trends conveyed the message that (4) an important function of young jazz musicians was "preservation." Just as the Preservation Hall Jazz Band had been maintaining the work of its New Orleans ancestors, the Lincoln Center Jazz Orchestra in New York, for example, was now attempting to preserve the work of several previous generations.

The combined effect of the music for the swing dance craze, the continuation of ghost bands, and the wide publicity for repertory bands and the "young lions" who were imitating earlier styles was to cause many outsiders to believe that jazz was experiencing renewed popularity. However, the truth was that popularity for most jazz at this time, including that of the young imitators, had actually hit a new low.

The most famous musician to emerge during this period and adopt this new attitude was trumpeter **Wynton Marsalis** (b. 1961). Widely respected for his career as a classical trumpeter, he also crafted believable imitations of Miles Davis in jazz recordings with Art Blakey and Herbie Hancock during the early 1980s. Then he made several albums imitating the mid-1960s style of the Miles Davis Quintet, with new compositions, solos, and accompaniment honoring the advances made by Davis, Wayne Shorter, and their innovative rhythm section of pianist Herbie Hancock, bassist Ron Carter, and drummer Tony Williams. (Listen to "Prince of Darkness" on *Jazz Classics CD2* Track 9 for the Miles Davis style that Marsalis imitated.) For this music, he hired musicians who could play in the style of Davis accompanists, such as Kenny Kirkland, who played remarkably like Herbie Hancock. He also hired his older brother Branford Marsalis, who at the time was the best Wayne Shorter disciple. Wynton Marsalis has since focused his career on learning earlier styles, such as Louis Armstrong's and the devices of the muted style associated with pre-modern trumpeters Bubber Miley and Cootie Williams. He spent much of the 1990s recreating the music of Duke Ellington. He even learned how to compose in the style of Ellington and won a Pulitzer Prize for one such piece. An articulate spokesman for jazz, Marsalis has ultimately reached a large audience, achieved wide name recognition, and has become an effective educator. He cultivated respect for jazz as a serious art form in ways similar to Leonard Bernstein's educational programs during the 1950s and 60s that spread understanding and appreciation for classical music.

Collectively these styles were variously pegged (1) **"neo-classical,"** (2) **"neo-traditional,"** or (3) **"retro."** They were the most-played (4) **"classic"** or (5) **"mainstream"** styles during the 1980s and 90s. Musicians themselves generally refer to their music as (6) **"straight-ahead"** and (7) **"acoustic."** The broadcasting industry confused the matter by using the term "classic jazz" to designate almost all non–avant-garde jazz styles other than smooth jazz. This included not just the neo-classicists, but also older musicians themselves and those who offered original twists on older styles. This included bebop and bebop-derived styles as well as the 1960s approaches of Miles Davis and John Coltrane. The term "mainstream" was widely interchanged with "classic," and some broadcasters also used (8) **"traditional"** to designate all but smooth and avant-garde styles of jazz. These terms were unfortunate choices because (a) "classic" and "traditional" had long been the accepted descriptions for the original New Orleans and Chicago combo styles of the 1920s and the subsequent Dixieland revival, and (b) "mainstream" had been coined in the 1950s to classify swing era musicians who were still active. The "traditional" term did, however, distinguish them from "smooth jazz" because many referred to smooth jazz as "contemporary jazz," quite the opposite of traditional. The "acoustic" term succeeded in distinguishing them from the electronically processed sounds of funk and fusion bands as well as most "smooth jazz" productions. The "acoustic" term failed to distinguish them from the New Age music that was created without electronics and from various combinations of jazz with world music such as Klezmer jazz.

Neo-classical jazz Revival of earlier jazz styles, also known as **"retro"** or **"neo-traditional."** During the 1980s and 90s it referred mostly to young musicians emulating the hard bop of the 1950s and 60s and the mid-60s style of the Miles Davis Quintet.

POPULAR APPEAL

With the exception of a few standouts, jazz had less exposure and fewer performance outlets during the 1990s and the beginning of the twenty-first century than at any other time in its history. The number of night clubs featuring jazz on a regular basis was smaller than ever before, and the fees paid to the musicians in them were lower. The number of musicians able to extract a living by performing jazz decreased, too. Those few non-smooth jazz musicians who managed to live on earnings from playing jazz usually depended heavily on appearances at European jazz festivals. They could not survive from performance opportunities in the United States alone. Many depended partly on fees as touring instructors at jazz clinics in schools and colleges. A number of eminent jazz musicians acquired full-time positions as college instructors and would not have been able to remain in the field of music without such jobs. Hundreds of excellent jazz players served as adjunct professors in colleges and universities. In fact, most of the jazz improvising going on in America during this period occurred in high school and college bands. Despite the decrease in paid opportunities for performing jazz, more and more students chose to learn how to play it. Jazz majors proliferated in college and university music schools, and the level of musicianship among many young players was so high that a number of high school and college bands were better than some professional bands.

SUMMARY

1. Smooth jazz was the most popular jazz style after the mid-1980s.

2. Kenny G was the most popular saxophonist in history, surpassing 50 million albums sold.

3. David Sanborn was the second most popular saxophonist during the 1980s and 90s.

4. Michael Brecker, Joe Henderson, and Wayne Shorter were the most important saxophonists concerned with complex, noncommercial jazz.

5. A swing dance craze during the 1990s boosted interest in 1930s band styles and "jump bands" of the late 1940s and early 50s.

6. Backward-looking "neo-traditional" musicians and their repertory bands received the most media attention, though not substantial record sales. Even musicians who had been originators in the past tended to devote part of their output to older styles of others.

7. Fresh styles were devised by saxophonist John Zorn, trumpeter Dave Douglas, and their colleagues, frequently incorporating Yiddish Klezmer music with Ornette Coleman and Don Cherry approaches.

8. A number of musicians combined jazz improvisation with accompaniment styles from hip-hop, acid jazz and other pop genres, some of which resulting in "Drum 'n' Bass."

9. The period was marked by continuing vitality in the careers of several musicians who had innovated in prior decades: Cecil Taylor, Sonny Rollins, Ornette Coleman, Herbie Hancock, Chick Corea, Joe Zawinul, Keith Jarrett, and John McLaughlin.

10. Combinations of jazz with Latin American pop music gained new respect, and "Latin Jazz" made several Cuban musicians into mainstays on the U.S. jazz scene.

11. Carla Bley and Maria Schneider wrote distinctive original works for their contemporary big bands.

KEY TERMS

Afro-Cuban music	Klezmer	neo-classical jazz
Drum 'n' Bass	Latin jazz	smooth jazz
hip-hop		

FURTHER RESOURCES

✓●—[Study] and **Review** on **mysearchlab.com**

Test your knowledge with the chapter quiz.

VIEW

Kenny G Greatest Hits Video Collection. BMG. Short (40 minutes) collection of his commercial videos.

Keith Jarrett: The Art of Improvisation. Euroarts. Documentary with many interviews and performances with Jarrett and his associates.

Masada Live at Tonic 1999. Tzadik. Features John Zorn and Dave Douglas in Zorn's Klezmer-jazz band.

Tito Puente: King of Latin Music. Hudson video. Documentary with performance clips.

Carla Bley: Live in Montreal. Image Entertainment Recorded at the Montreal Jazz Festival in 1983.

LISTEN

George Benson—*Breezin'* (Warner Archives 76713) and *In Flight* (Warner Brothers 2983) are among the albums that set the pace for smooth jazz.

Birth (Josh Smith, Jeremy Bleich & Joe Tomino)—*Birth, The Live Disc,* and *Find* (available from *www.birthsound.com*) are albums that illustrate Drum 'n' Bass with avant-garde improvisations atop it.

Carla Bley—*The Very Big Carla Bley Band* (Watt/ECM: 23, 1990, c1991). Bley, *The Carla Bley Big Band … Goes to Church* (Watt/ECM: 27, 1996, c2000). *Looking for America* (Watt/ECM: 31, 2002, c2003); *4x4* (Watt/ECM: 30, 1999, c2000). Bley, *Escalator over the Hill* (Watt/ECM: 1802 [EOTH], 1968–71, c2000). A good overview is Carla Bley, *Selected Recordings,* :rarum xv (Watt/ECM: B0002795-02, 1971–1999, c2004).

Michael Brecker—*Michael Brecker* (MCA 5980), *Don't Try This at Home* (MCA 42229); also see Horace Silver, *In Pursuit of the 27th Man* (Blue Note 35758), The Brecker Brothers, *Heavy Metal Bebop* (One Way 31447), and Claus Ogerman, *Cityscape* (Warner Brothers 23698).

Peter Brotzmann—*Sacred Scrape* (Rastascan RAST 15) illustrates contemporary free jazz.

Hank Crawford—*Soul Survivors* (Milestone 9142) and *Mr. Blues Plays Lady Soul* (Collectables 6244) illustrate one source for the sax styles of Kenny G and Dave Sanborn.

The Crusaders (Joe Sample & Wilton Felder)—*Street Life* (Blue Thumb 701); *Southern Comfort* (MCA 6016); *The Best of the Jazz Crusaders* (originally on Pacific Jazz; now on Blue Note 89283) illustrate one source for Kenny G's sax style.

King Curtis—*King of the Sax* (Fuel 2000 Records 302 061 378), *Have Tenor Sax Will Blow/ Live at Small's Paradise* (Collectables CCL 6418) and *Soul Meeting* (Prestige 24033) illustrate one of the soul saxes. Also see Oliver Nelson, *Soul Battle* (Prestige OJC 325).

Dave Douglas—*Parallel Worlds* (Soul Note 121226) and *Witness* (Bluebird 63763) illustrates his poly-stylistic postmodern compositional style. *Constellations* (hatOLOGY 542) and *Tiny Bell Trio Live in Europe* (Arabesque Jazz AJ0126) illustrate his blending Klezmer music with jazz. *The Infinite* (RCA Bluebird 63918) is his homage to late-1960s Miles Davis. *Prentice Hall Jazz Collection* (ISBN 0–13–111674–6) has his "Kidnapping Kissinger" (2000). *Jazz Classics CD3* for *Jazz Styles, 10th Edition* (0-13-600561-6) has his "Red Emma."

Kenny G—*Breathless* (Arista 18646), *The Moment* (Arista 18935), *Duotones* (Arista 8496), *Silhouette* (Arista 8457); also see Jeff Lorber, *The Definitive Collection* (Arista 14639).

Charles Gayle—*Consecration* (Black Saint 120138) and *Kingdom Come* (Knitting Factory KFW 157) illustrate contemporary free jazz.

Joe Henderson—*Double Rainbow: The Music of Antonio Carlos Jobim* (Verve 527222); *In 'n' Out* (Blue Note 96507); *The Milestone Years* (Milestone 4413); also see Horace Silver, *Song for My Father* (Blue Note 99002) and *Cape Verdean Blues* (Blue Note 90839).

Irakere—*The Best of Irakere* (Columbia 57791) with Chucho Valdés, Paquito D'Rivera, and Arturo Sandoval; and *Live at Ronnie Scott's* (World Pacific 80598) with Chucho Valdés. *The Best of Paquito D'Rivera* (Columbia CK 85342).

Bob James—*Fourplay* (Warner Brothers 26656), *Between the Sheets* (Warner Brothers 45340), and *One on One* (Warner Brothers 45141) exemplify smooth jazz of the 1990s.

Keith Jarrett—*Staircase* (ECM 1090) is his most stunning unaccompanied piano album. *Radiance* (ECM 1960/61) is a 2002 example of his concert performances, demonstrating his stylistically wide-ranging solo work. Jan Garbarek, *Belonging* (ECM 1050) is one of Jarrett's best European Quartet albums. *Backhand* (Impulse! 9305) samples his American Quartet. *The Cure* (ECM 1440) samples his Standards Trio playing a 1990 concert.

Earl Klugh—*Living Inside Your Love* (Capitol 48385), *Low Ride* (Capitol 46007), *One on One* (Warner Brothers 45141) exemplify smooth jazz.

Buckshot LeFonque—*Buckshot Lefonque* (Columbia 57323) illustrates mixing rap, hip hop and jazz, in the acid jazz manner.

Wynton Marsalis—*Black Codes From the Underground* (Columbia CK 40009) and *Wynton Marsalis* (Columbia CK 37574) illustrate his Miles Davis phase. *Blood in the Fields* (Columbia 57694) illustrates his Ellington phase. *Prentice Hall Jazz Collection* has his Ellingtonian "Express Crossing." See Art Blakey, *Album of the Year* (Timeless 74503) and *Keystone 3* (Concord 4196) for examples of his Lee Morgan/Freddie Hubbard phase.

Wes Montgomery—*Bumpin'* (Verve 539 062) and *A Day In The Life* (A&M 75021 0 816) were important models for smooth jazz.

Eddie Palmieri—*La Perfecta* (Fania 8170); *The Sun of Latin Music* (Music Productions 6253); *Unfinished Masterpiece* (Music Productions 6259); *Palmas* (Elektra Nonesuch 61649); and *Vortex* (TropiJazz/RMM 82043).

Maceo Parker—*Roots Revisited* (Verve 843751) illustrates one source for Dave Sanborn's sax style.

William Parker—*In Order to Survive* (Black Saint 120159); also see Peter Brotzmann, *Sacred Scape* (Rastascan 15) illustrates contemporary free jazz.

Tito Puente—*Mambo Diablo* (Concord Picante 4283); *Royal T* (Concord Picante 4553); and *Special Delivery* (Concord Picante: 4732).

The Royal Crown Revue *Mugsy's Move* (Warner Brothers 46931) provided music for the swing dance craze.

David Sanborn—*Upfront* (Elektra 61272), *Straight to the Heart* (Warner Brothers 25150); also see Bob James, *Double Vision* (Warner Brothers 25392).

Maria Schneider—Maria Schneider, *Evanescence* (ArtistShare: 0006 [ENJA], 1992, c2005); *Concert in the Garden* (ArtistShare: 0001, 2001–04, c2004). *Coming About*

(ENJA: 9069, 1995, c1996); *Allegresse* (ArtistShare: 0005 [ENJA], 2000, c2005); *Days of Wine and Roses: Live at the Jazz Standard* (ArtistShare: 0017, 2000, c2005). All albums are available on-line via artistshare.com.

Brian Setzer—*The Dirty Boogie* (Interscope ISC 90183) illustrates new music for the swing dance craze.

Wayne Shorter—*Beyond the Sound Barrier* (Verve B000 4518) from the 2002–2004 tours with Danilo Perez; *Native Dancer* (Sony 46159) with Brazilian musician Milton Nascimento is a desert island pick for many jazz musicians; *Speak No Evil* (Blue Note 99001) with Freddie Hubbard and Herbie Hancock is an all-time favorite with musicians; also see Art Blakey, *Roots and Herbs* (Blue Note 21956), *Witch Doctor* (Blue Note 21957); Miles Davis, *E.S.P.* (Columbia CK 65683) and *Sorcerer* (Columbia CK 65680); Weather Report, *Mysterious Traveler* (Columbia CK32494) and *I Sing the Body Electric* (Columbia CK 46107). Also see *Jazz Classics CD2* for *Jazz Styles* (ISBN 0-205-03686-4) for "Masqualero" with Davis and "Surucucu" with Weather Report.

Chris Speed—*Deviantics* (Songlines SGL 1524) illustrates Klezmer jazz and Drum 'n' Bass.

Junior Walker—*Shotgun* (Motown 530245) and *The Ultimate Collection* (Motown 530828) illustrate one source for Michael Brecker's sax style.

Grover Washington, Jr.—*Mr. Magic* (Motown 530 103) and *Winelight* (Elektra 305) were very influential in smooth jazz, particularly pop saxophone styles of the 1980s and 90s such as Kenny G.

John Zorn—*Masada Live in Jerusalem 1994* (Tzadik 7322) and *Masada Live in Middelheim 1999* (Tzadik 7326)

READ

Beal, Amy C. 2011. *Carla Bley*. Urbana, Illinois: University of Illinois.

Carr, Ian. 1992. *Keith Jarrett: The Man and His Music*. New York: Da Capo.

Loza, Stephen. 1999. *Tito Puente and the Making of Latin Music*. Urbana: University of Illinois Press.

Mercer, Michelle. 2007. *Footprints: The Life and Work of Wayne Shorter*. New York: Tarcher-Penguin.

Powell, Josephine. 2007. *Tito Puente: When the Drums Are Dreaming*. Bloomington, IN: AuthorHouse.

Zorn, John, ed. 2007. *Arcana II: Musicians on Music*. New York: Hips Road/Tzadik.

Zorn, John, ed. 2000. *Arcana: Musicians on Music*. New York: Granary.

Elements of Music

In describing the nature of jazz and the characteristics of different styles, several basic musical terms are quite helpful. This chapter is devoted to defining some of these terms, and I urge all readers, including those who are musically knowledgeable, to examine them carefully.

When people think of jazz, they usually think of rhythm first. But because the word rhythm is often used to describe a large variety of musical characteristics, some uses convey inaccurate or contradictory meanings. Much of the confusion can be avoided by first understanding three related terms for which rhythm is often mistaken: beat, tempo, and meter.

Beat

Music is often said to have a pulse. The unit of pulse is called a beat. When you tap your foot to music, you are usually tapping with the beat. Here is a visualization of the pulse sequences we call beats.

Tempo

((•─Listen on
mysearchlab.com

Listen to audio-visual explanation of tempo on mysearchlab.com

Tempo refers to the speed or rate at which the beats pass. If you describe a piece of music as fast, you probably mean it has a rapid tempo, not that it occupies a short time span. When the beats continue at a regular rate, we say the tempo is constant. A clock's ticking is a good example of constant tempo. If the passage of beats is rapid, the speed is called "up tempo."

Meter

The beats in music are rarely undifferentiated. They are usually heard as being grouped. Meter describes the type of grouping. Our perception of grouping results when sequences of beats are set off from each other. This occurs in several ways. Every third or fourth beat may be louder or longer than the others. It may be distinctive because it has a different pitch or tone quality. Those differences are perceived as emphasis or accent. If we hear a sequence of beats grouped in fours, it may be due to a pattern of accents which creates this effect: ONE two three four ONE two three four. That pattern represents a meter which musicians simply call "four."

((•─Listen on
mysearchlab.com

Listen to audio-visual explanation of meter on mysearchlab.com

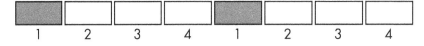

If the beats fall into the pattern, **ONE** two three, **ONE** two three, **ONE** two three, musicians say that the music "is in three" or in "waltz time."

Meters of four and three are quite common, but there are also meters of five, six, seven, and others. A meter of five might sound like **ONE** two three four five **ONE** two three four five, **ONE** two three four five, with a large accent on the first beat and no other accents. Or there may be a strong accent on the first beat and a smaller accent on the fourth: **ONE** two three **FOUR** five **ONE** two three **FOUR** five **ONE** two three **FOUR** five; or a smaller accent on the third beat: **ONE** two **THREE** four five **ONE** two **THREE** four five **ONE** two **THREE** four five. A meter of six usually feels like **ONE** two three **FOUR** five six **ONE** two three **FOUR** five six.

Each group of beats is called a **measure**. When the meter is three, there are three beats in a measure; when the meter is four, there are four beats in a measure.

Rhythm

In the broadest sense, rhythm simply refers to the arrangement of sounds in time, and therefore encompasses beat, tempo, and meter. But rhythm has come to mean something more specific than these features. In fact, beat, tempo, and meter furnish the framework in which rhythm is described.

Imagine a continuous sequence of beats occurring at a constant tempo, with four beats to a measure. The steady beat which in musical notation is represented by a string of quarter notes can also be visualized as a series of boxes, representing equal amounts of time. Our meter would be called "four." Each beat is called a quarter note, and each unit of four beats constitutes a measure.

The sound within a measure can be distributed in an infinite number of ways, one of which includes "filling" the measure with silence. Rhythm is the description of how that measure or a sequence of measures is filled with sound.

Let us take a few examples, numbering the four parts of the measure one, two, three, and four, respectively. We shall create rhythms by using a single sound mixed with silence. First, divide a measure into four equal parts, filling only the first and third with sound.

We have a rhythm. It is not complex, but it does what a rhythm is supposed to do: it describes the distribution of sound over time. In fact, this is the bass drum part in numerous marches, and it is the string bass part in many slow dance pieces.

Now, instead of taking just one measure, take two measures as a unit of repetition. In other words, the rhythm is two measures long.

Finally, repeat a one-measure rhythm to fill two measures's worth of time. This might be heard as a two-measure rhythm or as two one-measure rhythms.

Rhythm is the distribution of sound over time, but rhythm also refers to the way sounds are accented. Usually, the first beat of a measure is accented. An example would be the typical OOM pah pah accompaniment for a waltz. In a measure of four, the first and third beats are often accented, as in the BOOM chick BOOM chick drum pattern used in much popular music.

Syncopation

Examining our use of accents can lend understanding to a rhythmic element called *syncopation*, a crucial aspect of jazz feeling. For example, if we expect to hear a sound on every beat but only hear it in a few odd places, the upset we feel is the result of syncopation. This upset can be very stimulating and contribute a prime component of jazz feeling.

Examine this manner of filling two measures.

Note that the sounds which occur, bordered by silence, in positions other than on the first and third beats seem to stand out. They seem to be self accenting. If we additionally stress these odd positions by making the sounds in those positions louder than the sounds in other positions, syncopation is enhanced: one TWO three four ONE two three FOUR.

The concept of syncopation partly depends on a listener's expectations. For example, if we are expecting to hear ONE two THREE four, but we actually hear one TWO three FOUR, we are experiencing syncopation. Jazz drummers often keep time by playing boom CHICK boom CHICK (one TWO three FOUR) instead of BOOM chick BOOM chick. This syncopation is part of what makes a performance sound like jazz. Another frequently used syncopation occurs when we hear one two three FOUR when we are expecting to hear ONE two three four. So you see that rhythm involves the arrangement of stresses in addition to just describing the arrangement of sound over time. We have also seen that a phenomenon called syncopation results when the sounds are arranged or stressed in unexpected ways. Of course, what is expected depends on what the listener is accustomed to hearing. Therefore the statement that syncopation consists of unexpected accent is inadequate. Perhaps a more useful definition involves the accent of beats other than the first and, in measure of four beats, also the third beat. Silence can also be syncopating. For example, if we encounter silence at a time when we are expecting to hear ONE, the feeling of syncopation results.

Eighth Notes

To understand more complex syncopations and another essential element of jazz feeling, the swing eighth note, requires an acquaintance with ways in which beats are divided into smaller units. Here is a measure in four, with four quarter notes to the measure. We can divide each quarter note in half to produce eighth notes.

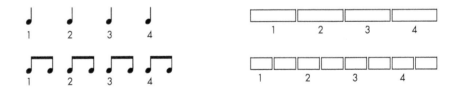

There are two eighth notes for every quarter note. If we place accents on the eighth notes according to the way we previously accented the measure of quarter notes, we have ONE two three four FIVE six seven eight. The time span for a measure of eight eighth notes is identical to that in a measure of four quarter notes, but keeping track of eight eighth notes is cumbersome. So we express the eighth notes in terms of subdivided quarter notes, saying "and" for the second half of each quarter note (every other eighth note): one and two and three and four and. Each word, whether it is the name of a number, called a **downbeat**, or the word "and," called an **upbeat**, represents an eighth note.

Syncopation occurs when any upbeats receive more emphasis than downbeats. Accenting the "and's" is essential to rhythms frequently employed in jazz. The final two beats in a measure are often divided into eighth notes with the last one accented the most: three and four AND. Many notes that appear in written form on the first beat of a measure are played on the and of the fourth beat in the preceding measure when given a jazz interpretation. The practice of playing a note slightly before or slightly after it is supposed to be played is a syncopating device that jazz musicians apply to pop tunes in order to lend jazz feeling to a performance.

Triplets

The quarter note can also be divided into three equal parts to produce what are called eighth-note triplets.

Sixteenth Notes

Here, each quarter note is divided into four equal parts, called sixteenth notes.

Dotted Eighth-Sixteenth Note Pattern

So far we have examined equal divisions of the quarter note. But it is also possible to divide it into notes of unequal value, for instance, a long note and a short note. One such pattern consists of a dotted eighth note followed by a sixteenth note. A dot after a note means that the note receives one and a half times its usual value; therefore the dotted eighth note has the combined value of an eighth note and a sixteenth note.

Tied Triplet Figure

Another long-short pattern is based on the triplet division of the quarter note. The pattern is called a tied triplet figure. Here, the first note has the value of two-thirds of a quarter note, and the second has the value of one-third.

Jazz has one rhythmic quality that, to my knowledge, is not found in any other kind of music: jazz swing feeling. A discussion of it appears in the "What Is Jazz?" chapter, but that discussion hinges on the swing eighth note which is examined next.

Having heard the term "*swing eighth note*," you might wonder how, if an eighth note is simply half the duration of a quarter note, we can have different types of eighth note, swing eighth note being one of them. Strictly speaking, you cannot have different types. An eighth note is an eighth note. Our descriptive language is loose enough, however, that we can use the term to label notes of slightly more or less duration than the eighth note is understood to receive.

Legato and Staccato

This looseness in applying the term "eighth note" is not exclusive to jazz musicians. Non-jazz musicians often use terms such as **legato**, which means long or slurred together or connected. They use the term **staccato**, which means short, abruptly separated. A legato eighth note equals a full-value eighth note. A staccato eighth note, on the other hand, has variable duration. Its length depends on the style of performance, and its value may actually be less than half that of a legato eighth note. It can be called an eighth note only because it is immediately followed by silence which fills up the remaining time that a full-value eighth note requires. Perhaps a staccato eighth note should be called a sixteenth note, or it should bear some designation that is more precise than the label of "staccato eighth note."

Listen to examples on *Demo CD* Tracks 44–45.

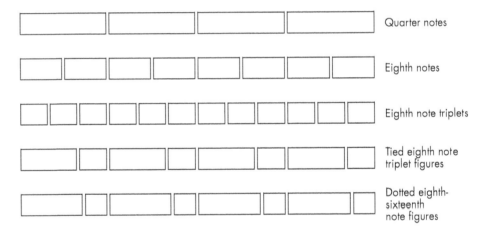

Quarter notes

Eighth notes

Eighth note triplets

Tied eighth note triplet figures

Dotted eighth-sixteenth note figures

Swing Eighth-Note Pattern

A wide assortment of eighth note durations and stresses are found in jazz styles. There are no jazz musicians who divide the beat in only one way. But there is a pattern that is more common than any other. It is a long-short sequence that is close, but not identical, to the pattern of durations found in the tied-triplet figures. The tied-triplet figure, you may remember, consists first of a long sound, then a shorter sound that is half the duration of the first sound. The two sounds together fit the duration of a single beat in the manner of a quarter-note triplet. The duration pattern most commonly employed by jazz musicians, the **swing eighth-note pattern**, falls somewhere between the tied-triplet figure and a sequence of eighth notes having identical durations. In other words, the first member of the pair is shorter than the first member of a tied-triplet pattern, and the second member is somewhat longer than a triplet eighth note. But neither member's duration is truly equal to an even eighth note, what musicians call "a straight eighth." Researcher Mark C. Ellis has found the duration ratio to range from 1.474:1 to 1.871:1, with a grand average ratio of 1.701:1. Stated differently, the ratios of long-short subdivisions ranged from approximately 3:2 to 9:5 (*Perceptual and Motor Skills*, 1991, 73, 707–713).

Listen to examples on *Demo CD* Track 43.

The stress patterns for swing eighth-note patterns are distributed differently from player to player. Sometimes within the work of a given player, the stresses are distributed differently from performance to performance, sometimes from passage to passage.

Basically, however, the first in a group of such swing eighth notes is softer than subsequent notes that occur on upbeats.

There is considerable confusion about notation of swing eighth notes. Such lack of uniformity exists in this regard that about the only accurate statement is that, when reading eighth notes, the desired choice of duration patterns usually depends upon the particular band and the style of arrangement being played. A little history might make this point a bit clearer. In countless written arrangements of jazz-oriented pieces that were published before the 1960s, dotted-eighth sixteenth figures appeared whenever the arranger wanted a swing eighth sound. (The arranger did *not* want true dotted-eighth sixteenth note patterns in which long-short meant the long member sounded three times the duration of the short one.) The notation appeared as even eighths thereafter in most arrangements, but the intention was for those notes to also be played as swing eighths. (If an arranger of this period wanted *truly even* durations, a written message appeared above the notes: "even 8ths." The musician's assumption was to otherwise play all the written eighth notes in a swing rhythm.)

Polyrhythm

To appreciate the rhythms that typify jazz, we should keep in mind the fact that several rhythms are usually played simultaneously. *Polyrhythm* (meaning *many rhythms*) is very important to jazz. When you listen carefully to a modern jazz performance, you should be able to hear several different rhythms at the same time. These include the rhythm in the melodic line, that of the bassist, the rhythm played by each of the drummer's four limbs, and each of the pianist's two hands.

Polyrhythms are often created by patterns that pit a feeling of four against a feeling of three. In other words, two measures can be played at the same time, with one being divided by multiples of two and the other being divided by multiples of three. In addition to that, the onset of one pattern is often staggered in a way which results in something less than perfect superimposition atop another pattern. Pitting three against four and staggering the placement of rhythms can project the feeling that the rhythms are tugging at each other. The resulting combination of stresses can be extremely provocative, and it can produce new syncopations in addition to those already contained in the separate patterns.

You can now understand why to say that jazz is quite rhythmic is to make an almost meaningless statement. All music has rhythm, and most music has syncopated rhythms. What sets jazz apart from many other types of music is the preponderance of syncopated rhythms, the swing eighth-note sequences, and the frequent presence of polyrhythm.

Scales, Keys, Tonality, and Modality

Understanding scales is basic to appreciating chord progressions, and an acquaintance with scales and chord progressions aids our knowledge of the rules that guide jazz improvisation. Everyone is familiar with musical scales. No one has been able to live very long without hearing a friend, neighbor, or family member practice "his scales."

Scales comprise the rudiments of beginning practice routines for singers and instrumentalists alike. Even people who cannot read music are familiar with the sequence *do* (pronounced "dough"), *re* (pronounced "ray"), *mi* (pronounced "mee"), *fa, sol, la, ti* (pronounced "tee"), *do*. Those eight syllables do not represent exact pitches as C, D, E, F, G, A, B, C; they are only the names of acoustic relationships. (Do not let that term, acoustic relationships, scare you. It is one of the simplest concepts in music. It means only that no matter what frequency of so many vibrations per second is assigned to *do*, the remaining seven pitches are determined by set multiples of it, for example twice the frequency, $1\frac{1}{2}$ the frequency, and so forth.)

"*Do re mi fa sol la ti do*" numbers eight elements, the eighth element carrying the same name as the first, *do*. Its relationship to the first is exactly double the frequency of the first. For example, if the first *do* were 440 vibrations per second, the next higher do would be 880. It is no more complicated than that. That last *do* ends one sequence and begins another. The relationship between the bottom *do* and the top *do*, the first and eighth steps of the scale, is called an *octave*. The sound of two notes an octave apart is so similar that if they are played simultaneously, you can easily mistake the pair for a single tone. Most naturally produced tones contain an octave as one component of all the frequencies that combine to give a tone its own characteristic color or quality. The octave is called a harmonic or an overtone of the tone's fundamental pitch. That is the reason two tones an octave apart sound like one when they are played at the same time.

Since the interval of an eighth, from *do* to *do*, represents a doubling of frequency, you have probably guessed that those intervals between the first and the eighth must be fractions. You guessed correctly. The ratio of the fifth step (*sol*) to the first step (*do*) is $3/2$; that of the third (*mi*) to the first (*do*) is $5/4$, etc.

The seven-note scale has many labeling systems. We have already used three of them: (a) do, re, mi, fa, sol, la, ti, do; (b) first, second, third, fourth, fifth, sixth, seventh; and (c) the frequency ratios: re/do = $9/8$; mi/do = $5/4$; fa/do = $4/3$; sol/do = $2/3$; la/do = $5/3$; ti/do = $15/8$. Next is the system that uses alphabet letters A, B, C, D, E, F and G.

Look at the diagram of the piano keyboard printed here.

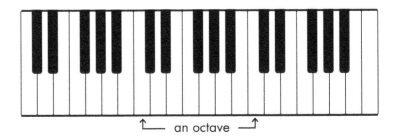

an octave

It is constructed so that the pattern of eight white keys and five black keys recurs again and again. The distance, or interval, between the beginning of one pattern and the beginning of the next is called an "octave." The scale that beginners usually learn first is the C scale; the C scale is obtained by playing eight of the white keys in succession, starting with the one labeled C. That scale, C, D, E, F, G, A, B, C, contains the same note relationships that we know as do, re, mi, fa, sol, la, ti, do. Play the notes of the C major scale in the order in which they are numbered in the diagram.

C	D	E	F	G	A	B	C
Do	Re	Mi	Fa	Sol	La	Ti	Do
1	2	3	4	5	6	7	8

Look again at the piano keyboard.

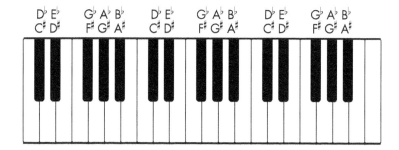

The black keys are known as sharps and flats. Sharp is symbolized # (like the number sign on a keyboard) and flat is symbolized b (like the lower case b on the keyboard). The black keys derive their names from the white keys that are next to them. The black key to the right of A is called "A-sharp" because it is slightly higher than A. But it is also referred to as "B-flat" because it is slightly lower than B. If we want only a C scale, going up an octave from C to C, we use none of the black keys. But if we want scales that begin on any note other than C, we have to employ at least one (and sometimes all) of the black keys. For instance, to play a major scale on D, it is necessary to make use of two sharps, F-sharp and C-sharp.

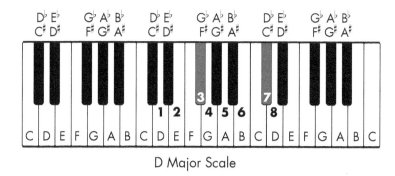

D Major Scale

((⋅•─ **Listen** on
mysearchlab.com

*Listen to audio-visual explanation
of scales on mysearchlab.com*

A scale may be played starting from any black or white key. Altogether there are twelve such scales. Going up (moving left to right) from C, they are the scales of C, C-sharp, D, D-sharp, E, F, F-sharp, G, G-sharp, A, A-sharp, and B. Or, naming them in descending order, C, B, B-flat, A, A-flat, G, G-flat, F, E, E-flat, D, and D-flat.

When musicians say that a tune is in a certain key, for instance, the key of C, they mean that the song is played with the notes of the major scale beginning on C.

The relationship of the notes of the major scale gives a song a particular kind of sound and structure that is called **tonality**. Although tonality is a complicated idea, it can be understood as the feeling that a song must end on a particular note or chord. A key defines a scale which, in turn, defines that key. If a piece of music has the feeling of reaching for the same note, the key note, or it seems loyal to some note more than to any other, the overall harmonic character of the piece is called **tonal**.

There is another term like the term "scale" that is not interchangeable with "key." The term is **mode**. Like a scale, a mode describes a sequence of acoustic relationships. Some modes even have the same number of elements as the scales we just explored. In fact, the C scale has a mode name: Ionian. But if we use the notes in the C scale and start the sequence on D, we produce another mode, Dorian. In other words, if we go from D to D in the key of C, we have constructed the Dorian mode. (See page 302.)

Dorian mode

For each of the seven scale steps in a key, there is a corresponding mode. The major scale itself has a mode name: Ionian; beginning on the second step produces the Dorian mode; the third step, the Phrygian mode; fourth, the Lydian mode; fifth, the Mixolydian mode; sixth, the Aeolian mode; and seventh, the Locrian mode. Each has a different sound because each has a different sequence of acoustic relationships that results from starting on different steps of the scale. I urge you to find a keyboard and play these modes. The concepts outlined here mean little without the sounds they describe.

We have seen that there are twelve keys, C, C# (or Db), D, and so forth. We also know that for each key there is a corresponding seven-note scale starting on the note that bears the name of the key (C D E F G A B for the C scale). Within each key there are modes, one mode beginning on each of the seven steps. The mode constitutes an octave of its own. Scales (modes) of fewer than seven notes and greater than seven notes also exist. (See page 301.) The most common scale constructed of more than seven notes is the chromatic, meaning simply that sequence of all the piano keys in an octave, white ones and black ones. Scale is a poor name because **the chromatic scale is actually just another way of dividing an octave into twelve equal parts.** It does not indicate a key as the C scale and the Bb scale do. *The chromatic scale is only a sequence of very small intervals called half steps.*

The chromatic scale has twelve steps: C, C#, D, D#, E, F, F#, G, G#, A, A#, and B. Unlike the modes, which have to be started on certain scale steps to guarantee their unique qualities, the chromatic scale can be started on any note, proceed through an octave and create the same identifiable chromatic quality no matter what note is chosen for its starting position. That means the C chromatic scale is identical to the C# chromatic scale (and all others). Perhaps it should be called "chromatic scale starting on C" or "chromatic scale starting on C#," specifying exactly what tone is to be the reference note.

The chromatic scale is very important because it expands the number of acoustic relations possible. Given twelve different tones in place of only seven, we have the option of raising and lowering (sharping and flatting) virtually any note we wish. Most Western European music of the past two centuries uses the chromatic scale instead of limiting itself exclusively to notes within one key at a time or, what is even more restrictive, only one mode at a time. Music was produced during the twentieth century that used all twelve tones equally and discarded the feeling of particular keys. Tonal music, you remember, is simply music that seems to be loyal to a certain note, always reaching for that note. Music without tone center is called *atonal.*

Most music has key feeling even when employing all twelve tones in the chromatic scale. This is just another way of saying that most music has tonality. During improvised music, tone centers might shift, but they usually remain long enough for their effect to be perceived. Most jazz employs tone center. It is extremely difficult to improvise without at least implying temporary tone centers and key feelings. The twelve tones are usually employed to enrich the conventional do re mi tonal orientation instead of providing a harmonic orientation all their own, one of atonality. Keep in mind that some music employs more than one key at once, but this type of music is not generally termed atonal. It is called *polytonal*, which means many keys.

If you play within the do re mi scale and enrich your melody with chromatic tones, the character of your playing can be partly described by how often you employ certain chromatic tones. Many people consider *bluesy quality* essential to jazz. A central component of bluesy quality is the frequent use of chromatics, three chromatics in particular: the *flat third*, *flat fifth*, and *flat seventh* notes of the scale. In other words, chromatic scale tones are employed to enrich the seven tones already available.

In the key of C, the blue notes are E-flat, G-flat, and B-flat. Remember the C scale consists of C, D, E, F, G, A, and B; there are no sharps or flats (none of the piano's black keys). To create a blue note we lower the third step of the scale. In the key of C this means changing E (a white key) to E-flat (a black key). We use both E *and* E-flat in constructing jazz lines, but the E-flat stands out because it is not one of the notes in the C major scale.

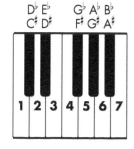

C scale without any blue notes

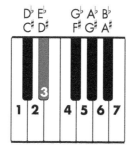

C scale with the flat third blue note

Listen to *Demo CD* Track 55 to hear these sequences.

The second most common blue note is achieved by lowering the seventh step of the scale. In the key of C, this means changing B (a white key) to B-flat (a black key). Again we use both B *and* B-flat for our lines, but the B-flat is more distinctive because it is not in the key of C.

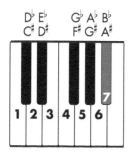

C scale with the flat seventh blue note (B-flat)

((••[**Listen** on
mysearchlab.com
Listen to audio-visual explanation of major and minor harmonies on mysearchlab.com

Note that the concepts of regular third step and blue third step are like the concepts of major chord and minor chord (the sounds of which you can demonstrate for yourself, using the following keyboard diagram as a guide to positioning your first, third, and fifth fingers).

((••[**Listen** on
mysearchlab.com
Listen to audio-visual explanation of blue notes on mysearchlab.com

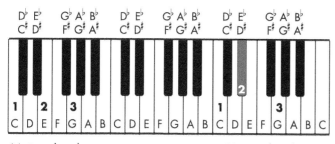

Major chord   Minor chord

The third most used blue note is the lowered fifth. Its use was not frequent until modern jazz began in the 1940s, but thereafter it became a standard device to convey a bluesy feeling, much as the lowered third and seventh had been in early jazz. In the key of C, a flat fifth is achieved by lowering G (a white key) to G-flat (a black key).

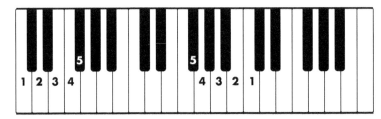

Going up to the flat fifth (G-flat)   Coming down to the flat fifth (G-flat)

Blue Notes

The term "blue note" does not have a single, universally accepted use. Some writers use it to designate the flat third and flat seventh that were discussed above. These sounds might best be termed "chromatically lowered" pitches because they are lowered by one step of the chromatic scale, the interval known as a "half step," a "chromatic semitone." Some writers use the term "blue note" to designate any pitch that is not completely a half step below another. This makes its classification "indeterminate" because, instead of being a clearly identifiable pitch of the chromatic scale, it is a pitch we might obtain only if we could play a note from the region within the cracks between the piano keys, so to speak. Musicologists variously call such pitches "neutral thirds," "heptatonically equidistant," or "indeterminate pitches." (For a closer examination, see "Blue Notes and Blue Tonality" by William Tallmadge, *The Black Perspective in Music*, 1984, Volume 12, Number 2, pages 155–165.) These pitches cannot be produced on the piano, but that does not mean that pianists have not wanted to produce them. The recent proliferation of synthesizers in the hands of jazz-rock pianists saw the molding of numerous solos employing this second kind of blue note, apparently because synthesizers are capable of generating pitches that represent fine gradations between those found on the piano. Playing with pitches is termed "pitch bending." (Listen to Track 58 of the *Demo CD* for examples.)

The attraction that jazz musicians have for out-of-tune thirds and sevenths might be the result of differences between European and African preferences for tuning. One origin is suggested here. The European seven-tone scale (do, re, mi, fa, sol, la, ti, do) is not based on equal divisions of the octave. It is a sequence of whole steps and half steps (the "diatonic" system) in which each half step represents about one twelfth of an octave. (The interval between C and D is a whole step, as is that between E flat and F. The interval between B and C is a half step, as is that between E flat and E.) A mix might have resulted between the European seven-tone approach and a West African seven tone (heptatonic) approach in which the interval separating each successive scale tone is equal, not the unequal pattern we find in whole steps and half steps. This African "equidistant heptatonic" scale has pitches that coincide fairly closely to those in the European diatonic scale. However, the third and the seventh steps are flat in relation to their counterparts in the European scale. This means that if an African sang his own pitch in a European piece, the third and seventh steps would sound "blue" or not perfectly in-tune to the ears of a listener who was accustomed to the European scale. If African-American singers and musicians retained their taste for this particular kind of tuning, and seasoned European music to suit their tastes, then they performed European-style music in the "blue" manner we today associate with jazz.

Chords and Chord Progressions

Familiarity with the concept of scales allows us to explore the concept of chords and chord progressions, which, in turn, is essential to appreciating the harmony that jazz improvisers follow. These concepts are quite simple, but they have far-reaching applications, not only in jazz, but in all music that uses harmony.

A chord is obtained by sounding three or more notes simultaneously. Try these:

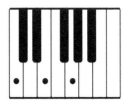
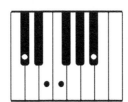
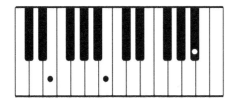
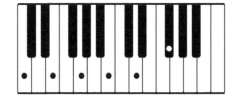

Although chords can be constructed from any tones, they are usually described in terms of scale notes and given Roman numeral names. The most common chord, one alternately described as a tonic chord, a major triad, the key chord, or a I (Roman numeral for 1) chord, employs the first, third, and fifth notes of the scale: do, mi, and sol. In other words, this chord is produced by simultaneously sounding do, mi, and sol in any key, any register, with any loudness or tone color.

Chords are named for the scale step on which they are based. A I chord is based on the first step of the scale, do; a II chord is based on the second step, re; a III chord on the third step, mi; a IV chord on fa; a V chord on sol; a VI chord on la; and a VII chord on ti. This system of naming is very handy for describing chord progressions. (See page 301 for notations.)

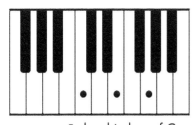

I chord in key of C

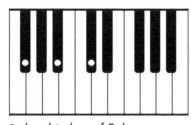

I chord in key of F-sharp

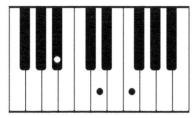

I chord in key of B-flat

A chord change is simply what it says, changing a chord. If we move from one chord to another, we have executed a **chord change**. We have moved forward, progressed, from one chord to another. In other words, a **chord progression** has been made. If the chords involved are those based on the first and second steps of the scale, respectively, we could describe the chord change as a I-II progression. If we move from a chord based on the first step to a chord based on the fourth, we create a I-IV progression. The reverse of that is a IV-I. If we move from the I chord to the V chord, and then back to the I chord, we create a I-V-I progression.

To hear the sound of a very common chord progression, the I-IV-I-V-I blues progression, find a piano, an organ, an accordion, or any other keyboard instrument and strike all the keys simultaneously, the number of counts (1234, 2234, etc.) indicated in the diagram below. You need not worry about what fingers to place on what keys. In fact, go ahead and use fingers from both hands if necessary. Try to keep a steady rate for striking the keys. If you can keep a steady rate, you may find that you are sounding like you have heard pianists and guitarists in rhythm and blues bands sound.

Demonstrated on *Demo CD* Track 19.

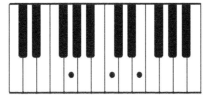

1234 2234 3234 4234 (**I** chord for 4 measures)

1234 2234 (**IV** chord for 2 measures)

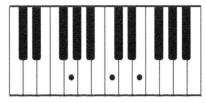

1234 2234 (**I** chord for 2 measures)

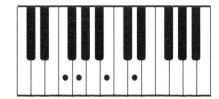

1234 2234 (**V** chord for 2 measures)

((•⏛**Listen** on
mysearchlab.com

Listen to audio-visual explanation of chord changes on mysearchlab.com

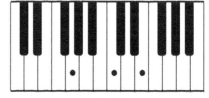

1234 2234 (**I** chord for 2 measures)

Chord Voicing

Most music uses chords that have been **voiced**. The concept of voicing is a very simple concept. It involves the fact that the keyboard is a succession of repeating octaves.

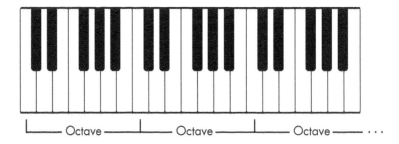

L—— Octave ——L— Octave ——L— Octave —— · · ·

With the resulting repetition of notes available, we can pull each chord note away from the position it holds within a single octave and spread the chord over the range of the keyboard. We can also include additional notes and/or omit some of the original notes. All these manipulations fall under the heading of "voicing."

The same chord (three notes) arranged in different positions across the keyboard.

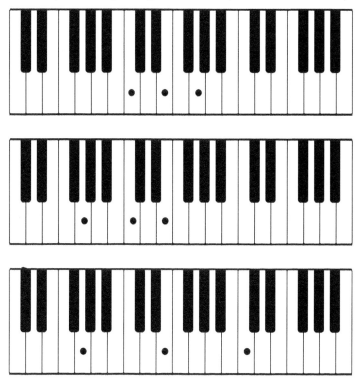

Jazz pianists can often be identified by the way they voice chords, and characteristic preferences in piano voicing are important components of the style in almost every period of jazz. In recent jazz, for example in the work of pianists McCoy Tyner and Chick Corea, voicing in fourths is quite common. Voicing in fourths means that chords are made up of notes four steps away from each other. In other words, a chord voiced in fourths might contain do, fa, and ti instead of do, mi, and sol. (The interval between do and fa is called a perfect fourth. To create a perfect fourth between fa and ti, the ti must be flatted. In building a chord composed of perfect fourths, each successive note is considered do of a new scale and the fourth note, fa, in that scale is used.) You can hear the sound of a chord voiced in fourths by playing this:

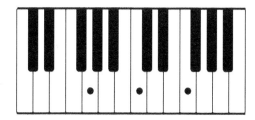

Voicing in fourths

The term "voicing" also refers to how the notes of a chord are assigned to instruments in an orchestra or band. The ranges of the instruments as well as their tone colors are taken into consideration in voicing chords. Characteristic voicings serve to identify the work of different arrangers. Duke Ellington, for instance, voices chords in a manner distinguishable from Stan Kenton. Both Ellington's chords and his choice of instruments differ.

Voicing is also a term used to identify the instruments playing a melody. For example, we might say Duke Ellington "voiced the lead (the melody) for clarinet, trumpet, and tenor sax," meaning that those instruments played a unison passage in a particular Ellington arrangement.

The Blues

The term "the blues" has several meanings. It can describe

1. a sad feeling, or music that projects a sad feeling;

2. a rhymed poetic form (paired couplets in iambic pentameter);

3. a slow, funky, earthy type of music;

4. a type of chord progression, usually contained in twelve measures, that has certain predictable chord movements in the fifth, seventh, ninth, and eleventh measures;

5. any combination of the above.

((•—Listen on
mysearchlab.com
Listen to audio-visual explanation of twelve-bar blues progression on mysearchlab.com

Blues poetry is so common in popular music that a technical description of the positions of accent and rhyme is not necessary in order for you to recognize the form. A single, very characteristic example can serve to illustrate the structure of blues poetry:

My man don't love me, treats me awful mean. (pause)

My man don't love me, treats me awful mean. (pause)

He is the lowest man I've ever seen. (pause)

((•—Listen on
mysearchlab.com
Listen to audio-visual explanation of paired couplets in iambic pentameter on mysearchlab.com

The I, IV, and V chords are basic elements of harmony used in the blues. In the twelve-bar blues, which is the most common blues form, these chords are distributed over twelve measures in a particular way. Although many variations are possible, the basic form is always the same. The chords and their respective durations are shown in the following chart. Each slash (/) indicates one beat. Perhaps it is helpful for you to think of a chord played on each beat by a rhythm guitarist. Note that the principal chord changes occur in the fifth, seventh, ninth, and eleventh measures.

I				IV		I		V		I	
////	////	////	////	////	////	////	////	////	////	////	////

Although the chord relationships of the fifth, seventh, ninth, and eleventh measures usually hold, the remaining measures are the scene of countless alterations. Modern jazz blues progressions often employ more than one chord in a single measure and at least one change every measure. It is not unusual to have ten to twenty chord changes in the space of twelve measures. Sometimes the principal chords of the fifth, seventh, ninth, and eleventh measures are also altered. When the blues is sung, the words are often distributed in a standard way over the twelve-bar progression (see page 278).

A blues can be fast or slow, happy or sad. It may have lyrics, or it may be a purely instrumental piece, and its chord progressions may be simple or complex. For a piece to be a blues, the only requirement is that the I-IV-I-V-I chord progression or a variant of it be presented in a twelve-measure form.

The Thirty-Two-Bar A-A-B-A Tune

Another form on which jazz musicians often improvise is the thirty-two-bar A-A-B-A tune. The thirty-two-bar tune is made up of four eight-measure sections. The opening eight measures, called the A-section, is repeated in the second section. The third part is the B-section, sometimes referred to as the bridge, release, inside, or channel. The last eight bars bring back the material of the first eight. So the tune falls into what is called A-A-B-A form. Thousands of pop tunes composed during the 1920s, 30s, 40s, and 50s were thirty-two bars long in A-A-B-A form.

Listening for the Twelve-Bar Blues and Thirty-Two-Bar Forms

To gain a practical familiarity with chord progressions, glance at the list of tunes on page 279. These are categorized as twelve-bar blues or thirty-two-bar tunes in A-A-B-A form. Go to a record collection and find performances of tunes on the list, and choose one of them. Listen to approximately the first thirty seconds to determine whether this rendition has an introduction or begins immediately with the tune itself. Also determine how fast the beats are passing. A clue can often be found in the bass playing. If the bass is walking, there is a bass note for every beat, four beats to the measure. Listening to that sound, you should be able to hear the pulse as though the bassist were a metronome. The sound of the drummer's ride cymbal may also be a good indication of where the beats lie.

Having listened long enough to determine the tempo, you will also have discovered whether there is an introduction, and the point at which it ends and the tune begins. If you are not sure whether the beginning of the piece is an introduction or part of the tune itself, wait a while and listen for it to recur. If it does not recur, it is probably an introduction. In A-A-B-A form, the first part, A, is immediately repeated, A-A, before a new section, B, occurs. The routine for most twelve-bar blues tunes consists of repeating the entire twelve bars before beginning improvisation. Musicians occasionally use the same music for an ending that they used for the introduction. So if you hear something familiar at the end that does not seem to fit exactly in twelve or thirty-two bars, it may be the introduction attached for use as an ending.

By now you should know both the tempo at which to count beats and the moment to begin counting. Start when the tune itself starts (right after the introduction, in most cases). For a twelve-bar blues count: "1234, 2234, 3234, 4234, **5**234, 6234, **7**234, 8234, **9**234, 10 234, **11** 234, 12 234." Listen and count until you can detect the chord changes in measures five, seven, nine, and eleven:

I				IV		I		V		I	
////	////	////	////	////	////	////	////	////	////	////	////

If your counting is accurate, you will eventually be able to anticipate these important chord changes. That should provide some insight into harmonies that the jazz musician uses in his improvisation.

Count like this for a thirty-two-bar A-A-B-A tune:

	"1234,	2234,	3234,	4234,	5234,	6234,	7234,	8234,
repeat	234,	2234,	3234,	4234,	5234,	6234,	7234,	8234,
bridge	234,	2234,	3234,	4234,	5234,	6234,	7234,	8234,
back to A	234,	2234,	3234,	4234,	5234,	6234,	7234,	8234."

Listen and count over and over until you can not only hear the bridge and the repeated sections, A-A, when they occur, but anticipate them. Do not become discouraged if you find it necessary to start and stop many times. Counting beats and measures requires practice. It is very important because it may be your only clue to the tune's form once a soloist has begun improvising. Learning to count accurately may take a few minutes, a few hours, or even a few days, but it is essential to an understanding of jazz improvisation. It will be well worth the effort. You might get especially good at anticipating the B-section. If you know the tune, or can learn it by listening a few times, try humming it while listening to the soloists improvise on its chord changes. This will help clarify the relationship between the improvisation and the original tune. It will also help you keep your place.

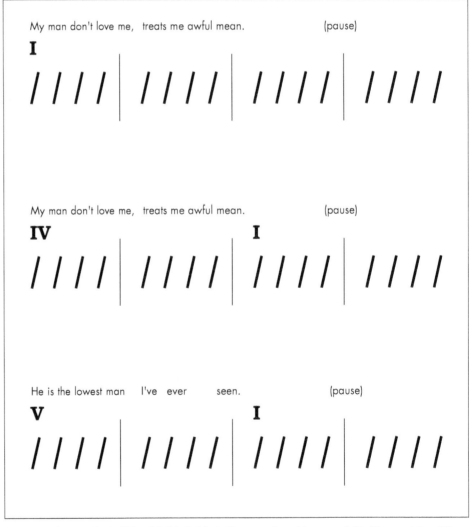

Blues poetic form in relation to the twelve-bar blues chord progression. The lyrics shown are from Billie Holiday's "Fine and Mellow." Available on LP as *The Sound of Jazz* (Columbia: CK 45234, 1957), on video as *The Sound of Jazz* (Idem: 1058, 1957), on CD as *The Sound of Jazz* (Columbia: CK 6608, 1957). Also available on *Prentice Hall Jazz History* DVD (ISBN 0-13-6026435)

Detecting Other Forms

Not all tunes fit into the twelve-bar blues form or the thirty-two-bar A-A-B-A form. "I'll Remember April" is a forty-eight-bar A-B-C-D-A-B form. "I've Got You Under My Skin" is a fifty-six-bar A-B-A-C-D-E-F form. Together, the twelve-bar blues form and the thirty-two-bar A-A-B-A form probably describe more tunes than any other single form, but they actually describe less than forty percent of all tunes written between 1910 and 1960. Let us examine a few other forms.

The twelve-bar blues is a particular set of chord progressions (I-IV-I-V-I) in a twelve-measure package. There are twelve-bar forms that are not blues simply because they do not follow the I-IV-I-V-I progression or any variation of it. For example, Richard Rodgers's "Little Girl Blue" is an A-A-B form in which each section is twelve bars long, but it is not a blues. It is also not uncommon in pop tunes to find a twelve-bar section that is actually an eight-bar progression with an extra four-bar progression connected to it.

The word "blues" in a song title does not necessarily signify the twelve-bar blues form. Both musicians and nonmusicians use the term "blues" to describe any slow, sad

Compositions with Thirty-Two-Bar A-A-B-A Construction

"Ain't Misbehavin"	"Have You Met Miss Jones?"	"Moten Swing"
"Angel Eyes"	"I Can't Get Started"	"Move"
"Anthropology"	"I Cover the Waterfront"	"Oleo"
"Birth of the Blues"	"I Love You"	"Over the Rainbow"
"Blue Moon"	"I'm Beginning to See the Light"	"Perdido"
"Body and Soul"	"It's Only a Paper Moon"	"Robin's Nest"
"Budo" ("Hallucinations")	"I Want to Talk About You"	"Rosetta"
"Darn That Dream"	"Jordu"	"Round Midnight"
"Don't Blame Me"	"Lady Be Good"	"Ruby, My Dear"
"Don't Get Around Much Anymore"	"Lover Man"	"Satin Doll"
"Easy Living"	"Lullaby of Birdland"	"September Song"
"52nd Street Theme"	"Makin' Whoopee"	"Take the 'A' Train"
"Flamingo"	"The Man I Love"	"Well, You Needn't"
"Four Brothers"	"Midnight Sun"	"What's New?"
"Good Bait"	"Misty"	"What Is This Thing Called Love?"

Twelve-Bar Blues Compositions

"Bags' Groove"	"Blue Trane"	"Mr. P. C."
"Barbados"	"Cheryl"	"Now's the Time"
"Billie's Bounce"	"Cool Blues"	"One O'Clock Jump"
"Bloomdido"	"Cousin Mary"	"Sid's Ahead"
"Bluesology"	"Footprints"	"Soft Winds"
"Blue Monk"	"Freddie the Freeloader"	"Straight, No Chaser"
"Blues in the Closet"	"Goodbye Porkpie Hat"	"Walkin"
"Blue 'n' Boogie"	"Jumpin' with Symphony Sid"	"Woodchopper's Ball"

tune regardless of its chord progression. "Birth of the Blues" is a thirty-two-bar A-A-B-A tune and "Sugar Blues" is an eighteen-bar tune. The "St. Louis Blues" is actually a twelve-bar blues plus an eight-bar bridge and an additional twelve-bar blues. Performers sometimes choose to repeat, delete, and reorder sections of "St. Louis Blues" when they play it.

Some people use the terms "eight-bar blues" and "sixteen-bar blues." Usually the tune they are describing has the I-IV movement in the first five bars and deviates from the twelve-bar I-IV-I-V-I progression thereafter. Some tunes of lengths other than twelve bars sound very much like twelve-bar blues simply because they contain the I-IV-I-V-I progression, but the durations of a few chords may be changed, and certain sections may be repeated. Herbie Hancock's "Watermelon Man," for example, has been called a "sixteen-bar blues."

Unlike the twelve-bar blues, the thirty-two-bar A-A-B-A form is not always based on the same basic chord progression. Many different chord progressions have been used in the A-A-B-A form. Fats Waller's "Honeysuckle Rose" and Erroll Garner's "Misty" are both thirty-two-bar A-A-B-A tunes, yet they have almost completely different chord progressions.

The form A-A-B-A does not always contain thirty-two bars nor does each section necessarily have the same number of measures. In "Girl from Ipanema," which is A-A-B-A, the A-section has eight bars while the bridge has sixteen. In "Secret Love," another A-A-B-A tune, the A-section has sixteen bars while the bridge has only eight.

There are also elongated versions of the basic twelve-bar blues and thirty-two-bar A-A-B-A forms. Lee Morgan's "Sidewinder" is a twenty-four-bar blues: each chord lasts twice as long as it would in a twelve-bar blues. Another example is the sixty-four-bar A-A-B-A form in which each section is sixteen bars long instead of eight. Ray Noble's "Cherokee" and Lerner and Loewe's "On the Street Where You Live" are both sixty-four-bar A-A-B-A tunes. Charlie Parker's "Ko-Ko" is based on the chord changes of "Cherokee"; consequently it is also a sixty-four-bar A-A-B-A tune. There are shortened versions of the thirty-two-bar A-A-B-A, too. Sonny Rollins' "Doxy" is a sixteen-bar A-A-B-A tune; each section is only four bars long.

A-A-B-A is not the only common thirty-two-bar form for pop tunes. Numerous tunes fit an A-B-A-C form (both the C-section and the B-section differ from the A section). "My Romance," "On Green Dolphin Street," "Indiana," "Sweet Georgia Brown," and "Out of Nowhere" all fall into a thirty-two-bar A-B-A-C form. In addition to the thirty-two-bar A-A-B-A and A-B-A-C, there is also the thirty-two-bar A-B-A-B. "How High the Moon" is an example. There are shortened versions of these, also. "Summertime" is a sixteen-bar A-B-A-C tune.

Hundreds of tunes fit into sixteen measures. "Peg o' My Heart" is a sixteen-bar pop tune. Horace Silver based his "The Preacher" on the sixteen-bar pop tune "Show Me the Way to Go Home." Wayne Shorter has written many sixteen-bar tunes, including "E.S.P.," "Nefertiti," "Prince of Darkness," etc. Some chord progressions are used in sixteen-bar tunes almost as often as the I-IV-I-V-I progression appears in the twelve-bar blues. Certain sixteen-bar progressions have become standard.

Verse and Chorus. It is important to note that the forms we have been examining refer only to chorus length. A large number of tunes consist of two major parts: a verse followed by a chorus. The verse traditionally differs from the chorus in tempo, mood, and harmony:

1. The chorus might be played at a faster tempo than the verse.

2. Verses are often performed freely, with accelerations and decelerations of tempo.

3. The verse might feel as though it is leading up to something, whereas the chorus usually has the stamp of finality to it.

4. There may be little similarity between chord progressions used in the verse and those in the chorus.

5. The key of the verse is sometimes different from that of the chorus.

6. Choruses are repeated, but once a verse is played, it is usually over for the entire performance.

7. The chorus is the section of the tune jazz musicians usually choose as basis for improvisation.

Breaking into Multiples of Two. When you are listening to performances and trying to detect forms, be aware that arrangements of thirty-two-bar A-A-B-A, A-B-A-C, and A-B-A-B tunes sometimes depart from strict repetition of those thirty-two bars. Arrangements sometimes contain four-, eight-, and sixteen-bar sections, formed by omitting or adding to portions of the original thirty-two-bar tune. Note also that many tunes, especially pre-1930s Dixieland tunes, have long, elaborate forms similar to those of marches and of nineteenth-century European dance music (such as the quadrille). Forms for many tunes in pre-1920s jazz were derived from march music. A piece might have a series of sections consisting of multiples of eight bars. Designating each section by a letter of the alphabet, a piece might conceivably follow a pattern like this:

$$A - A - B - B - C - D - E - F - C - D - E - F$$
$$16-16-16-16-16-16-24-32-16-16-24-32$$

When listening for form, keep in mind that even in the most intricate pieces, forms can usually be broken down into two-bar segments. So if you are unable to divide a piece neatly into either four-bar or eight-bar sections, try using a few two-bar sections. "Sugar Blues" can be heard as 18 or as 8+10 or as 8+8+2. That form poses problems for the improviser because it tends to break the flow of ideas conceived in four- and eight-bar melodic units. It is like being forced to walk left, right, left, right, left, left, right. The form of the original "I Got Rhythm" is:

$$A — A — B — A + tag$$
$$8 — 8 — 8 — 8 + 2 \text{ or}$$
$$8 — 8 — 8 — 10$$

When jazz musicians improvise on its chord progression, they omit the two-bar tag. If included, the tag would interrupt the flow of the improvisations and again be like having to take two steps with your left foot before going back to an alternation of right with left. Another popular tune that has an unusual structure is "Moonlight in Vermont." It follows the form:

$$A — A — B — A + tag$$
$$6 — 6 — 8 — 6 + 2$$

Modal Forms

During the late 1950s and especially during the 60s and 70s, modal forms practically eliminated the "change" part of "chord change." In modal music, improvisations are based on the extended repetition of one or two chords. Those chords contain so many notes that they either include or are compatible with all the notes in a scale. The term mode is synonymous with scale, hence the term "modal music." Although this is not the definition of modal employed by classical composers and in textbooks on classical music, it is what jazz musicians and jazz journalists have come to mean by "modal." In most instances, jazz musicians also employ notes that are not contained in the mode or in the repeated chords. Some of John Coltrane's work, for example, is not strictly modal, but has the flavor of music that is.

In modal music, the entire improvised portion of the performance is often based on a single chord and scale. Usually the chord and its scale are minor, Indian, Middle Eastern, or in some way more exotic-sounding than the chords used in most pop tune progressions. Because it is based on a single scale, the music has no real chord changes, just a drone.

Sometimes a melody containing chord changes of its own precedes the improvised section of a modal performance. John Coltrane's recordings of the Rodgers and Hammerstein tune "My Favorite Things" are good examples. Coltrane played the original melody while his rhythm section played the appropriate chord changes. Then the entire group improvised only on the primary chord of the tune (and the scale compatible with that chord). Near the end of their improvisations, they switched to another chord, that lent the piece a slightly different character. Coltrane could have retained the chord progressions of the tune and used them as the basis for improvisation, but he chose not to.

Some modal music does have chord changes, or "mode changes." One rich chord (or scale, depending on how one cares to conceive it) is the basis for four, eight, or perhaps sixteen measures. Then a different chord is in effect for another similar duration. The Miles Davis tune "Milestones" is based on one mode for the first sixteen bars, a different mode for the second sixteen bars, and a return to the original mode for the final eight bars. The melody has the form A-A-B-B-A, and each section is eight bars long. Herbie Hancock's "Maiden Voyage" has a thirty-two-bar A-A-B-A construction; here each mode lasts for four bars. The A-section is based on two different modes, each lasting only four bars. The B-section makes use of another two modes also lasting four bars each. If each mode were labeled by letter name, "Maiden Voyage" could be described as X-Y-X-Y-Z-W-X-Y. "So What" (on the Miles Davis album *Kind of Blue*) has a melody in thirty-two-bar A-A-B-A form, and the use of modes corresponds to that form: there are sixteen bars of one mode, eight of another, and a return to the original mode for the last eight bars. John Coltrane's "Impressions" not only takes the same form as "So What" but also uses exactly the same modes. (See pages 304-306 for modes on "Milestones," "Maiden Voyage," and "So What.")

Much jazz of the 1960s and 70s was based on infrequent chord changes (another way of saying modal) instead of the frequent chord changes found in most twelve-bar blues and thirty-two-bar forms. Many groups abandoned both the blues form and the thirty-two-bar forms. Some groups used complex melodies and intricate rhythm section figures, yet their improvisations were based almost exclusively on one or a small number of chords ("Freedom Jazz Dance," for example).

The Effects of Form on Improvisation

Song forms of four- and eight-bar sections tend to break improvisations into small segments of similar length. Divisions of form, in other words, can influence the flow of improvised lines. This is not necessarily a disadvantage, however. The divisions in form can frame well-chosen melodic figures, and they can provide a means of transition from one figure to another. This creates more continuity than a solo might contain without chord progressions. Forms based on single modes sounding indefinitely tend to free the improviser, enabling him to create lines that are as long or short, tense or relaxed as he desires. No preset tension-relaxation devices in the form of chord progressions are there to suggest construction patterns for his improvised lines.

Bridges. The B-section of an A-A-B-A tune is called the bridge. It bridges the gap between repetition of the A-sections, and it usually provides a contrast to the material in the A-sections. The bridge can break up or lift the mood established by repeated A-sections. Many bridges are placed a few keys higher than the A-section. A key change can be a boost in any situation, but is especially effective after the repeated A-sections.

The bridge is important to improvisers because a good improviser can capitalize on the bridge's natural capacity to provide contrast. Some of the greatest solo segments in jazz are those improvised over the chord progressions of a tune's bridge. The rhythm section also takes advantage of the bridge and is often especially active just before the bridge is entered and just before it is exited. Heightened rhythmic activity can announce the arrival or departure of the bridge.

Combos often use the bridge as a container for solo spots. Sometimes a tune's melody will be played for the final time in the performance, and when the bridge occurs, everyone stops playing except the drummer. It becomes his feature. Then the entire band returns precisely on the first beat of the final A-section.

In some jazz tunes the bridge consists only of chord changes. Such pieces require improvisation during the bridge but return to the written melody when the final A-section is reached. Sonny Rollins's tune "Oleo" is an example. Many groups also use that approach on "The Theme," a popular up-tempo number for jazz combos of the late 1950s and early 60s.

Turnarounds. Another important part in the construction of standard tunes is the turnaround (also known as the turnabout or turnback). In many, perhaps in most songs, the seventh and eighth measures of each section are occupied by a single sustained tone or two long tones (see below). That part of the tune might be considered dead space due to the lack of melodic movement, but the jazz musician uses that space. He fills it with chord changes that lead directly to the beginning of the next section. Jazz musicians are expected to know a variety of chord progressions common to turnarounds. The manner in which they fill that space with chord changes and improvised lines is the art of the turnaround.

The whole combo digs in when a turnaround comes up. Drummers tend to kick more and, thus, tie together the musical statements of one section and bring in the next. Those bassists who almost invariably walk are more likely to vary this pattern in a turnaround. Tension can be built during a turnaround and resolved by the onset of the next section of the piece.

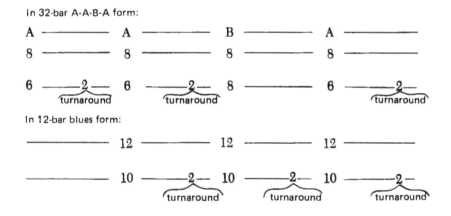

In 32-bar A-A-B-A form:

In 12-bar blues form:

Turnarounds in 32-bar A-A-B-A pieces and 12-bar blues pieces.

Phrasing in Relation to Form

Jazz musicians prior to the mid-1940s tended to improvise phrases that coincided with the tune structure. Most progressions consist of two- and four-bar units, and improvised solos often proceeded in phrases of similar length. Furthermore, soloists tended to make larger silences at or near the end of an A-section or B-section. They rarely connected tune sections by continuing phrases through the turnarounds. They stopped at or before the turnarounds, and then started anew at the beginning of the next section. They treated the eighth-bar line as a barrier. Twelve-bar blues solos often contained phrases that started at the beginning of each chorus regardless of what happened at the end of a previous chorus, thus treating the twelfth-bar line as a barrier.

One characteristic of modern jazz (beginning in the 1940s) and the music of the players who most influenced it was the use of phrases that began somewhere within an eight-bar section and continued into the next section without a pause. There was no lull during the turnaround.

A characteristic of some modern jazz during the 1960s and 70s was the absence of preset chord progressions. That free approach significantly loosened the tendencies of jazz phrasing. Although players retained patterns common to preceding jazz eras, they were free to phrase with greater variety due to the lack of underlying chord movements. Some jazz of this type projects a feeling of expansiveness quite unlike the crowded feeling often projected by modern jazz of the 1940s and 50s.

Some tunes that appeared during the 1960s, especially those of Wayne Shorter, were sixteen or more bars without any repeated sections. The A-section was not repeated, there was no bridge, no turnaround. These tunes were "all A." That form enabled improvisers to play with great continuity yet without the crowded, segmented feeling which sometimes characterizes improvisations based on standard A-A-B-A and A-B-A-C forms with the usual turnarounds and bridges. Sometimes a free, floating feeling could be projected by improvisers using these "all A" forms.

Tone Color

((•⦿ Listen on
mysearchlab.com

Listen to audio-visual explanation of timbre (tone color) on mysearchlab.com

An important element of music, usually the first to be perceived, is tone quality or tone color. This element is also known as timbre (pronounced tamm´ burr).

How can you tell the difference between the sound of a flute and the sound of a trumpet if they each play only one note, and it is the same note? The difference is tone color, the spectrum of frequencies generated by each instrument in its own unique way.

This definition is an oversimplification of a complex situation in which many factors come into play.

The spectrum of frequencies produced by an instrument is not fixed. The spectrum varies depending on the pitch and the forcefulness with which it is played. The ways in which a player starts and stops a note, the attack and release, also are important in determining tone color. The attack and release are accompanied by temporary changes in a tone's frequency spectrum.

Another complication arises from our tendency to associate an instrument's tone color with the aggregate effects of all the notes being played on it rather than the spectrum of frequencies present in a single note.

Finally, when sounds come to our ears, they are modified by room acoustics and by recording and playback techniques. The way our ears deal with that variability is quite involved.

Tone color varies greatly from one instrument to another, and there are also especially discernible differences in tone color among jazz musicians playing the same instrument. For example, to speak of the tenor sax tone color of John Coltrane or Stan Getz is to describe sounds so unique that some inexperienced listeners could differentiate them as easily as they could distinguish flute from trumpet. The evolution of jazz tenor saxophone playing reflects not only changes in the phrasing and rhythms, but also changes in tone color.

Tone color is a very personal characteristic of a player's style. Jazz musicians place great emphasis on creating the particular tone colors they want. A jazz musician's attention to tone color is comparable to an actor's concern for costume, make-up, and voice quality combined. Tone color is so important to saxophonists that many spend lifetimes searching for the perfect mouthpiece. They also experiment with different methods of blowing and different ways of altering the vibrating surface of the cane reeds that are attached to their mouthpieces.

Because the tenor saxophone is capable of producing an exceptionally wide variety of tone colors, it is easier to differentiate jazz tenor saxophonists by tone color alone than it is to recognize a particular trumpeter or pianist. That is not to say that differences are absent from trumpeter to trumpeter or from pianist to pianist. The differences are just more subtle.

Two pianists can play the same piece on the same piano and produce quite different sounds. No two pianos have the same tone color, and one piano can produce distinctly different tone colors, depending on how hard the keys are struck. The use of the pedals and a pianist's timing in releasing one key and striking the next are cru-cial to the sound. A key may be released before, after, or at the same time as the next is struck. When a note is short and ends well before the next note begins, we call it a staccato note. If one key is released after the next is struck, the two sounds overlap in time. Notes played smoothly one after the other are said to be legato. The amount of overlap influences the clarity of attack and the dimension of legato-staccato. Our ears hear sounds in combined form rather than as single tones. Whatever is left in the air from a preceding sound mixes and colors the subsequent sound. The relationship between consecutive sounds, ranging from complete separation to extreme overlap-ping, are resources that contribute to the personal character of a pianist's style. Count Basie's touch and tone color differ remarkably from Duke Ellington's. Perhaps you will perceive Basie's touch as lighter than Ellington's. No matter how you describe the sound, you will notice a difference if you listen carefully.

Mutes (Listen to examples on *Demo CD* Track 63.)

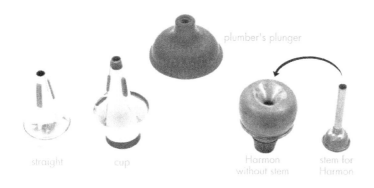

◀ Trumpet with Harmon mute.

◀ Trombonist Wilbur de Paris playing into plunger mute.

Photo by William P. Gottlieb, courtesy Library of Congress.

Guitarists's interest in tone color is manifested by their search for different types of picks, guitar strings, and amplifiers. Guitar amplifier dial settings are essential to the control of tone color. Bass players are also concerned with many of the same factors.

Trumpeters and trombonists explore available tone colors by experimenting with mouthpiece changes, methods of blowing, mutes, and instruments that represent different manufacturers and models.

Intonation is also an important aspect of tone. Intonation refers to playing in tune, playing sharp or flat. Playing sharp means playing at a pitch level somewhat higher than the average pitch of the ensemble. Playing flat refers to playing a pitch somewhat lower than that of the ensemble. Do not confuse the terms sharp and flat with words describing actual note names such as C-sharp and B-flat. These notes are raised (sharped) and lowered (flatted) by a larger amount than is usually the case in out-of-tune playing. That is, the interval between C and C-sharp is greater than the interval between C and that of a performer playing C a bit sharper than his fellow ensemble members. Small deviations of pitch occur all the time even in the best ensembles, but larger deviations lead listeners to comment "someone is playing out of tune."

Why is intonation described in this section on tone color? Intonation affects the tone color of both the soloist and the ensemble as a whole. If a group of musicians played the same piece twice, once without listening or adjusting to each other's pitch (perhaps by pretuning their instruments and then wearing ear plugs for the performance), and then a second time, listening carefully to each other's pitch and continuously adjusting accordingly, you would hear two performances, each having distinctly different tone colors. Ensembles that lack precisiontuning have a thicker, rougher sound than precisely tuned ensembles. One element of a slick ensemble sound is careful and consistent tuning.

For tone color reasons, some soloists systematically play a little "high," meaning a bit sharp. Intonation is a musical resource for them. This is common in most types of music, including symphonic, but it is especially true for jazz soloists. A tone cuts through an ensemble if it is a bit sharper than the average pitch of that ensemble. Some jazz soloists, Johnny Hodges, Stan Getz, and Paul Desmond, for instance, play at the average pitch, whereas Charlie Parker and John Coltrane, for instance, tend to various degrees of sharpness. That is another component of tone color that helps us identify a particular player's work.

▲ Miles Davis playing into cup mute.

Courtesy of Frank Driggs

▲ Trombonist Dicky Wells playing into straight mute.

Photo by William Gottlieb

Music Buying Strategies

One key to being a happy jazz fan is finding the right albums. This section of the text book provides guidelines and short cuts to help you.

Minimizing Risk in Selecting Albums

1. **Beware of endorsements in newspapers and magazines.** They represent knowledge and understanding no greater than that of one individual. The reviewer might not be knowledgeable or perceptive. Moreover, his tastes might differ from yours. For instance, staples in the record collections of musicians are sometimes unknown by many critics, and some of these masterpieces were given only lukewarm reviews by the critics who did notice them. Albums that win Grammy awards are not necessarily outstanding, either. Usually they are merely among the albums that the largest companies want to promote. They nominate these for consideration by recording industry members who have not heard most of the jazz albums released within the preceding twelve months. (Over a thousand albums are issued each year in the U.S. alone.) A parallel might be helpful. You probably remember a few Academy Award winning movies you did not find enjoyable. Conversely, you might have also found yourself liking a few movies that received bad reviews. You may have been impressed by a few movies that no one was talking about, too. Similarly, *albums receiving the most press and airplay are not necessarily the highest quality*. Extent of press and airplay is determined largely by the record company's promotional budget, luck, and persistence, plus the tastes of disc jockeys and journalists. Some of the best albums never get publicized.

2. **Listen to the music before you buy it.** Try to avoid album buying as an impulse purchase. Unless you want a record for purely academic reasons or historical perspective, you might realize too late that you spent your money on something you don't enjoy. This is worth keeping in mind unless you can afford to experiment expensively. Friends, libraries, jazz courses, and internet services can often expose you to new albums. If there is a jazz radio program broadcasting near you, don't hesitate to phone the station and ask them to play a particular album. (College radio stations not only broadcast more jazz than commercial stations, but they are also more likely to be interested in your requests.) And when you hear something you like, you could also phone the station and ask for its album title and record company name. If you want to sample a particular musician's work, you can Google his name and then look for free downloads of his music.

3. **Use a broad sampling of recordings before forming your opinion of a particular player.** One good reason is that *few jazz improvisers are extremely consistent in producing inspired recordings*. Some of even the greatest jazz musicians have had whole strings of unexciting albums. This means that, if the only recording you hear is from an off day for that player, you derive a nonrepresentative view of his talent. You are not fair to him.

   Another reason for using a broad sampling is that, *if the player had more than one style period in his career, you cheat yourself if you draw a conclusion from sampling only one of them*. For instance, Sonny Rollins had a creative peak in the middle 1950s, and another in the 1990s with a different style. This means that, if you heard a few recent Rollins records and did not like them, you might not seek any mid-1950s Rollins material, even though you might have liked it. The converse would also be true.

4. **Don't accept substitutions.** The quality and character of improvised music can vary drastically from album to album and from selection to selection, even if made by the same band during the same period, and even from the same record date, as the music you seek. So once you decide which albums you really want, don't get others first, merely because they are available or look similar.

Confusing Album Titles

Be suspicious of titles for compilations. Let's examine reasons for caution with two categories of compilations: (a) *Greatest Hits* and (b) *The Best of, The Indispensable,* and *The Essential.* **Problems for both categories often occur when the compilation comes from only one company's recordings,** and that particular company did not record the artist during his creative peak (invalidating *The Best of* designation) or during his height of popularity (invalidating the *Greatest Hits* designation). Another company did. For example, a Verve album of 1950s recordings called *The Essential Lester Young* is probably "essential" only to those Lester Young collectors who already have much of Young's creative peak represented in his 1930s Count Basie recordings, reissued by Columbia/SONY and Decca/MCA/GRP.

A second set of problems arises **when musicians have had several different styles during their careers** and a creative peak for each. They may have been recording for a different company during each important period. For example, John Coltrane made important recordings as a bandleader for three different companies (Prestige, Atlantic, and Impulse). Each company documented a stylistically different stage in his career. (And some of his best work was recorded with Miles Davis' bands for Columbia, a *fourth* record company.) This means, for example, that an Atlantic album called *The Best of John Coltrane* cannot contain Coltrane's best work from all three periods—although it could sample some of his best Atlantic sessions if the compiler knew what he was doing.

A third set of problems results **when musicians made their best recordings as sidemen in the bands of others,** not as bandleaders, yet the compilation draws only from recording sessions where they were bandleaders. For instance, Lester Young's best work was done as a sideman with the 1936–41 combos and big bands associated with Count Basie. The music on his combo recordings as leader does not sound like his music on the Basie recordings. This means that an Emarcy album called *Pres at His Very Best*, containing music from 1943–44 in which Young was bandleader, is probably not his "very" best recorded improvisations, though it might represent the best playing he recorded as a bandleader. The Emarcy album title is misleading.

Here are some other examples of the confusion arising from album titles not coordinated with varied careers. In the 1960s, pianist Herbie Hancock and saxophonist Wayne Shorter both recorded for Blue Note as bandleaders. During much of that time they were also recording for Columbia as sidemen in the Miles Davis Quintet. Most of their playing on the Davis recordings is superior to that on their own records. But since they were bandleaders for Blue Note, the Blue Note recordings, not the Columbia recordings, provide the pool for albums titled *The Best of Herbie Hancock* and *The Best of Wayne Shorter.* Hancock's and Shorter's work on Blue Note is excellent music, and it also features the outstanding composing for which Hancock and Shorter are distinguished. But when heard strictly as piano and saxophone improvising, their work on Blue Note may not be the absolute best of either man's career, as claimed by an album title. Incidentally, a Columbia album called *The Best of Herbie Hancock* (JC 36309) contains neither his innovative playing with the 1963–69 Miles Davis groups nor his distinguished composing within the Blue Note work. The album samples a third facet: Hancock's jazz-rock material of the 1970s.

A fourth reason for approaching compilation titles with caution is that **sometimes compilers are not qualified for their task.** This means that, even if an artist recorded solely for one company during his creative peak, a *Best of* album might omit his *best* work because the person in charge of preparing the compilation was not familiar enough with all the artist's work for that firm. The compiler might not have had sufficiently developed taste, either, or he did not realize how much he needed to call upon the taste and knowledge of consultants. This may explain why a number of single-company compilations of several jazz giants, that emerged on compact disc during the 1990s, had knowledgeable consumers wondering why so many unremarkable selections had been included while outstanding performances remained untapped in the company's vaults. It might also explain why even a few multi-company compilations have had jazz fans puzzled about odd choices.

Greatest Hits can be misleading as an album title because, in addition to all the previously mentioned problems, a player's best-selling material might not even appear on it. For example, the largest-selling Miles Davis recording for Columbia was his 1969 *Bitches Brew* (GP 26). Yet it is not represented on the Columbia album *Miles Davis' Greatest Hits* (PC 9808). The 1964 recording of "Girl From Ipanema" for the Verve company was the highest selling recording of Stan Getz's career. Yet there is an album titled *Stan Getz's Greatest Hits* (Prestige 7337) drawn from 1949 and 1950 sessions made for the Prestige company. The Prestige material is excellent, perhaps better than the Verve material, yet it does not include his largest-selling hits as the album title deceptively implies.

To avoid being misled by compilation titles, first learn about the musician's career. Then check details on the album wrapper or box insert to confirm that recording dates, titles, and personnel match what you seek. It is also wise to consult authorities to determine what companies were recording the artist during critical portions of his career and what selections are deemed outstanding. Some such sources are available online.

By seeking prescreened items such as the types of anthologies discussed above, rather than making impulse purchases, you lessen risks in finding music you will want to keep. Ultimately you need to remember, however, that the main reason for buying compilations and samplers is to become familiar with a wide range of music for a small price. But also bear in mind that just because selections on the samplers are critically acclaimed or generally popular does not guarantee you will like them.

About Reissues

When seeking out-of-print recordings, there are several things to keep in mind. Many jazz recordings that have disappeared from catalog listings return later in altered form. This includes the category known as *reissues*, *re-releases*, and *repackages*. Before we discuss them, here is some relevant history. Prior to the widespread use of twelve-inch, 33⅓ rpm (revolutions per minute) LP (long play) records, most jazz was issued on ten-inch, 78 rpm records. Twelve-inch 33s were not common until the 1950s, so many bebop- and cool-style bands—in addition to Dixieland and swing bands—were initially presented on 78s. Due to the size of the record and the speed of rotation, most 78s could accommodate only about three minutes of music per side. An *album* consisted of several records packaged much like a photo album. Each disc had its own pocket or sleeve. The set was bound in cloth or leather. Then when the LP arrived, many of the three-minute selections originally on 78 were issued again (reissued) as compilations within 33⅓ rpm albums. This time, the word *album* meant one disc containing many selections. All the recordings in this book's premodern section and a few modern items are to be found in this kind of "reissue." Later on, LPs themselves began to be reissued, re-released, and repackaged as "new" LPs. Then when compact disc technology emerged, the contents of old LPs began appearing in CD format. Sometimes additional selections were included when the album was reissued on CD because the CD could accommodate up to about 79 minutes of music instead of the 50-minute limit that was common for LPs. Sometimes two LPs were represented on one CD. This is the altered form in which you can often find music originally available on records which have "disappeared" from the catalog.

There is something else to consider when searching for a reissue of a particular recording. *It is common for jazz groups to record several versions of the same tunes, and some players record the same tunes with different groups.* Since you are a jazz fan, you are seeking recordings of particular improvisations, not merely the tunes they are based on. So you must find the actual performances you want. A musician's improvisations on other versions of the tune might not even resemble what you want.

You might be able to locate an out-of-print album through such online services as amazon.com and www.eBay.com. Alternately, you may contact the auctioneers and rare record dealers that are often advertised on the back sections of jazz magazines. But when you are trying to locate music from a recording that has gone out of print you might find it in new compilations of old material. For these new packages, album titles are sometimes changed, and material from the original album is scattered over several different compilations. Another common problem is that the recordings may have belonged originally to companies that later sold their material. The original company's name helps you identify reissued material. For instance, one group of important Charlie Parker recordings was originally made for the Dial company, and its reissued form is called *The Dial Masters*. However, when record companies are bought and sold, sometimes the music is reissued intact, causing you no headaches. For example, Impulse was bought by ABC, then by MCA, then GRP, then by Universal, but many of the important albums John Coltrane made for Impulse during the 1960s continued to be distributed intact, though with new catalog numbers.

Another key to locating material in reissued form is that it is often identified by where it was recorded. For example, the pivotal Bill Evans-Scott LaFaro music originally made at New York City's Village Vanguard night club for Riverside record company, originally issued on albums titled *Sunday at the Village Vanguard* and *Waltz for Debby*, has been reissued by Fantasy-Prestige-Milestone as *The Village Vanguard Sessions*. Recordings from an outstanding 1953 concert by Charles Mingus, Charlie Parker, Dizzy Gillespie, Bud Powell, and Max Roach are frequently identified only by recording site: Toronto's Massey Hall (*The Massey Hall Concert*).

When seeking music that you think is out-of-print, you need a complete listing of the musicians, the pieces, the recording dates, the original album title, and the name of the record company. It also sometimes helps to have the original catalog numbers. Personnel listings can be especially useful because material is sometimes reissued under the name of a musician who was a sideman on the original recording session but has now become more significant than the leader. It is packaged as though he were leader at that original session. For example, a 1956 Tadd Dameron album called *Mating Call* was reissued under John Coltrane's name and called *On a Misty Night*. Coltrane was a sideman on it but is now in much demand in his own right. Several reissues of Joe Oliver's Creole Jazz Band have come out under Louis Armstrong's name, even though Armstrong was a sideman, not the leader, on Oliver's recordings. Much pre-1940 Lester Young material is available in reissues under Young's name, though it was originally recorded under Count Basie's leadership.

There are several ways you can keep up with what is being reissued. Internet sources may be the most efficient. Many new albums and reissues are announced by jazz magazines, such as *Jazz Times* (85 Quincy Avenue, Suite. 2, Quincy, MA 02169; 800-437-5828; *www.jazztimes.com*) and *Down Beat* (P.O. Box 11688, St. Paul, MN 55111-00688; 630-941-3210; *http://www.downbeat.com*). Several mail order services give information and take orders over the phone. One is J&R Music World (800-221-8180; *http://www.jr.com*). Another is Downtown Music Gallery (800-622-1387; *http://www.dtmgallery.com*).

Many Versions of the Same Tune

The problem of a single tune recorded many times by the same artist increased substantially during the past forty years. This was due to increases in: (1) legitimate reissue programs by major firms, (2) illegitimate releases (called bootleg or pirate records) by numerous small firms, (3) the issuing of alternate takes and rejected takes from the same recording session, and (4) the discovery, or rediscovery, of a seemingly endless variety of broadcast performances, called *air shots* or *air checks*. (Music of the 1930s and 1940s, unlike that of the 1950s and 1960s, is well documented by air checks because most jazz groups made live radio broadcasts in those days.)

Beginning in the 1960s, record companies began massive distribution of repackaged material. Hundreds of albums with new titles were introduced. Many contained music originally on 78s. Other albums had music originally available on LPs. In the 1990s huge reissue programs began making even more vintage music available because of CD technology.

Albums flooded the market from companies, both American and foreign, which operated without the consent of the recorded artists (or of their estates, in the case of deceased artists). Those albums constitute the illegitimate releases mentioned earlier as *bootlegs*. The companies were small and disappeared quickly. Some of their material had appeared previously on other records, but much of it had never been available before. A lot of it came from homemade recordings of night club appearances and radio broadcasts. Many albums have incorrect tune titles. Few contain complete personnel listings and recording dates. Internet file sharing similarly opened listeners to huge numbers of both legitimate and illegitimate recordings. Beware, however, that selections often download without band personnel or recording dates being identified. Many display poor sound fidelity. But if you can tolerate all those weaknesses, you might be well rewarded by the music itself. It is also worthwhile to be aware of bootleg recordings because the appearance and distribution of them is very common and likely to continue.

With the bootleg material added to the legitimate releases and reissues, it became possible to own, for instance, more than eighty albums of Charlie Parker, or more than one hundred of Duke Ellington. The record collector might be confronted with five to ten Parker versions of "Confirmation" and "Ornithology" and just as many Ellington versions of "Mood Indigo" and "Sophisticated Lady." Keeping track of recording dates and band personnel became essential to discussing particular performances of these frequently recorded tunes.

A few Charlie Parker classics illustrate the usefulness of having band personnel, tune titles, recording dates, and original record company name before you begin seeking a particular recording. The much praised music that Parker originally made in the form of 78s for Dial Record Company has been sold in numerous forms, some of them offered by tiny, obscure record companies that worked without the consent of Parker's estate. Take "Embraceable You," for example. Parker recorded different versions of it. But if you want his famous Dial recording of it, remember that he made two different versions at the same session in 1947 with pianist Duke Jordan, bassist Tommy Potter, and drummer Max Roach. Any deviation from that particular combination of identifiers will indicate that you are holding another version of the tune instead of the famous version. It is also essential to note the record company name and recording date if you want to locate Parker's famous 1945 "Now's the Time," which was made for Savoy record company with the Miles Davis trumpet solo that was later adapted and recorded by pianist Red Garland on the Miles Davis *Milestones* album. It is especially easy to become confused in this instance because another version of the same tune was also recorded by Parker without Davis in 1953 and released on a Verve album called *Now's the Time*. If you seek the Miles Davis recording of "Spanish Key" containing Chick Corea's piano solo analyzed in this book, you may be confronted with more than fifty listings for "Spanish Key" on any given download service. Crucial information may be missing from a given download's content, even when you are using a legitimate service such as Rhapsody or iTunes. You might not be able to verify band personnel, recording date or the actual version ("take" number), which means that you might not get the same improvisation you seek. There are instances in which historic figures recorded only one version of a given tune, but the more you study jazz, the more you will find it beneficial to **keep track of details to ensure you're buying what you originally set out to buy.**

One final example is offered to illustrate the usefulness of having complete information about an improvisation you seek. If you have a transcription of a Miles Davis trumpet solo from a performance of "Joshua," and you want to hear the original or play along with it, you cannot just run out and buy the correct album, even if you already have the personnel listing and the year of recording. Miles Davis recorded "Joshua" at least three times with saxophonist George Coleman, pianist Herbie Hancock, bassist Ron Carter, and drummer Tony Williams. Two out of the three times were in the same year, 1963. One version was released on *Seven Steps to Heaven*, an album which was issued with two different catalog numbers: Columbia CS 8851 and CL 2051. Another version was released on *Miles Davis in Europe* (Columbia CL 2183 and CS 8983). Then Davis recorded another version in 1964 that was released in *Four and More* (Columbia 9253 and CL 2453) that was reissued on CD under a new title and new catalog number in 1992.

Rare Record Dealers, Importers, and Auctioneers

Worlds Records
P.O. Box 1992
Novato, CA 94947
800-742-6663;
www.worldsrecords.com

Cadence Record Sales
Cadence Building
Redwood, NY 13679
315-287-2852
orders@www.cadencebuilding.com

www.amazon.com

www.ebay.com

International Association of
Jazz Record Collectors
www.iajrc.org
(Write for a membership listing, then determine who specializes in the style you seek, and write that member.)

Jazz Record Mart
444 North Wabash Avenue
Chicago, IL 60611
800-806-1115
www.jazzrecordmart.com

Downtown Music Gallery
www.dtmgallery.com
800-622-1387

Mail Order In-Print Albums

J & R Music World
800-221-8180
www.jr.com

Mosaic Records runs a broad-ranging program of reissuing hard-to-find items. Their reissue packages are prepared in a very intelligent and conscientious manner with excellent annotation. As this book went to press, Mosaic was still carrying material by Stan Kenton, Duke Ellington, Louis Armstrong, George Shearing, Miles Davis, Nat Cole, Don Cherry, Charlie Parker, and others. Mosaic also was running a subsidiary, called True Blue, which distributed Blue Note recordings, a source for pivotal music from the 1950s and 60s that has become difficult to locate. Request a catalog from Mosaic Records, 425 Fairfield Ave., Suite 421, Stamford CT 06902–7533; phone 203-327-7111; *www.truebluemusic.com* or *www.mosaicrecords.com*.

A SMALL BASIC COLLECTION OF JAZZ VIDEOS

Listening to Jazz by Steve Gryb (Prentice-Hall) 60 minutes; demonstrations of instruments and their combo roles, corresponding to the audio illustrations on *Demonstration CD* for the *Jazz Styles: History and Analysis* textbook by Gridley; ISBN 0–13–601053–9; phone 800-947-7700.

Prentice Hall Jazz History DVD. Historic Footage of performances by Louis Armstrong, Duke Ellington, Billie Holiday, Miles Davis, and others. ISBN 0-13-602643-5

The Sound of Jazz (Idem 1058) 58 minutes; an unedited copy of the 1957 kinescope of the CBS broadcast with performances by Count Basie, Lester Young, Coleman Hawkins, Ben Webster, Billie Holiday, Roy Eldridge, Thelonious Monk, Jimmy Giuffre, and others.

Trumpet Kings (VAI 69036) 60 minutes; hosted by Wynton Marsalis; includes Louis Armstrong, Bunny Berigan, Roy Eldridge, Red Allen, Dizzy Gillespie, Miles Davis, Freddie Hubbard, and others.

Piano Legends (VAI 4209) 63 minutes; hosted by Chick Corea; includes Earl Hines, Fats Waller, Art Tatum, Thelonious Monk, Bill Evans, Cecil Taylor, and others.

Reed Royalty (VAI 69072) 58 minutes; hosted by Branford Marsalis; includes Johnny Hodges, Charlie Parker, Gerry Mulligan, Eric Dolphy, Lee Konitz, Sidney Bechet, Ornette Coleman, Benny Goodman, Sonny Stitt, and others.

Tenor Titans (VAI 69073) 60 minutes; assorted tenor saxophonists: Coleman Hawkins, Lester Young, Stan Getz, John Coltrane, Wayne Shorter, Sonny Rollins, Dexter Gordon, and others.

Jazz Masters Vintage Collection, Vol. 2: 1960-61 (A-Vision 50–239–3) 45 minutes; Ben Webster, Ahmad Jamal, Miles Davis Quintet with John Coltrane, Miles Davis with Gil Evans Orchestra.

One Night With Blue Note, Vol. 1 (Blue Note/EMI 96008) 55 minutes; Bobby Hutcherson, Herbie Hancock, Ron Carter, Freddie Hubbard, Joe Henderson, Tony Williams, Stanley Jordan, Art Blakey, Curtis Fuller, Johnny Griffin, Walter Davis, and Reggie Workman.

One Night With Blue Note, Vol. 2 (Blue Note/EMI 96008) 60 minutes; Kenny Burrell, Grover Washington, Grady Tate, Reggie Workman, McCoy Tyner, Jackie McLean, Woody Shaw, Cecil McBee, Jack DeJohnette, Charles Lloyd, Michel Petrucciani, Lou Donaldson, Jimmy Smith, and Cecil Taylor.

Sun Ra: A Joyful Noise (RHAP) 60 minutes; documentary and much live music.

Satchmo (CBS 49024) 86 minutes; documentary on the career of Louis Armstrong.

Duke Ellington and His Orchestra (JCVC-101) film clips of the Ellington band, 1929–52.

After Hours (RHAP) 27 minutes; 1961; featuring Coleman Hawkins, Roy Eldridge, and Cozy Cole.

Thelonious Monk: Straight, No Chaser (Warner Bros.) 89 min.; performances and recording session, some dialog.

Bill Evans: The Universal Mind (RHAP 9015) 45 minutes; Evans talks and plays.

The Coltrane Legacy (VAI) 61 minutes; John Coltrane, Eric Dolphy, Elvin Jones, McCoy Tyner, Reggie Workman, Jimmy Garrison; performances; interviews with Jimmy Cobb, Elvin Jones, Roy Haynes, Reggie Workman.

Note: These videos can sometimes be found in video stores, libraries, and music stores. To keep up with new and reissued videos, watch for reviews and advertisements in jazz magazines. At the time we went to press, some of the above videos and several others were available by mail from these distributors:

Rhapsody Films (RHAP)
46-2 Becket Hill Road
Lyme, CT 06371
860-434-3610
www.rhapsodyfilms.com

Jamey Aebersold
P.O. Box 1244
New Albany, IN 47150
800-456-1388
www.jazzbooks.com

Jazzland
P.O. Box 366
Dayton, Ohio 45401
800-876-4467
www.landofjazz.com

Spectrum Music Videos
P.O. Box 280
Oaks, PA 19456
800-846-8742
www.musicvideodistributors.com

Cadence Record Sales
Cadence Bldg.
Redwood, NY 13679
315-287-2852
www.cadencebuilding.com
www.amazon.com

Glossary

acid jazz   usually the creation of a disc jockey who takes funky accompaniments that have been synthesized electronically and/or sampled from jazz recordings, then repeats them continuously with raps and/or jazz improvisations superimposed atop them.

antiphonal   an adjective describing a common pattern of interaction between improvisers or between sections of a band, taking the form of a question and answer or a call and response.

arco   the technique of playing a stringed instrument with a bow.

atonal   the character and organization possessed by music that has no key (see page 270 for further explanations and illustrations).

attack   the very beginning of a sound (opposite of release).

back beat   strong accent on the second and fourth beats of every four-beat measure; a term usually applied to the work of a band's drummer.

ballad   a slow piece.

big band   an ensemble of ten or more players.

blue note
   1. a pitch somewhere between a major third and minor third or between a major seventh and minor seventh step of the scale (see pages 270–272).

   2. minor third or seventh scale step (see page 271).

blues
   1. a simple, funky style of black music separate from but coexistent with jazz; beginning at least as early as the turn of the century, probably much earlier; exemplified by such performers as Blind Lemon Jefferson, Leadbelly, Lightnin' Hopkins, Muddy Waters, T-Bone Walker, and Robert Johnson. It has been and continues to be an influence on jazz and rock. The majority of blues compositions employ the I-IV-I-V-I chord progression or a variation of it.

   2. a piece characterized by any one or any combination of the following:

      a. the I-IV-I-V-I chord progression or some variation of it in a twelve-measure package

      b. a sad feeling

      c. a slow pace

      d. poetry in the form of paired couplets in iambic pentameter

      e. many lowered third, fifth, or seventh intervals (see pages 271–272 for further explanations).

bomb   a pronounced accent played by the drummer.

boogie woogie   a premodern jazz piano style associated with Meade Lux Lewis and Albert Ammons. It is characterized by a repetitive left-hand bass figure that states almost every beat by dividing it into dotted-eighth sixteenth-note patterns.

bop (bebop)   the style associated with Charlie Parker, Dizzy Gillespie, Thelonious Monk, Bud Powell, Dexter Gordon, and Sonny Stitt (see pages 98–102).

break
   1. the portion of a piece in which all band members stop playing except the one who improvises a solo. The tempo and chord progressions are maintained by the soloist,

but, because the band has stopped, it is called a stop-time. Rarely do such breaks last longer than two or four measures (see *Demo CD* Track 34).

  2. the solo itself.

bridge   the B part of an A-A-B-A composition; also known as the channel, the release, or the inside (see page 282 for further information).

broken time
  1. a style of rhythm section playing in which explicit statement of every beat is replaced by broken patterns which only imply the underlying tempo, exemplified by the 1961 Bill Evans trio with Scott LaFaro and Paul Motian.

  2. the manner of playing bass or drums in which strict repetition of timekeeping patterns is not maintained, but constant tempo is; exemplified by the 1960s and 70s playing of Elvin Jones.

chart   the jazz musician's term for what is written as musical arrangement. This is distinguished from the classical musician's "score" because not all the notes are present. Many spaces in the chart are filled only by symbols indicating the chord progression that guides improvisation. Often the drum "parts" are almost blank.

chops   instrumental facility

chord progression
  1. when one chord changes or "progresses" to another chord.

  2. a set of harmonies in a particular order with specified durations; for example, the twelve measure I-IV-I-V-I blues progression (see pages 272–274).

  3. the sequence of accompaniment chords intended for a song but used instead as the basis of a jazz improvisation.

chorus
  1. a single playing through of the structure being used to organize the music in an improvisation.

  2. a jazz solo, regardless of its length.

  3. the part of a pop tune performed in constant tempo and repeated several times after the verse has been played, usually the only portion of a tune's original form used by the jazz musician (see pages 11 and 280–281 for further explanation).

collective improvisation   simultaneous improvisation by all members of a group together.

comping   syncopated chording which provides improvised accompaniment for simultaneously improvised solos, flexibly complementing the rhythms and implied harmonies of the solo line (see *Demo CD* Track 20 for further explanation).

cool
  1. an adjective often applied to describe the subdued feeling projected by the music of Bix Beiderbecke, Lester Young, Claude Thornhill, Gil Evans, Miles Davis, The Modern Jazz Quartet, Gerry Mulligan, Lee Konitz, and Jimmy Giuffre (see pages 123–136).

  2. sometimes used as a synonym for West Coast style.

  3. sometimes used to denote modern jazz after bop.

counterpoint   two or more lines of approximately equal importance sounding together.

Creole
  1. French- or Spanish-speaking individual born in the New World.

  2. a person who has mixed French and African ancestry and was born in the New World (also known as "Creole of Color," as opposed to the white-skinned Creole defined above).

decay   the very end of a sound; also known as a release. Opposite of attack (see *Demo CD* Tracks 46–53 for discussion).

Dixieland style
  1. Chicago combo style that was prominent during the 1920s.

  2. a synonym for all pre-swing-era combo jazz.

double stop   sounding two bass strings at the same time.

double-time   the feeling that a piece of music or a player is going twice as fast as the tempo, although the chord progressions continue at the original rate.

Fender bass   electric bass guitar, used to play bass lines instead of chords; common in jazz rhythm sections after 1970.

fill   in general, anything a drummer plays in addition to basic timekeeping patterns; in particular, a rhythmic figure played by a drummer to:
  1. fill a silence

  2. underscore a rhythm played by other instruments

  3. announce the entrance or punctuate the exit of a soloist or other section of the music

  4. stimulate the other players and make a performance more interesting.

free jazz   an approach associated with Ornette Coleman and Cecil Taylor, in which the music contains improvised solos which are free of preset chord progressions, and sometimes also free of preset meter (see pages 163–175).

front line   musicians appearing directly in front of the audience, not blocked from view by another row of musicians. This designation is sometimes used to separate hornmen (because they stand in the front of a combo) from accompanists (who usually appear to the rear of the hornmen).

funky
  1. earthy or dirty

  2. mean, "low down," evil, or sexy

  3. bluesy

  4. gospel-flavored

  5. containing a predominance of lowered third, fifth, and seventh steps of the scale.

  (*Note: During the 1970s this adjective was applied to describe rhythms as well as melody, harmony, and tone color characteristics.*)

fusion   a synonym for jazz-rock style (see pages 195–226).

fuzak   music that blends the characteristics of jazz-rock fusion styles with the characteristics of Muzak. It tends to stress electric instruments, steady funk rhythms, smooth textures, without many surprises. Used as background music during the 1980s and 90s by listeners who liked the softer variants of fusion and funk. Often applied to music of Kenny G, Grover Washington, Jr., Earl Klugh, and Najee.

growl style   a method used by some trumpeters and trombonists in which by unorthodox use of mutes, lips, mouth and blowing techniques a sound is produced that resembles the growl of an animal. Despite the odd assortment of sounds that the growl includes, recognizable melodic figures can be played with this alteration of tone quality (see Bubber Miley, Cootie Williams, and Joe "Tricky Sam" Nanton).

hard bop   the jazz style associated with Horace Silver, Art Blakey, and Cannonball Adderley (see pages 137–167 for further explanation).

head the melody or written theme for a piece.

head arrangement a band arrangement that was created extemporaneously by the musicians and is not written down.

high-hat (sock cymbal) an instrument in the drum set which brings two cymbals together by means of a foot pedal (see pages 11, 13 and 14 for illustration and *Demo CD* Track 2).

horn general label for any wind instrument; sometimes includes stringed and percussion instruments as well (the most general term for all instruments is ax).

jam session a musical get-together where improvisation is stressed and prewritten music is rare (jam means to improvise); may refer to a performance which is formally organized or casual, public or private, for profit or just for fun.

jazz-rock a variety of styles beginning in the late 1960s that use electric instruments, funk rhythm accompaniments and jazz improvisation; also known as fusion music; often applied to the post-1968 music of Miles Davis, Spyro Gyra, Weather Report, the Crusaders, John McLaughlin, the electric music of Herbie Hancock and Chick Corea (see pages 195–226.)

laid back an adjective used to describe a feeling of relaxation, laziness, or slowness; often describes the feeling that a performer is playing his rhythms a little later than they are expected, almost after the beat or "behind" the beat.

lay out to stop playing while other players continue.

legato a style of playing in which the notes are smoothly connected with no silences between them (opposite of staccato).

lick a phrase or melodic fragment.

locked-hands style a style of piano playing in which a separate chord parallels each note of the melody because both hands are used as though they are locked together, all fingers striking the keyboard together; also known as block chording, playing the chord notes as a block instead of one at a time. (Listen to Milt Buckner, Lennie Tristano, George Shearing, Ahmad Jamal, Red Garland, and Bill Evans.)

modal music in which the melody and/or harmony is based on an arrangement of modes. In jazz, the term can mean music based on the extensive repetition of one or two chords or music based on modes instead of chord progressions (see pages 175–180, 280–282 for further explanation).

mode
1. the manner of organizing a sequence of tones, usually an ascending sequence of an octave.

2. the arrangement of whole steps and half steps common to scales.

(See pages 269, 280–282, 302–306 for further explanation.)

mute an attachment which reduces an instrument's loudness and alters its tone color (see pages 285–286 for illustrations).

New Age music that is soft and soothing, lacks variety in rhythm, loudness, and chords. Often applied to the work of George Winston, selected works of Pat Metheny and others who recorded for Windham Hill, Narada, and ECM record companies. It tends to combine characteristics of:
1. the minimalist style associated with nonjazz composers Philip Glass, LaMonte Young, and Steve Reich.

2. the style that Keith Jarrett developed for his unaccompanied solo piano improvisations of the 1970s and 80s.

3. music of classical musicians, including members of the Paul Winter Consort and Oregon, who improvised soft, smooth sound textures that did not swing.

pedal point   low-pitched, repeated, and/or sustained tone. It usually retains its pitch despite changes in chords and improvisations occurring around it; common in the 1960s work of John Coltrane and McCoy Tyner.

pitch bending   purposeful raising or lowering of a tone's pitch; usually done for coloration or expressive purposes (see *Demo CD* Tracks 46–53 for illustrations and explanation).

pizzicato   the method of playing a stringed instrument by plucking instead of bowing.

polyrhythm   several different rhythms sounding at the same time (see page 267).

progressive   jazz music associated with Stan Kenton (see pages 130–134).

ragtime
   1. a popular turn-of-the-century style of written piano music involving pronounced syncopation.
   2. a label often applied to much pre-1920 jazz and pop music, unaccompanied solo piano styles as well as band styles, improvised as well as written music.
   3. the style of music associated with composers Scott Joplin and Tom Turpin.

release
   1. the manner in which a sound ends or decays (opposite of attack).
   2. the bridge of a tune.

rhythm section   the group of players whose band function is accompanying. This role is particularly common for pianists, bassists, and drummers, but it is not exclusive to them (see pages 12–14 for explanations and *Demo CD* Tracks 1–8, 20, 23–26, 29–30).

ride cymbal   the cymbal suspended over a drum set, usually to the player's right, struck by a stick held the drummer's right hand; used for playing timekeeping patterns called ride rhythms (see pages 13 and 14 for illustration).

ride rhythm   the pattern a drummer plays on the ride cymbal to keep time, the most common being ding-dick-a-ding-dick-a (see *Demo CD* Track 3).

riff
   1. phrase
   2. melodic fragment
   3. theme

rim shot   the drumstick striking the rim of the snare drum at the same time as it strikes the drum head.

rip   an onset ornament in the form of a quick rise in pitch directly preceding a tone. (Listen to Bix Beiderbecke or Louis Armstrong.)

rubato   free of strict adherence to constant tempo.

scat singing   jazz improvisation using the human voice as an instrument, with nonsense syllables (dwee, ool, ya, bop, bam, etc.) instead of words.

sideman   a designation for each musician in a band except the leader.

smooth jazz   a designation for the styles of music played on radio stations subscribing to "The Wave" format of the 1980s and 90s: a blend of Kenny G, Grover Washington, Jr., Earl Klugh, Lee Ritenour, Larry Carlton, George Benson, Bob James, and their disciples.

sock cymbal   see high-hat

staccato   brief and separated (opposite of legato).

stride

1. left-hand style used by early jazz pianists. It usually employs a bass note on the first and third beats of each measure and a chord on the second and fourth.

2. the piano style of James P. Johnson and Willie "The Lion" Smith.

swing

1. a word denoting approval—"It swings" can mean it pleases me; "to swing" can mean to enjoy oneself; "he's a swinging guy" can mean he is an enjoyable person.

2. the noun indicating the feeling projected by an uplifting performance of any kind of music, especially that which employs constant tempo (see pages 3–5 for further explanation).

3. the feeling projected by a jazz performance which successfully combines constant tempo, syncopation, swing eighth notes, rhythmic lilt, liveliness and rhythmically cohesive group playing (see pages 3–5 for further explanation).

4. the jazz style associated with Count Basie, Duke Ellington, Jimmie Lunceford, Benny Goodman, Art Tatum, Roy Eldridge, and Coleman Hawkins, as in the "swing era" (see pages 58–97).

syncopation

1. stress on any portion of the measure other than the first part of the first beat (and, in meter of four, other than the first part of the third beat), i.e., the second half of the first beat, the second half of the second beat, the fourth beat, the second half of the fourth beat, the second beat, etc.

2. stress on a portion of the measure least expected to receive stress (see pages 263–265 and *Demo CD* Track 20 for further explanation).

synthesizer   any one of a general category of electronic devices (Moog and Arp, for example) which produces sounds or alters the sounds created by other instruments.

third stream   a style that combines jazz improvisation with the instrumentation and compositional forms of classical music.

tonal inflection   alteration of a tone's pitch or quality, done purposefully at the beginning, middle, or end of a sound (see pitch bending, and see *Demo CD* Tracks 46–53).

tone color (timbre, tone quality)   the characteristic of sound which enables the listener to differentiate one instrument from another, and, in many cases, one player from another.

tremolo

1. fluctuation in the loudness of a sound, usually an even alternation of loud and soft.

2. a manner of playing a chord by rapidly sounding its different notes in alternation so that the chord retains its character, but also sustains and trembles (*Demo CD* Track 42).

3. the means of sustaining the sound of a vibraharp (see *Demo CD* Track 47).

4. an expressive technique for use by instruments in which vibrato is very difficult (flute, for example) or in which the variation of pitch necessary for vibrato may not be wanted (some styles of oboe playing, for example).

5. the rapid reiteration of the same note.

turnaround (turnback, turnabout)   a short progression within a chord progression that occurs just prior to the point at which the player must "turn around" to begin another repetition of the larger progression (see page 282 for further explanation).

two-beat style   a rhythm section style which emphasizes the first and third beats of each four-beat measure, often leaving the second and fourth beats silent in the bass; sometimes called boom-chick style.

vamp   a short chord progression (usually only one, two, or four measures long) which is repeated many times in sequence. Often used for introductions and endings. Much jazz and pop music of the 1960s and 1970s used vamps instead of more involved chord progressions as accompaniment for melody and improvisation.

vibrato   the slight fluctuation of a tone's pitch, alternating above and below its basic pitch; used as an expressive device, varied in speed and amplitude by the performer to fit the style and feeling of the music (see *Demo CD* Tracks 46–49).

voicing

1. the manner of organizing, doubling, omitting, or adding to the notes of a chord (see pages 274–275).

2. the assignment of notes to each instrument (see page 276 for further explanation).

walking bass   a style of bass line in which each beat of each measure receives a separate tone, thus creating a moving sequence of quarter notes in the bass range.

West Coast style   the jazz style associated with Gerry Mulligan and Chet Baker during the 1950s (see **cool** and page 128 for further explanation).

For Musicians

You have now entered the technical part of the appendix. This section is designed to give musically literate readers a chance to experience some of the musical elements discussed in the main body of the text. Keep in mind that it is possible to learn more by playing the examples at the piano than by merely reading the attached explanations. Once you have played these demonstrations yourself, the principles will be more obvious to you when they occur in jazz recordings.

Chords and Chord Progressions

One way to understand how chords can be constructed is to imagine them as being built from tones in the major scales. For instance in the key of B♭, tones for the chords can be drawn from the notes in the B♭ major scale (B♭ C D E♭ F G A B♭). In the key of C, they can be drawn from the notes in the C scale (C D E F G A B C). Beginning with a single tone, the chord is made by adding every other tone in the scale. In other words, the first, third, and fifth tones are used when the beginning tone is the key note (first tone of the major scale). The second, fourth, and sixth tones are used when the chord is based on the second step of the scale. The third, fifth, and seventh tones are used when the chord begins on the third step of the scale.

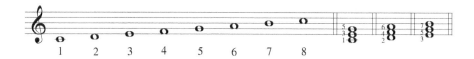

If a chord is based on the first tone of the major scale, it is called the "one chord," symbolized by the Roman numeral for one, I. The chord based on the second step of the major scale is a II chord. The labeling system continues through the VII chord.

I   II   III   IV   V   VI   VII

The system is more involved that what we have discussed. Before you can apply chord knowledge to studying improvisation, you must become acquainted with construction of many type of chords: dominant sevenths and major sevenths; major, minor, diminished, and augmented chords; chords with added ninths, elevenths, and thirteenths; chords with added fourths and sixths, flat fifths, raised ninths, etc. You will also need to confront a collection of different chord labeling systems.

Twelve-Bar Blues Progressions

Though basically a I-IV-I-V-I progression, the twelve-bar blues may contain a huge assortment of chord progressions. Here are three possibilities for a blues in the key of C.

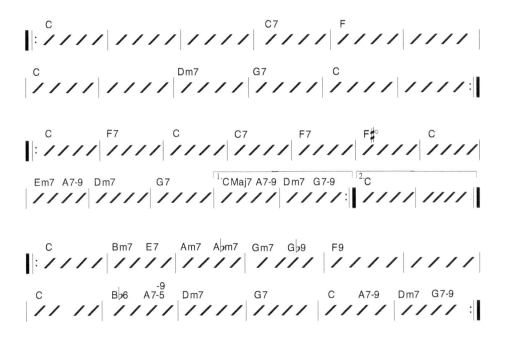

Modes

Though used for centuries in classical music, modes just recently became popular harmonic bases for jazz improvisation. To get a rough idea of what is meant by the term "modes," we can use the tones of the major scale to produce different modes if we play ascending sequences, starting on different steps of the scale. Each mode's unique sound is the result of its particular arrangement of whole steps and half steps. For example, in the Ionian mode (also known as the major scale), half steps occur only between the third and fourth steps and the seventh and eighth steps. (The eighth step is an octave up from the first step.)

The Dorian mode is constructed from the same tones as the Ionian, but it begins on the second tone of the major scale. The Dorian mode has half steps between its second and third and its sixth and seventh tones.

There is a mode for each step of the major scale. Each mode has a distinct musical personality because its half steps fall in different places.

Examine the following modes. Play them, and listen carefully while you play them. Find the positions of the half steps in each mode. Once you know a mode's pattern of whole and half steps, you should be able to begin it on other notes. Remember that the interval between Bb and C is defined as a whole step, as is that between E and F#. Remember also that the interval between B and C is a half step, as is that between E and F.

Ionian (also known as major scale)

Dorian

Phrygian

Lydian

Mixolydian

Aeolian (also known as ancient, minor, pure, natural)

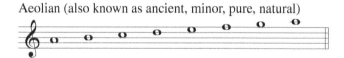

Locrian

Kurd (Arabic)

Hungarian

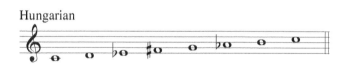

Byzantine

Charhargah (Persian or Gypsy)

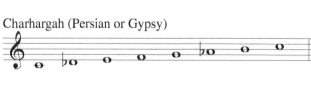

Balinese

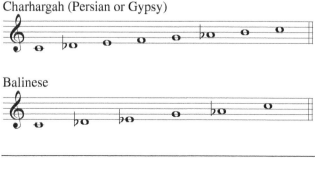

Spanish

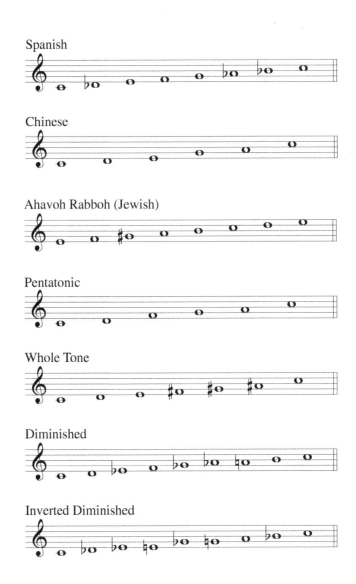

Chinese

Ahavoh Rabboh (Jewish)

Pentatonic

Whole Tone

Diminished

Inverted Diminished

Modal Construction of "Maiden Voyage"

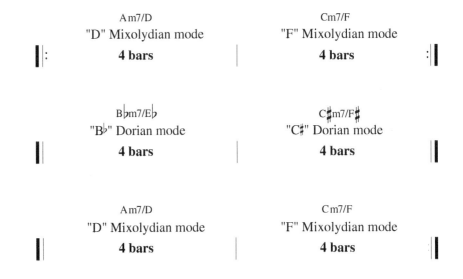

Am7/D	Cm7/F
"D" Mixolydian mode	"F" Mixolydian mode
4 bars	**4 bars**

B♭m7/E♭	C♯m7/F♯
"B♭" Dorian mode	"C♯" Dorian mode
4 bars	**4 bars**

Am7/D	Cm7/F
"D" Mixolydian mode	"F" Mixolydian mode
4 bars	**4 bars**

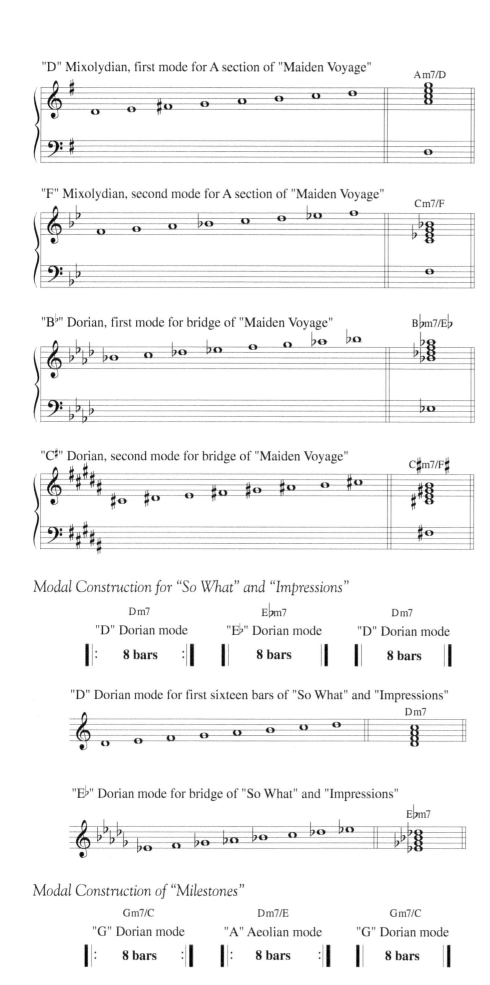

"D" Mixolydian, first mode for A section of "Maiden Voyage"

Am7/D

"F" Mixolydian, second mode for A section of "Maiden Voyage"

Cm7/F

"B♭" Dorian, first mode for bridge of "Maiden Voyage"

B♭m7/E♭

"C♯" Dorian, second mode for bridge of "Maiden Voyage"

C♯m7/F♯

Modal Construction for "So What" and "Impressions"

Dm7
"D" Dorian mode
‖: 8 bars :‖

E♭m7
"E♭" Dorian mode
‖ 8 bars ‖

Dm7
"D" Dorian mode
‖ 8 bars ‖

"D" Dorian mode for first sixteen bars of "So What" and "Impressions"

Dm7

"E♭" Dorian mode for bridge of "So What" and "Impressions"

E♭m7

Modal Construction of "Milestones"

Gm7/C
"G" Dorian mode
‖: 8 bars :‖

Dm7/E
"A" Aeolian mode
‖: 8 bars :‖

Gm7/C
"G" Dorian mode
‖ 8 bars ‖

"G" Dorian mode for first sixteen bars of "Milestones"

"A" Aeolian mode for bridge of "Milestones"

Walking Bass Lines

Walking is meant to provide timekeeping in the form of tones chosen for their compatibility with the harmonies of the piece and style of the performance. Ideally, the walking bass complements the solo line.

Three choruses of walking bass are shown here. They display three increasing levels of complexity for walking bass lines for the 12-bar blues in the key of C (conceived and notated by Willis Lyman).

Comping

Here are two examples of piano accompaniments, or comping, for a jazz twelve-bar blues solo. Comping is accompaniment that is simultaneously composed and performed to fit the style of a piece and the directions in harmony, rhythm, and melody that are taken by the soloist. Comping usually contains pronounced syncopation.

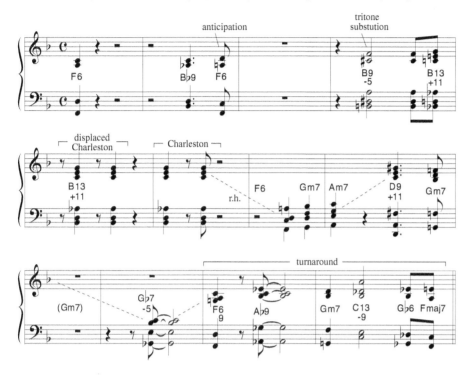

Bebop-Style Comping (notated by David Berger)
(*Reprinted by permission of David Berger, Such Sweet Thunder, Inc.*)

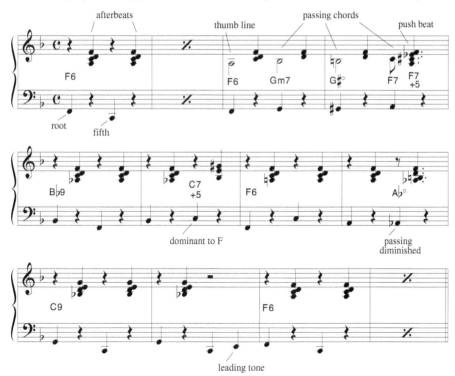

"Boston" or Two-Handed Stride-Style Comping (notated by David Berger)
(*Reprinted by permission of David Berger, Such Sweet Thunder, Inc.*)

Comping Figures for "Rhythm Changes"

This is a typical example of piano comping for improvisations that follow the chord changes used by George Gershwin to accompany his melody "I Got Rhythm." This would also fit "Cottontail," "Shaw Nuff," "Lester Leaps In," and "(Meet the) Flintstones." Other comping examples for Flintstones can be heard on the *Demo* CD, with and without the Flintstones melody. (Reprinted by permission of Jerry Sheer.) (Composed and notated by Jerry Sheer.)

Index

polyrhythms, 267
Powell, Bud, 89, 94, 98, 103, 109–113, 124, 176, 209
Preservation Hall Jazz Band, 54, 256
Prince of Darkness, 188–191
Progressive jazz, 130
Puente, Tito, 244–246

Q

Quiet Nights (Davis), 253

R

ragtime, 17, 18, 24–25, 32, 36, 40, 41
Ravel, Maurice, 49, 176, 180, 254
"Reckless Blues" (Smith and Armstrong), 54–55
Redman, Dewey, 192, 236
retro jazz, 257
Return to Forever (Return to Forever), 210
rhythm, 263–267
rhythm guitars, 61, 64, 78, 100
rhythm section, 10, 12–14, 69
Rich, Buddy, 106
ride cymbals, 13, 14, 101, 182, 188
ride rhythms, 13, 69, 70, 101, 178, 182
riff band style, 68
riffs, 60, 68
"Riverboat Shuffle" (Beiderbecke and Trumbauer), 50–52
Roach, Max, 101, 110
"Rockit" (Hancock), 207, 208, 220, 240
Rollins, Sonny, 158–160, 165, 232, 237, 239

S

sampling, 218, 240
Sanborn, Dave, 199, 211, 228, 230
Sandoval, Arturo, 246–247
Satie, Erik, 248
saxophones, 50, 59, 66–67, 102–103, 124–128, 132, 157–161, 177–180, 189–191
scales, 267–272, 303–307
scat singing, 47, 49, 83, 86, 88, 117
Schneider, Maria, 227, 249, 253–254
Shakti, 202
Shorter, Wayne, 4, 14, 138, 139, 140, 181, 188–191, 202, 204–206, 231, 237–240, 257
Silver, Horace, 137–139, 143–145, 165, 209, 217, 232, 237, 243
"Sittin' In" (Eldridge and Berry), 64–65
sixteenth notes, 265
slap-tongued, 35
slaves, 20
Smith, Bessie, 53, 54–55, 81, 196
Smith, Josh, 240
smooth jazz, 7, 164, 210–211, 217, 228, 229, 257
snare drums, 13, 64, 72, 78, 101, 178, 182
"Solar" (Evans, LaFaro, and Motian), 182–187
solo breaks, 34, 64
soprano saxophones, 39, 175, 177, 198, 200, 201
"So What," 166–167, 176, 193, 282
soul-funk music, 197

soul jazz, 137
soul music, 197, 221
soul saxophone style, 227–232
Sousa, John Philip, 25
Sousa phone, 38
South American music, 200, 253
"Spanish Key," 212–216
Speed, Chris, 240, 242
staccato, 64, 159, 162, 188, 266
Stone, Sly, 197–198, 208, 228
Storyville, 26
straight-ahead music, 257
straight eighth notes, 132, 264–267
straight up and down, 197
stride style, 38, 41–43, 46, 50, 64, 112
string bands, 24, 27
string bass, 4, 12, 61, 69, 198
"Subconscious-Lee" (Konitz and Tristano), 126
substitution, 89
sweet bands, 94, 224, 244
swing bands, 58–95, 222, 242, 244
swing dancing, 58, 94–95, 254
swing eighth notes, 48, 83, 132, 254–256, 266–267
swing era, 58–95, 94–95
swinging, 3–5, 48, 68–69, 234, 263–267
swing style, 3–5, 58–95, 113, 255
syncopation, 4–5, 24, 48, 83, 92, 162, 182, 263–264
synthesizers, 198, 204–205

T

Tatum, Art, 43, 44, 88–91, 98, 100–102, 104, 109, 113, 124, 255
"Taxi War Dance" (Basie and Young), 68, 70–72
Taylor, Cecil, 89, 132, 169, 172–175, 178–180, 182, 187, 188, 222, 232, 234
techno, 220, 240
tenor saxophones, 11, 59, 63– 66, 70–76, 113–117, 132, 140, 144, 155, 158–161, 168, 188–189, 230–231, 234–240
Thornhill, Claude, 125, 127, 130, 132, 148
"Tiger Rag" (Tatum), 90–91
timbales, 244, 245
Time Out (Brubeck), 129
tom-toms, 13, 62, 178, 188
tonal, 269
tonality, 269
tone color, 252–253, 283–285
tone quality, 150, 170
trading fours, 65, 106
trading twos, 71
traditional jazz, 53–54, 257
triplets, 182, 255, 265
Tristano, Lennie, 89, 94, 123–127, 132, 134
trombones, 31, 34, 50, 60, 70, 72, 78, 131–134, 140
Trumbauer, Frankie, 50
trumpets, 31, 45, 48–53, 60, 62–66, 64, 78, 103, 132, 143, 148, 150–157, 189, 240–241, 243–247, 255–257
trumpet-style piano, 44–45, 46–47
tubas, 37, 38, 39, 127, 198

tumbao, 246
turnaround, 182, 183, 282–283
turntablists, 219–220
Turrentine, Stanley, 228, 231
twelve-bar blues, 21–23, 46, 54, 100, 104, 115, 146–147, 274, 276–280
"Two Bass hit" (Davis, Adderley, Coltrane), 146–148, 178
two-beat style, 61, 63
Tyner, McCoy, 139, 168, 177, 199, 200, 209, 232, 246

U

up-beats, 182, 264

V

Valdés, Chucho, 246
Vaughan, Sarah, 81, 116–118
verses, 50, 280–281
"Vijay Iyer," 238
Vitous, Miroslav, 203
vocal blues, 53
vocalists, 53–55, 81–88, 116–118
voicing across sections of the band, 76, 93

W

Walker, Junior, 144, 199, 228, 231
walking bass, 12, 61, 64, 69, 70, 78, 104, 110, 140, 182
Waller, Fats, 41, 42–43, 92, 254
Walton, Cedar, 140
Washington, Grover, Jr., 199, 211, 228, 229
Weather Report, 202–207, 222, 223, 238, 239
Wells, Dicky, 70, 71
West Africa, 21
West Coast Cool, 128
West Coast Jazz, 123–124, 128
"West End Blues" (Hines and Armstrong), 44
"West End Blues" (Oliver), 46
"What Is This Thing Called Love," 126
Williams, Cootie, 76, 78, 79, 80
Williams, Mary Lou, 89–94
Williams, Tony, 139, 181, 188–191, 198, 199, 201, 236, 257
Wilson, Teddy, 44, 74, 84, 85, 91, 113
"Wind-Up, The" (Jarrett and Garbarek), 233–235
wire brushes, 62, 69, 78, 132
woodblocks, 33, 34, 39, 62
wordless vocal, 77, 86
World music, 170

Y

Young, Lester, 11, 67, 69, 70–74, 83, 84, 92, 98, 102, 103, 113, 114, 123, 124, 151, 206, 255
"Your Lady" (Coltrane), 177

Z

Zawinul, Joe, 202–207, 232, 239
Zorn, John, 242–243, 247

Media Reviews

"The best approach to contemporary classroom jazz extant."—*Jazz Times*

"...clearly a text designed to fit a ten-week college quarter; but it can also serve nicely as an informative introduction to jazz for novice fans...Gridley manages to touch most of the important musical bases with chapters devoted to early jazz, swing, bebop, cool jazz, hard bop, avant-garde and fusion...a few hours with *Concise Guide to Jazz* will add immeasurably to one's enjoyment of the music."—*Jazz Forum*

Author Biography

Mark C. Gridley is an active professional jazz saxophonist-flutist-bandleader in Cleveland. His *Jazz Styles: History and Analysis* and its abridged edition, *Concise Guide to Jazz*, are America's most widely used introductions to jazz. He has also written for The *Musical Quarterly, Black Music Research Journal, The Black Perspective in Music, Encyclopedia of African American Music, College Music Symposium, Current Musicology, The Instrumentalist, Jazz Educator's Journal, Grove Dictionaries of Music*, and *Encyclopaedia Britannica*. His research on perception and preferences in music and art appears in *Creativity Research Journal, American Psychologist, Psychological Reports, Psychology Journal*, and *Perceptual and Motor Skills*. He has been honored by the Educational Press Association of America's Distinguished Achievement Award, and he is listed in *Marquis Who's Who in America*.